All Tigers, No Donkeys

A Canadian Soldier in Croatia, 1994–1995

KURT GRANT

Vanwell Publishing Limited
St. Catharines, Ontario

Copyright © 2004 by Kurt Grant. All rights reserved. No part of this book may be reproduced or used in any form or by any means, electronic or mechanical, including photocopying, recording, or in any information storage and retrieval system, without permission in writing from the publisher.

Vanwell Publishing acknowledges the financial support of the Government of Canada through the Book Publishing Industry Development Program for our publishing activities.

Vanwell Publishing acknowledges the Government of Ontario through the Ontario Media Development Corporation's Book Initiative.

Design: Carol Matsuyama
Cover: Carol Matsuyama

Vanwell Publishing Limited
1 Northrup Crescent
P.O. Box 2131
St. Catharines, Ontario L2R 7S2
sales@vanwell.com
tel: 905-937-3100
fax: 905-937-1760

Printed in Canada

National Library of Canada Cataloguing in Publication Data
Grant, Kurt, 1959–
All tigers, no donkeys: a Canadian soldier in Croatia, 1994–1995/Kurt Grant.
ISBN 1-55125-091-8
1. Grant, Kurt, 1959–   —Diaries. 2. Peacekeeping forces—Croatia. 3. United Nations Protection Force. 4. Canada. Canadian Armed Forces—Biography. I. Title.
DR1605.2.G72A3   2004   355.3'57'092   C2004-905450-3

CONTENTS

- 4   Acknowledgments
- 5   Foreword
- 6   Preface
- 9   Canadian Military Terms
- 12   Map

13   PART ONE GETTING READY

20   PART TWO TRAINING

72   PART THREE THE FIRST HALF OF THE TOUR

176   PART FOUR THE SECOND HALF OF THE TOUR

317   EPILOGUE

ACKNOWLEDGMENTS

A BOOK OF THIS NATURE DOES NOT COME TOGETHER WITHOUT THE HELP OF A CAST OF characters. During its creation many have given advice and guidance along the way. Chief among them is my wife Catherine. Without her help, understanding, love, patience, and guidance, I don't think this book would ever have come to fruition. She is the rock upon which my life is built.

To my friend Andrew Stirling, and the Hon. Douglas Young, former minister of National Defence, thank you for taking the time to put the book into context for the reader.

Thanks also to the members of the "Gentleman's Night In" group who grace my dining room on an irregular basis (and shall remain nameless to protect the innocent as well as the guilty). Your fellowship has been a tonic and an inspiration for me over the years.

To Bob Coldwell and Dr. Steve Harris of the Department of History and Heritage, your guidance and encouragement inspired me to be a better writer and for that I am more than grateful.

To the men and women of the 1 RCR Battle Group, though your names have been changed I trust you will recognize yourself in these pages, and it brings back many fond memories. It was an honour to serve with you.

Finally, my thanks to Vanwell publishing for their patience and faith in this work. The list goes on of course, but rather than risk offence by omission I'll stop here and simply say thanks to all of you for your kindness: you know who you are.

FOREWORD

ONE OF THE GREATEST CONTRIBUTIONS CANADA HAS MADE TO THE WORLD OVER THE LAST few decades is its commitment to Peacekeeping. As a "middle" power, Canada has participated in numerous military ventures with the singular purpose of securing peace. These enterprises have not, however, been without their cost. As this book reminds us, "The public has been largely unaware that Canadian troops have been killed and wounded by hostile fire and land mines in many of the missions they have participated in." Indeed, the author knows intimately the costs and dangers of being a Peacekeeper. As a Reservist with the Canadian Armed Forces, Kurt Grant voluntarily agreed to serve the cause of peace. His fascinating account of the challenges he faced not only takes the reader into the mind of the chronicler, it also sheds light on the context in which he operated. The reader will feel his apprehensions, fears, joys and frustrations as he takes us on a daily journey through his experience as a Peacekeeper, and the cost that he and his family bore. Nevertheless, having witnessed so much violence throughout the world, Kurt Grant concludes, ". . . above all, I am grateful to be Canadian." I am sure his prophetic insights will cause the reader to affirm the same.

The Rev. Dr. Andrew Stirling,
Senior Minister, Timothy Eaton Memorial Church,
Toronto, Ontario

THIS BOOK PROVIDES VALUABLE INSIGHT INTO THE WORLD OF TODAY'S CANADIAN CITIZEN soldier.

There is a wealth of material written on our nation's involvement in conflicts from the Indian wars to Afghanistan but not much specifically about our Reservists. Kurt Grant makes a significant contribution to a better understanding of the role of Canada's Reserve Force members. He has added to the history of Canada's Militia with this record of his tour of duty as he and his colleagues followed in a long and honoured tradition of bravery and compassion.

Arguments have raged for a hundred years on whether Canada's Armed Forces are properly trained and adequately equipped yet time and time again men and women from across the country have responded with valour when called to war or peacekeeping, silencing the naysayers. Rarely is doubt expressed about the calibre and commitment of the men and women in Canada's military, as they go about their dangerous and complex missions abroad, however there is little appreciation of the challenges faced by their families.

Catherine and Kurt Grant are inspiring examples of the courage and commitment, service and steadfastness, that are the hallmarks of the members of Canada's Armed Forces and their families.

Hon. M. Douglas Young P.C.
Ottawa, ON

PREFACE

THE CONCEPT OF THE "CITIZEN-SOLDIER" IS NOT NEW IN CANADA. WHILE WE CANADIANS tend not to dwell on the fact that we own a rich and diverse military tradition, recorded history reminds us that from our earliest days the citizenry was largely made up of those with a military background. Research soon reveals how large portions of the St. Lawrence Valley, then Upper Canada, were settled by entire regiments of soldiers who disbanded from the British army after the Anglo-Spanish and the Peninsular wars. In exchange for a land grant, each soldier was expected to belong to the local militia, and to rendezvous each year for a week's training—admittedly as much a reunion party as an arms training refresher. In my own area of the country, the rendezvous was at Fort Wellington in the town of Prescott. People of the region from as far away as Carleton Place, Morrisburg, and Brockville, made their way on foot to Prescott for this yearly gathering. Ever since the Battle of the Plains of Abraham determined the course of history for North America, there have been many examples of citizens setting aside the tools of their trade to take up arms at the request of the parliament of the day.

In recent years the primary role of the reserves has been to augment the regular forces in times of need. From the beginning, the militia and the regular forces have worked closely together whenever necessary. Regiments such as the Governor-General's Foot Guards; the Cameron Highlanders of Ottawa; the Stormont, Dundas, and Glengarry Highlanders of Cornwall, and my own Brockville Rifles, fought side by side with the regular force regiments of the Royal 22nd Rifles (R22eR), the Royal Canadian Regiment (RCR), and the Princess Patricia's Canadian Light Infantry (PPCLI). In many cases the reserve units have more battle honours than these regular force regiments.

However, from the beginning the relationship between the two has been rocky. The regulars fostered the feeling that a professional army could always do the job better than a part-time one. The reserves, in spite of receiving exactly the same training, contended that despite going into the field only once a month they were just as good because they actually wanted to be there. What they might lack in intense training, they made up for in a willing attitude. This feeling of us vs. them, real soldiers vs. weekend warriors, meant that any reservist applying as an augmentee for a peacekeeping tour was viewed with suspicion and an animosity bordering on rivalry. The reservist invariably has had a serious uphill battle to fight before winning respect in the battalion ranks.

In 1993, after years of government cutbacks, the regular forces found themselves in a situation where, in order to meet the operational demands of maintaining a battalion on the ground for the newly formed UNPROFOR mission in Yugoslavia, they had to rely heavily on the reserves to fill the gaps in the ranks. Indeed, the majority of the "bayonets-on-the-ground" in the Medak Pocket in 1993 were in fact reservists. By late 1994, the Armed Forces introduced a policy restricting the number of reservists on any deployment to no more than 20% of the personnel. The Canadian forces were being called upon to fulfill an ever increasing number of missions, but with fewer resources and fewer trained personnel in situations like the Somalia and Rwanda—missions that clearly contained no fewer dangers. They had to rely heavily upon the battalions as the backbone for each mission, the bulk of whose troops were fresh out of battle school, having just completed trades training. Searching through the ranks of sister battalions and transferring people filled holes in its leadership structure and manpower. In Afghanistan for example, the PPCLI had to scour the ranks of four different battalions in order to reach the required number of personnel needed for the mission.

For the reserves about to deploy, we had to confront the artificial barrier between them and us. For some it was easy, for others it was hell. The reservists on my tour were all trade-qualified, many of whom—myself included—had completed advanced leadership courses like the infantry section commander's course, and held the rank of Master Corporal or Sergeant. Still others had at least two and more likely three or more trade qualification courses (TQ) in addition to their basic infantry training. Yet because the military didn't have the money to pay its augmentees anything above the rank of private, we all chose to forfeit our rank (and pay) so that we might be considered for this tour.

What follows is the diary that I kept as I went through the process of being chosen as an augmentee to go with 1 RCR as part of UNPROFOR, Rotation 5 to CANBAT One in Croatia, in the fall-winter of 1994–95. First came the selection process within the reserve unit, then the training, then the mission itself, and finally my return home.

It was a journey; not just to the other side of the world, but it was a journey from civilian life into the bowels of the military—and almost back out the other end. Along the way the uninitiated will encounter the unique language and inner workings of the military, while those who have served will recognize much. Yet it remains a very personal journey. This book is as much about perception as it is about reality. What is written here is about how I and the people in my section, platoon, or company *perceived things to be*, not necessarily how they were. It can be taken as a way of getting a better feel for what was going on at the time, in simple and colourful terms. This is the view from the bottom of the pile, from the pointy end of the stick as it were, not from the lofty heights of the Headquarters shack. So, if at times our situation seems confused, it probably was, and we probably were.

This work is both a book and a diary. As a book, I compiled it as a record for my family. My motivation was simple. I once had an uncle who fought on the Eastern front for the Germans during the Second World War, and who was subsequently captured in 1942 by the Russians and sent to Siberia. He did not return to his home in Germany until 1956, some 14 years later, among a group of the last German prisoners to be released from Russia. From his return until the day he died, he never spoke of his experience in Russia. I always felt this as a loss to history, not to mention as a loss to my family, and I promised myself that if I went to Yugoslavia, I would leave a legacy for anyone in the family who wanted to know more. This was the most compelling reason for my transformation into a chronicler.

As a personal diary, this work was written simply to have an emotional outrigger. A quiet place where I could go and talk about how I was feeling without being judged and without burdening anyone else. My need for such a diary became even more urgent when, with only a few short weeks remaining before I went on tour, my wife Catherine was diagnosed with Multiple Sclerosis.

Kurt Grant
Brockville, ON
August 2004

CANADIAN MILITARY TERMS

2IC—Second in command
9er—Commanding officer
AK47—Rugged, fully automatic assault rifle exported widely by the former Soviet Union
APC—Armored Personnel Carrier. Also means "*a pieds, calice!* " as in, "How are we getting there?" "*APC!*" (i.e. *on foot, dammit!*)
ARC—Alcohol Rehabilitation Center, also known as the *spin dry* course
AWOL—Absent Without Leave (usually involves drink or a woman)
BgodO—Base God Officer; the Chaplain
C3—Parker Hale sniper weapon.
C6—7.62 platoon support machine gun. Best support weapon the army has
C7—Personal weapon of every infanteer. Looks like an M-16, with a scope
C9—Section support machine gun. Two in every section, belt, box, or magazine fed. Second best support weapon the army has
Carrier—Slang reference to an M113 APC
CB—Confined to Barracks. Punishment for minor transgressions (usually involves drink or a woman)
CFSAC—Canadian Forces Skill at Arms Competition. National level competition between Army, Air Force, Navy, civilian and police teams from across Canada
Chetniks—Serbian extremist group
Class A contract—part time work with the military at reserve pay rates
Class B contract—full time work with the military at reserve pay rates
Class C contract—reservist filling a regular force position at regular force pay rates
CO—Commanding Officer
Combats—Uniform used for field operations
CQ—Company Quartermaster. Supply
CSM—Company Sergeant Major. Highest ranking NCO in the company. One step down from the RSM
C/S—Callsign. Term used to describe both radio nicknames and identify small units or individuals
DND—Department of National Defence
Dragonov—Russian-made semi-automatic pistol
.50 Calibre—Large machine gun normally mounted on vehicles and aircraft. Each Canadian M113 mounted one on the top of the vehicle
Fart Sack—Sleeping bag
Flack Vest—Protective Kevlar vest worn by all soldiers. Designed to stop shrapnel, not bullets
HASMAT—Hazardous Materials
Hard rations—Dehydrated boil-in-a-bag rations used in place of fresh food when on a field exercise. Each carrier carried three days' worth of water and food in case they couldn't make it back to camp
HLVW—Heavy Logistics Vehicle Wheeled. A five-ton truck
HQ—Headquarters

IAs—Immediate Actions. Term used in conjunction with weapons, as in "IAs and stoppages of the C7"
Iltis—German designed, Canadian made, four cylinder light vehicle
JNA—Yugoslavian National Army. Serb controlled both before and during the war
Junior Ranks—refers to the ranks of Private, Corporal, and Master Corporal. Short form for the term Junior Ranks club (or JR club), a drinking mess for the junior ranks
Karl Gustav—81 mm Anti armor weapon. With new RAP round it's effective out to about 750 metres. One per carrier or one per platoon when on foot
Lt—Lieutenant
M113—1960-vintage, aluminum, armored personnel carrier. The standard *battle taxi* of the Canadian Forces. Also know as a "carrier" or a "track"
M72—Fiberglass tube housing a 66-mm rocket. Used primarily against soft skinned vehicles
Mess—Structure wherein meals and social functions are held by members of similar rank. As in Junior Ranks' Mess, or Sergeants' Mess
MLVW—Medium Logistics Vehicle Wheeled. A two-and-a-half-ton truck
MP—Military Police
NATO—North Atlantic Treaty Organization
NDHQ—National Defence Headquarters. Sometimes referred to as *Disney Land on the Rideau*, or *Fort Fumble*
OC—Officer Commanding. Refers to the company commander
Ogroup—Orders Group. Meeting held regularly by leaders to inform subordinates of upcoming plans
OP—Observation Post
Ops—Operations
Padre—Military clergy. Sometimes referred to as *BgodO*
PMQ—Permanent Married Quarters
POL—Petroleum, Oils, and Lubricant. A POL point is a common location for all these items
Pte—Rank of Private
Pull Pole—The act of breaking camp. Comes from the act of taking down the tent pole
PWT—Personal Weapons Test. A shooting test, conducted on a range where the infanteer must complete a set course of fire
QRF—Quick Reaction Force
RCR—Royal Canadian Regiment
Regs—Regular Force personnel, or Regulations. Depends on context
REMF—Rear Echelon Mother Fucker. A derogatory phrase coined by the Americans, it refers to any non-combat military personnel in an operational theater
RPG—Rocket Propelled Grenade. Refers to a Russian shoulder-fired missile weapon used by infantry forces as an anti-tank weapon. Comes in several variants such as the RPG-16, and RPG-18
RSM—Regimental Sergeant Major—God. His appearance on the scene strikes fear equally into the hearts of both the guilty and the innocent
Salvage—All the bits and pieces left over after ammunition has been fired. Boxes, bandoleers, casings, pieces of plastic
SOP—Standard Operating Procedures
Sunray—Radio nickname for the commander of any unit

Sunray Minor—Radio nickname for the 2IC of any unit

SVK—Serb Army

TOW—**T**erminally operated, **O**ptically tracked, **W**ire-guided missile. A standard NATO anti-tank system, it could be mounted on a variety of vehicles and even broken down and hand carried

Track—Slang term for M113 armored personnel carrier. Also the part of the M113 that provides propulsion and comes in constant contact with the ground. Depends on the usage

UNCIVPOL—United Nations Civilian Police. Policemen and women who work for the UN and are used for dispute resolution

UNHCR—United Nations High Commission on Refugees

UNMO—United Nations Military Observers. These are military personnel who are unarmed and observe the goings on within a war zone

UNPROFOR—United Nations PROtection FORce. The name of our mission in Yugoslavia

VCFA—Violation of the Cease Fire Agreement

VCP—Vehicle Check point

Webb Gear—Also known as "Webbing." The sturdy pouch-covered belt-with-shoulder-straps worn by infantry soldiers, attached to which are ammo pouches, water bottles, grenade pouches, bayonets, gas mask, and other assorted goodies. Weight: up to 12 kilos. Known in the ranks as "the military's idea of bondage"

Went to ground—Set up camp, or went to bed

Y101—A building number. Home of 1 RCR

What is a Veteran? As defined by the Concise Oxford Dictionary, it is one who has long experience in some area of endeavour including fighting war. This may be extended quite clearly to Canada's long-term commitment to peacekeeping and the continuing employment of the Canadian Armed Forces in the service of peace

What is a Peacekeeper? A Peacekeeper is a member of the Canadian Armed Forces who has been sent by the Government of Canada to participate in peacekeeping missions sanctioned by the United Nations (UN), or the North Atlantic Treaty Organization (NATO), or any other instrument of collective defence that may be entered into by Canada

What is the difference between Peacekeeping and Peacemaking? The United Nations Charter authorizes both peacekeeping and peace enforcement. A peacekeeping mission is established only when both antagonists request one. A peace enforcement mission may be established by the United Nations to intervene in the internal affairs of a state or between states in order to reestablish peace in the area of conflict. Both the Former Yugoslavia and Haiti are examples of peace enforcement. The difference is that peace enforcement may result in the use of arms to impose peace upon the warring factions in order to establish the basis for political reconciliation. In peacekeeping, the arms carried by the soldiers are for self-defense.

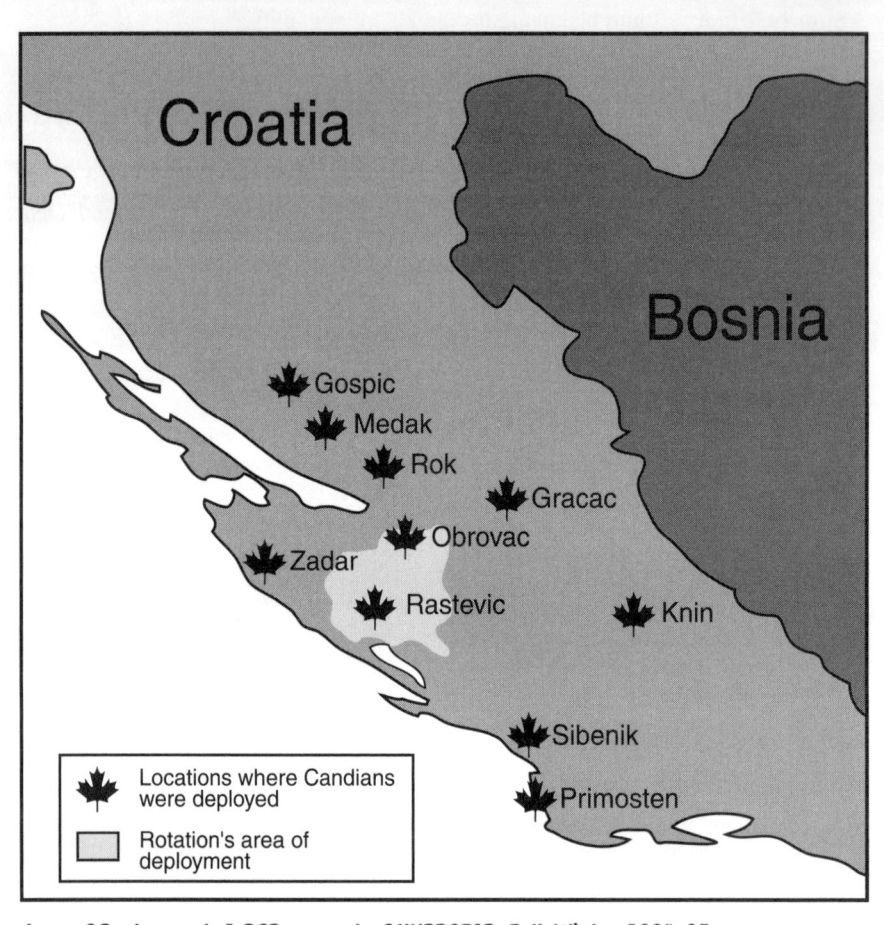

Area of Deployment, 1 RCR, as part of UNPROFOR, Fall-Winter 1994-95

PART ONE GETTING READY

The Sergeant-Major stepped out of the training office and approached us from the left side of the parade square. With his barrel chest, infantry knees, and short legs he appeared to waddle toward where we, the members of Alpha Company of the Brockville Rifles, had formed up.

Without a word, he pointed at one of the troops on the end of our formation, then up at the overhead blowers, which were cranking heat—and enough noise to drown out a car with a bad muffler. The young man in question quickly left the formation and ran over to the panel on the wall that controlled the fans. He threw the switch.

In the ensuing silence, the air of the Brockville Rifles armouries seemed to echo while the people on and around the parade square, rubbed their ears with the sudden drop in air-pressure.

"OK troops, listen in here," the Sergeant-Major began, glancing down at the piece of paper he held before him, "I have here a message from LFCA requesting nominations for OP Harmony, rotation five to Yugoslavia. Is anyone interested?" Several hands including my own shot up. "After dismissal tonight, come to the company office, and I'll take your names so we can start the process."

Finally, I thought to myself. It was now the seventh of January, already 1994, and rumours had been running rampant since September that there would be a new UN tasking coming. The only question had been when. The last three UN tours had shown a marked increase in the number of Reservists brought in to fill out the ranks of the regular force battalions. With each successive six-month rotation, a different militia area in Canada was offered the opportunity to send troops to try out for the tour. Now it was Land Forces Central Area's (LFCA) turn, and it was official. No one knew if there would be another UN tour offered to the reserves again, or when it would be LFCA's turn to work with the regular forces again. This was the closest I was ever going to get to a shooting war, since Yugoslavia represented the most dangerous, public, and toughest of the UN tours Canadian soldiers had been involved in since Korea back in the fifties.

I knew at the time that I was sufficiently suited to the upcoming challenge, for it seemed to me that I'd spent my entire life in and around the military. My dad was in the Air Force, so we traveled every couple of years to a new base. I was in Air Cadets throughout my teens and I had joined the Reserves when I was 20. For the past 14 years I had been in and out of the Reserves three times as jobs and life permitted, and I'd always had goals I'd wanted to achieve while in the reserves.

Most military people will tell you that it's a noble and honourable thing to train to be a soldier in the service of your country, but it leaves you with a hollow feeling when you end your career without ever being tested in the environment for which you trained. That's how it was with me when I left the reserves to pursue a business opportunity without ever even getting close to a war environment. To walk away from years of training left me wondering, could I have cut it when the bullets started to fly. I had returned to the military this time, in the hopes that I might have the chance to put my training to the test, and the only way that I could do it, short of becoming a mercenary, was to get myself onto a UN peacekeeping tour.

For those of us in the reserves, the process of signing on for a UN tour is rather lengthy and exasperating. Over the next three months, bits and pieces of information would be fed to us, only to be changed on the following parade night. For instance, at the end of January we found out that our report date to the Royal Canadian Regiment (RCR) at Canadian Forces Base Petawawa—the RCR was the battalion assigned for this rotation to Yugo—was to be the 14th of June. Then we found out in February that the report date had been changed to the 21st of June. Now, if you have any military experience at all, the term "SNAFU" (Situation Normal All Fucked Up) will immediately come to mind. The only real defense for this kind of situation is to sit back and ride it out, because as every experienced soldier will tell you, things are going to change right up to the last minute. There is another saying which has come to define the attitude of many soldiers in the Canadian Forces when faced with situations which involve timings (which is most of the time), namely, "Max Flex." Maximum Flexibility is that which a soldier must be capable of when faced with ever-changing situations. This, along with the ability to think on your feet and retain a wry sense of humour, generally gets you through most situations.

We were soon to experience first-hand the vast number of things that the modern volunteer soldier is required to do before even reporting for training. The extensive check-off list begins with submitting your name for nomination. That first night in early January 1994, thirteen people signed up. There is no limit to the number of nominees a Regiment may put forward; the only restriction is that each candidate must survive the selection process, and then be properly kitted with all necessary personal gear prior to arrival in Petawawa.

Once your name has been submitted to the company, the next step is to go through your service record to ensure that all the information contained therein is correct and complete. This task is usually completed with the help of your Section Commander, Section 2IC (the second in command), or, if you are a section commander, as I was, you direct any questions you might have to the platoon warrant officer. When this first bit of paperwork is completed, the interview process can begin; and for the average infanteer at the rock bottom of the ranks, it starts with a talk to the platoon warrant.

Each warrant has his own style and his own idea of how the process should work. In our case my platoon warrant was a tall, lean man who prided himself in his ability to know his troops. While he was a superb field soldier, to say that he was strong administratively would be to overstate the case more than a bit.

Clipboard in hand, the warrant parked himself outside his office on the edge of the parade square, and using the principle that if you stand still long enough, the world will pass by your doorstep, he waited in ambush for all thirteen of the applicants. One by one he stopped us long enough to confirm that we indeed wanted to go on tour, and perhaps ask a question or two. Content with our answers and his judgement of us, and whether he thought we'd actually survive the process, he added his comments to our files and passed them on to the next level, the Platoon Commander.

It is the role of the platoon warrant to collate each trooper's information and provide an assessment of the individual. It is the role of the platoon commander to sort through each troop's records and interview the individual. Like so many other things in the military, there is a prescribed list of questions laid out for the platoon commander to ask during the interview. Following the format, they ask questions like "are you sure you want to go on a UN tour?" "which courses do you have?" and "are there any personal problems which may get in the way of your going on a tour?" The questions are designed to touch on almost all aspects of a soldier's life, from financial issues, to how well trained he is and thereby ensure that the soldier is, if not mentally, at least administratively prepared for the tour.

At the end of the interview, the commander would usually ask any personal questions he feels he needs to ask in order to satisfy himself that the soldier is prepared to move on to the next level. Once satisfied, he adds his comments to the file and passes it along the chain.

At the time of our interviews I was 34 years old, married, and a successful project management consultant working at Canada Post. My mind had been made up for a long time that this was something I wanted to do and the platoon commander, who was a friend of mine, knew this. So the questions in my interview were strictly a formality. The platoon commander did ask if I thought I was perhaps a little too old to do this kind of thing. After all, the infantry is known as a young man's game and being 14 years older than the next oldest candidate has a way of making you stand out in a crowd.

For most reservists, going on tour represents their first trip out of the country. Most of these young men were fresh out of high school, and still didn't know what they wanted to do with their lives. For their first trip abroad to be a UN tour to a country where war has been ongoing for the last two years can be an eye opening and traumatic experience. Understandably, each Regiment would have to look closely at its candidates to make sure they weren't getting in over their heads.

Unlike the others, I had the advantage of having lived in Europe for five years while I was growing up. In that five-year period our family traveled to almost every country in Western Europe, and thus we were exposed to a wide variety of cultures and experiences. A fact that weighed heavily in my favour was that I spoke German well and French passably.

Whether I'd be recommended for the tour by the Brockville Rifles was in little doubt, but that is not to say that I could circumvent the system and just go ahead on my own to the training base. Like everyone else I had to be interviewed at all levels. The Regiment wants to be absolutely certain that each candidate is fully prepared before being sent off to the Regular Force as the Regiment's representative.

Assuming that the Platoon Commander likes you and deems you fit for service, he then recommends you to the next level, which is the Company Commander. After the first two rounds of interviews our numbers had dropped to 12 from the original 13. The Company Commander went through the file and asked many of the same questions the Platoon Commander had asked. And again at the end of the interview he asked some questions of his own. By the time we were through this interview, our numbers had dropped to eight. Perhaps it was just my perception of the situation, or the fact that I was pumped for each interview, but it felt like my interviews were shorter than everyone else's.

The next step in the process is an interview with the District Personnel Selection Officer. This would be an officer whose job it is to go from regiment to regiment within the district and interview prospective candidates for the tour. All of our interviews were slated for a Saturday morning.

We all gathered in the armouries on the appointed morning, and everyone showed signs of being nervous. This was probably the biggest hurdle we'd faced so far. If this guy said no to our application, that was it. For us, our chances of going to Petawawa to begin the selection process hinged on a good interview and everyone knew it.

This late in the process it was down to seven men, and one woman. As we waited outside the RSM's office, each person who went in came out slightly shaken, not knowing for sure what kind of impression they had made. And, of course, the instant each of us stepped outside the door the questions started. What did he ask you? He really grilled me on. . . . I imagine things had to be particularly hard for the woman. She was the only female trying out for a position with a regiment with a reputation for not wanting women on the front lines beside their men. In a sense, she was doomed from the beginning. Yet, although she was well aware of the potential hurdles her gender presented, she was bound and determined to be on the tour. Knowing her as I did, I'd have bet my next paycheque she'd stick with it till the bitter end.

When my turn came to be interviewed, I walked in, introduced myself, and took a seat. The PSO was a tall man, or so he appeared, seated at the RSM's desk. He took one look at me and leaned back in his chair, lit a cigarette, and smiled. Here we go, thinks I.

"You're a lot older than the others," he said eyeing me through the smoke he'd just exhaled. It was said in a tone that was as much a question as a statement of fact.

"Yes sir, 34 this summer."

He took a moment to consult the papers he had laid out before him.

"I imagine you know what you're getting yourself into?" he asked with a tired voice, without looking up. Clearly he'd asked this question more than once.

"I imagine." I answered without expanding.

He grunted his acknowledgement, then paused again, as he flipped the page of the form.

"Ever travelled outside the country?" he queried, raising an eyebrow.

" Yes sir. I grew up in Europe, and have been to most of the countries there. I've been back and forth across Canada more than a few times, through the States and to the Caribbean as well." I answered, not taking my eyes off him for a second.

He gave a short grunt and said, "You'd be surprised how many of these kids have never been outside of the province, let alone the country." He paused again and looked back at the form, made some notes then flipped it to the last page.

"So, what would you do if you were surrounded by a group of angry Serbs?"

Interesting question.

"Well," I paused, not quite knowing what to say next. "I expect I'd try and talk my way out of the situation," I paused, "and hope to Christ that someone was calling for backup."

He just smiled, and said "Fine," stubbed out his smoke, signed the papers, asked if I had any questions, and said he had no problems recommending me.

That was it. Interview over.

I stepped outside the office, and stopped to wonder. That was shortest bloody interview I'd ever had. I suppose being a little older has its advantages.

In the end, of the eight who had been interviewed, only seven of us were accepted. One of the guys fell by the wayside. It is greatly suspected that his answer to the question about being surrounded by Serbs played heavily against him. I seem to recall him having said something about letting the bastards have it and shooting his way out; but when I asked him again later he wouldn't own up to it. I guess we'll never know.

Medicals were next on the list, and due to our proximity to Kingston we were dispatched there to have the requisite "turn your head and cough" performed. Eye exams, hearing exams, dental exams, and please pee in the bottle exams, were all performed during the month of April as scheduling permitted. Most of this was pretty routine and didn't really faze any of us. In fact, it wasn't until we caught one young man looking at an x-ray of his scull showing the precise location of all his teeth and fillings (and what little gray matter he might be in possession of, we teased) that it began to sink in that this was for real. This was not a "one by one" square of film that your local dentist slips into your mouth we were looking at. No sir, this was a stick your chin on the pad and wait for the gizmo to circle your head type x-ray.

The experience lasted only a minute or so as this whirring and buzzing piece of machinery circled your head, but looking at the 11" x 14" piece of film it produced really had a sobering effect on all of us.

"Why do I have to have such a large x-ray?" he asked the nurse, as he looked down at the big x-ray sheet of his head.

"Oh, that's just to help identify you if you get blown into little tiny bits," she said, a twinkle in her eye as she took his x-ray back from him. This left the poor guy with a stunned look on his face and the rest of us in stitches. Evidently the question was not new to her.

A Saturday in March had been set aside for a group interview with the district stress people. This was an opportunity to bring all the candidates and their families together and fill them in on what to expect during the tour. Information packs were handed out that contained contact numbers of organisations within the military establishment that had been set up to support those staying behind. By calling one of the numbers you could get a recording of the daily reports the battalion commander in Yugoslavia was giving to NDHQ.

We gathered in the Junior Ranks mess at the armouries, and listened for about two hours as the presenters went through their routine. It seemed to both my wife Catherine and myself that what was being proposed was a whole lot of common sense. Being independent people, we were already doing many of the things that they were proposing. Things like having a close group of friends to consult with when you were down, belonging to a church or club to stay occupied. That sort of thing.

Towards the end of the session, one of the mothers broke down and started to cry. She was worried to death that her son was going into a war zone and was going to get killed, an unlikely yet very real possibility. Everyone in the group tried to reassure her that everything was OK, but I'm not sure how far it went to allay her fears.

In the end, it was a good session. Everyone left with a better feeling about whom to contact if something happened at home, and who would contact them if something happened in country.

Last on the list of compulsory interviews were interviews with a padre and with the CO. Our Unit Chaplain was a Vietnam veteran, and brought unique insight to the interview process; an ability to see past the bullshit and adrenaline and make a realistic assessment of each individual. The "been there, done that" factor weighs heavily in the military, and the perception was that he had plenty of that.

By now everyone up the chain knew what questions were being asked of each of the soldiers at the previous stage. The padre, knowing this, chose a different line of questioning. Being the only married applicant, I was asked to have my wife Catherine along for the interview and as one might expect from a chaplain, it was a quiet affair held in the officer's mess. "Was I committed to the tour?" "What do you think of his going over?"(this question directed to Catherine). "Do you have any family problems that we would like to discuss, or the Unit should be made aware of?" (No and I wouldn't mention them at this late stage and jeopardize my chances if I did). "Do I feel prepared?" (for blood and guts? Is anyone? And just how would you suggest I prepare myself?) "Are all your affairs in order—financial and family?"

In retrospect, I have to say the hardest question he asked, which at the time didn't seem so, was "Are you prepared emotionally for the tour?" I say this only because I didn't know what the hell I was getting into emotionally. Not knowing exactly what we were going to see, or the kind of situations we'd be faced with, rather leaves things open as to how you are going to react. What I did know, or at least suspected, was that I was about to immerse myself in an alternate culture, and that the attitudes of a "pure army environment" were going to take an enormous toll on my civilian outlook. As it should be. I would need to harden myself if I were going to do well at this.

By now I had pretty much decided on the age-old practice of keeping a diary. My reasoning was that it would serve as an emotional outlet for me, and something that I could bring back for Catherine and other members of the family to read. The Padre agreed that this was a great idea and hoped that I would follow through with it.

Catherine, of course, sailed through the interview without blinking an eye. And in truth, the interview was more of a friendly discussion. I always liked the Padre, and talking to him was easy. Catherine felt the same. We felt when it was over that he would have no problem recommending me—us—for the tour. Another hurdle down, on to the last stop: the CO.

The CO's office is located in the corner of the armouries, in the base of one of the building's two towers, just a short walk down the stairs from the officers' mess. It's an oddball-shaped room, with high ceiling, angled and curved walls, and kind of octagonal layout. The room is complete with the requisite fireplace, wood panelling and leather chairs. The desk is a marvellous oak affair that fits the room perfectly, and seems to be made for it. On the back wall behind, of course, is Her Majesty the Queen's portrait, flanked by windows draped in rifle green and red, the Regimental colours.

Going into this office is always an intimidating affair for a soldier, because the CO is perceived as God's representative on earth—within the small universe known as the Regiment, that is—with the RSM coming a close second as his appointed right arm. Usually the only reason you get to see the inside of this office is when you've really screwed something up, and you are in there doing the hatless tap dance (being charged for some crime, perceived or otherwise). Our CO was a tall, well-groomed man, with a magnificent white moustache (all moustaches should look this good). Elegantly spoken and quiet of manner, he rose from his chair to greet Catherine when we entered the room.

Actually, as I think back now, I can't for the life of me remember what was said at that meeting. Catherine and the CO got along famously, and I'm told we were in there for at least half an hour. I do recall smiling and making small talk, but beyond that it is just a blur. I suppose we made all the right noises, and bobbed our heads at the right times, because the CO signed the papers in due course and wished us well.

Whatever have I got myself into?

Once it was official that you were going to Petawawa, the lengthy process of sorting out and upgrading your personal kit began. Most of May and part of June were devoted to it. All of our clothing docs were pulled, and compared to the kit list sent to us from area headquarters. Any deficiencies would be identified at this point and corrected.

This was like Christmas to us. We were being issued with kit I didn't even know CQ had. Things like barrack boxes, something I'd never seen in the armouries, mysteriously appeared out of thin air. Gortex bivi-bags were another item none of us had even known to exist; yet we were told the Regs had been using them for more than a year now. It seems like the Reserves are always the last to receive any new kit that the military issues.

Having at long last cleared all the hurdles required to get us to Petawawa, each of the candidates were told to come into our Regimental orderly room to sign our class B contracts, and pick up our clearance documents before departing for Petawawa on Monday the 17th of June. The contracts were to cover us for our term of employment during the trials.

Assuming we passed through the training without problems, some time in July we were to be offered a class C contract that would take us to the end of the tour. We'd each been given our assignments at the same time. Myself and one other were to report to Duke's Company; he to 2 Platoon, and me to 3 Platoon. Two others were assigned to Bravo Company. One, because he was mortar-qualified, was sent to Echo Company, mortar platoon. And finally the two driver-qualified guys went to Foxtrot Company as drivers in the transport section.

So now it was official. I had everyone's blessing to go to Petawawa and try to make the list of supplementary soldiers who were going off to a war zone to keep the peace. I would be competing against guys who were fifteen years younger than I was. In this profession physical fitness and how well you got along with "the guys" were probably the biggest test of whether you were suitable for the tour, really in a way more meaningful than the long series of official screening interviews. All that was left now was for me to end my contract with Canada Post, put in two weeks of hard work on the house making last minute renovations so things would be easier for Cat, pack my bags, pick up the last of my kit, and get a haircut. The adventure was about to begin.

TRAINING PART TWO

Friday, 17 June 1994 It was a sunny spring day, with a cool breeze blowing from the northwest and nary a cloud in the sky. I hadn't been able to sleep hardly at all last night for thinking about the journey I was about to embark upon.

I walked into the armouries at the appointed hour of 9:00 to pick up the package with all my docs in it, prior to making one last stop at home before hitting the road for the four-hour trip to Petawawa. As I appeared in the door, the Sgt looked up from his desk and said "you're here for your docs, right?" I nodded and then said, "I'm sorry to disappoint you but they're not ready." I didn't know whether to be very angry or laugh out loud. These admin weenies had a full month to get my docs together and they still couldn't get it right.

"It seems," he went on, "that there has been some sort of mix-up at district and they are still trying to compile some information on you. The soonest it will be here is Monday, so you might as well go home and wait for us to call."

We exchanged knowing looks and just shook our heads. Screw-ups like this were a common occurrence when you have to deal with central command. I always hated showing up late for a tasking, it has a way of making you stand out, and besides you can never tell what you've missed. All I could do under the circumstances was smile, turn around and leave. Oh well, at least I'll have a couple more days to putter around the house.

Monday, 20 June No call. Fought off the urge to call the Regiment and enquire. They know the score, no point in bugging them.

Tuesday, 21 June Call came at 8:00 A.M. I'd been up for two hours. Told them I'd be there at 10:00 (it's a 20-minute trip). No point in seeming too anxious.

Picked up the package without incident and drove home. Cat had to leave early to go into Ottawa, so we only had a little time together before I left.

Time to go.

Thursday, 23 June Well, after nearly a week of wondering if I was ever going to be offered a contract, I'm finally on the ground here in Petawawa.

WOW! A lot has happened in the past 30 hours.

The trip up was uneventful, though I will confess that my mind was turning somersaults wondering just what I'd got myself into. The combination of anticipation, and apprehension kept me so occupied during the drive that I hardly noticed the time pass, or how truly lovely a day it was. It had been years since I'd last been to Petawawa, and at first glance it appeared little had changed since my last visit back in 1987. At least the landmarks were the same.

My first stop was the front gate. Twenty minutes inside the gatehouse secured me

Y101, the home of 1 RCR in Petawawa

a map of the base with directions to RCR headquarters, the place I had to report, my car registered with the MPs, and a pass for my car, which expired at the end of September, though my contract was only to mid July. Interesting.

Next on the list was the RCR orderly room. I found Y101, the building they called "the Chicken Coop" quite easily, as it was right at the end of the road. The fact that it was sitting on what I recall was an ammo depot was a trifle confusing. I inquired at the gate and the guard informed me I was quite right. There had indeed been an ammo depot at that location; it just hadn't been there for the past five years.

Driving up to the building I spotted an entrance that looked likely. Not seeing any "No Parking" signs I pulled up and parked the car in a clear area near the door and proceeded inside. I managed to make it about halfway down the corridor when someone stepped into the hallway and bellowed, "Who owns the silver car outside the door?" "Oh brother," thinks I, "here we go."

Turning around I responded "I do," forgetting to add the requisite "sir" to the end of the sentence when you don't know who it is you're addressing. Looking down the end of the hall, all I could see was a silhouette of a tall thin man with a pace stick under his arm (pace sticks are never a good sign).

"Good" he said in a calm, authoritative, bass voice, "would you kindly remove it from my parade square, and park it in the spaces provided!"

"Yes of course, sir" I said as I scurried past him on my way out the door. As I passed the man I caught a glimpse of his rank. Oh God, I thought to myself, a bloody company sergeant major no less.

I pause here to point out that if the individual in question had been a sergeant or a warrant officer, the infraction, perceived or otherwise, wouldn't have been so bad. But in this case I had chosen to offend a CSM. These guys are next to God himself in the world of an Army Regiment (for the lowly infanteer, God can be loosely defined as the Regimental Sergeant Major, or RSM, whose every word has been accorded the weight equivalent to that of the big guy upstairs), and this guy was next in line to be the "god" of this Regiment some time after the end of this tour, as I was to find out later. Not an auspicious beginning.

As I went out the door, a corporal who'd witnessed the incident, chuckled and quietly told me where I could park the car, and thus properly parked, I made my way back into the building and tried to find the Orderly Room.

The world of administration within the Army, is, as many have learned, a world unto itself, with its own language, acronyms, and structure. My arrival on the scene was nothing out of the ordinary that day. I was only one of several Reservists trying to get their paperwork sorted out. The only real difference was that I was in civilian attire rather than the combat uniform everyone else in the building was wearing. This aside, when it came my turn to check in, I was mistaken for an officer and immediately addressed as "sir." The problem was that I was only a Corporal and the young lady addressing me was a Master Corporal, and thus outranked me. For her to address me as sir was just plain wrong and I felt it prudent to inform the young female clerk of my correct rank. Besides, with all my paperwork sitting in front of her, she would have discovered the mistake sooner or later.

The initial in-clearance paperwork thus completed, I was told to report to Dukes Company, which was just down the hall on the right. Upon arriving at my destination, I was greeted by a plaque on the wall that proclaimed that this was indeed Dukes Company, thus called because of an affiliation with the Duke of Edinburgh.

The clerk behind the desk was a French-Canadian fellow who stood a little taller than me, with a bushy moustache, and a thick French accent. "Oui, 'ow may I hep you?" he asked as I walked in.

"Yes, my name is Cpl Grant, from the Brockville Rifles, and I've been told to report here." He gave a look of recognition as I mentioned my name and he reached for a file and began thumbing through it. Just then another individual walked through the door whom I recognized as Paul Sharpe, a guy I did my mortar course with last summer. He was from the Hastings and Prince Edward Regiment, otherwise known as the Hasty P's of Farley Mowat fame, and he too, had only arrived the previous day and was assigned to Dukes Company. As we were chatting away the clerk interrupted and asked if I was the Grant who had the Mortar course.

"Yes I was," I replied but I had signed on as an infanteer, and that I hadn't touched a mortar in almost a year.

He paused and then turned and said, "What do you want to do with him, Warrant?" Up to this point I hadn't noticed the man; in fact, I thought the clerk was addressing a rather large plant at the end of the counter. The warrant was sitting behind a desk next to the counter and the plant and a conveniently placed stack of magazines had obscured him from view. Now that I think back, it's a bloody wonder I didn't see him sooner. When he stood up it was like watching a leviathan rise from the deep. I kid you not, when I tell you that he had to stand 6'5," and had shoulders on him wider than a doorframe. He sported an enormous barrel chest, and the sleeves of his uniform were rolled up just past the elbow, because it was clear his arms were so thick he couldn't have rolled them any higher if he wanted to. Sharpe and I just stood there dumb struck, as we watched him move around the desk. And so it was that Sharpe and I were introduced to Warrant Officer Fuller.

There was a brief pause as he looked at the file, then he said, "mortar-qualified eh, the guys over in mortar platoon are looking for people, you may be reassigned to them."

There was no way in hell I wanted to go to mortars, the chances of my being chosen to go to Yugo would be greatly reduced if I was sent over to train with them. For me it would have meant going back to school again just to relearn the basics, not to mention all the regular training I'd have to do. I figured my chances were best if I stayed with what I knew best, namely being an infanteer.

"I'll be straight with you Warrant," I said "I have no desire to go to the Mortar Platoon. I came up here under the assumption that I'd be going infantry and that's where my preference lies if it's all the same to you. Besides," I added "Sharpe here is mortar qualified and from a mortar Regiment to boot. No doubt he's more up to date on the tubes than I am so you could always send him over."

Sharpe shot me an evil glance then presented his argument for not wanting to go. Oh well, it was worth a try.

The Warrant just smiled then said "OK, the boys are in the field right now, and I'm due to join them in about an hour," he turned to the clerk and continued "give Grant here a room, and then he can meet me and Sharpe down in CQ, before we go out in the field." He then turned to me and said "once you get your room assigned, I want you to get changed and pack your overnight kit, and don't forget your webbing and helmet, we're on the range, I don't have weapons for you Reservists yet, but I'm sure there's lots of things I can find for you to do," he added with an evil smile.

The thought of protesting on the grounds that I hadn't completed my in clearance crossed my mind, but was stopped before it got to my mouth. The sheer size of the guy, despite his gentle manner, intimidated the hell out of me, and in light of my earlier encounter with the Sergeant Major, I thought it prudent to keep my mouth shut and meekly go wherever he wanted me to.

And so the race was on. I had to find a building I hadn't seen in more than half a dozen years, put all my kit into my assigned room, change, pack, then get back in time to catch the MLVW —the Medium Logistics Vehicle, Wheeled.

I figure I would have had lots of time (two or three minutes anyway) to spare if, when I arrived at the appointed room in the barracks, I hadn't discovered that all the bloody beds in the place had been taken already. So now what the hell do I do? I have a timing to meet, and the room I've been assigned has been taken. SHIT, I thought, this is just my luck.

In situations like this, I've found it best to decide on a plan of action, then carry on and sort things out later. I thus brought all my kit up to the room and put it in as neat a pile as I could make, changed, then wrote the following note, "Sorry for the inconvenience, have to go into the field for two days, I'll sort this out when I get back," signed Cpl Grant, Brockville Rifles.

With my rucksack on my back and webbing and helmet in hand, I dashed out the door to meet up with the warrant and Sharpe for a two day trip into the field. Thank God I had a car. Trying to meet timings is one thing, but trying to meet them when you have a carload of kit to carry halfway across a base would have been damn near impossible. Fortunately, the warrant was running a couple of minutes late, and I managed to park the car, and get myself and my kit loaded into the back of the MLVW before he showed up. When he arrived, we loaded a few extra stores and then headed into the field to link up with the rest of the company.

We arrived on the ranges just after 4:00, and Sharpe and I off-loaded the stores and our kit in an area next to the MLVW. The Warrant then told us which sections and platoons we were to report to. I was assigned to 3 Platoon, 2 Section. My section commander was Master Corporal O'Grady, and after stowing my kit in the area assigned to his section, I asked around and discovered that he was on the other side of the range doing weapons testing.

I looked at my watch then looked across the field. Supper was being set up and it was getting close to the time when things were going to shut down. In spite of being told to report immediately to my section commander, I made a decision to wait till things shut down for supper before reporting to him. At least this way I wouldn't walk into the middle of a lesson or testing session. In the meantime I joined the others milling about waiting for supper to start, and joined in the conversation.

Half an hour later, supper rolled around and people started drifting in from various testing stations. I watched as O'Grady crossed the field and went and ate his supper. I waited until he finished eating before I went to introduce myself. Unfortunately the Warrant beat me to him.

Watching from a distance, I could see the Warrant enquiring after my whereabouts. Of course, O'Grady knew nothing about me because I hadn't reported to him yet. Even from a distance I could see the Warrant getting wound up. He jabbed his finger at O'Grady a couple of times to emphasize a point, and he had a real ugly look on his face. From what little I could make out, it was clear I was in a world of hurt when O'Grady got hold of me.

I watched for a bit as O'Grady turned and started walking towards the section area. "OK," thinks I, "the best defense is a good offense. Let's get this over with." I stood up and walked straight towards him. Fortunately he didn't see me coming until I was about 10 feet from him.

"Master Corporal O'Grady, I've been looking for you." I smiled in the hopes that it might disarm him a little. "The Warrant informs me that I'm in your section."

Momentarily caught off guard by the forwardness of my approach, he stopped in his tracks and thought for a second. Then he let me have it. "That's right, and he also told you to report to me immediately after you got here," he said pointing his finger at me and filling the air with his barely disguised Newfoundland accent. He paused for a moment to think and then he said less forcefully "OK Grant, I understand this is your first day here, but let me tell you how it works around here. If the Warrant tells you to do something, then you bloody well do it. You were supposed to come see me as soon as you got off the ML, and you didn't, and that's not on. Don't let it happen again, OK?"

I nodded in understanding, and he then inquired after my kit to ensure it was with the section's then he told me to just hang with the other guys until something came up. Well now, that wasn't so bad, I thought to myself. Not a great beginning but a beginning nonetheless.

They didn't have rifles for all the Reservists, so we spent that evening, from about 6:00 till 11:00 in the butts working the targets for the Regs so they could complete the night shoot portion of their personal weapons qualifications. The following morning we were back again doing the same thing for the daytime re-shoots.

After lunch we marched back from the ranges (roughly 4 km) with rucks and webbing—and it was a hot steamy one for sure; the humidity had to be around the 80% mark and the sweat flowed freely as we humped our way back at a quick pace. I managed to sweat clean through the straps of my webbing. Nobody dropped out though.

After weapons cleaning back at the company area we were cut free to do as we wanted. Tomorrow is the Battalion change of command parade. It's one of the major events of the summer. People would be promoted, and a new CO would be brought in, so attendance is considered mandatory. No administrative leave permitted for this one.

The only warning pertaining to the next few hours prior to the parade came from warrant Fuller. If anyone faints on tomorrow's inspection, they don't go to Yugo. From what I've been able to gather, nobody even went near the mess.

I have to admit this first taste of the RCRs had me somewhat shaken. From being told by an in-clearance clerk that I was different from all the other Reservists—much more together—to being shit on by the warrant, through my section commander, for not reporting to the section soon enough, I find myself a little off-balance and working hard to fit in. Am I really cut out for this life? Am I too old? The first real test comes tomorrow when we have a 3.2 km run in the morning after the parade. How I do there will determine my standing within the platoon and how much work I have to do.

I left a high paying job to do this—have I lost my mind? I'm surrounded by kids, for God's sake!

These past couple of days I've been focusing on trying to get acquainted with the various players and understanding what's expected of me. I've also been wondering what I've gotten myself into. Not a great way to start the tour that I thought I was looking forward to. Note: There are 40 Reservists in our Company. 28 are going, better than 50% odds. I know I can do this—but still I wonder.

Warrior testing can best be described as a basic skills review. By this I mean that the infanteer is tested on a number of basic skills in which he must be proficient in order to do his job effectively. Some of these skills include the load and unload drills on six different weapons, sentry and patrolling drills, skill at arms (which was why we were on the range), and a timed 3.2 km run with weapons, helmet and web gear.

Usually this type of review training and testing is left to each individual Regiment to perform at its own discretion. In Ontario, however, it has been determined that in order to guarantee a consistent level of basic training between the Reserves and the Regular Force Regiments, each Regiment will conduct the review training on a yearly basis, according to the standard as laid out in the Warrior Pam (a publication created by Maj.-General Vernon, Commander of the Army in Ontario). Depending on which level of proficiency the infanteer attains during the run, a pin of gold, silver or bronze is awarded and worn on his uniform.

This is the first year it's been in effect, and because it's a new directive and thus unfamiliar to us, our Regiment (and every other Regiment in Ontario that I'm aware of) spent the entire training year reviewing and testing the troops. A large part of my time at my Regiment was spent teaching and testing everyone else in the Regiment.

In theory, it's not a bad idea, despite all the grumbling that goes on. With the Canadian Army being asked by the UN to take on more and more missions, the Regular Force Regiments simply can't keep up with the demand. The result has been that more and more Reservists are being asked to fill regular force positions within these Regiments to bring their battalions up to strength. By ensuring that the Reservists and regular force personnel are trained to the same standards on a yearly basis, the transition from Reservist to regular force is thus eased, without the need for a massive amount of additional training by battalion to bring their new personnel up to speed. In the end it all comes down to money.

Monday, 27 June Friday was a real bad day! It started with the Battalion parade. My bowels were so upset I actually thought they might let go right on parade. I had an inkling that something was wrong shortly after we formed up. My stomach didn't feel right, and the gurgling sounds it was making were loud enough that the people standing next to me were inclined to comment.

The usual routine for these types of parades is as follows. The Battalion Commander sets a parade time of, say, 9:00 o'clock. The RSM then sets a form-up time of 8:30 so that he can do spot inspections and ensure that everything is to his liking. The Company Sergeant Majors then move that timing up to 8:00 so that they may inspect their troops prior to the RSM's inspection. Of course, the platoon warrants want to make sure that their troops look good prior to being inspected by the CSM and the RSM so they in turn bump up the timing to 7:30. The Section commanders have to ensure that the troops have actually dragged their arses out of bed in time to draw weapons, and that they look presentable. To do this requires time, therefore the timing now gets set at 7:00. This means in order for the poor slob at the bottom of the heap to be on time he has to arrive at the form up point at 6:55, for to arrive on time is to arrive 5 minutes early.

So you can see that on this day we all arrived at 6:55 to be inspected by various personnel of ever increasing rank. For the most part we just stood around, shooting the shit, as we waited to be moved into position prior to being marched onto the parade square.

During the hour and a half preceding the parade, I contemplated more than once asking to be dismissed to go to the washroom, but there never seemed to be a correct or opportune time to ask. Besides, being on the ground for less than two full days, I was unsure how much liberty I could take, and how much the warrant was willing to give. As time passed, the discomfort increased. It is a difficult thing to pass gas without shitting one's pants. But when faced with no other alternative, one tends to focus a great deal of energy on determining whether one or the other is going to happen.

At long last the parade began to move. We marched on in fine military order and took our positions according to a predetermined routine. While moving, the pain in my bowels seemed to subside. Swinging my arms and moving my legs helped to move things around. However, once we stopped and stood at ease, the pain began to return. Both focus and control were required in order to avoid an accident and that necessitated tremendous concentration on my part.

Warrant Fuller appears to have been observing me during my weakest moments because he managed to sneak up behind me when I least expected it. I'd had my eyes closed and was concentrating so hard on keeping my knees from buckling from the pain rumbling around in my belly, that when he whispered in my ear "Grant, are you sleeping on my parade?" I swear to God, I just about lost control of my sphincter right there. Partly from the pain, and partly from being shocked that someone so big could move so quietly, and I hadn't even heard him coming.

I cleared my throat, but a very meek "No, warrant" was all I could manage in response.

Fortunately, about three-quarters of the way through the parade, just when the gas pains were at their worst, the guy behind me decided to faint, and in the process damn near took me with him. As he went down, I heard his rifle clatter behind me, then felt my knees being knocked out from under me. Luckily, I managed to shoot one foot forward and catch myself before I took the guy in the front rank down with us. This afforded me the opportunity to move around a bit, as I was quickly nominated to walk the guy off the back of the parade square, and over to the medics. Believe me, I took as much time as I thought I could get away with to walk off the cramps before returning to my position on the parade square. Going to the washroom was out of the question, because I was wearing too much kit to get it on and off again without being missed on parade. So it was grit your teeth and hope to last.

When I did return, the warrant began a mind-game, which really added to the stress all the Reservists were feeling. It began with him talking in a low voice, just above a whisper, to everyone in the platoon. He was addressing his boys, the Regs, and was badmouthing all the Reservists. "Ya see, boys," he started, "these goddamn weekend warriors aren't worth a shit. That guy"—referring to the guy who fainted—"may as well pack his bags and head for home. He ain't coming to Yugo with us, not if I have my way."

This is all I need to hear, a warrant who has it in for the reserves. Some of the guys were saying that on the first day he had taken all the reserves into a room and laid it on pretty thick with threats to run us into the ground and whatnot. With this monologue the stress levels amongst the reserves have hit a new high for the week. The parade, the cramps, and the monologue went on.

Right after the parade I moved as quickly as possible to the nearest washroom where I had the most violent case of the runs I've ever had. It's a wonder anybody could go in there without a gas mask after I was done. As with all things military, shit flows downhill (no pun intended). Somewhat relieved after my visit to the facilities, I made my way to the platoon form up area to wait for the run.

It didn't take long for MCpl O'Grady to find me and give me the once-over for sleeping on parade. Flanked by Cpl Wyatt, the section 2IC, he stood in front of me with his hands on his hips, and a total look of disgust on his face as he started his grilling. "All right Grant, lets hear it, what's yer excuse DIS time?"

When faced with this kind of attitude the infanteer's only line of defense is to plead ignorance. Snapping to attention I replied "No excuse, Master Corporal!" as I looked at the top of his beret (he was a full 6 inches shorter than I was).

"I didn't bloody tink so" the words coming slowly and were loaded with loathing.

This, dear friends, is not the way to make an impression. At least not a good one. Cpl Wyatt shot me a glance as they walked away. It was clear from his expression that he sympathized with me for whatever reason. This at least was some comfort.

We ran the 3.2 km that morning which helped to knock some of the stress off the morning festivities. Most of us in the section finished in good shape, but some of the regs were hurtin' bad and finished well behind the section. The remainder of the morning passed pretty uneventfully and we were sent home at lunch for the weekend.

There was lots to think about on the three-hour drive home. I recall thinking before I went to bed Friday night that there was a remarkable similarity between the stress I was currently experiencing and that which I experienced in a former job I had as a production manager for a sign company. Something is wrong. I can't put my finger on it, but it's definitely there.

Monday morning—this morning—I woke up at 4:30 A.M. with a start. Something was definitely wrong. I was sweating and my heart was pounding. Over the next half-hour as I waited for my alarm to go off, the same questions kept running through my head. Am I cut out for this? Why am I doing this to myself? Is this really what I want? What do I do if I get cut? By the time the alarm finally went off, I'd resolved to try to deal with the whole situation one day at a time. I think it was Napoleon who said, "Never fight a war on two fronts." I can't please the warrant and my section commander at the same time, so I've resolved to just do the best I can. Cliché perhaps, but at this point it appears to be my only means of self-defense. The culture shock of leaving a civilian environment and coming to a military one had left me unbalanced. This, I thought to myself, is not me. This is not the way I handle things. Get your act together! Oddly, as the day progressed the stress abated. Whatever it was that was out there bugging me is mostly gone now. I have very few days to make an impression, there are too many of us competing for too few jobs. I'm a long ways behind because

I got here a week late, but that's not my fault. What I'm going to do now is stay tuned to the day's task and the rest can take care of itself.

Some good news, MCpl O'Grady is leaving us, he's going over to Transport where it appears they need Master Corporals. Warrant Fuller addressed the platoon and put up a good argument for his transfer, but it was easy to read between the lines. I confirmed my suspicions by talking to some of the Reg force guys who knew him—they all agreed he was a first rate weenie anyway, and his leaving was no great loss. It seems he was a newly promoted Master Corporal and was looking to make a name for himself on the backs of his troops. The result of which was he was real hard on his men. Making them do things like kit inspections that lasted for hours, which were uncalled for. Micro-managing your troops like that is both unnecessary and detrimental to morale. Everyone understands the need to be good at your job, but not at the expense of your people. The rumour is that Fuller had him transferred because he didn't want him in his platoon. I cannot speak to the validity of that, but it seems from what I've heard, to be a likely supposition. I now understand Wyatt's look the other day. At least now I know it wasn't all me.

Tomorrow is new kit issue and a new day. The remainder of today was taken up with an 8 km ruck-march and first-aid classes. I'm glad I decided to start training weeks before I came up here. All the training I did is paying off because the ruck-march presented no problems at all.

The issue of my room was resolved this afternoon when I managed to find a room with an empty bed in it next door to the one I was originally assigned. Man, it's a small army. One of the guys in this new room was in Florida on exercise with me this spring. He's from 4RCR and his name is Ryerson. Nice guy too.

All in all I'd rather be in this new room than the one I was assigned. These guys, two cooks and Ryerson, are older, late twenties and early thirties, and we're considerably more organized than the room next door. That place looks like a disaster area, or as we like to say in the army, like a kit-bomb went off.

Tuesday, 28 June A reasonably good day today. One of those days that fit into the 90% inactivity category. (Military life has been described as 90% inactivity, 8% work, and 2% Holy Fuck! Ratios may vary according to unit involved, and proximity to the front line).

We started the day with a 5 km run which was interrupted by doing crunches by the roadside. Led by WO Fuller, the crunches started out to be a drill, but ended up being a punishment for a guy who kept falling out. He was a new guy named Wilcox, and couldn't run to save his life. We'd start to run and a hundred yards or so down the road he'd start to drop back and after 500 metres we'd have to drop and do crunches until he caught up.

The run ended on Passchendaele Hill, which, being the tricky hill that it is, from the bottom only LOOKS like it's 30 degrees incline, but halfway up you KNOW it's really 60 degrees, and magically gets steeper towards the top. Myself and another fella wound up almost carrying Wilcox up the hill after which, he decided he didn't like the way breakfast went down so he brought it back up again to the cheers and encouragement of our entire platoon who were flat on their backs doing crunches.

After showering and cleaning up, the rest of the morning was spent cleaning the platoon support weapons. Three 50's, a 60 mm mortar, Karl Gustav, and a C-6 came out of the lockup dirty, and went back sparkling.

After lunch we sat around till 2:30 waiting for our turn to draw special kit for Yugo. We arrived at base stores just as another of the companies was finishing up. With so many people in the company, a great deal of our afternoon was spent just sitting and soaking up the sun until it was your turn to go in. By 4:30 I was at the front of the queue. It only took me twenty minutes to go through my kit issue, as my CQ had done his best to get me as much as possible beforehand. Even so, I didn't get back to the shacks until 6:15.

Tomorrow is the first leg of the 2x10 (the old term for back to back 10-mile marches). The first leg is 13 km with rucksacks, webbing, and weapons. I've never done one of these before so it should prove to be an interesting go. The rumour is that we'll be doing a reasonably quick pace with light running as the last of the 3 Platoons in the company leapfrogs to the front of the column.

The rucks have to weigh a minimum of 55 lbs, or 22 kg, your weapon, helmet and web gear are extra. My guess is that my ruck alone weighs 60 lbs when loaded with my regular field kit.

The day after it's a 16 km march with helmet webbing and weapons only. Should be fun. I'm feeling better all the time. I'm getting back to my old self and I'm fitting in well.

I mentioned before that the Regiment doesn't have enough personal weapons to go around for all the Reservists. What they've done is issue rubber training weapons to those who don't have weapons. These things look like the real thing, weigh roughly the same amount, but are made out of the same rubber as a hockey puck. I got one the first day I got here, and the implication is that we're not good enough to carry the real thing, so like the rest of the guys issued with them, I feel slightly insulted having to carry the damn thing around. We've been assured it's a temporary situation, but it doesn't dispel the discomfort—or the snide comments.

Wednesday, 29 June Today our section was introduced to our new section commander. His name is Sgt George Macari, and our first impression is that this guy is a P.T. god. Sgt Macari comes to us from the Airborne by special request, and from all accounts this is a guy who knows his shit. Hopefully I'll get along better with him than with O'Grady.

Day one of the 2x10. Joy of joys, because of my size, and because I don't have a real rifle, I was given the C-6, 16 lbs of automatic weapon, to carry for the duration. Two hours and 15 minutes later I could have sworn I had an enormous blister on the ball of my left foot. We all lined up and plopped ourselves down on the grass and took our boots off. A quick inspection revealed that it was only a hot spot, and no blister. Wilcox developed a blister on his heel early into the march and didn't say anything. By the time he got to the end, the blister had broken, and his sock was soaked with blood. When the medics cut the sock away, it revealed a flap of skin the size of his whole heel, had become detached from the sole of the foot and was hanging only by a little strip of skin. Even the medics had never seen anything so awful. Debate runs hot and heavy whether he'll be charged for a self-inflicted wound because he didn't have insoles in his boots, a classic no-no for a route march.

Immediately after completing the march, we had to move to complete part two of the march requirements. This meant dropping our ruck-sacks and strapping on our web gear and helmet, grabbing our weapons and doing a running jump over a six-foot gap which simulated jumping a trench. We then jog over to a six-foot wall, and pull ourselves over it without any assistance, then complete a 100-metre fireman's carry of someone roughly your own size.

As soon as I started to move through the course my foot felt like someone had stuck a hot knife into it, the pain was so intense. Grin and bear it. No time to quit now. I finished the rest of the course easily.

The funny of the day came when we all stopped what we were doing and watched this little Reservist try to carry one of the reg force master corporals who weighted roughly fifty pounds more than him. You begin to get an appreciation for the hard work the guy put in when you realize that at roughly five foot two, he had to carry a pack and kit that weighed nearly half his weight and he nearly had to run to keep up with the rest of us. The fact that he finished with the rest of us is more than worthy of respect.

He took a long run at the six-foot jump and had to do it twice to clear the distance. It was agony to watch this guy try to pull himself with all his webbing and rifle over the wall. He succeeded only when the warrant quietly hinted that he should use one of the support legs holding the wall up to boost himself over the wall. Virtually everything came to a standstill as we all watched, then shouted encouragement to him as he struggled with the fireman's carry and a weight that was a full third again more than his own. As he approached the half-way point he began to slow down, and at the 75-metre point he had to stop to adjust the body draped across he shoulders. He struggled valiantly to keep going as the rest of us shouted encouragement from the sidelines, but alas, five metres short of the 100-metre mark his legs finally gave out and he collapsed in a heap with the guy he was carrying nearly smothering him in the process. When he finally managed to stagger upright everyone erupted into cheers as they applauded his efforts, and the CSM took pity on him and didn't make him do it again.

The rest of the day we DAGed. Don't ask me what DAG stands for. No one that I've asked can tell me either. I can tell you that it is a process that clears up all your paperwork prior to leaving on tour. UN and Military ID cards, passports, interviews with the padre, life insurance, medicals, separation allowances, and final will and testaments are all addressed at this time.

E-1, the building set aside for the process, had stations set up in rooms along the corridors on two floors, each with a different task to perform. Each soldier is given a checklist and a station to start with, then sent into the fray. It can be slow, but it's probably the most efficient way of dealing with the plethora of paperwork that needs to be seen to.

Good day today.

Thursday, 30 June Day two of the 2 x 10. Up again at 4:30 to be at the RCR building at 5:30. Carried the C-6 again today.

After yesterday's march it became obvious that I had developed a bad case of chafing because of the cotton boxers I was wearing. For this morning's march I solved my crotch rot problem two ways. First, I wore spandex running shorts instead of boxers under my uniform. And then I applied a liberal amount of silicone blocking gel that I picked up from the medic yesterday when it became obvious that I was going to have a problem. Boy, how do you spell relief? This stuff is great! No chafing at all. Of course that doesn't help me with the fact that every other muscle in my body still aches and I'm walking like a hunchback.

We marched the 16 km out into the training area to Delta range in just over two hours. Some running, mostly walking—good pace though. Some of the Regs said it was the slowest they'd ever done it. Even so, there were some hurting people. One guy finished the distance and promptly collapsed. The medics pumped 4 bags of IV solution into him before he started to come around again.

The march ended at one of the ranges where we were broken into relays to do some shooting. Several of us didn't shoot because we didn't have weapons, so we spent the rest of the day in the range shack doing drills on the .50 calibre machine gun. We're told there will be one per section vehicle, so we have to know the load and unload drills cold. What an impressive piece of kit. 129 lbs of pure business. Capable of cutting through a cement block wall a kilometre and a half away, yet accurate enough to cut a man in half at 2500 m on a single shot. Scary is the best word I can find for it.

We all gathered in a large circle around the instructor who proceeded to walk through the drills. Essentially they are the same basic drills as for the other machine guns in the company. Each person went through the load, unload and simple stoppage drills. Again, the funny for the day was provided by the same guy who had so much trouble yesterday with the fireman's carry. It came while he was attempting to perform the load drill. The .50 sits on a tripod that has a traversing bar between the two back legs. The act of cocking the machine gun requires a real snap and pull action, and involves the whole upper body. There's a real knack to it, and most people don't get it on the first try. If you don't get it the first time, what can happen is the bolt can jam and no matter how hard you pull the action will not cock. This little guy on his first try only managed to pull the action part way back, and had to let it go and try again. On his second try it wouldn't budge. Part of the problem was that the machine gun weighed more than he did, so the instructor suggested that he brace his feet on the traversing bar and try again. Well, he did this, and promptly jammed the action again, only this time he didn't let go and just kept pulling, he was going to cock that action if it killed him. He pulled so hard that he actually managed to pull himself right off the floor. With both feet on the tripod, both hands on the cocking handle, and someone holding onto the barrel, his butt was a full six inches off the ground, and the weapon refused to cock. It provided a lot of entertainment value for everyone, and even the CSM had a good laugh over it. This was one battle this guy simply couldn't win!

Around 4:30 the CQ showed up with supper. By now the weather had turned lousy with driving rain and cold winds. It seems somehow ironic that the kitchen would choose this day to serve stew. There was no room in the range hut to set up the serving tables so serving was done outside in the rain. The stew, which was already watery, was further diluted by the driving rains. Any bread you could get was soggy, and you could forget about the peanut butter, jam, or butter.

We found out today that the cuts will be made on the 15th of July. I'm feeling better about my chances. I don't feel nearly as intimidated as the first couple of days.

P.T.—Physical Training, otherwise appropriately known as "pain time'—starts on Monday with flack vests and webbing. This should prove interesting!

Monday, 04 July "Pain Time" was BRUTAL this morning. While we were stretching WO Fuller came over to us and said to Sgt Macari "Sergeant, I want you to run these guys into the ground. I want to see who has enough balls to keep up. "Aw crap...." was all I could think. Looking around the circle of our section, it was obvious that everyone else was thinking the same. The sergeant just smiled (evil bastard!).

We went out to the biathlon trail and ran hills in flack vests, webbing and helmet. Shortly into it we lost one guy who couldn't stop throwing up his breakfast. Henry Wyatt valiantly volunteered to stay with the guy as the rest of us slogged on.

The run started on pavement, but that quickly gave way to dirt road, followed closely by sand. I believe there is nothing worse in the world than running in sand, unless of course it's running in sand in formation! Thankfully the sand gave way to pine needles and a bit firmer footing.

There were seven of us trying to keep up with Macari, who appeared to enjoy trying to run us into the ground. As we got into the hills, five down and five up, by necessity we had to string out. It was pure hell for me trying to keep up with those young guys. Fourteen years takes its toll no matter how much you work out. Subsequently, as the elder statesman, I felt obligated to bring up the rear. At one point during the run I honestly believed that if I made it to the top of the next hill I was going to leave my breakfast at the side of the trail. I didn't but by now I was in a fair amount of pain, and sounded more like a blown horse than a guy trying to catch his breath. I was breathing so loudly going up the hills that later the guys commented that they could hear me coming from the back of the pack. On the whole the group kept together, never stretching out more than ten metres during the run.

The run ended with us coming out of the woods at the top (thankfully) of Passchendaele Hill. Sgt Macari had been leading the way on a narrow trail and we were stretched out behind him. When we cleared the woods, the formation closed up to four ranks of two.

When the Sergeant turned around to see who he'd lost, he was greeted with a tight formation and smiling faces. Judging by the look on his face, I think he was genuinely shocked to see us all there. From that point on 2-Section started to gel as a unit. When we ran back to our company area, we were greeted by the warrant who didn't quite know what to make of us. Here were eight guys running in tight formation, with all their kit on and soaked to the bone with exertion. Yet to a man we were smiling, as if to say "Fuck you warrant. You gave it and we took it."

Skeptical that perhaps the sergeant hadn't run us hard enough, the warrant quizzed Macari about the run. "George, what the hell did you do with these guys? I thought I told you to run these bastards into the ground?" Sgt Macari, much to his credit, stuck up for us. "Warrant, trust me, these guys earned their pay this morning. I ran them hard and they kept up."

The warrant just smiled at us and shook his head, then walked away to harass the next section. Smiles all around.

The rest of the day was spent taking the first aid and CPR practical testing. I managed to breeze through both tests with compliments from the instructors. I hadn't let on that I used to teach CPR and was trained as an EMT. Sometimes it's better just to keep your mouth shut.

The written portion of the tests went easily for me as well. While I know that I passed, what our scores were remains a mystery. We were later told that 50% to 60% of the people failed the written exam. I can assure you that this fact raised more than a few eyebrows. We've been told that there will be make up training scheduled later.

The final activity of the day was .50 cal drills. We're on the ranges for a support weapons shoot tomorrow, and they want us up on the immediate actions (IA's) and load and unload drills. Tomorrow's the first ride in the section carrier, our armoured personnel carrier. Nothing like a ride in a tank to put a smile on the face of an infanteer.

Tuesday, 05 July Support weapons shoot today. M72 anti-tank weapon, C-6 and .50 cal machine guns, and grenades.

This morning on parade, Warrant Fuller asked me to stand for him in the platoon warrant's position during morning parade. I was the most senior person left in the platoon, as most of the Regs were off to the ranges to set things up. Nice to be asked.

It was 3 km to the ranges and we covered it on foot—just far enough to work up a sweat. Upon arrival at the range, we were broken into teams and sent up a small hill to the various stations. At the top of the hill was a cement platform roughly 30 metres deep and 100 metres long. On the left were two carriers with .50s mounted, then next in line were several C-6s, followed by the Karl Gustav, and further along the M72 stand.

We'd been broken into three man teams and our team was first on the .50. I climbed up onto the front of the carrier and was first behind the gun. Once I got the knack of cocking the weapon with the back end of it nearly in my face, myself and the instructor fought with the dammed gun for half an hour trying to get more than one or two rounds to fire in a row. We finally gave up and called the weapons tech for help. It turned out that one of the pieces in the feed mechanism had been installed backwards and when we turned it around, I laid down a couple dozen rounds of continuous fire. What a thrill! What power. A very impressive weapon, but what a pain in the back when shot from the turret of an APC. I got lots of practice loading and unloading with all the stoppages.

The next person behind the gun was a young kid named Ingersol from one of the regiments in Toronto. I was in the process of getting into position to act as number two on the gun—you kneel beside the gunner and ensure there are no feed problems with the belt ammunition—and the instructor had his back turned momentarily while talking to the weapons tech. This kid decides he's going to cock the gun without any direction, and proceeds to start yanking on the cocking handle. The only problem is, he hasn't got the knack of cocking the weapon, so, to better facilitate the cocking action, he spins the gun so the barrel is pointing right down the firing line! And then he proceeds to push, rather than pull, on the cocking handle, while holding onto the handle beside the trigger. The instructor and I moved as one. I jumped forward and grabbed onto the back end of the gun, and swung it around so it was pointing back down range, and the instructor, on the opposite side of the hatch from me, grabbed onto the kid by the shoulder to stop his motion. There was a momentary pause, followed by a severe dressing down from the instructor for acting without direction or supervision.

Had the kid succeeded in cocking the action, his hand was on the trigger and could easily have fired the action. With the barrel pointing across the range, and directly at the others on the range at the time, there was a very real possibility that there would have been numerous casualties. .50 calibre rounds tend not to stop after hitting one body, they have a nasty habit of carrying on through anything in their way including the sides of armoured personnel carriers. It was a very close call indeed, but we worked through it and carried on shooting.

The last activity of the day was the grenade range. Service Battalion was on the range ahead of us and seemed to take forever to put everyone through. They wound up taking all morning and half the afternoon to put through one company of troops, 124 people. We, by comparison, took less than an hour to test the same number of troops. It just shows you what good organization and control can accomplish.

At the end of the day someone left an M72 with sabot insert out on the range. Someone had to drive all the way out to the range and try to find it. In the end, the delinquent M72 turned up in the salvage.

Gas huts tomorrow! Oh joy!

Wednesday, 06 July Finally, at long last, I've been issued with my own weapon, and I get to fire the PWT—the Personal Weapons Test.

We took the trucks out to the range early this morning (no Physical Training) and set up to shoot right away. When the dust settled, I managed to come away from the shoot with a 77/84. Not great but certainly in the top ten in the company.

At the end of the day the section sat around one of the picnic tables by the back door, and decided who would take what training. My score on the PWT was good enough to get me listed as an alternate for marksmanship training to work with the snipers. If that came to pass it'd be great. The training I could bring back to the unit would be outstanding.

Sgt Macari needed someone to take famil training on the HF (high frequency radio) sets. Wyatt (the 2IC) was chosen, but may have a conflict with some of his other scheduled training, so I was nominated again as a standby. All of this is good stuff, and leads me to believe that my chances are better than ever for staying on.

The gas hut was rather surprising today; not at all difficult. We were only in the hut for less than 2 minutes. Outside we all put our rain gear and masks on before we went in. The object of the exercise was to check the seals on our masks. Very professional, very quick in and out—not at all like the basic training as I recall. We use CS gas, which reacts with moisture in the eyes, mouth, sweat and that sort of thing. During basic training the instructors tried to make you sweat and/or puke by making us run on the spot and doing pushups. You had to remove, talk to the instructor, and then replace your gas mask, which stung like hell when the gas attacked the moist areas around your face. Occasionally someone would make a mistake and not clear the mask properly, and inhale a lung full of gas, which usually resulted in breakfast or lunch coming back up and filling up the inside of the mask.

In today's exercise, the only minor hitch with me was my glasses. I have a special pair of low profile glasses designed for use with a gas mask that I was testing, and I found a bit of a leak around the seal on the right side. Not much, but enough to make my eyes water until I readjusted my mask.

Tomorrow, they tell us we're learning to emergency-drive the 113', and we're dividing up into teams for the Battalion sports parade.

Thursday, 07 July This morning we sorted out the teams for the first of the regular Friday sports. I had joined the group for the floor hockey team when the CSM called me by name from halfway across the parade square. "Grant!" he bellowed "get your ass over here for the tug-of-war team." Holy shit, I thought, how does the CSM know my name? More importantly, *why* does the CSM know my name? Trust me when I tell you I didn't waste any time in joining his group. While everyone else went off to practice their various sports, the CSM took us aside and said that he didn't believe in practicing tug-of-war, so bugger off and do what you want.

I can deal with this, I thought; so, not wanting to be seen in the local area, one of the guys and I linked up and went for a 3.2 km run. We surprised ourselves by completing it in 15:12. Not so bad for an old fart, if I do say so myself.

With PT out of the way, the rest of the morning was spent in the 113s. We went out to the Mattawa plain and each of us took turns driving around a sand pit. What a blast! We drove around this sandy area about the size of a football field at full speed and wound up tearing the place all to hell. It was great fun.

The remainder of the afternoon wasted away with kit exchanges. Because I had a car, I arrived at base supply first and so cleared through very quickly. That left the remainder of the afternoon to do as I pleased, so I took the opportunity to head back to the shack and snag some zzz's before reporting to the company area for dismissal. A very slack day.

Friday, 08 July, Sports day At day's end the tug-of-war team had won against all comers. The final match was brutal—having to go three pulls to decide the winner. Our opponent was Headquarters, and their team was stacked (so was ours but that's not the point). They had a lot of short heavy guys pulling for them (being HQ, what else would you expect?). Most of their people came out of the Maintenance pool, and let me tell you, there are some pretty strong lads in that group. When it was over I had bruising on the inside of my right arm, and all along my rib-cage from the rope, reason enough to take the rest of the day off and watch the rest of our teams play.

Dukes Company wound up finishing tied for second with our arch-rivals, Charles Company. It was a good day, and yet, so fair and foul a day I have never seen! (apologies to the Bard) for it went from being hot, to muggy, to raining, and then sunny by turns throughout the day.

Warrant Fuller took all the reserves aside later in the day and told us in no uncertain terms that the crunch comes on Monday.

I believe I'm in a good position for several reasons. First, I'm older, and in spite of this fact I've yet to drop out of P.T., which is a strong point in my favor. It seems P.T. has become the place where the section commanders are judging the mettle we're all made of. Second, I've been chosen for additional training in marksmanship and radio. And finally, because of my Emergency Medical Technician training it looks like I may be slated for additional medical training as front line medic if the shit ever hit the fan.

The tension is killing us. All we Reservists are talking amongst ourselves, and in our own minds trying to decide who will go and who won't. I don't think there's any question in my mind that I'm going, yet the speculation runs high, as does the stress. I keep wondering if perhaps I've made a mistake in shutting down my business. Consulting work can be hard to come by at the best of times, so if I get cut on Monday it could leave me in a real pickle. Warrant Fuller has a way of making everyone so bloody insecure. A guy could develop ulcers worrying about it.

Yet, we must always look on the bright side, mustn't we? The weekend is here and I'm going home to my lovely wife. This is a good thing. Monday we're supposed to be doing a live fire section attack. These are always lots of fun. Something to look forward to anyway.

Monday, 11 July Physical Training this morning was once again…brutal! I'm almost beginning to think I'm getting too old for this shit. Sgt Macari decided that for section P.T. someone different should set the run each time. This time it was John

Renwick's turn. I'd like to think that the guy actually had a choice in where we were going for the run, but the truth is, he was told where to go and with the Sergeant running beside him, he didn't have any choice at all. This, of course, didn't stop the rest of us from cursing him roundly under our breath when we realized that we were headed for the biathlon course again.

As with all training of this nature, the more you do it the better you get. The problem is, no matter how good I get at it, I still feel like I'm dragging my ass and bringing up the rear on these runs. The only consolation is that I'm not really. The section tends to split itself into two groups during the run. There's a couple of the Regs who have a great deal more trouble with morning P.T. than I do, and are consistently way behind us at the finish. This is good for my morale if nothing else. Knowing that I can run ahead of a bunch of 20-year-olds is its own satisfaction. As for the six of us who stay together up front, I'm still looking at their back at the finish line, which isn't necessarily a bad thing. After all, keeping up I can do, it's the keeping up and not preparing to have a coronary that's the tricky bit! To help stave off the impending heart attack, I've decided that I'm going to start running at night whenever possible and I'm also going to try and hit the gym from time to time. It's the only way I can get in shape to move up on these guys.

Today's training involved piling into a truck and heading out into the training area to a gravel pit where a hasty trench system had been established. John Renwick, myself, and a couple of guys from the other platoons were tasked with setting up the targets and trenches. Figure 11 targets, roughly 48" x 18", represented the enemy, and holes in the ground and small mounds of dirt represented the trenches. The entire company had to go through the attack one section at a time, so the day went pretty slowly. The only real hard part was doing the dash-dive-crawl bit on gravel. Landing on your knees in this stuff tends to be a bit painful so you tend to spend a fair amount of time checking out where your next landing spot is going to be rather than shooting at the target. But in our favour was adrenalin and endorphins to kill any discomfort.

At one point in the attack, right after we threw the simulation grenades into trenches, I got up and made a mad dash at a trench. Carrying my rifle in one arm and firing madly at the target while screaming at the top of my lungs I ran as hard as I could. When it was over the platoon commander chastised me a bit for not having two hands on the rifle (safety rules). Oh well, I know my target died a glorious death in the defense of his little bit of ground, and went straight to hell for it. What I wasn't going to admit to anyone was that with the flack vest on, I could barely reach around to my right side to put my left hand on the rifle.

As to the matter of the cuts, we've been told they're coming in two phases. Part one involves removing the deadwood. In our platoon at least eight people have to be cut. Pretty much everyone knows who it's going to be. You work with people long enough, you get to know who the workers are and are not. Part two involves making up the reserve platoon.

The last thing the warrant did before dismissal today was take our preferred leave dates while on tour. He provided us with a list of dates for each leave block as they currently exist and asked us to tell him our three preferred dates, ranked from most to least preferred. The rules are that married guys get preference over the single guys when they make up the lists. So, with this in mind I set about the task of choosing the dates I'd like to go on leave.

I chose to stay away from the Christmas holiday season, even though it would divide the tour neatly into two blocks. Chances would be slim of my getting chosen over someone with children to go home at that time of the year. So I decided to choose a time that would mean something to both Catherine and myself. We were married on 28 January 1990, so I thought it would be a nice gesture as a fifth anniversary present, to take her to England for two weeks. She loves England, and I could think of no better gift for her. For the third week of the block, I could visit my relatives in Germany that I haven't seen in years, and then link up with everyone in Rome.

The dates I've chosen are all around the end of January and the beginning of February. With a little luck, I might have something special to give to Cat this anniversary.

My chances of going to Yugo just went up a notch! Each platoon had to put forward two people to act as the platoon medics. Of all the Cpl's and MCpls chosen from the battalion I'm the only Reservist. For the next two weeks I'm taking advanced first aid training with additional training in morphine, IV treatment and oxygen therapy.

It seems pretty clear that they want me to go, so all that is left for me to do is study hard and pass the course, while getting in shape at the same time.

Tuesday, 12 July Today was another one of those days. P.T. was non-existent, partly because it was pissing to beat the band at 7:30 this morning, and partly because being on course we are technically not part of the section for the duration of the course. Therefore we are left to do P.T. on our own based on the timings laid out by the course. And, truth be told, I just didn't feel like it.

From the battalion, they have selected 65 of us for this training, enough to have to split us into two groups so we could all fit into the two classrooms. As it was our first day on course, the entire day was spent in the classroom getting lectures on the 10 body systems. It ended with a discussion on the reproductive system. In our class the instructor was female and the room was full of guys. Hoots of laughter were heard from both classrooms, and speaking for my class, there was an abundance of snide and witty comments loaded with sexual innuendo. I have little doubt that the other class was any different. But, credit to the instructor, who gave as good as she got, and only added to the fun.

They tell us that next week we get to start sticking each other with needles. This is going to be a hoot. The joke going around is that we'll all be up on charges for suspicion of being drug addicts with all the needle tracks in evidence.

As mentioned I've decided to do my own P.T., and tonight it started with one circuit of the biathlon course. Wearing only a T-shirt, combat pants and combat boots, I completed the course in 23 minutes. I was most pleased with myself for running all the hills without walking.

The next step is to dig out my webbing and start running with it on. With time I can add the flack vest and helmet, but for now I'll just use the webbing, and on rain days I'll hit the gym and push some light weights. Finally, I'm going to try to get out on the Saturday and do between 6 and 10 km at a good steady pace. Then take Sunday off and start the routine again. Great plans I know—I'll let you know how it goes.

Wednesday, 13 July P.T. this morning was something from another planet. We, on the first aid course, were supposed to be cut free to do our own P.T., but this morning the Platoon Commander had different plans.

He decided he was going to do "FARTLEC" training. I tell you a lot of us would like to Fartlec him. The bastard ran us into the ground! We started out at a fast pace and it didn't take long for the platoon to string out. Our first stop involved fifty pushups and as many sit-ups. We formed up again and had no time to catch our breath before we took off at a full sprint. Two more stops brought us to the base track where we did laps. 100-metre sprint, and 100-metre jog to catch our breath. Guys were dropping out all over the place, despite the platoon commanders yelling encouragement from the middle of the field. Thankfully the run back to the chicken coop was at a slow pace and everyone managed to keep up.

Throughout the run, I wasn't with the lead group, but I did manage to stay in the middle. The whole platoon, at one point, was strung out over 300 metres, with the young P.T. gods up at the front, and the overweight, smoker types at the end. Some of us just gave up trying to keep up, and set the fastest pace we could manage. We must have looked pretty bad with the whole platoon stretched out along the road. It kind of destroys the image you might have of a tightly packed platoon running in close formation. Mutiny was on the minds of most of us this day.

Today's first aid training involved 1- and 2-man, child, and infant CPR. We also did some work with the oxygen bottles. The day was extremely boring. I'm not sure which took more out of me, the morning training or the slow pace of the classes, but I found it exceedingly difficult to keep my eyes open. Thirty-five guys packed into a classroom makes for a warm room, and a lot of us were fighting to stay awake—something the instructors noted and much to their credit did their best to rectify by keeping the material moving.

Tonight I decided not to work out because of the beating I took at this morning's P.T. I thought it best to give my body a chance to recover (that's my story and I'm sticking to it).

Thursday, 14 July P.T. this morning was on the Company scale and the Dukes tug-of-war team remains undefeated. We were finished in about 5 minutes flat. Two pulls was all it took and WO Fuller didn't even try on either of them. In fact, spectators told us later that there was slack rope at the end (he of course is our anchor). Fuller in his usual showy style, taunted the other team by waving to them and holding up the end of the rope during the pull. Of the eight men on the rope, only six or sometimes seven of us were actually pulling. Nothing like demoralizing the other team.

Prior to going to class I dropped my barrack boxes off at company CQ to have my name, Service Number and Unit painted onto the tops, in preparation for shipment overseas. Because I'm on course one of the guys in CQ will make sure it gets done.

The remainder of the day was spent listening to first aid lectures. They're good lectures but tiring as hell. Everyone feels like shit at the end of the day, worn out from all the sitting, if you can believe it.

Tonight I went for another run on the biathlon course and shaved 30 seconds off my time. Next week I start wearing my webbing.

Tomorrow's the CO's parade. It'll be the first time this week I'll be with the guys from the section. Being on the course is great, and it feels good to be singled out for special training, but being away from the section stinks. It's like being disconnected. You miss out on all the "in" jokes, and the personal dynamics as the section gels as a unit. When you come back to it, you feel a little like an outsider.

Friday, 15 July Training today finished off the classroom work. We took the rest of the morning and afternoon to do backboard training and vehicle extractions. I must admit, it was good hands-on training. Some of the guys really got into it with the play-acting, and half the fun was in trying to stop laughing at the guy as he pretended to be hurt. All in all it was a really good day.

After work I grabbed my webbing and headed for the biathlon course again. I managed to complete it without stopping in just under 24 minutes. Each time I come off the course, I feel like I have a great big lump in the back of my throat. A couple of years ago I strained my diaphragm during a rowing competition, and I feel like it's acting up again. It feels like my esophagus is pushing against the back of my throat. This is one bit of information that will not get out, for fear it will affect my chances of going overseas. You never know how "higher" will react to something like this.

Monday exams start. CPR on Monday, then Tuesday the written First Aid portion. Wednesday, Thursday and Friday are the practical exams. Time to hit the books.

Monday, 18 July P.T. this morning was on the Platoon level. We tackled the Airborne obstacle course. Four hundred metres from Hell—one walk through, one run through.

There wasn't enough time to take a shower when we were finished, so myself and two other guys from the course showed up dripping with sweat to write the CPR exam. When the dust settled, myself and one other guy on the course managed to come away with perfect marks (50/50). The practical portion went equally well and I managed to duck out around 11:00 for a shower.

After lunch we were introduced to IVs and we began the process of sticking ourselves with needles. IV needles to be precise. I missed on both of my attempts, and subsequently couldn't find any volunteers so I could try again. I'm dejected that I missed both times, but I feel confident that the next time I'll be successful.

Tonight I studied like mad trying to pack as much information into my tiny little brain as possible. I'm going to try and raise a few eyebrows and top this course. As the only Reservist on it I suspect my performance is being closely monitored. It's kind of an unwritten rule, but most Regs consider the reserves as inferior soldiers. Therefore topping the course will put all Reservists in a better light.

They caught up to me today—the rank police that is. I have to remove my Cpl hooks, and put up Private hooks. They're claiming that I signed on as a Private, and that's the rank I should be wearing. What a drag! Sgt Macari told me today when he brought around the class C contract for me to sign. It seems that despite my time in, they (LFCA) are making me go over as a Private. Well, Private it is. I'll put them up tomorrow.

Warrant Fuller told us on dismissal that if he gives you a leave date tomorrow you're going. If he doesn't "guess what boys? That should tell you something." Tension runs VERY high amongst the Reservists.

Tuesday, 19 July Another slack day. No P.T. this morning. The platoon went into the field for the day and I went back to the shack to change and study for my First Aid exam.

WO Fuller inquired as to why I wasn't a Cpl anymore. He asked me to have the unit send a message to promote me up to MCpl, so that he could then promote me back to Cpl. He also said that he was looking to WSE (While So Employed—temporary promotion) me to MCpl and move me to another platoon in Dukes Company. That came as a complete shock, but it sure felt good to know that I was being considered for a leadership role.

As soon as we were finished talking, I immediately got on the phone to the Brocks and tried to talk to Capt Jamison, our liaison officer. He wasn't in, so I'll have to try again tomorrow. Wow, what a feather in the cap this would be.

The testing went well. I pulled off a 74/80, which is acceptable to me. The highest mark is 75/80, so just for the fun of it myself and another guy protested the marking of one of the questions. We'll find out tomorrow if we get it or not. Either way, from what I've seen of the marks, out of the 65 people taking the course, there are only two of us with a mark higher than 70. This is a good thing.

Most of the rest of the day was spent in the field doing Casualty Simulation. We were broken into teams of five, and I was nominated team leader for our routine. The instructors seemed impressed and I was told that I did very well. The next couple of days will be spent doing more of the same. Friday is supposed to be a run through with IVs and make-up. That should be neat.

Tonight I went to the gym for a light workout; a little rowing, a little upper body, and some pushups. I'm still a bit sore from yesterday's run through the obstacle course. All in all, not a bad day.

Wednesday, 20 July P.T. this morning was actually not bad. I worked my way up to the front of the platoon as we started off and ran beside the platoon commander. We went out at a fairly fast pace and let me tell you, it's a whole lot easier to run at the front of the platoon than at the back.

We ran from the chicken coop to the track at the base gym (about 1.5 km) and did more pushups than I can ever recall doing in any given time in my life. I'm going to be sore as hell tomorrow—I can already feel it. We then ran some sprints around the track, and did a pile of chin-ups before heading back.

I called the unit before class this morning and managed to get hold of Capt Jamison. I told him about the RCR's plans to promote me, and his immediate response was to ask if I was calling to get myself promoted on my own. Now, Capt Jamison and I have never seen eye to eye on very much, and I know he doesn't like me, but I had no idea it was this bad. There was a long pause before I decided it would be better not to comment upon his remark. I chose to tell him instead that I was under direct orders to call and pursue this request. I later went back to the warrant and asked him to follow up—which he assured me he would. I must admit that I was quite taken back by the Captain's comment. I find it hard to believe he would think I'd even consider such a course of action, let alone follow up on it. It pissed me off so much that it took quite awhile for me to forget about it and get on with things. What an ass.

The remainder of the day was spent doing CAS SIM (casualty simulation) with make-up and lots of blood. In one scenario I wound up as a patient who had an abdominal wound, with my guts hanging out, and spitting chewed tomatoes over the first person to show up on the scene. They tried three times to put an IV into my arm but all I wound up with were needle tracks.

The funny of the day came when one of the instructors assigned this huge strapping lad to play a pregnant woman. After the initial shock of realizing what he'd been asked to do, (and all the ribbing instantly heaped on him from the rest of us), the guy really got into it. When the rescue team arrived, his voice went up two octaves and he started screaming and wailing pretending he was in labour. It didn't take long before all the victims, the rescue team, and the entire instructing staff were in stitches, laughing at this guy's impression of someone about to give birth. What made it funnier was that we couldn't see him. He had walked around behind the over-turned truck that served as our "crash site," and all we could hear was his flailing about back there. The poor guy assigned to "rescue" him played right along saying in a loud voice (and a thick Newfoundland accent) things like "it's ok moiy dear, I'm here t' help. Now spread yer legs apart soz oi can get at yer." It didn't take long before we had to stop because we were laughing so hard no one could concentrate on the job at hand. When they came out from behind the truck, the two received a standing ovation from everyone and we all took a smoke break. All in all it was a fun day of training.

My leave dates have been confirmed (which means in Warrant Fuller's language that I'm going to Yugo). My block leave dates are from 28 December to 21 January. Oddly these are not the dates I chose at all. Luck of the draw I guess.

So the section has been chosen, in fact, except for one or two cuts, the entire platoon has now been chosen. Our section consists of Sgt George Macari, formerly of the Airborne, and now back with the Regiment, as our section commander. MCpl Henry Wyatt, wit a tic Newfoundland ack-cent byes, and a hell of a nice guy, is the 2IC. Cpl Ted Newman, who at 33 is still running the Ironman, and hopes to remain a Cpl till the day he retires, is our section driver. Pte Jim Tennant, with three years in will be our section's second driver. New to the Regiment, and fresh out of battle school is Pte Bruce McMillan, a short tough, and very strong little guy. Pte Robert Nowlan, our resident Italian, and Pte Jay Palmer. On the reserve side, and rounding out the section are Pte David Kini, who has a promising career lined up as a professional football player. Pte John Renwick, a third year chemical engineering student from the E and K Scottish Regiment; and yours truly from the Brockville Rifles. As good a section as any, and from what I've seen, it looks like we're going to get along well.

As a final note, I lost my protest on the exam so I only scored 74/80. Oh well, I guess I place second on the course and not first.

Thursday, 21 July Company P.T. this morning and once again the Dukes tug-of-war team squared off against an opponent and soundly trounced them. This morning the victim was Headquarters Company. These were the guys who gave us a run for our money during the battalion P.T. day.

During the first pull things were going so well that Warrant Officer Fuller decided to wave to the opposing team, and taunt them with insults. This is all in good fun of course, but for the fact that no one on our team expected it. If he had stuck to a few simple insults it wouldn't have mattered, but Fuller, as he is wont to do, turned it into a regular stand up comedy routine. This, of course, broke not only the opposing team's concentration, but our own as well, resulting in us laughing so hard that we almost screwed up the pull at the last second.

The Company Sergeant-Major, our team captain, was unimpressed enough that he gave us all the evil eye. The second pull was over in seconds, for fear of suffering the CSM's wrath.

So once again P.T. lasted a grand total of 10 minutes. I might add that I'm not sure which caused me the most pain, the pull this morning or the pushups from yesterday. Either way, I'm stiff as a board now.

The rest of the day was spent watching videos and poking ourselves with IVs. One video was from the Afghan war, and let me tell you, it was some gruesome. Two hours of war-wounds and amputations. It was enough to turn anybody's stomach.

I tried my hand again at poking someone with an IV. This is the fourth time I've tried and I still haven't been successful. This time I actually thought I had it, but it was another false alarm. I tell you, those veins can be pesky little buggers to try and find sometimes. Victims . . . I mean volunteers are getting hard to find, word's got out to stay away from me.

Early dismissal today. Final testing is tomorrow.

Friday, 22 July This morning's P.T. was at the Company level again, and lead by none other than our fearless company commander. We only went 6 km, half walking, and half running, with flack vests and web gear.

Towards the end the OC said "flack vests off and hold them over your heads." Now, it had just begun to rain at this point, and everyone around me in the formation, including WO Fuller and Sgt Macari, all thought that we were doing this to keep ourselves dry. This wouldn't have mattered anyway because with 100% humidity everyone had soaked through their uniforms, and the rain only made sure we were completely wet.

Then the OC said "hold it out in front of you," and just as if someone had switched on a big light, we all realized at the same time that we were doing flack vest P.T. And for the rest of the run we proceeded to get soaked.

My next timing wasn't until later in the morning, so I took the opportunity to take a long shower and dry my clothes. The first aid class had been divided into two groups so the limited number of instructors could test everyone. Because I was in group two, I didn't have to report to the pick up point until 11:15, when we'd be given a ride into the field. Once out there, we waited till nearly 1:00 to take our turn through the simulations. Our group had been split into teams of five or so men. That way there would be one casualty per person on the team. Once again the team nominated me the leader, and it fell to me to direct traffic at the scene as we paired off with a victim.

The casualty I had, had a "neck wound" and "open stomach wound," so moving him quickly wasn't the first thing on my mind. I took a little too much time to try and assess and stabilize the injuries before starting to move him away from the burning truck (read truck on its side with a smoke grenade placed on it). The truck "exploded" (read someone dropped a thunder flash to simulate an explosion) and I was supposedly injured in the arm by the blast. Thus injured, I had to attend to my injuries before finding someone to help me move the other guy away from the truck. It was mayhem there for a while as I tried to pick an area for triage, assess my victim, fix my arm, direct traffic, go through the triage process and set victim priorities, and issue orders for the removal of the priority cases.

It appears I did everything in the right order, once I recovered from the "blast" (it was a bit odd waiting for the instructor to tell me what kind of injury I had, as everyone was running around). My assessment was good and I passed with flying colours, which I can tell you was a huge relief.

With the course finally over, next week I go back to the platoon. Who knows what that will bring. I haven't really spoken to anyone because of all the studying, so I don't know what's going on.

At dismissal today we got a reminder to ensure the non-essential kit we were sending ahead was packed in our two barrack-boxes. They have to be loaded into sea containers for the long trip overseas. They leave next week, and we'll link up with them in Croatia. The anticipation factor just went up a notch or two.

PS: Today was my birthday. I'm 35 now, and officially the third oldest man in the Company behind the OC (38) and the CSM (36).

Monday, 25 July P.T. this morning was at the section level. Sgt Macari and Cpl Wyatt were both off doing something else, so I was assigned to take what was left of the section—5 people and myself—and went and ran the biathlon course one way, then jogged back along the road to camp. All the extra P.T. I've been doing really paid off today, because I managed to set the pace in our small group and kept ahead of everyone.

After P.T. we started to get a company level lecture on fire safety. I say started, because just after it began, WO Fuller came to the front of the class and quietly pointed to six of us (two from each of the Companys' 3 Platoons) and we excused ourselves. He then pulled us aside and informed us that for the next three days we were to report for CIS—Combat Incident Stress—training. Asking around, the one question on just about everyone's mind was "this is nice, but why me?"

The CO provided the answer to that one. Gathered in a classroom on the other side of the base, he told us that we had been "hand-picked" by our warrants because we were considered the "informal leaders" within each platoon.

Speculation runs high as to just how hand-picked we all really were. It's the general consensus that most of us were picked because of our advanced first aid training (infanteers tend to be a distrustful lot). While I acknowledge the compliment the CO paid us, I'm afraid I don't have the perspective that the warrant and Sergeants have, so I cannot pass judgment on his statement. In spite of this, one of the other guys from my platoon is adamant that the CO is just blowing sunshine up our collective asses for whatever reason. True or not, having a little sunshine blown up your butt every now and then feels pretty good.

This course is proving to be really interesting stuff. We're covering what to look for and how to defuse stress after an "incident," both one on one and as a facilitator for a larger group.

Tomorrow we start at 08:00 for a long day of group therapy (practice only, sadly—I'm sure some of these guys could really use it), on top of which at 7:30 we have to hand in our two barrack boxes so they can be loaded on the sea containers, which leave this week for Yugoslavia.

Tuesday, 26 July No P.T. this morning. A quick stop at the CQ to drop off my barrack boxes, then off to meet my first timing at 8:00 so I didn't have go to out with the guys. Just as well, I didn't really feel like running 3.2 km carrying someone on a stretcher. The poor guy nominated to ride on the stretcher gets the shit knocked out of him from the uneven rhythm of everyone running, and by the end of the run, all the carriers feel like their arms are about two feet longer than when they started. Better them than me.

They have been training us to act as defusers, either one on one, or for larger groups. It's really not unlike taking a guy aside in the bar and saying "hey, I heard about what happened, so tell me what really went down," and letting the guy rant on from his perspective.

We are told to try and break the incident into three parts or questions; what happened? what was the worst part for you? (instead of how do you feel—avoid the "feel" word at all costs); and how are you now?

At the end of the day, it was my turn to lead a group discussion. Everyone seemed to think I had done particularly well. The assessor even said that I was a born defuser. In reality I think I just knew what questions to ask to draw the info out of each speaker without badgering them. It's easy really, some of the guys are so tightly wound, with so many internal walls up that with a couple of pokes and prods in the right place they spin like tops.

The most interesting part of the day came when the session was officially over and we still had some time to kill, so everyone started talking. Fully half the class had gone to Yugo on the very first tour. They started telling stories and making observations. I learned more in one hour listening to these guys, than I did in the six or so weeks I've been here. In short, the Regs feel that this battalion flinches far too easily, is charge happy, and that the "Red Sash Society" (Sergeants and above wear red sashes with their full dress uniforms) generally ignores what the troops have to say. They feel the officers are "right out there," and that the Regimental Sergeant-Major is an egomaniac.

How much of it is just blowing steam and how much is true remains to be seen, but in light of the fact that everyone in the room agreed with what was being said, it makes one wonder. Certainly it's not very encouraging considering where we're going. To say the very least, it was illuminating.

Wednesday, 27 July No P.T. again today. My 8:00 am timings saved the day yet again. This is the second morning in a row I've been able to have a full breakfast without threat of bringing it all back up on the morning run.

This morning was spent listening to testimonials from various people who have been in theater. A sergeant from the Engineers told us about mines, bridges and booby traps. A captain told us about his experiences as someone who had to collect dead bodies. He had us rolling in the aisles as he told a story about how his driver and he had been called out to collect a body in a minefield. After getting lost several times on the way there, they finally arrived and stuffed the several day old—and bloated from the heat—body into a body bag, then struggled as they loaded it onto the back of a 5/4 ton truck. I should point out at this juncture, that the body collection team had taken to calling all the bodies "Bernie's" after the movie about the two guys in "Weekend at Bernie's."

As he told it, after loading the body, they started off down the dirt road. He and his driver were following the 5/4 ton truck in an Iltis, and after going over one particularly bumpy part of the road, noticed that the tailgate of the 5/4 had dropped open. As the truck bounced, the Captain and his driver watched in horror, as the body bag worked its way closer and closer to the edge of the tailgate. Anticipating what was about to happen next, the Captain reached for the microphone of the radio to warn the driver in the truck ahead. Unfortunately, he wasn't fast enough, and hitting another series of bumps in the road, the body-bag flew out of the back of the truck and skidded to a halt on the shoulder of the road. The driver of the Iltis slammed on the brakes and slid to a halt only metres from the body-bag, both driver and Captain staring aghast at the bag on the road before them. The driver of the truck must have noticed what happened because he stopped the truck immediately, and jumped out, ran up to the body-bag, and assuming the position of a major league umpire, yelled at the top of his lungs "-and Bernie slides into home plate and he's SAFE!!" After a moment's pause, both driver and captain broke out in howls of laughter and nearly fell out of the Iltis. The truck driver manhandled the decomposing body back into truck, secured the tailgate and took off down the road, leaving the captain and his driver to compose themselves before following. We of course were equally amused by the story, and continued to get a chuckle out of it the rest of the day.

On a more sobering note, we listened to a private who was in Bosnia on a soccer pitch that was being used by the UN as a staging point for a refugee evacuation by helicopter. He had been assigned as security detail for the evacuation of a local hospital. During the loading of the helicopters the Serbs began shelling the field with mortars, and in a desperate race to get to cover, he was hit in the back of the head with a piece of shrapnel. As he told it, the last thing he remembered was running for cover. He woke up 3 days later in hospital wondering where the hell he was.

For the past year and a half he's been trying to get past the experience. As he stood before the class, he fought hard to control the tears as he described the drinking problems, bad sex, lack of communication with his wife, keeping things to himself, and his initial belief that he could deal with everything himself, but finally coming to the conclusion that he couldn't. He spent a lot of time in the messes just hanging with the guys, and avoiding going home. He finally broke down and saw a counselor when one day he was sitting on his porch steps and his three year old daughter came up to him and put her arms around him and said, "it's going to be OK daddy." He burst into tears and realized then that he needed help. He's been in counseling for six months now, and has requested not to be sent on this tour. All of this was meant to bring to light the items or elements which might cause stress in the soldier. And I can tell you the light was a bright one.

The morning was capped with another gab session under a tree, which lent further credence to those points raised against the battalion yesterday.

All in all it was a great course to have. Everyone agreed that the best part was to have privates and corporals as counselors. In the past, men who were "shell-shocked" during the First World War were treated as cowards and shot. In the Second World War the army treated shell-shocked troops as cowards and painted yellow crosses on their backs. Between 1945 and 1992 the problem of combat incident stress was ignored. With the start of hostilities in Yugoslavia, the medical establishment finally won the battle and had CIS identified as a legitimate medical condition. Earlier tours brought people over from Canada to do the debriefings, and the troops reacted predictably (who the hell are you and what the fuck do you know about. . . ?) With the introduction of this course, we will be the first troops trained to talk infanteer to infanteer. It makes a difference.

In the afternoon it was back to the platoon where we rode around in carriers on simulated VIP escort. Riding in carriers is going to be a problem with me, because I develop motion sickness really quickly if I'm stuck in a hole and can't see out. I am not looking forward to this part of the training.

Thursday, 28 July Company P.T. again this morning, and as boring as it sounds the tug-of-war team won yet again. In fact, Dukes beat Charles Company so badly in 6 of 7 sports that their CSM took the whole company out for a punishing run late this afternoon. I have to admit that I felt a little sorry for them because their CSM is a runner, and in REALLY good shape. Everyone just winced as we watched them run down the road in formation. You gotta know it was going to be a painful run.

The morning was spent in the theater doing vehicle recognition. We were off between noon and 3:00 for personal administration, then down to Kiska beach for a company smoker and family day. After the party a bunch of us wound up back in the barracks for continued drinking and philosophical discussion (as infanteers tend to do when they are plying themselves with excessive drink). Some great tunes were played, some god-awful singing was heard, and I drank entirely too much. It was so good to sit with guys who understood how I felt about Canada, honour and getting the job done.

Stomping Tom Connors was a hit with his song " the Blue Beret." In these parts, it's become something of an unofficial anthem. There's actually quite a story as to why this is so. As the story goes, one of the lads first heard the song on one of Tom's albums, and wrote to him, explaining that the Battalion was about to go overseas and would he consider doing a concert for them. Not only did he do the concert free of charge for the Battalion, but he brought a film crew to Petawawa, and shot the Blue Beret video on the base using the soldiers as a backdrop all wearing their blue berets.

Now I know there's a lot of people out there who don't care for Stompin' Tom, but having seen him once in concert years ago, I have to admit there's just something about him and his songs. There's no doubt about it, he ain't pretty, and I doubt his songs would win any rewards for composition, but like Bob Dylan, it's what he says with his music that reaches people. The Blue Beret is a simple song, yet his simple act of kindness and the respect he showed for the soldiers of this base have won the hearts of everyone here, and in simple terms, ya gotta respect that. What a great night!

Friday, 29 July Morning parade was at 9:00 instead of 7:00. And a damn good thing too, much earlier and I probably wouldn't have made it. I never suffer from hangovers, and the last time I howled at the moon was just before I got married, but this morning I was suffering from a whopper of a hangover.

We didn't do very much in the morning, mostly running around getting administrative problems solved (pay etc). In the afternoon we watched the movie "Sniper" with Tom Berringer. Hollywood crap! At times it was hard to hear the movie for all the heckling. It's hard to argue with a guy when you know he's sniper-qualified. George (Sgt Macari) led the heckling, being a Master Sniper, and many others joined in. Dismissal was at 4:00 and I'm off home for the weekend.

Monday, 01 Aug. No P.T. this morning, we formed up at 7:00 and moved all our vehicles out of the vehicle compound for reasons unknown. We then waded through a day of Mine Awareness. This is all good stuff—but my god it's boring. The only really interesting part came when we did the "what to do when caught in a minefield and your lead man is down" drills (in the rain no less—if it aint rainin' it aint trainin'). At least then we were doing something. At least we were moving around.

On dismissal we got the worst news I've had since I arrived. All Reservists are to go to CAC—summer concentration of reserve units in Petawawa for training—during block leave. No time off. That's all the warrant said. Just the thought of 10 days in the field turns my stomach, let alone going back to my unit just to do this exercise. All of us feel that we've earned our place in the Battalion and that it's not right to send us back. To say that there were some very disgruntled people on parade, would have only begun to describe the situation. They call it "getting the big green cock," and man, it looks like we'll get it big time.

Tuesday, 02 Aug. P.T. this morning consisted of a platoon run of 9 km. It wasn't all that bad, but the platoon commander insisted on stopping every 2 km and doing pushups. Even that wasn't so bad, but on the last stop I started cramping up pretty badly, so the last bit of the run was pretty hard.

All the stops along the way took up time, and some of the guys today were pissed at the platoon commander for leaving them too little time after P.T. to clean up and meet their first timing. There is much truth in this because I was some miffed about the situation. He seems to have forgotten that some of us have to go clear across base to get to our shacks. For the guys who live in single quarters the situation is not so bad because they're located right next to the Battalion complex. But for the married guys, the Permanent Married Quarters are located on the far side of the base. And if you have a house you're off the base. I'm located in the transient quarter near the PMQs, so for several others besides myself, a car is the only solution to meeting the timings. This problem is compounded by the traffic jam which occurs after P.T. because everyone is trying to get out of the parking lot (which, by the way, is wholly inadequate for the number of people who try to park there), in an effort to get home and back on time.

Fortunately I made my timing, but I feel badly for the guys who had to ride bikes home and back. They could legitimately ask why bother showering?

Mine awareness was the theme for today's classes and was a good go. We were in class all morning. I fought through every class to stay awake, as did so many others. In the afternoon we walked out to the old airfield to do identifying unexploded bomb drills, and how to report them.

All in all it was another slack day. Tomorrow we run the 3.2 km for good. Our times will be recorded and will count towards our final standing and the colour of badge we will wear. It's supposed to be a free-for-all, but Sgt Macari wants to run it as a section in formation, and in under 18 minutes. We'll see what happens tomorrow.

Wednesday, 03 Aug. P.T. this morning was the timed 3.2 km run I mentioned yesterday. This is part of the required training for Warrior testing, and all the P.T. we've been doing has been to keep us in shape to complete the run. The run itself must be completed while wearing your helmet, webbing, and carrying your rifle. Running shoes are not permitted, as you must be in full combat uniform, which means running it in combat boots.

The standards to meet are; gold, if you finish in under 18 minutes; silver, if you finish between 18 and 22 minutes; and bronze, if you finish in between 22 and 24 minutes. If you take longer than 24 minutes, you have to do it again and again until you pass.

I took the car over the course last night to figure out where the ¼, ½, and ¾ points were so I could pace myself. I like to start off a little slower and gradually build my pace, so knowing where the various marks were lets me know how I'm doing. My plan is to finish in around 17 minutes. Not too fast, but fast enough to get gold.

Each platoon in the company was given a time to report to the start line to ensure sufficient spacing on the course (each company ran the course on different days). Our company formed up, and each platoon, then each section broke off to do our warm ups and stretches prior to reporting to the start line. Between us we had agreed that our section was going to do the run in formation, as a section. This would help some of the slower runners break the 18-minute mark. So much for my plans.

The platoon formed up again and we marched over to the start line. As we approached the line one of the timers stepped forward and shouted "GO!" It caught everyone off guard. All the carefully laid plans went out the window and we took off in a mad dash of assholes and rifle butts, everyone fighting for open space. Back to plan A. It took a lot of discipline not to run out at the same pace as all the others, and just let the pace develop. I wanted to hit my marks and finish in good time.

Around the 500m mark I came up fast on WO Fuller. He's a huge man, and by this point he was already drenched in sweat, and it was clear he was working hard. As I passed him, I took a quick glance sideways and made eye contact. I came very close to blurting out the thought that came instantly to mind, come on warrant, you're not going to let an old man beat you are you? but the thought of him strangling me in one of those big meat hooks of his stopped me from saying anything. In spite of this, I think he got the message anyway, because he just smiled at me as I went past. In retrospect, I probably should have said something. I figure he would respect me for being older and taunting him, and besides, he has to carry at least 50 more pounds than me, and I'm certain I can run faster scared than he could mad, so I figure chances are pretty slim of him catching me (but then what do I do when the race is over? . . .)

As I rounded the ¾ mark on the trail, a Sergeant. whom I recognized, came up beside me and ran with me for a while. "Good pace you've got going, mind if I run with you for a while?" he asked.

"Not at all" I replied, between breaths.

"What time are you hoping to finish in?" he inquired.

"Around 17 minutes. Why?" I asked.

He just smiled and said, "because I want to finish around 13 minutes." Momentarily confused by his statement, it suddenly occurred to me that this guy must have started behind us and he was in the process of running our entire platoon down. Just to rub salt into the wound the bugger turned to me with a smile and said "your pace is too slow for me. See ya", and promptly sprinted off ahead of me.

"Well, fuck you, Sergeant," was my immediate reply, and I picked up the pace and tried to catch him (I never claimed to have brains). For the next kilometre, I ran my heart out trying to catch the bastard, and try as I might do you think I could close that 5 m lead he had on me? Not a hope in hell.

When I crossed the finish line, I was winded and a little dizzy, but for the most part none the worse for wear. Looking around, I began to wonder if I'd stopped at the right place because there were only a couple of runners about catching their breath. I found Sgt. Macari and John Renwick together, and knew then at least that I was in the right place. It was only later that I found out that I'd finished in a time of 16:18 and posted one of the faster times in the company behind only a handful of others.

After a quick shower and change we did some FIBUA—Fighting In a Built Up Area—lectures, and another stress lecture at the platoon level, which I promptly slept through.

The afternoon was spent in a lecture given by the Officer Commanding. He gave us a breakdown of the area we were going to, and some of our responsibilities. It looks interesting but it's boring as hell. The worst part is that all the Observation Posts are built with biodegradable sandbags, so guess what we'll be doing when we get there?

Block leave starts for the Regs on Friday, and the word about the reserves staying behind is that we do not have to do CAC, thank the gods, the Lord be praised. Fuller let on that the CSM was having us on. I'll tell you, a lot of sphincter muscles were working overtime thanks to him these past two days.

Thursday, 04 Aug. The final company sports parade was this morning. Once again our tug-of-war team beat the doodoo out of the opposition. Fuller has become quite showy in his taunts of the opposition, with waves, and swinging the end of the rope in the air to show that he's not adding his weight to the pull. Meanwhile the rest of us are too busy pulling our hearts out to really take notice of him. I'm told he was quite entertaining.

All the Regs are talking about block leave and razzing the Reservists about it (they're leaving and we're staying for the two weeks). This has all of us rather upset. We feel we've earned our right to be part of this battalion and to be left behind only emphasizes yet again the difference between Regs and Reserves. My understanding of the situation is that we're staying because of "contractual reasons." This may be so, but it doesn't make it any easier.

While the rest of the guys went off to do FIBUA training I went upstairs to the pay office to try and sort out my separation allowance (it only took me an hour and a half!). During the discussion in the BOR my promotion to Cpl was brought up yet again. Why I wasn't one, basically. A review of my record showed that I have the equivalent of four plus years of full time employment, sufficient to warrant promoting me to the rank of Cpl on Class C. Despite this, LFCA is insisting that I be a private. I'm told it's a money thing. With all the cutbacks, they can't afford to promote anyone, and as a result I have to draw private's instead of corporal's pay. The difference is about $10,000 in take home pay.

At lunch Warrant Fuller read a memo to the platoon about direct entry opportunities offered to Reservists, then later he came over to me and asked why I hadn't signed up. I just looked at him and said "Warrant, I'm 35 years old, what kind of career opportunities do you think I'll have?" That made him think, I don't think he really realized what he was asking when he talked to me. It's obvious he thought I was a natural for the job, but hadn't considered my age or the fact that I had been self-employed before joining up. For me, the army was more of a hobby than a job, and I had no desire to change that. Going overseas was one thing, but asking Catherine to pull up stakes and move on base would be a fast way to end a really good relationship. The discussion then turned to my rank. He promised to look into the problem over block leave. (It appears that the unit, when WO Fuller called and spoke to them, promised to look into the situation and never called back. It also appears that the Bn.CO can promote me at his discretion so Fuller is looking into that possibility as well).

Early dismissal at 2:30. Everyone buggered off but agreed to meet after supper to party. The guys are really coming together. Everyone in our platoon likes everyone else, which is kind of odd really, and it's the general consensus that 3 Platoon is the best place in the company to be, because of its leaders and troops. We've called ourselves the "3rd Herd," and the name's caught on.

The party went long and hard. I begged off at 11:00 and headed back to the shacks. This time out I didn't drink as much as the last time. Maybe it's old age, maybe it's experience, but my desire to party is out-weighed by my desire to remain vertical during the parade tomorrow.

Friday, 05 Aug. Late to rise this morning. Up at 6:30 and took my time getting ready. I had a good breakfast to combat any ill effects I might suffer from last night's excesses, but I don't think that will be a problem.

It's amazing the number of guys who were wearing ribbons on parade today. Cambodia, Kuwait, and Yugoslavia were prominent as well as Cyprus. One guy in my section, Cpl Ted Newman, had five of the darned things (our last CDS only sported a

CD which in itself is a bloody disgrace). Even the CSM commented on it (he only had three).

The parade was mercifully short, which was a good thing, because we were formed up on tarmac, and the sun was awful warm. It didn't take long for the polish to start melting off the boots.

It's kind of funny to see how everyone gets to know the people in command. I was standing beside MCpl Ray Labell throughout the parade, and through our conversations (very quiet, and under our breath), it became obvious that he could anticipate everything that was going to happen. RSM Bennett for example, is known far and wide for his "all tigers, no donkeys" speech. Before the parade, as we waited for things to get started, speculation ran high as people argued back and forth as to whether or not the RSM would indeed give the famous speech.

As the parade drew to a close, and the various commanders commented upon how well we performed during training, Ray whispered over to me to listen up for Bennett's approaching speech. Sure enough, when the RSM stepped forward to give the last address of the parade, it was as if everyone had been given a copy of the speech ahead of time and was reading it along with him. He talked of pride of Regiment, of quality soldiers, and doing your job, something everyone bobbed their heads to and made little grunting noises of agreement ala Tim Allan. And then, as he came to the climax of his speech, it was as if everyone held their breaths in anticipation, then repeated the words at the same time in quiet unison when he said "and remember, this regiment has all tigers, and no donkeys in it!" Whether he actually heard us is unknown, but I can assure you that everyone in our platoon repeated the words along with him, and we all walked off the parade with a knowing smirk on our faces.

The post-parade dissemination of information was short, everyone wanted to get out of there and start their leave. Dismissal was at 12:00. I took my time to get changed and have a decent lunch before I hit the road for home.

Just an observation. I'm finding it more and more difficult to switch off after I leave this place. I get home and my mind is in neutral. I listen to Cat talking to the animals sometimes and I wonder if she's not from another planet.

I also find I don't want to be around other people. Catherine's sister's kids came up this weekend (Derek and Meaghan) and the minute they walked through the door the noise level jumped about 100 decibels. Cat was stressed from the 14-hour drive from Sault Ste Marie where she'd gone to pick them up, but said it was "happy noise", which it probably was, but it still pissed me off.

Sunday we went for brunch at a local pancake place, and at one point in the meal I just about reached over and clubbed Derek for misbehaving. No fault of his, he was just being a kid. I'm still not sure how I managed to control myself, but it surprised me how strong the feelings of anger were.

This base, perhaps this army, does something to you. It's a world unto itself, and it breeds a certain kind of toughness that you don't find in the civilian world. Shutting your emotions off in an effort to block what you've just seen or done creates a time bomb in people, which in the end catches up with them. There's a lot of people here who are on short fuses and are barely holding it together. You can see it in the eyes of the guys who have done more than one tour. They've suffered bullshit, bad rations, cold weather, and poor living conditions, and below-the-poverty-line pay, and the strain of trying to keep their family together while they're away. All of which would break any civilian asked to walk off the street and do our job. There's a toughness, an attitude, about them. Nobody here talks about "feelings." It's not a manly or macho thing to do. And if you did, you would open yourself up to ridicule and razzing so fast that you'd never recover.

Everything here is about being tough. Put a bunch of guys in a barrack block and magically the skin-mags appear, and the walls get papered with centerfolds. Not long after the porno flicks are being shown, and then the tough-guy commentary starts. Self-images are fostered through magazines, war novels, and videos. Left too long in the cycle, the internal walls become impenetrable. Is it any wonder that after these guys get married they suffer from drinking problems, wife abuse, and a seriously unbalanced self-image.

I'd like to think my viewpoint is seriously skewed, but everyone I talk to tends to agree completely. I worry sometimes that I'm being drawn, unknowingly, into the same cycle. I've noticed that the longer I'm here the more separation there appears to be between myself and the outside world. In a way I know it's a form of self-defense. I'm going to a tough place where to survive I too must be tough. Part of me loves this shit, and part of me can't stand it. I know now that I would have made a damn good infanteer, had I joined when I was twenty, but also clearly, I don't belong in the ranks.

I've been asked by warrant officers and sergeants alike, why it is that I'm not an officer, and my stock answer is that I'm having too much fun in the ranks. Besides, there's no way I would be on this tour if I had joined the reserves as an officer.

I've noticed I'm becoming increasingly intolerant of people outside the military, and that I'm more forceful in my beliefs. Most of the time I can control it but other times I feel like popping someone (I wish I could give you an example but nothing comes to mind). On the other hand, I got angry with Cat a couple of weeks ago for complaining about a pain she has been having in her back. I became intolerant and made a very uncharacteristically unkind remark, the gist of which was you don't hear me bitching about my aches and pains, which are many, so why should I listen to you whine? I apologized this weekend for that. There's a war going on inside of me, and I feel like the part of me that is civil, caring, and tolerant, is getting the shit kicked out of it. If this is what happens after seven weeks, what will happen after eight months?

What this really boils down to is that life on this base has no connection to the outside world. We train to do things in an environment that most people can't even imagine let alone understand, and yet civilians seem to think they have the right to pass judgment. The longer I'm here, the more isolated I become. Life is the Army, the Army is life.

Monday, 08 Aug. P.T. was the CO's route today, 8.8 km in 40 minutes. Not a bad run at all.

I've been appointed the platoon warrant for the next two days, section commanders rotate every day. Now that the Regs are on leave, we're moving the positions around within the platoon.

Today we went to the rappel tower. Showing up at the site, getting organized, then progressing through the various levels on the tower took most of the day. By the time the last guy went off the top of the tower, it was close to 3:30, so we knocked off early. It was good to skip off the side of the tower again, it's been quite a while since my last rappel. Next week, they tell us, we're going to the Ottawa River to a rappel sight that has a 60-foot drop right down to a raft on the water. That is going to be fun.

All in all it was a slack day. The funny for the day came when we lost a section commander. He showed up an hour-and-a-half late looking a little sheepish. I guess what happened was he reported to the wrong classroom first thing in the morning, and got stuck in a lecture for the duration, being unable (or unwilling) to leave the class until they took a break.

The platoon commander (Mr. McConnell) suggested we charge him, but I convinced him not to. This is a slack time until everyone else comes back, charging him would be a waste of time and bad for morale. Tomorrow we're scheduled for track maintenance—oh joy!

Tuesday, 09 Aug. Today's P.T. involved a fast run to the gym, followed by lots of upper body work and two laps of sprints, then a casual run back to the RCR building. We even had time for breakfast before starting the day's training. Damn decent of the Lieutenant to make the training work out that way.

The powers to be have decided that this two-week period will be fairly easy on us, because when it's over the field training starts. In talking to the platoon commander it seems that no real training plan has been laid out for us, so they're flying by the seat of their pants for the time being.

Training today, if you could call it that, was track maintenance. This involves stripping down the vehicles, 113s, and washing them out with a high pressure water hose, doing inventory, and learning how to change the tracks and road wheels.

Fortunately, I was spared much of the drudgery by using the excuse of platoon administration. Weekend leave passes take a long time to fill out, and there always seems to be some little problem to look after. Odd how that happens really.

After lunch I thought I should put in an appearance, so I went over to learn how to change a road wheel. The operation involves having someone crawl under the vehicle and carefully place a fifty-pound piece of steel, nicknamed the torpedo, on the track at an angle, so as the vehicle advances slowly it wedges itself into position. Once properly placed, the guy then crawls out from under the vehicle, and it is slowly advanced until the jack is in the upright position compressing the suspension leaving the road wheel off the ground, where it can then be changed. On hard pavement this is a fairly straightforward operation. But I'm sure you can appreciate that as terrain degrades (mud, water, etc) the level of difficulty increases. The danger in the operation is if the tool is incorrectly placed. Thirteen tons of track can shoot this fifty-pound tool out from under with amazing velocity. For that reason, every effort is made to do it safely, and everyone stands well back.

I figured I'd better get my hands dirty, so I volunteered to place the torpedo. Lying on my side I held the torpedo in both hands and in the correct position to engage the rocker arm of the road wheel. I then told the guy directing the driver to slowly advance the track. When the driver pushed the starter button to fire up the vehicle, the whole thing jumped three feet forward and stalled—with me still under it holding the torpedo.

Everybody stopped and held their breath. I slowly put the torpedo down and crawled out from under the track. With all eyes on me, I slowly stood up and turned to face the driver, and very quietly said "get out of the vehicle."

The driver was Ingersol of rifle range fame. He'd never been around one of these vehicles before, and, just like a kid who sits behind the wheel of a car for the first time, he had jumped into the driver's seat thinking it would be cool to play at being a driver. Now, all thoughts of being cool vanished as he took one look at me and started jabbering. I swear, in thirty seconds, he came up with more bloody excuses than I thought humanly possible. That's all it took really, as soon as everyone heard his excuses, half a dozen guys started verbally abusing him for lack of responsibility, being an idiot, and damn near everything else under the sun. At the same time three guys stepped between me and the vehicle to ensure I didn't try to lay a beating on him or something equally vile. I guess I had a pretty mean look on my face.

The truth is, the thought of beating him up never really occurred to me, though I don't think anybody would have blamed me if I had. What he did ranked about as high as it gets on the stupid scale. All I wanted was for him to be replaced as the driver, because it was painfully obvious that he didn't know what he was doing. And if I was going to crawl back under this thing to try again, I sure as hell didn't want this guy in the driver's seat.

In the end, the reg force Cpl who had been sort of in charge of the whole training session, stepped in and told Ingersol to get his sorry looking ass out of the drivers seat so he could get in. Ingersol kept well away from me the rest of the day.

I finished the day with a range Orders-group for Thursday, which, all things considered, was a hell of a lot better than waking up in the hospital, which might very well have happened.

Wednesday, 10 Aug. This morning we ran the Commanding Officer's route again; this time in 35 minutes. It would have been a great run if my calves didn't hurt so much.

The guys are talking back a lot more now that there are no Regs around. Everyone is still pissed at being left behind during block leave, and it seems every break I hear someone saying something about it.

Right after P.T., Lt McConnell told me Cpl Scarth was the new Platoon Warrant. I felt like shit. I was really getting into the job and quite enjoying myself. The reason the lieutenant gave for the change was that I clearly knew what I was doing, but Scarth needed the experience, and the object was to get as many people into command positions as possible. Sounded good, but didn't help much. Oh well, soldier on.

Training today was Method of Instruction, more commonly known as M of I. This is where you get up in front of a classroom and teach a lecture. Some people it scares the hell out of, others do just fine. I've been teaching on and off now for close to twenty years, so I really didn't want to have to go through it all again. Fortunately, I was able use the hand over the platoon administration to Scarth excuse to get out of the classroom for most of the morning. Unfortunately, I couldn't drag it out much past 11:00, and wound up getting tagged for a lecture.

The lecture had to be 10 minutes in length, and when faced with this type of situation, I rely on the ever trusty lecture, The Strip And Assembly Of The Zippo Lighter. It's a fast and effective way to cover all the required parts of a lecture, while injecting a little light-heartedness into the proceedings. The lighter only has half a dozen parts so it's easy to split the lecture into "field stripping" and "detailed stripping", to stretch things out a bit.

Throughout the remainder of the day people kept asking me questions thinking I was still the Platoon Warrant. To add to the confusion Scarth kept coming back to me for guidance on various things. All in all it was a pretty confusing time.

Tonight on the way back to the barracks, I met up with Margret Fielding. I'd only seen her at a distance on P.T., or as Bravo Company went by. She stopped me to ask my advice. It seems she's gotten the hint/feeling that she won't be permitted to go overseas as a part of the infantry company. She's been told that she'll be in the reserve platoon left behind and she doesn't feel good about it. To be honest I don't blame her. She is arguably one of the best infanteers I've come across in a long while. She's dedicated, tough, knowledgeable, and in really good shape.

Her choices were to stay behind on the off-chance that she'd get a chance to go overseas, or return to the unit to continue her training. The first option meant she'd get a regular paycheck for the next eight months, the other was less dependable. We talked things out for a while and we came to the conclusion that the cards were stacked pretty heavily against her. While she might be a better infanteer than a large number of the Reservists trying out, it's become obvious that the company commander and others are dead set against having women in their ranks. You can say what you want about affirmative action, but in this case it falls to the OC to make the call, and I don't think there's any real chance of her making it to Yugoslavia.

I think she knew what her decision was, but needed someone else to tell her. It was tough to watch her dream die as we spoke. It was like watching the air go out of someone. She, like the rest of us really thought she stood a fair chance of making it. It was sad to see that the reality was different. I expect she'll be returning to Brockville sometime soon.

Thursday, 11 Aug. Shooting!! My favorite pastime. This morning I got up at 4:45 in order to meet a 6:30 timing for weapons draw, only to end up sitting on the range most of the morning because the Airborne were jumping, and they were in our range safety template. The afternoon went much faster.

My rifle kept double feeding and stove piping rounds, so I had to borrow a rifle to shoot my relay while the weapons tech worked on my rifle. 60 rounds; 30 grouping and 30 on score. I felt like I was shooting fish in a barrel at 300 yards with the new scopes. I'm used to using iron sights, but this new scope is great. If shooting at 300 was easy, the 200 and 100 were child's play.

Once sighted, the course of fire was fairly easy. The target we were to shoot at is called a figure 11. It's 18" wide, and 48" tall, and has the image of a charging man on it. At 300 metres we were to fire 5 rounds at a figure 11 from the prone position. We then got up and moved to the 200 m point where we fired 5 rounds from the prone and 5 from the sitting at the same figure 11. Then we moved up to the 100 metre point, where it was 5 from the prone, 5 from the sitting, and 5 from the kneeling positions. No scoring rings, all you have to do is hit the target.

Of the one hundred and twenty Reservists shooting today, only myself and one other had a perfect 30/30. Unbelievable!!!

If the politicians want to see what effect budget cuts have on the Reserves, all they have to do is read the score sheet. The average score was around 12/30, which is embarrassing as hell. A more realistic result would have close to 50% of the shooters scoring 30/30. After all, these are troops planning to go to an area of the world where good marksmanship could save your life.

It appears that someone forgot that the role of the infantry is to close with and destroy the enemy. What the hell's the point of closing with the enemy if you can't hit what you're aiming at when you get there?

Friday, 12 Aug. We played baseball all morning in lieu of P.T. Unfortunately Dukes Company got our collective butts whipped in both our games.

We were all dismissed before noon, and I drove Bob VanBeek to Brockville before I went home for the weekend. Bob, too, was cut from the roster. He was assigned to Recce platoon, and was one of the last six to be reassigned to the Reserve platoon. He and Margret have been going out for more than a year now, and he thinks he'll return to the unit with her.

I found out that Briggs was put on Reserve, along with Bowes. Both had problems with P.T. and had trouble keeping up. That means that Gary Ennis, Kevin Hodges and myself are the only ones going over. Bowes and Briggs stay behind in Reserve, and VanBeek and Fielding are going home.

Sunday Night, 14 Aug. Something is wrong with Catherine. All through the weekend her motor skills got worse and worse. By this afternoon the right side of her face was numb, she could hardly raise her right arm above her shoulder, and her right leg flopped as she walked. In spite of my badgering her to go to the hospital today, she insisted that she's fine, and whatever she has will pass. She has an appointment with her doctor on Wednesday, and doesn't want to go to the hospital without talking to her doctor first.

It's frustrating as hell watching her limp around, but she is in reasonably good spirits, and she doesn't think it's anything serious. I have to believe she's telling me the truth. Only she knows for sure what's going on inside her.

Before I left I made her promise to call her doctor on Monday and see if she can get her appointment moved up. We talked for a while, and she tried to reassure me she was OK, but I don't feel good about this. I don't know what's wrong, but as I sit here on my bunk, I can tell you it's weighing heavily on me.

Monday, 15 Aug. P.T. was floor hockey, the great Canadian pastime. Good fun and lots of body contact. After we got cleaned up, we loaded up onto the trucks and headed out into the training area. We helped the instructors build a rope bridge and then took turns pulling ourselves along it to the other end. You start by tying on a rope harness and hooking up over dry land with a carabiner, and hanging upside down under the rope. 80 feet doesn't seem that far, but when your arms start to give out about halfway, you begin to realize that there's no turning back. Hanging upside down over the water has a way of motivating you. I thought I was in good shape till I hit the $3/4$ point when my arms started to give out and I had to stop for a rest. To be honest, it was pretty tough.

Once finished with the bridge, it was on to the rappelling. One of the troops said it best at the rappel site: "I used to hate Mondays, but now I think it should be mandatory for everyone to go rappelling in the morning." What a scream! Dropping off the ledge and racing to the raft below only to stop yourself short from leaving a hole in the floor boards was great fun! I managed to get in 5 rappels," and each one better than the last. I couldn't believe there were people who didn't want to do it. Ah well, each to his own.

We pulled into Y101 at the end of the day and I was given a message to report to the company orderly room. When I walked in and identified myself, I was told to report to the CSM immediately. As soon as I stepped into the door of his office, he looked at my nametag and told me that Cat had been admitted to Emergency at the Ottawa Civic hospital. He gave me a number to call, and found me an office with a phone to use.

As soon as he said she was admitted to Emergency, I felt a cold chill run down my back, and all the hair stood up on the back of my neck. Holy shit, I thought she wasn't supposed to see her doctor until tomorrow.

I immediately tried calling, but couldn't get hold of her, the nurse who answered informed me that she was in for tests at the moment. For the next hour or so I was on pins and needles, my stomach doing somersaults with worry, and it feels like I've been calling every five minutes, even though I haven't. Mr. McConnell said that if I needed it, I can take tomorrow off to visit, and I may just take him up on it.

I finally got through around 5:00, and Cat did everything she could to reassure me that she was OK, and that I shouldn't come to her until they know what's wrong. Right!

The doctors are stumped right now, and probably will be for the next couple of days. That doesn't mean that I can't or shouldn't be there to help her though this. I feel like I'm stuck between a rock and a hard place. On the one hand I should be by her side, on the other, there's no point being there if there's nothing to do or learn. At times like this you should trust your heart, and my heart tells me her side is where I belong right now.

God I hope this thing she has isn't anything serious. I'd be utterly lost without her. She's the most important person in my world, and I wouldn't even consider going anywhere if I wasn't absolutely sure she was OK.

Tuesday, 16 Aug. I drove into Ottawa today to see Cat, and I'm sure I broke every speed record there was for getting to Ottawa from Petawawa. Before I left, I checked in with the Company Commander to get permission to leave for the day. The Company Commander didn't want to let me go. He was worried about my annual leave, and wanted to save it for a "real emergency." Christ, if my wife in the hospital with an unknown disease isn't an emergency, I don't know what is. I was floored when he told me that.

The Company 2IC was a little better, he caught me coming out of the OC's office and asked how things were. After I told him, he told me to bugger off during the afternoon admin time. When I reported back to Lt McConnell and told him what the OC had said, he couldn't believe it either. It didn't take him long to make his mind up. He took me aside and said "get the fuck outta here, don't get caught, and don't get in an accident in the morning." I'm outta here! I was out the door before he was finished talking. He's a good man in my books!

I arrived at the hospital about mid morning, dressed in full combats, and wasted little time finding out where she was. I felt like a bull in a china shop. There wasn't anything that was going to stop me from seeing my wife, even if I had to kick some ass on the way there.

The instant I walked through the door, Cat came apart. I moved quickly to her arms, where we stayed for a very long time. Winnie, a long time family friend who had been in the room chatting with Catherine, quietly excused herself until we could compose ourselves again.

The doctors don't know what's wrong with her. We sat and chatted until late afternoon. Winnie left us shortly before lunch, and others came to visit throughout the afternoon. As I think of it now, I can't recall who was there, it's all sort of a blur to me. I left about 5:00 to have supper with some friends who live just down the road from the hospital, then stopped by to visit Cat again before I left for the base. During our discussion the story of how she ended up in hospital came out. I discovered that Cat had loaded the kids up and driven the hour into Ottawa and dropped them with her father, then drove to the west end to her doctor, and from there drove back across the city to the hospital. All of this with no feeling and limited movement on her right side. She used her left foot for the gas and brake, and drove with her left hand. All of this with a car full of kids. It's a wonder she made it at all.

Cat's being a real trooper about this. She's putting up a good front, but I can see she's scared. For my part I'm confused as hell, worried, and a little angry, but I'm trying hard to keep my emotions in check. The waiting game is always the hardest.

It's agony to watch her walk around like someone who's suffered a stroke. She can hardly control her right side, or feel the soles of her feet. I have to help her get up, and hold her steady as we shuffle around. If I let her go, she'd just fall over, her balance has been affected so much. This is a woman who used to be a semi-professional sprinter for the Ottawa Harriers track team. It's easy to see the confusion in her eyes.

Wednesday, 17 Aug. Went out to the range to sight my rifle in today, while everyone else did the NAVEX from hell. Swamps, thick brush, and a checkpoint on a raft in the middle of a lake were the order of the day for them. I overheard two of the officers talking about it while I was drawing my weapon. That was one exercise that I was just as glad not to participate in. With my attitude right now, it'd be more of a chore than fun.

I came back from the range early only to end up working in the BOR for the afternoon, looking up postal codes for one of the clerks. I found it difficult to focus at times, thoughts of Catherine seem ever present. Late in the afternoon I managed to call Cat to find out how she was doing and what's going on. The doctor had her in for an MRI today, so the testing goes on. Catherine hates loud noises and confined spaces. I can't imagine what an ordeal that must have been for her. Still no word yet as to what's wrong.

This has to be hell for her. She has no distraction to take her mind off things! And what a mind it is. She is one of the smartest people I know. I hate to think what she must be going through. Lord knows I haven't been able to focus to clearly these past two days. God I love that woman! But I just don't know what to do except wait.

Thursday, 18 Aug. We did a 13 km march and shoot this morning, and completed it in 1:32. I actually enjoyed the whole thing. Pushing myself physically has always had a way of clearing my mind. I must be getting in shape, because nothing hurt when it was over. In spite of the fact that our platoon turned in the fastest time and left the fewest number of plates standing at the end of the shoot, we still lost due to penalty points. Oh well, it just doesn't seem important now. Still, it was nice to take my mind off Catherine for a while.

Cat talked to her neurologist this morning. They're still non-committal, it could be a stroke, or a tumor or something equally vile. It's scaring the shit out of her—I could hear it in her voice when I called this evening—and it's got me worried sick. Even so, she puts up a brave front, not wanting to commit herself to anything until we know for sure what's wrong. I feel terrible being so far away from her during all of this, but despite my request to take a couple of extra days off, I've been refused at every turn.

Visions of her in a wheelchair have been plaguing me all day. We've talked about this possibility before and I know she won't let it go that far. Best not to think about that sort of thing until we know more. Still the possibility scares the hell out of both of us.

There were times today I felt close to tears with the frustration of it all. I feel so bloody helpless. Dealing with emotions is like fighting an invisible opponent. You never know where the next punch is coming from or where and how it will affect you. The worst part is all you can do is stand there and take it.

Friday, 19 Aug. We found out late last night. It's been confirmed—Cat has Multiple Sclerosis.

The MRI the other day confirmed the doctor's suspicions, so a lumbar puncture isn't really necessary. Cat was in pretty rough shape when I called—we both were. This was the one thing she was scared of. I think this is the closest I've come to packing it in and going AWOL. They've got her hooked up to an IV drip of steroids, and they're pumping her as full of them as they can. The side effects have already started and she's antsy as hell. This does not make me feel good.

I called my Dad last night to give him the news, and asked if he would spread the word around the family. That was a tough call. There were a lot of pregnant pauses, as I fought to find the words, and control my voice. I hung up the phone and paused for a moment. The hallway was dark and lit only by the red glow of the exit signs. In one of the rooms a party was going on and the deep bass thumping of the techno-music was pushing out the sounds of silence and invading my thoughts. I don't think I've ever felt so hollow . . . or alone. Thank God we've been given this coming week off, I need the time to sort this all out, and see what we're dealing with.

P.T. today was soccer and floor hockey, we had a choice. I played goal for the soccer team, but in truth, my heart wasn't in it at all. I just couldn't seem to focus on the game.

I ran into Padre Rembaldie after the game. We'd met in the halls of Y101, and talked several times during the past couple of weeks, so it was easy to talk to him. In retrospect, I'm not sure the lieutenant didn't have a hand in his magical appearance at our game, or the way he just seemed to appear at my side. It was appreciated though. We talked for ten or fifteen minutes, and despite his best efforts to reassure me, I just couldn't get my head around what he was saying. It didn't help.

Monday, 29 Aug. Back off leave. I started letting people in the platoon know what's been happening. Pretty much everyone seems genuinely shocked and concerned for us. That's nice.

This past week has been harder than I thought. Fielding phone calls, dealing with kids and dogs, and having to inform friends. In a way it was like going back to school, trying to learn everything I could about MS, and its effects. The worst part was watching Catherine suffer with the side effects of the steroids she's on. When she was in hospital, they gave her mega doses of the stuff by IV. The doctor gave her three sheets of known side effects of the drugs, and it appears she has all of them, plus a few not on the list. Some of the visible signs are she takes shorter steps because of her balance problem. She uses a cane around the house, and she hangs onto everything she can reach as she walks. She's also much slower. Her movements, once quick and decisive, are now slow and deliberate. She hasn't gone near the piano, as much because she can't control her fingers, as because she's scared. This is particularly tough for her, because she makes her living as a music teacher, and she's damned good at it. The thought of not being able to earn a living doing what she loves has her frightened beyond words. On the up side, she is in good humour, and she seems to be coping well enough.

It really hit me this morning how much all of this has taken out of me. I felt like a wet dishrag. Something I know the warrant picked up on when I stood in front of him and tried to explain what happened. It was tough talking to the warrant. I didn't realize how screwed up I was over this thing until we talked. I felt like I was shaking like a leaf, and stumbling over every word that came out. To his credit, the first words out of his mouth were "do you need time off to be with her?"

Shortly after our conversation, WO Fuller came back to me and said that he and the CSM wanted to have a private conversation with me in the CSM's office. The CSM, WO Fuller, and I talked for about half an hour. Actually I did most of the talking while the other two listened. It was a tough half hour. I tried to sound coherent as I sifted through all the facts I'd learned during the past week in an effort to explain what MS was, and what its effects were. Mostly, I tried to stay in control.

I remember trying to explain that MS had three main characteristics; it's incurable, unpredictable and almost untreatable. I also remember saying it at least three times during the course of the interview. I felt it was important for them to understand these points, if they were going to take the next step and keep me on the active list for the tour. Catherine and I had talked long and hard on this topic during the past week, and we came to the consensus that we would put this behind us. Her biggest fear is that I'm going to be left behind on account of her. We decided not to put our lives on hold on the off chance that she could suffer another attack while I was away, and that we both want me to go overseas, so I guess it falls to me to make the case. Weighing heavily in this choice was the offer our friends had made to move in with Cat if anything ever went wrong. Still, it wasn't easy to convince me to stay the course and go on tour.

When I left the interview, I felt like I'd made a hash of it. Maybe I didn't explain myself well enough, maybe I should have been more forceful in explaining my desire to go, after all, I'd signed on the dotted line and was committed to fulfilling my obligations and not have this affect my performance. I replayed the interview a dozen times before I made it back downstairs to the platoon area.

At this writing, I've not heard anything back, so I presume the jury is still sitting.

Through all of this our friends have really come through. Elizabeth, Winnie and Judy have proven to be really solid. Everyone else has really shown their support as well. Of all our friends, Andrew Stirling, Cat's minister and coworker at Parkdale United, seems to have taken it the hardest. He and Cat share a special friendship, based on mutual respect of the other's intellect and sense of humour.

I'm confused sometimes. I know there's nothing I can do for Catherine, but there are times I get this overwhelming urge to stay and not leave her side. Maybe it's a little apprehension slipping in about the upcoming tour. I'm sure I've done all I can to prepare, but there's still just a little doubt left. Perhaps, too, it's just the guilt of leaving her behind to face this thing on her own. I don't know. The fight between the heart and the mind is as old as time itself, and I feel I'm not going to win this one any time soon.

Today was largely admin time. The Regs are back and we moved into the field at 7:00 this evening in preparation for tomorrow's training, and went to ground in a boy-scout camp located in the training area. We've been quartered in log cabins with bunk beds, so this is pure luxury compared to sleeping under the stars in the back of a carrier. We'll see what tomorrow brings.

Tuesday, 30 Aug. Up at 6:00 to shave and eat. We sat around until 9:30, then I got tasked out to fill sandbags. Thus the morning passed. The afternoon was supposed to be a live fire section attack range but endless check fires put an end to that. The Airborne were jumping in the area again, so we couldn't fire any live rounds lest we knock one of them out of the sky by accident. We wound up doing dry runs instead. Nothing like grown men running around in the woods yelling "bang, bang" or "government cut backs, government cut backs", to put a real sarcastic bent on things. This is your army in action.

The evening was spent as staff on an ambush range. The object was to have a convoy of vehicles hit a mine, and then test the section commanders and everyone else's reactions. Three sections were to have gone through, but endless delays resulted in only one actually doing it. We spent more time swatting flies than anything else. All of this leads one to question. Why the hell are we doing this? It's a question everyone is asking, but we soldier on.

Tonight we're on Quick Reaction Force, which means if some joker decides to fire a few rounds off in the middle of the night, we're the first to react. We'll see how much rest I get.

Wednesday, 31 Aug. How much sleep did I get you ask? Lots! No one woke us up last night so we slept straight through.

Today was broken into three distinct parts. The morning we did a live fire section attack. At one point I got up to take a bound and wound up doing a forward roll to avoid falling flat on my face. Our attack only took 15 minutes but took most of the morning to get the whole company through.

In the afternoon we were in "UN mode" and doing a jungle lane. This was to test our reaction to a UN situation. It was good training but I felt out of it for some reason. My scenario was to walk up a road with Jim, and react to what we found. We got jumped by two targets in the woods, and I missed calling for backup and doing a SITREP—Situation Report. As well it was pointed out that because we were only a two man patrol, we should have chosen a tactical withdrawal instead of going into section attack mode and being so aggressive. I don't agree with this assessment. If we come under fire, I'm not about to run away, I'm going to shoot back. It was hard to switch from infanteer to UN man. I don't think anybody really knows what's expected of us.

The evening was also a UN-type scenario. Our section, down to a strength of six because of various taskings, was to advance on a Serb Observation Post in the zone of separation—at night. Henry Wyatt was last man in our foot patrol, and he got blown up when he supposedly stepped on a mine. I was wounded (flesh wound to the arm). We had to probe 35m back to our carrier, on a gravel road on our hands and knees, and my back hasn't been the same since.

Wyatt wound up dying despite our best efforts to save him (he did a great dying man routine in a thick Newfoundland accent), but we all got a good chuckle out of it.

It was actually really good training. This is the kind of training we should have been doing back in July, so that by now we would have the drills down. Tomorrow I've been tasked to work in the kitchen. This is something I have never, in all my many years in the military, had to do. I guess there's a first time for everything.

Thursday, 01 Sept. I slept in the mess hall last night. They brought everyone tasked for security and kitchen duty, into the mess so that they wouldn't have to go looking for us out in the company lines. I don't seem to be getting much in the way of sleep while out here. I keep waking every couple of hours. Must be the fresh air.

Kitchen duty isn't all that bad, if you don't mind dish pan hands. My job was to clean pots, and help out cutting food and prepping for the next meal. It goes in spurts of course, the pots start piling up after the meal and it takes me about 2 hours to get through them. I'm finding I really don't mind this work at all. In fact, if I wasn't in the infantry I wouldn't mind trying my hand at becoming a cook. At least they appreciated the hard work I put in.

Tomorrow is supposed to be a short day ending with a Barbecue and beer, some time around 3:00. Cat isn't expecting me home this weekend so that will be a nice surprise for her. And me.

Friday, 02 Sept. More jungle lanes this morning. This is great training. The more of this we can do the better. Today was situational training. Walk up the road in pairs, and deal with what you find. Jim was my partner again—we work well together. Our situation involved a mix up on the "Serbs" part, which put them in the zone of separation. It got tense for a bit but we managed to talk our way out of it.

The opposition turned out to be the section commanders, Warrant Fuller, and the officer, Mr. McConnell. Because we had to go in pairs, it took the better part of the morning to put the platoon through. Sitting at the bottom of the hill, a group of us decided that the instructors had had their way with us most of the day and that it was our turn to get even with them. As the last pair of the day worked their way up the road, everyone else gathered together to decide on a plan. After a brief discussion it was decided to get even by rushing the "Serb" position en masse. As it turned out the patrol involved in the last scenario had just called for the QRF, and were working their way back down the hill in a tactical retreat, when all of a sudden 20 guys came rushing around the corner. What followed was a mass charge with a lot of laughing and yelling, and hurtling of insults at the "Serbs." The instructors were caught completely off-guard and were forced to fight a tactical withdrawal. It was the perfect end to a perfect morning.

We got back to Y101 at 3:00 and cleaned and put stores away before 4:00. Unfortunately we all had to stay for a steak and beer supper that had been laid on, and orders were that we couldn't leave before 5:30. A lot of the troops were pissed about that, but the beer helped to ease the tensions a little. Home for the long weekend.

Tuesday, 06 Sept. Today begins two weeks in the field. It's our big shake-out exercise and it's on a Brigade level. We got up at 3:30 AM, and our section packed into our carrier, and was in the field at our assigned position by 8:00, where we established an OP. We dug sandbags from 9:00 till 4:00 then did up a shift list and grabbed some sleep, rotating through OP duty which was up a tower overlooking Duke Plain.

OP duty has to rank as one of the most boring jobs in the world. Thank goodness we won't be doing much if any of it over there, if what we're told is correct. I'd go crazy. So far it's been a pretty slack Ex. We'll see what the rest of the week brings.

The section had a good chat and card game before darkness put an end to the game. The section is coming together well. It should be a good tour with these guys.

Wednesday, 07 Sept. Last night Jim and I pulled duty between 2300–01:00 hrs. Not too bad a time. Once again, I have to reiterate that OP duty has to be the most boring of duties. I did, however, manage to get some sleep on the floor of the carrier when we were done.

Around 6:15 as I was happily dozing, two TOW tracks pulled into our position to relieve us. No one had told us of this, so George spent a bit of time trying to confirm the orders as the rest of us packed up to leave. We got back to Landries Crossing (exercise headquarters) and lay about and cleaned weapons until noon.

Around 1:00 we went on a wild goose chase, and set up a VCP—a vehicle check point. We were in position for a grand total of 40 minutes when we got the call on the radio and were sent back to base, just in time to be sent out for a 24 hr VCP at a different location. We were supposed to have fresh rations but we left just as the mess opened, so we missed lunch. Instead we wound up eating ration packs (Individual Meal Packs). Trust me when I tell you, a VCP is no more fun than an OP.

Thursday, 08 Sept. Last night I slept a sleepless night on the side of the road. Literally. Here's the road, here's the track, and that's me, the little green lump on the side of the road, all bundled up in my sleeping bag. It took most of the day to get the kinks out of my back. With Ted acting as chef, we polished off a loaf of bread cooked up as toast and Cheese Whiz, done on the open-flame of a Coleman stove off the back of the carrier. We packed everything up and drove in to Landries Crossing for breakfast. The food we've had in the field these past two weeks has been great. The cooks we have are excellent.

The morning was spent on the crack-thump range, to familiarize us with locating the enemy. The crack-thump range is where someone fires a shot from your left at a target on your right—preferably far enough in front of you that the bullet doesn't pass through your ranks.

It took us an hour by truck to get there. But once there it only lasted twenty minutes, because it took only two shots to identify the location of each of the shooters, both within 100 metres of us. The range was a good idea but the shooters were less than 100 m away from us, so there little distinction between the "crack" of the bullet passing and the "thump" of the round being fired.

The afternoon was better because we were on an artillery impact range. They showed us the difference between 81-mm mortar impacts and 105-mm artillery impacts. It was really neat to hear the rounds coming in and watch them explode about 500 m below our position. After a couple of demos we did up ShellReps—shell reports—in the format they require for Yugo. Good practice.

After supper I did something really stupid. When the WO asked if anyone had ever done a live fire FIBUA (Fighting In a Built Up Area) range, I was stupid enough to say I had. In answering the question I guess I was a little too "direct" and the WO took exception. Not only did I end up replacing someone in the kitchen who had never been on this type of range, but I had to attempt to extract myself from the kaka by humbly apologizing to the warrant in a quiet moment later in the evening. He smiled when I told him I had been having a shit week, but I would try to not let it happen again.

The good thing about KP was that I didn't have to do pots, much to the consternation of the other guys assigned to the kitchen. I did such a good job the last time that the cooks went easy on me. Also I managed to get a good hot shower without having to fight for a spot, as I was the only one in the shower at the time. Tonight I'm looking forward to a good night's rest.

Friday, 09 Sept. This morning the Ironman competition is being held. This is a pretty elite competition, as only those Regiments that are part of the Special Forces are permitted to compete. Still, people come from all across Canada to try their hand. And it ain't easy. Each competitor must run 30km, paddle 2km, and run carrying a canoe for 5km, the whole time carrying a pack weighing no less than 55lbs., his weapon, and do it all while wearing his combat boots. We all grabbed a coffee and cheered them on as they passed by us.

The front runner had a 24-minute lead on his nearest competitor. He wound up turning in the fastest time ever posted in the history of the competition, just over 5 hours. As it turns out he's our company signaler, Arthur Madison. Ted Newman surprised everyone by passing us in 12th place. He was later to finish 13th over all. A very respectable finish.

At 8:30 a group of us jumped in the trucks (section Cmdr, 2IC and 2 extras per section) and came into Y101 for a CP Ex. We'll be here till tomorrow morning then I have to go back to the camp for the weekend and do camp security (they say its the luck of the draw, but I think its because I pissed off the WO).

The purpose of the exercise we're engaged in is to give us each experience with radio procedures and to train the HQ staff in directing radio traffic. We've been set up in the drill hall at Y101. There are half a dozen tables spread out across the parade square, with the HQ table in one corner. A company net has been established with everyone being hooked up with a land line over which we give our radio reports.

The scenario the staff have put together for us, was for a patrol to go through it's normal routine, and then to react to effective enemy fire directed at it from a village they were supposed to be passing, and for them to call for QRF support.

The umpires would walk around between the tables and pass notes with instructions to each of the teams, in accordance with a pre-set timetable. The notes would say things like "take a break from the patrol to check out a house on your route", and we'd then call in a SITREP telling HQ what we were doing. HQ would record the information and keep track of our position.

I have to admit tonight was a lot of fun. 3 Platoon really had the CP hopping. Around 01:00, we came under enemy fire while on patrol, and decided to degrade our situation into an all out firefight complete with QRF support and Karl Gustav deployment. The tables were close enough that all it took was a wink and a nod from table to table, and all the section commanders followed Sgt Macari's lead. HQ kept trying to break in to the radio traffic, but couldn't get a word in edgewise, and when they did were told "wait, out." It was a riot to watch George go at it. After he conveniently killed off the platoon commander and the platoon warrant by reporting their carrier hit by a Serb anti tank missile, he stood up, and just held the microphone to one side while he talked in a loud voice (using proper radio procedure of course) to the other sections, as he directed the fictional battle through the streets of a nonexistent village. When the battle was over, we went through the usual AMMOCAS (ammunition and casualty) reports, and called them in to HQ according to the proper net priority. With the last report being called in at 01:32, we had successfully hijacked the entire scenario, and finished the exercise a full two hours ahead of schedule. Even the umpires had to laugh at it. We found out later that the CP was completely overwhelmed by our radio messages, and simply couldn't keep up.

End-Ex was called, because we had taken the situation a little further than they had wanted it to go. Maybe so, but we had a ball doing it.

Saturday and Sunday, 10-11 Sept. Both these days are the ultimate in uneventfulness. I pulled three shifts, including one from 0200 to 0400 A.M. Aside from working on my new kevlar helmet for 10 minutes, and a couple of odd jobs, I've either slept or watched movies the whole time. I don't know what's up for this week but I'm sure it'll be on the boring side.

Monday, 12 Sept. Last night around 9:30 we packed all our worldly possessions and headed to the DZ Anzio shack. We set up our cots and hit the sack. At 6:00 we were up again and cleaned up and ate breakfast. Because I had to go in for a medical, I was fasting. A subtle but important point I forgot about until I took the first bite of my breakfast sandwich, where upon I realized the error of my ways and spit it out into the garbage can, followed closely by the remainder of the sandwich. The medical took all of ten minutes, so I took the opportunity to cut out to the shacks to clean up before going back to our company lines to get a ride back to the camp.

When I got back our section was tasked to do a four-hour roving patrol of all the OP positions put out for the exercise. It was a dusty ride to say the least. When we got back to the shack, we were told to pack up and grab a quick supper because we were leaving soon. As it turned out, we wound up sitting and waiting (as is usually the norm) and myself and John got snagged for unloading the MLVW back in Landrie's Crossing. That took all of 20 minutes and I spent the next two hours sitting on ammo cans waiting for the rest of the platoon to arrive. When they did, we were told to unpack and go to ground in one of the shacks because we were doing a road move to the Pembroke airport the following day.

Forty guys closely packed in a tiny room with the windows closed makes for a muggy night, and an awfully stale awakening.

There was a phone available to us in the camp, so I took the opportunity to call home before I hit the sack. Cat told me today that she went out and bought a walking-stick to help her with her balance. We hope it's temporary but I fear her balance has been permanently affected. Hearing her like this makes me that much more desperate to be with her. I feel like she's slipping away from me, and there's nothing I can do. God, I miss her.

Tuesday, 13 Sept. The road-move to the airport was uneventful. We heard over the radio that the column had been stopped by belligerents, but we were too far back in the line to see anything. The stop only lasted a short while and then we were on the road again. When we arrived in position we quickly unloaded and set up a shift list. I wasn't on so hit the sack for a couple of hours.

Orders came down that we're here till Thursday, 12 hours on, 12 hours off. My shift is at night with Sgt. Macari, Renwick and Newman. We've hit the sack in tents set up near the mobile kitchens, and we start at 7:00 tonight.

I have to say something about the cooks. Without doubt they are the best in the Battalion. The meals they've prepared have been outstanding. I gotta admit, this UN duty is a strange sort of job. It's not hard, but it's not easy either.

Tuesday Night: 7:00 p.m. to 7:00 A.M., 12 hours on OP duty. Two men on and three off. Every two hours we patrol up the road to the next OP position and back.

That was what was supposed to happen. What really happened was 5 guys played cards in the back of the carrier till the wee hours of the morning, with two of them going for a stroll every couple of hours. In the early hours we all hit the hay, but kept an ear out for the radio.

The most interesting thing to happen was when we shut off the radio to start the

Training 65

track and forgot to turn it back on. All told it was off for about half an hour and we missed our radio check. In the end we realized our mistake when our patrol came back and tried to call in.

Sgt Macari had a friend who lived 300 m up the road so he snuck off while on patrol and had a shower, shave and a hot coffee. He came back smelling pretty, while the rest of us suffered in our smelly clothes.

Wednesday morning we "pulled pole" and returned to our new camp and were promptly designated QRF. I'm going to sleep now and wait for the call.

OP duty at the airport

Wednesday, 14 Sept. We, as a section, had a rehearsal as the QRF, to familiarize ourselves with our duties, then we bolstered the wire around the camp by adding another layer to it. Camp, it should be pointed out, is defined as roughly a two hundred square metre square carved out of a farmers field, surrounded by barbed wire, sleeping tents for three forty man platoons, and a complete field kitchen and ablution area.

The rest of the day was my own until we were called out. As it happened it was after 2:00 pm, I was in the mess tent watching porn movies supplied for our viewing pleasure by the cooks when the call came. I'm sure I broke the overland speed record getting from one tent to the other to pickup my flack vest and weapon, then back again to the gate.

As it happened most of the guys were racking when I came flying in, so I woke them up then took off. Kit was flying everywhere as everyone went from sound asleep to fully awake, and trying to put on their flack vests and helmets at a full run. The call out was for a friendly protest (about 75 people). It lasted for about 45 minutes then everyone went home.

The rest of the day was quiet. That is, until 10:30. It was then that we got the call to pack everything up and hit the road again. It was amazing to see. What had been a fully functional camp with barbed wire, sandbags, working kitchen, and sleeping quarters, what was essentially home to 120 men, completely disappeared in less than an hour and a half.

3 Platoon as usual, was better organized and we subsequently finished our duties before all the others, and then spent an hour waiting for everyone else to catch up. We didn't leave our position until 00:15 and didn't arrive at the DZ Anzio shack until 01:00. The ride in the carrier was boring, uncomfortable (10 guys plus kit in one carrier—my knees were up around my ears for most of the trip) and loud. In spite of that, most of us slept.

As soon as we arrived we started working to unload the flatbed that had arrived loaded down with filled sandbags, and in less than an hour had built a complete OP and road-block. We strung wire, put in road-blocks and completed a hasty perimeter fence. Good work for an hour.

Robert Nowlan and I were tasked with the first watch and drew straws to see who would do the gate and who got the radio. I got the gate while he stayed inside by the fire. The shift wasn't that bad, the stars were out in force, and the air was crisp if not cool. It was a beautiful night to just sit and contemplate whatever came to mind. I got to bed at 04:20.

Thursday, 15 Sept. Today was once again one of those slow days. Guard duty for our section continued until 13:00 with me on the final shift. It was kind of nice actually. The sun was warm, it was fairly quiet out, I had a good book and the company of two chipmunks to share my sunflower seeds with.

After duty I decided to lie down for a while, and surprised myself by sleeping right up to supper. After supper our section received a warning order to establish a roadblock no later than 7:00 PM. So, we grabbed two carriers and off down the road we went.

What we were expecting was a demonstration by a mock group of protesters. We had been given orders to delay them as long as possible, so we had settled on letting them through the road-block one at a time, delaying them as long as possible by doing a full body search, and taking extra time to register each person. This would have used up masses of time.

What happened was absolutely nothing. We sat and played cards until 2300 letting the occasional car or truck through, but nothing else happened.

We had just received orders by radio, to pack things up and return to our temporary base. As it happened, I was on the top of the carrier and had to jump off to help pack things up. I moved to the front of the carrier and in an effort to save time I attempted to slide down the trim vein and jump the final three feet to the ground. As luck would have it I hooked a heel on something, and off into space I went.

As I sailed through the air I had enough time to realize that I really wanted to be somewhere else at that precise moment. I hit the ground with a bone jarring thump, bouncing my head off the road a couple of times just to make sure I was safely down, and ground the palm of my hand into the gravel to stop myself and of course to make sure it was in fact a gravel road I'd just landed on.

Hearing the dull thud and the groan that accompanied my ignominious landing, Jim popped his head out of the driver's hatch like an oversized jack-in-the-box, to see what had happened.

"Hey, Grantpaw just fell off the carrier," he announced, trying to contain his glee, which was followed by hoots of laughter by the rest of the guys.

"Is he OK?" someone called up.

"I don't know. Let me ask. Hey Grantpaw, you OK?" he inquired, with an ear-to-ear grin.

By this time I had managed to roll over onto my back and was beginning to feel the pain that follows the shock of a sudden stop. "I'll be fine, just let me lie here and hurt a bit." Jim just chuckled.

As I lay there looking up at the stars and feeling the pain pulse through my body, I was struck by the thought that it would be just perfect if I hurt myself this close to leaving. God, I thought, I am truly getting too old for this shit. I slowly got to my feet, and walked the pain off as Jim continued to chuckle at me from the driver's hatch. End-Ex is tomorrow, which leaves just a wakie and I can go home to Cat and a soft bed. Oooooohhhh, but that's going to be nice.

Friday, 16 Sept. Up early this morning 05:00. We're doing a cordon-and-search exercise. Today I was tasked to be in the crew commander's hatch, which meant that I would be participating from a distance, watching everything go down from behind the 50.

We packed our kit and drove off to Landries' Crossing for breakfast, where we marshaled the vehicles. Then it was on the road to our FUP, or Form Up Point. From there, we moved to the start line and the game was afoot.

As we drove down the road to our appointed rendezvous, Jim, who was driving our track, and I started singing show songs and ballads in harmony over the intercom, ending with a heart-rending rendition of the "Jose Can You See by the dawns early search light . . ." a creative take on the American national anthem.

In the orders we were told that two armed men had been spotted in the Zone of Separation, carrying weapons, and had holed themselves up in an abandoned house. Our company was to go in and negotiate a peaceful resolution to the situation. Our convoy turned off the main road and down a side road where we came upon a couple of buildings at the edge of a large opening in the woods.

My carrier and another pulled up in a position to cover three sides of the building between us. Two sections of men off loaded and made their way up to the back of the building, then around to the sides within sight of the front door. At the front door Lt Alec Reid from 2 Platoon, tried to negotiate through the door with the two men. After fifteen minutes he turned and signaled to the two sections to make their way from the sides of the building and join him at the door. Some quick directions were given, and with one solid kick, Reid kicked in the front door, clearing the way for the two sections to force their way in and overwhelm the two men.

In all, the main part of the exercise lasted about an hour, with the whole operation taking about two hours. It was interesting and informative to see the level of professionalism shown by the boys. Everyone knew the exercise was fake, yet everyone did their jobs and no-one complained. Until we were done, at least.

After it was all over, we went back to Landries' Crossing for a debriefing by the company commander. Frankly we were all shocked by the OC's read of the situation. He had all the NCO's and Officers in one room and blasted them for being "too aggressive." From our viewpoint, the execution of the task appeared to be more on the "wimpy" side. If anything, it lacked aggression. Yet there it was.

Though all the NCOs tried to down play it, it was clear that they all had lost a lot of respect for the OC. If this were just another exercise loss of a little respect wouldn't be a big deal, but considering where we were going, it suddenly made things a little scary.

Back to the DZ Anzio shack to pack up, a task accomplished in less than an hour, then home to the Chicken Coop, unload, do a quick clean up of weapons and kit and get a final debrief and orders for next week. At 4:00 we gathered in the platoon area for orders. We were all standing in a semicircle around WO Fuller, and he was rambling on about this and that. Frankly I wasn't paying much attention, thinking instead of Catherine and what I'd like to do with her when I got home. What caught my attention was the letters "GD", which is short for General Duties or, in laymen's terms, shit jobs—something the army seems to have a never ending supply of. In this case it referred to helping tear down a temporary kitchen that had been set up outside on the north side of the building.

No sooner had the warrant uttered those two letters than he stopped and began to scan the room. People quickly averted their eyes for fear of being tagged with the dreaded duties. Seconds passed as he dragged it out, enjoying how uncomfortable he was making everyone feel. He stopped when his eyes landed on me. "Corporal Grant," he began, with a big smile while everyone else let out a collective sigh of relief, "I've been picking on you for three weeks now. After this, I promise I won't pick on you again. After dismissal I want you to help tear down the kitchen tent."

Hoping desperately to get out of the tasking, I immediately shot back, "Warrant Fuller, I've got a two-and-a-half-hour drive ahead of me tonight, with a beautiful woman at the other end waiting to make mad passionate love to me. Now you're asking me to stay behind and clean up? You're a cruel cruel man, Sir."

There was a momentary pause, then the entire platoon broke out in howls of laughter. It was a good come back. But it didn't get me out of the tasking. After dismissal, the warrant took me aside and told me to just put in an appearance then slip away when no one was looking. As I left the building on my way to put my kit into my car, it was plain to see that there were more than enough people tasked to take the tents down, so I just kept walking. Nobody was going to be the wiser anyway.

The past three weeks have not been particularly hard. In fact, I'd go as far as to say they've been slack. But it has been an education to see how the Battalion does things, and quite frankly, I like it. I can see now that I'm going to have trouble blending back into the Reserve way of doing things when I get back.

Monday, 19 Sept. Today, and all this week, has been set aside for administration. I spent the morning getting the last bits of my DAG items signed off so I'm good to go. The first item on the list was Hepatitis-A shots. One in each buttock. It felt like someone gave you a charley horse in each cheek. Two companys of men had to go through at once, so they had us lined up on the parade square in Y101, in front of some tables they'd setup at one end. The medics had set two tables to the sides with modesty screens, so you wouldn't be dropping your pants in the wide open for all-and-sundry to see. The procedure was for you to check in at the front table, then go to one of the open side tables, where two medics awaited your arrival. Drop your pants to mid-thigh, bend over and grab the edge of the table, and wait for the medics to stick you in each cheek at the same time. It was hilarious to watch some of the faces of the guys after they were stuck. If nothing else it made for light entertainment. Thus passed the morning.

The afternoon was just as relaxed. I had a medical at 1:00 (cough twice please) then over to E-1, the main administration building, to finally DAG green.

Just before dismissal the Blue Berets—or Blue Beanies as Cat is fond of calling them—were handed out. It was a mad scramble to find one that fit as they all seemed too big. Apparently they've been made in Belgium, and no one is overly impressed with the workmanship. That is not to say that they are not good, just to say that we're not impressed. Compared to our green berets, these ones have too much material in them, so when you fold the side down, it feels like the edge comes halfway down your ear. The edge of our green berets stop right at the band, so you end up with a beret that fit close to the head instead of something that looks like the deck on an aircraft carrier. The consensus is that the resulting LC (look cool) factor will be quite low.

Back at the shacks the first thing I did with mine was to cut the lining out of it so that I could get a nice clean edge and a smooth shape to it. The next thing I did was wear it into the shower so it could get drenched in hot water and thus be more easily formed. I must have looked quite the sight as I walked down the hall with nothing on but a blue beret and a towel around my waist. It was funny to see everyone running around with wet berets on their heads trying to form them to get just the right look. We're down to the short strokes now and these berets represent a confirmation that we've made it through the training, and we're going to go. It feels GREAT!!

Tuesday, 20 Sept. Today was not a particularly difficult day, but I'll be darned if I can remember what I did in the morning. I can tell you that in the afternoon our company held a sports parade where we ran a triathlon. Teams were made up and all sections entered one team. The three legs of the triathlon consisted of a 250-m swim, 5-km bike ride, and a 3-km run. When it was over, our platoon took 1st, 3rd, 4th, and 5th placing. It had to be agony for the participants, because no one has been working out seriously for the past seven weeks.

After the competition, it was passed that the Ogroup would be at platoon level, and would be held in town—at one of the local bars—so we all hopped into our cars and headed into town for the "Ogroup." We partied for hours at a local bar, then a bunch of us buggered off to the shacks and continued drinking well into the night. Today was a really relaxing and fun day.

Oh yes, I remember now what we did this morning. Mine awareness refresher, hygiene lecture, and AFV (Armoured Fighting Vehicles) recognition class. Three lectures that took up the entire morning.

Wednesday, 21 Sept. Today was something of a mish-mash. There was admin, stores cleaning, and all sorts of other things going on. We lost two guys from last night. They just failed to show up on parade this morning. Warrant Fuller was not impressed. The old rule, if you want to howl at the moon, you'd better be prepared to get up with the dawn, comes into play here.

A quick stop in the drill hall to check for TB reactions (serum infected on Monday) preceded a visit to base QM for issue of our new Gortex boots and any kit exchanges. Then back to the platoon area to sit around the rest of the morning and do odd jobs.

I took the time to sort out a pay problem then had a chat with the warrant. He said the darndest thing. First he thought I had been fucked by my Regiment (a point to be taken up with my CO) and LFCA. And that my final assessment would reflect that point. Second, that as far as he was concerned I had demonstrated that I was capable of being a section 2IC (MCpl). He also said that if the situation arises and a MCpl goes down that I was first on the list within the company to fill the slot. In spite of the fact that I only held Private's rank. Apparently people know (read CSM and OC) of my ability and it won't go unnoticed. Nice words. It's good to know I have the respect of the platoon warrant.

I also received my three-month assessment. In my eyes it wasn't very good. It said I needed to show more motivation and had to watch my attitude; after all, I was "only a private." Well bollocks! That's what happens when you take a MCpl and make him a private!

The platoon commander said in the interview flat out that he was more than satisfied with my performance and that he totally understood that I was being asked to play a role way beneath my capabilities. It was a case of "over-qualification without a doubt." In light of what Warrant Fuller said to me, I feel pretty good about myself. Fortunately the assessments are only for reference, and won't make it back to the home units.

Thursday/Friday, 22-23 Sept. Both of these days went fairly quickly. Thursday began with company and platoon photos being taken in the drill hall, followed by another pilgrimage to the ranges to re-sight our weapons. This was necessitated after the weapons techs made some modifications to the scopes. It was an easy day, as all range days tend to be.

Friday was only a half day with pictures being taken of the Battalion as a whole. It seemed that the parade lasted forever. My back was killing me when it was over. About halfway through, Buck Campbell—same guy who fainted on the first parade shortly after I got here—who was standing behind me decided to keel over. So, under the warrant's direction I led him to the MIR and took the time to stretch my back before rejoining the parade.

We've all been given two weeks off prior to departure for Croatia. Our report dates back to Battalion are determined by which "lift" you are on. As a whole, the Battalion has been broken into three lifts. Advance party, and lifts one and two. Advance party consists of all the command staff, section commanders, warrants, officers etc, plus a few extras, though I have to question the logic of putting all your commanders in one aircraft. From our section, George, Henry, Ted, and David went with the advance party, and the remainder of us slated to go on the second lift. This means I'll have the better part of two weeks off to spend with Cat.

With everyone keen to get home to the wife and kids and enjoy some time off, no one stayed after the parade and the parking lot emptied in record time. Judging by how fast people were moving, it's a wonder no one had an accident on the way outta here.

Monday, 10 Oct Well this is it. Forty-eight hours prior to departure I find myself back in my room—alone. Catherine and I have spent as close to an idyllic two weeks together as possible. We drove up here this morning and had lunch in the mess hall. In all my years with her, I don't think I've ever seen her look more lovely. As we walked arm in arm around the field by the barracks, and watched Rascal, our golden retriever running around and playing, I couldn't help but feel completely at peace. The sun was shining, the dog was playing, and I had my beautiful wife in my arms. Life was good.

It was really tough when Catherine left. We were both on the verge of tears as she got into the car and drove off. Standing there in the parking lot, I was torn by mixed emotions. On the one hand I was excited as hell to get the tour underway. On the other, I was wracked by guilt at leaving Catherine behind to deal with the house and her newly diagnosed disease. But mostly, I think I just felt lonely. I went to bed early tonight.

Tuesday, 1 Oct. 7:30 parade call at Y101 this morning. The final batch of kit—one barrack box, one duffel bag, and a rucksack—were weighed in and loaded onto the trucks bound for the airport. Passports, money—pay advance of 100 DM—and various pieces of paper were issued and shuffled. Then at 11:00 we were cut loose until tomorrow at noon.

I made a quick stop at E-1 to sort out my pay and life insurance. Because of Cat's MS, she's been rejected from the group life insurance plan which has caused no end of paperwork for both of us. I then headed back to the shacks to change. By 3:00 I had everything done—so I linked up with the rest of the section, and we all headed over to the mess to celebrate.

I recall somewhere around 10:00 that evening, I was trying to explain helicopter theory of flight, and gyroscopic effect to Jim. The poor guy was more confused than ever when I was done. I'm not sure if it was my explanation, or the fact that we were working on our 7th or 8th pitcher. We stumbled out of the mess a while later, and I recall falling into bed around 11:30 and passing out.

At times like these, when you are waiting to leave, one tends to think quite profound thoughts about life and such. It is tempting to try and write them down, but in truth I think that would be an exercise in futility, as I don't think I'd be saying anything that hadn't already been said a thousand times before.

Time and again my thoughts turn to Catherine. I am so proud of her! She is handling her illness with such style and grace that one cannot help but admire her. She constantly amazes me with her unfailing caring, and good nature. To a fault she always looks on the good side of a situation, and always tries to make the best of things. Words do not begin to describe my love for her. I turn instead to a poem by WH Auden that, with slight editing, begins to describe some of my feelings:

> *She is my North and South,*
> *My East and West,*
> *My working-week,*
> *My Sunday rest...*
> *She is my wife,*
> *She is my life.*

THE FIRST HALF OF THE TOUR PART THREE

Wednesday, 12 Oct., The Never-Ending Day Show time! We formed up at 12:15 in the company areas to draw our bolts, then up to the drill hall for final farewells. It was a good thing that the timing was so late. Much earlier and I'm sure we would have been missing more than a few people after last night's frivolities.

I sat in the bus watching all the women with their husbands and their children, and two things struck me. First, the quiet acceptance of the families as they said goodbye. There were no hysterics, or wailing and gnashing of teeth as one might expect. The good-byes were said with great dignity and calmness. It was quite moving to watch. And second, the curious mix of melancholy and excitement shared by those about to leave.

While we were at Y101, the regimental home building, I had a minute to slip away and call Cat. With all the farewells going on I needed to hear her voice again before I left. It was a short call, she fell apart, and I very nearly did as well.

The bus ride to Ottawa was to be the usual uneventful ride down old Highway 17. This time however, it held all kinds of pleasant surprises for me. For example, the air was crisp but warm, one of those classic fall days that always seems to refresh you, and there wasn't a cloud in the sky. There was a hawk gently floating over a field. A farmer was working to bring in an enormous field of corn, and just outside Cobden, there was a field of pumpkins, which someone had harvested and piled by the roadside. There had to be thousands of them, with the bright orange of the ripe pumpkins standing out against the green of the vegetation and the blue sky. The thought occurred to me that Canada truly was blessed. A land of peace and plenty!

When we arrived in Ottawa, we pulled in to the international airport. This struck us all as odd, as the plan called for us to go directly to the military side of the field, and offload at the old AMU. Turns out, we had a one hour layover before boarding, and the word got passed around that higher thought it would be more civilized to wait at a busy terminal (with a bar) than at the empty one. Finally, someone with forethought!

I quickly made my way to a phone and called Catherine, who was, if memory served, teaching in the west end of the city. She broke the overland speed record to make it to the airport, to my side. We only spent 20 minutes together, but I needed it. Our last conversation had been strained, and I wanted to put it right before I left. She was so beautiful, dressed in black pants and a black leather jacket. She quite took my breath away, as she walked through the terminal to my side. I was very glad to see her again; to inhale her scent, to hear her voice. It's going to be a long three months till the 30th of December when next we meet in England.

Under police escort we were bussed onto the tarmac in front of the AMU on the military side of the airport. Another delay allowed us to soak up some sun, take a few last minute pictures, and prolong the farewells. Several of the wives and girlfriends who didn't make it to Petawawa had come to the airport to say goodbye, and were gathered on one side of the fence while all the men were on the other. Those of us who had said our good-byes (Catherine had to get back to teaching) were gathered near the aircraft and were joking around trying to pass the time.

Then, to the strains of Scotland the Brave, and other inspirational tunes, played by a pair of pipers standing in the shade of the giant 747, things started to happen. Without anyone saying a word, we formed into one long snaking line, and we prepared to file onto the aircraft. Both the Brigade commander and the Brigade RSM were at the foot of the stairs to shake each man's hand as he prepared to board. Nice touch!

Another wait of 40 or so minutes, then at exactly 18:49, Tower Airways flight 5 to Split, Croatia, thundered down the runway into the cool Canadian night air.

We boarded to the strings of "Scotland the Brave"

Thursday, 13 Oct., Rodaljice Finally, at long last we've arrived. Eight-and-a-half hours, two movies, and two lousy meals after takeoff, we landed in Split.

Man it's hot! How hot is it? It's hot enough that by 9:30 A.M. local time, everyone was sweating freely. One guy even soaked through his shirt. His back looked like one giant wet spot. My impression of the place is that it's very Mediterranean in look and feel. Fancy that! There's lots of greenhouses, and market gardening in and around the airport area, while the surrounding terrain is barren, rocky, and covered in scrub brush, not unlike something you'd see in a desert. Everything seems to be a variant of the colour of sand. Yet, even here, away from where all the fighting is taking place, there is evidence of war. The control tower has been shot all to hell, and is no longer in use. Looking up at it in the early morning light, I saw clear evidence of the rocket fire that hit the tower. Wire and loose bits of concrete were hanging from what was left of the six-storey structure.

We had arrived at the airport before the outgoing troops, so to minimize the confusion inside the terminal, we were all moved out into the parking lot to wait. As the last of our guys cleared the terminal building, the PPCLI arrived in a convoy of buses. We stood around for about an hour as they offloaded and sorted themselves out prior to leaving. They formed a long line outside the front door of the building, as we gaggled our way slowly towards the buses. As we filed past them, no one said a word—we just looked at them as they looked back at us. It was like something out of the First World War. The green troops coming in to replace the grizzled old veterans. We with our pasty faces, full of piss and vinegar, and them suntanned and weary eyed. Everyone was pretty quiet. It was almost eerie.

The third leg of our journey lasted 40 minutes and took us to the port town of Sibenik. There, we were issued with 5 metal 30-round magazines of ammunition, a two-litre bottle of water, and a blue UN ball cap.

We also had to pick up our kit. But first, all the trucks had to be unloaded and the kit laid out so people could see the names stenciled on the top of each piece. It was a madhouse for about an hour, as 200 guys moved back and forth between trucks, each man having to find a barrack box, a rucksack, and a duffel bag. Thank God we colour coded each company's kit, otherwise we would have been there the better part of the day. As it was there was a whole lot of name reading going on, and shouting back and forth. Once claimed, we each removed our helmets and flack vests from the duffel bag, stowed our ammunition in the flack vests, then claimed our rifles from the special carriers. Once you'd finished collecting your personal items, the remainder of the kit then had to be reloaded onto specific trucks bound for your area of operation, then it was back on the buses, for the run to CANBAT One in Rastivic.

I don't know how long the bus ride to Rastivic took. I did a lot of head bobbing along the way. I hadn't slept on the flight at all, and was now pushing 26 hours without. The heat was killing us, and people were dropping off all over the place. I did, however, wake up, as did everyone else, for the border crossing. Word was passed quietly, as each of us replaced ball caps with helmets, did up our flack vests, and removed our weapons from the overhead racks and put them between our legs for quick access. The gentle click of magazines being pushed home echoed throughout the bus.

As we approached the Zone of Separation, it was clear a war had taken place. There were wrecked cars, burned out tank hulks, and demolished houses. Bullet holes pockmarked the facade of every house, and I don't think I saw a single unbroken pane of glass anywhere. Everyone was quiet as we approached the border, that is, until some joker in the back remarked, "hey, it's just like on TV." Life imitating art? It was good for a laugh, but it was at this point that it really began to sink in with us that this was no training exercise. As soon as we cleared the Serb side I fell asleep again.

I woke up as the bus slowed to make the turn to go up the final rise into Rastivic. You could almost drive by it and never know it was there. All you could see were evenly spaced OPs on the crest of a small rise like the towers of a medieval castle, but once you got through the gate it was a different world. Tents, ISO trailers, sandbags, razor wire, and as far as the eye could see there was gravel. The roads were made of it, the sandbags were filled with it, and the trailers sat on it. It was clear to see why this place had acquired the nickname Moon Base Alpha.

We got off the buses; laid out our vests, helmets and weapons by company; grabbed a quick lunch, and then did the kit shuffle again. From here we would split up and go to our various outposts. As per plan, the guys from our platoon piled our kit and ourselves into the back of an MLVW, and headed out into the countryside to drop everyone off. The first stop was a small village called Donja Bruska (where one of our

The First Half of the Tour 75

Looking for our kit at Sibenik

platoon's sections is located), then on to the town of Rodaljice where the remainder of the platoon is housed. We pulled into Rodaljice and were assigned our rooms (four men, four cots, and way too much kit in a dinky little trailer that's only 20' x 8') then broke off to have supper.

Supper consisted of pizza with all the fixins, some of which I didn't recognize, and it stayed in my stomach for a total of ten short minutes. Right after finishing the last bite, I was outside bringing it back up. There's me, leaning on the dumpster puking my guts out. Since arriving at Sibinek, I had polished off two 2-litre bottles of water without having to pee, and I was feeling slightly woozy. We were supposed to have 24 hours off after arriving to acclimatize, so with that in mind I headed to my little corner of this brave new world to get my kit sorted out and grab some shuteye.

It's got to be a rule or something, but I wasn't in my trailer 5 minutes when Sgt

Macari stuck his head in the door to ask me if I'd mind taking a shift for one of the guys who was off doing something else. What started out as a two-hour stand in turned into a full six-hour shift. George was good enough to join me for the last four hours, and we spent it doing the head-bob at each other. By the time we'd finished, I'd been up for 42 hours straight, traveled halfway around the world, puked my guts out, crossed I don't know how many time zones, and on the whole was feeling pretty good, but wow, talk about your culture shock. At 2:00 A.M. I went to bed . . . and passed out.

Friday, 14 Oct., Rodaljice After a few hours' sleep, I was awakened at 6:00 by the guys coming in and out of the trailer. I was in a trailer with John, Jay, and Robert, and believe me when I tell you, there wasn't much room. They were making so much noise trying to get things straightened around that it didn't seem worth it to stay in bed any longer, so I got up and went to clean up.

After taking in a late breakfast that actually stayed down this time, I was assigned to paint up a bunch of signs in Serbian, warning of the razor wire that lined the road. We were given a Serb-English dictionary to figure out the spelling. We thought we were painting "danger razor wire" but we could have painted "get a haircut here" for all we knew. The activity lasted until we broke just before lunch when the warrant came by to walk us around the camp and show us which sandbags were filled with bauxite and which ones we should stay away from—which was next to impossible because the damn things were everywhere.

After lunch David took John and I for our first foot patrol of the village. It was a lovely summer day for a walk, as we worked our way along the road. Our first stop was a Croat house where we were promptly offered a glass of wine. David was having none of it because on his first patrol he had so much to drink they almost had to carry him back. John and I, being the wine buffs in the section, chose to have a quick glass.

We worked our way along the various roads and back alleys, as David showed us where to walk, where not to, and which houses were occupied and which were abandoned. We walked past the village well that had an olive tree growing out of one of the retaining walls, and appeared to have been there a mere century or two. Then it was up into the hills.

Up here the scene was slightly different. The number of destroyed houses increased, and there were virtually no residents. David made a point of showing us which houses to avoid because the Engineers hadn't cleared them yet. We've been told that it's safe to assume that all the abandoned houses had been booby trapped—based on what the Engineers had found earlier—and it was probably safest to stay clear of them altogether. It was something to walk amongst the destruction that we'd only ever seen on TV. This was the real McCoy. It was here that the ethnic cleansing had taken place, and we were walking around in the remains of it. It had a sobering effect on our little group.

Upon our return, the heavy work started. Each section's carrier had to have everything stripped out of it, all the ammunition counted. This included our personal ammunition as well. They keep a very close count on the ammo we have (in spite of this, I know of at least two crates of unregistered ammo in the compound) and the serial numbers of all weapons are recorded. Then it had to be all put back in such a way that everyone knew where everything was. For instance, looking into the vehicle from the ramp, the .50-cal ammo cans were all stacked in a row along the floor at the front-end of the carrier, on the right side with handles up for quick access. On the left side, behind the driver's compartment, was all the 7.62 ammo for the C6, again stacked with handles up for quick access.

In the middle between the benches was the 5.56 ammo for the troops' personal weapons. This was left in a crate so the .50-cal gunner had something to stand on during a patrol. The right side bench held the section tent, rations and water for three days, the Coleman stove and lantern, and Karl Gustav ammo tubes. The left bench held the hand grenades, M72s, the tool bag and track repair kit and torpedo, 60 mm mortar bombs, and the 60 mm mortar, extra C9 belt ammo for the section gunners, plus various other items. The C6 was stored in a rack above the right hand bench, as was the 84 mm Karl Gustav anti tank weapon. And on the left side, below the carrier's radio rack, additional C9 ammo, a spare radio pack for foot patrols, and the emergency first aid kit were all kept. Because of my additional training in first aid, it fell to me to liaise with the medic and ensure that the kit was up to date, and contained everything that might be needed. With all the ammo and weapons stored there was enough room above each of the benches to stow an overnight bag and valise for each man.

Ingenuity is the middle name of the Canadian infanteer, and it wasn't long before Henry had put his hands on some bungee cord, and rigged a system to keep our kit from spilling out during a patrol.

What started out as 2 hours of work turned into eight, when it was announced that both of the tracks had to be taken off the vehicle, and all the road pads replaced and end connectors torqued. This involves swinging a 25-lb sledge hammer to knock the old pads off—which then became a game to see who could knock a pad the furthest—and leaning heavily on a 3 foot torque wrench to tighten up end connectors. When we were finished the beer never tasted so good.

The evening was spent playing pool (God only knows where they found the table), darts, and drinking beer, as we reveled in our first day on the job in a new country. The duty roster was posted shortly after supper, and my shift was set for 0600 in the morning, so sadly I had to limit my drinking. But, there's always tomorrow.

Saturday 15 Oct., Rodaljice Shift work. What can you say about it that hasn't already been said? Boring! Not much to it really. There are three of us on at a time. Two in the gatehouse and one in the radio room. Every two hours we rotate. At the gate we idle away the time, and give away bread and milk to locals when they ask for it. In the radio room, at least you get to talk to someone other than your partner, and besides, it can be interesting listening to some of the reports coming across the airwaves.

Today while I was on the radio, the electricians came by. In a prolonged discussion it was determined that the schoolhouse that we've occupied needs to be rewired. The electricians didn't have enough time so I volunteered to run all the wire so all they had to do was hook it up to the main circuit panel.

On another note, the camp is nearly empty. Warrant Fuller made a run to Donja Bruska with the ML and broke down on the return trip. He has been broken down for several hours, apparently he nearly sheared all the bolts off of one of the front tires on the MLVW, and he's not a happy camper. The rest of the boys are in Rastivic to trade the carriers around. We're having ceramic armour put on them.

I've just completed a double shift because the guy who was to replace me didn't get back on time. The lucky bugger gets my midnight to 6:00 shift. If nothing else it makes for a damn long day. But on the bright side there's filet mignon tonight for dinner. On the barbecue, no less. All the comforts of home!

Sunday 16 Oct., Rodaljice What did we do today? We went to the ranges this morning and fired in our weapons. Once again something is wrong with my rifle. This time we've figured out that the problem is with the extractor spring. Because the spring is too strong, it kicks out the casing too soon in the extraction cycle. This in turn causes endless jams. But at least we know what the problem is, and how to fix it.

After the range we stopped off in Donja Bruska to drop off 3 Section and pick up 1 Section. The rest of the day (from 12 to 6) I was on duty.

In our Ogroup tonight we were told again that the Croats are re-arming courtesy of the Germans. Apparently they have been given Leopard Tanks, fuel and arms. We've also been told that because the Jordanians go to bed at night and we don't, the Croats have been moving troops through their positions at night. The Serbs, on the other hand, need a port city to get around the arms embargo. There's going to be a fight and it will probably be in January or February.

Our policy has changed somewhat also. Up to this point we've been denied access to Camp Alpha, the primary Serb training base, which is just up the road from us. Sometime soon a group of officers are going to try to force their way in. Because our platoon is responsible for the area, we will be called in if something happens. We're not backing down and we all feel good about that.

Monday 17 Oct., Rodaljice For me, today was a day off. I managed to sleep in till 9:00 then had a light breakfast and went for my first workout of the tour. The rest of the day was just as slack. It actually caught me by surprise, I expected to get assigned to do some make-work projects today, but I didn't.

The warrant has pulled a few strings and had a "morale phone" installed upstairs in the school building. We've been told, on pain of death, not to let on to anyone that we have it. Today the CSM and the Company commander came by. For some reason a "condemned—do not enter" sign appeared at the base of the stair leading to the phone. (Both the CSM and the OC never made it upstairs). Though, how they missed the satellite dish sitting outside on the windowsill is beyond me.

Several things happened over the past two days. The best way to cover it is in point-form so here it goes:

—The platoon has been placed on 60-min notice to move. That means that all personnel leave the location, and only 3 people stay back with the kit.

— Position 6-1 had a drunken soldier fire 2 machine gun bursts at them. No shots were returned. Everyone is nervous. The harvest is in, and both sides seem to think there's going to be an offensive.

—3-1C had shots fired at it.

—A Charlie Company patrol found 10 fresh bodies yesterday. Apparently they've been dead less than 48 hours.

—An UNMO (UN military observer, unarmed) Vehicle was hijacked. Some Serbs rolled their vehicle on its side then pretended to be injured. When the UNMO stopped to help, they jumped up and stole his vehicle. Boy, I bet the UNMOs feel pretty silly.

—There is a platoon of Croat soldiers dug-in in the zone of separation. They've been doing some blasting to improve their trenches. Every time the UN sends out a patrol to investigate, they disappear over to their side of the line. So the strategy is to send a patrol in to confirm the position is empty, then follow it up with a platoon for security, and then send in the dozers to bury the place. This all will happen in the next day or two.

The First Half of the Tour 79

— Finally, something to inspire confidence in the admin section. The CQ has lost 42 vehicles. It's purely administrative but funny nonetheless. I'd hate to be the CQ at the mess tonight. The ribbing will be terrible.

I managed to get a call in to Cat today. It sure felt good to hear her voice again. The 15-minute limit on phone calls goes fast.

Tuesday 18 Oct., Rodaljice Up at 5:30 this morning for duty at 6:00. The shift passed with no incident. Our patrol was interesting. Everyone in the village is quite friendly. They offer us wine, or pivo (schnapps). They smile and chat with us. But there are a lot of abandoned houses in the area, and up on the hill there's a house where 29 people were decapitated, or so we've been told. When you look into the eyes of these people, you gotta wonder what they've seen and what they've done. Especially the Serb soldiers living here.

Twenty-nine people were decapitated at this house

It's a poor country, a harsh country. The size of the farm fields and the number of rocks in the fences and walls evidence this. Still, people continue to stop at the gate for daily rations of milk and bread. One wonders if it is because they need it or because it's free.

And now for the nightly update:

—6-1 took shots again today, apparently the whole Zone is active. Reason to take notice.

—Once again men in ski masks hijacked an UNMO. This makes #8 this summer.

—1 Nov is All Saints' Day in Canada but All Souls' Day here. Apparently there's a midnight vigil with candles. We may be tasked to provide security. More to follow.

—I've been given a night sight for my rifle. It's a laser that shows up as a dot on the target but can only be seen if you're wearing night vision goggles. Cool! Just like in the movies.

—Leave in Budapest. I got it from 1–5 Nov. More to follow.

—Our first vehicle patrol is tomorrow.

Wednesday 19 Oct., Patrolling A nice relaxing morning preceded today's patrol. We had our Ogroup around 11:30 to lay out the route, mission, and other pertinent information. The patrol itself started at 12:30 and was supposed to go till 4:30 but went long and didn't end until 5:45. I can see now why they want to build us up to two patrols per day. When we finally made it back to the camp, I was stiff as a board, covered in dust, and barely able to move my wrists. Everyone hobbled as they tried to make their way to their trailers. I guess six hours of standing in a hatch can do that to you.

What I saw on patrol today saddened me. We drove through entire communities where there wasn't a soul. One town had a school where a number of the students and teachers were simply lined up against the wall and shot. I'm told they were Moslems. You could still see the bullet holes and bloodstains on the wall. The houses all had their roofs blown off and were in various states of disrepair from piles of rubble to almost fully intact. Yet, even in the midst of decay there is beauty. I was looking to my right, when over the smell of dust and diesel fumes came the smell of roses. On the left side of the road, arranged in two long rows in front of what was left of a house were a dozen rose bushes. Each was about 5 feet high and absolutely drooping with blooms in red, white and pink. In the cool fall air and bright sunshine, they were in their glory. Once again the duality of man is illustrated.

Another place we drove through had a hospital—or what was left of it. Everywhere you looked there was evidence of fighting. Hull down positions, trenches, and bunkers were in abundance. Along one wall that had holes from rocket grenades, and hundreds of bullets, there was a bunch of graffiti. Nothing special, it's all over the place. But in the middle of all the Croatian lettering were words "welcome to hell" in English. An interesting concept in light of the surroundings!

I could go on forever about the destruction, but I won't. I'm sure in the days to come I'll have lots to say about it. There is one thing that I have to bring up that really makes you wonder. After the villages were "cleansed," the Serbs went into the graveyards and dug up the bodies and scattered the bones all over the place. Now it's one thing to kill a man for the way he worships his God, for his racial background, or even his political beliefs. Killing him puts him in the ground the first time. But you gotta wonder about digging him, and his family up, just so you can scatter their bones around. What kind of mind thinks up this shit? And who's stupid enough—or fanatic enough—to follow it through? I freely admit that I don't get it.

And now for today's news:

—6-1 once again came under fire. This is getting repetitive.

—Duck boys! we're being shot at. In Benkovac (a town we have to pass through to get to Dukes Company HQ, and numerous other places) UN personnel have reported being shot at with pellet guns. Christ, even the kids are getting into it. Fire will NOT be returned!

—To identify a Chechnik—Serb soldier—you must look for a beard, and a black wool cap with skull and crossbones on it. Is it me, or does this not sound an awful lot like a Second World War group?

—And finally, tonight we were called out to support our section on Donja Bruska. Between 6:30 & 7:00 the boys reported 11 grenades and prolonged machine gun bursts. Certainly cause for concern, particularly in light of the fact that Camp Alpha has never done night ops to our knowledge, and these rounds were going off within 200 yards of the village. We got an agitated call on the radio for backup, so we all piled into the three remaining carriers in camp and made the half-hour run to the village. By the time we got there all the excitement was over. We stayed for half an hour or so then came back to camp. False alarm!

As it turns out, the new camp commander and senior captain were in town. Both are particularly keen, and have stepped up training. Nice of them to let us know. And, here's an interesting note. Mercenaries have been seen in Camp Alpha wearing French Foreign Legion uniforms. Recruiting?

Today's patrol reminded me of a Sunday drive in the country with Cat. The fact that I'm sitting behind a .50 calibre machine gun, and rolling down the road in 13 tons of steel is incidental.

Thursday 20 Oct., Rodaljice There was no patrol for us today, so the day was pretty much ours. I took the opportunity to have a really good workout, then spent the rest of the morning working on the carrier. Now that it's reorganized, we finally have some room.

In the afternoon the electrician came by to do some work on the schoolhouse. After talking with him, I wound up with 75 metres of five wires (heavy-duty extension cord). A terrible waste, because all I'm doing is running lights and some outlets.

The supplies I ordered (cut plywood, 2 x 2s, nails etc.) arrived today as well. Instead of cutting the wood for me as promised, they sent 4 x 8 sheets of plywood. The 2 x 2s were 4 x 4 and the paint came in 5-gallon pails. Aside from the paint, the rest is pretty much useless to me until I get a skilsaw.

Last night several bursts of MG fire were heard from up the hill. We don't know who did it or why. But it means we'll have to be extra vigilant while on duty.

And now the news in brief:

—For the most part the sector was pretty quiet last night

—3-1, while on patrol, was offered wine and women in trade for fuel by some Serb soldiers. The offer was politely declined.

—A PPCLI officer has been charged with racking up more than 100 thousand DM in phone calls to his wife. As a result, the battalion has only 20% of its phone budget left. So we've been reduced to a 5-min call, once a week on our surreptitious phone hookup.

—And finally, last night the warrant decided he would finish a 750-ml bottle of Crown Royal by himself. It was his daughters second birthday and he wanted to drown his hurt, so we joined him. We talked about many things, as one tends to do when under the influence. We wound up talking about the Mafia, and John and Robert took the brunt of the warrant's wrath, simply because both were of Italian extraction. Well, the long and the short of it is that the warrant got pissed off, Lord knows at what, but he did, and he got up and headed for the door telling John and Robert to follow him into the foyer area. The next thing we know, the warrant is waving a loaded

9-mm pistol in their faces. After some more words were exchanged between the three of them, the warrant calmed down some and went outside.

Fortunately, MCpl Labell saw what was going on and spent a good bit of time trying to calm the warrant down. Eventually he convinced him that whatever he planned wasn't a good idea, and had him unload the pistol. Unfortunately, in his considerably intoxicated state, the warrant fumbled the unload drill, and he fired a round into an unloading bay outside the front door. We all thought that everything had calmed down until the round went off, then it was like a circus, as eight guys tried to make their way through the one door that led outside, as we tried to see what was happening.

John was first outside and approached the warrant, who by this time was leaning heavily against the kitchen trailer. As John approached he could see a dark stain on the warrant's pants and immediately thought the warrant had shot himself somehow. When John asked if he was OK the warrant informed him he was, but that he had involuntarily wet his pants.

Then Sgt Goldsmith, who was on duty, took control of the situation. John and MCpl Labell, under the direction of the sergeant, took the warrant by the arms and guided him back to his bunk. The sergeant relieved the warrant of his pistol. Nothing has, or will be said about it. The warrant looks out for us, and we'll do the same for him.

We all hit the sack at 1:30.

Friday 21 Oct., Rodaljice Today was also an off day—sort of. I was up for 7:20 to go with MCpl Labell to pick up our interpreter and our daily ration of 25 loaves of bread from a bakery in Benkovac.

The bread around here is like gold, and in the fine tradition of Radar O'Reilly, our CQ MCpl Labell uses it as barter for all kinds of things. Apparently we are one of only two camps in the battalion to get its own allocation of fresh bread. Labell is trying to get our allotment increased, thus increasing our local bargaining power.

The rest of the morning I worked on finishing the wiring. I got all the lines run, and the boxes installed, now I just have to wait for the electrician to come back so that we can hook up the main fuse box.

The warrant had tasked me with painting a giant Toronto Maple Leaf symbol on one of the walls in the common area of the school building. What started as a simple paint job turned into a painting party with more than 5 gal of paint ending up on the walls and two rooms being painted. When the paint dried, I started on the maple leaf. Working from the platoon commander's Toronto Maple Leaf coffee cup, I scaled the leaf up so that when I was done, the finished product was more than 6' high and 5' wide. It was really quite impressive, if I do say so myself.

During a break in the painting of the leaf, John and I had a quiet chat outside. What he told me surprised me to say the least. This morning after Jay, Robert and I had left the trailer, John was taking it easy reading a book while lying on his bed. The door burst open and the warrant reached in and grabbed John by his shirt and dragged him outside. Before John knew what was happening, the warrant had him slammed up against the outside of the ISO with his hand around his throat and his feet nearly off the ground.

"So Renwick, what'cha gonna say when someone asks you about last night?" he said in a low menacing voice.

"Nothing, Warrant," came John's strangled reply.

"That's a good little troopy, Renwick. Don't you forget it." Whereupon the warrant

Our Toronto Maple Leaf morale booster

loosened his grip on John's throat, and his feet came back down to earth. The warrant wandered away and John was left to massage his neck and wonder what the hell had just happened.

John and I talked around the subject for fifteen minutes or so, and came to the conclusion that neither of us would have said anything about last night no matter who was asking. So why did the warrant feel he needed to threaten his troops to gain their silence? Both of us have just lost a lot of respect for the warrant.

Last night some little shit tried to break into our compound and steal some gas. He was unsuccessful. As a result, tomorrow we're going to clear some of the bush around the POL point and lay out some extra razor wire. It's stacked 2 high on top of a wall now, but this will increase the depth and create more of an obstacle.

Starting in November some time, our platoon has been tasked to provide security for the town of Knin. That's north and east of here, so that will leave one section here in Rodaljice, one section in Donja Bruska, and one in Knin. We'll rotate through all the positions on a weekly basis for six weeks or so. If nothing else it will keep things interesting.

In January the QRF platoon, currently 1 Platoon, will be tasked for port security in Split. Subsequently 3 men per section will be sent to call sign "0" to provide local security. This too will be a six-week tasking.

It's funny what painting a place will do for morale. The atmosphere around here is that of a frat house. Paint brushes flying, MTV blaring, people laughing and joking. The walls are being painted white and tomorrow the doorframes will be UN blue. It's been said that this is the choice assignment. I believe it!

Saturday 22 Oct., Rodaljice I didn't really do very much today. Our section wasn't tasked with a patrol because one of our carriers hasn't come back from shop with its armour plating yet. They're putting ceramic steel on. This stuff is a little more than a half inch thick, can stop a .50 calibre bullet, and adds only 1000 lbs to the already 26,000 lbs the carriers weigh. The PPCLI appear to have left our carriers in a well-used condition and subsequently they are in need of many repairs, hence the delay.

We received some defensive stores which we laid out along the back of the camp around the POL point, which should make it harder to cut through the wire and steal our gas (mind you at 8 DM a litre I'd be tempted to break in myself).

I didn't actually participate in the laying of the wire, or the hacking down of trees and bushes. I'd just come off a 2 hr radio watch, and applying the rule of "old age and treachery will always triumph over youth and enthusiasm" (and being the oldest man in the platoon) I managed to take on the role of local security. That's where you stand around with flack vest and rifle, and watch everyone else do the work, while you provide security for them while outside the wire. This man's mama raised no fool.

The tasking took us from just after lunch until supper to complete, and being a Saturday it was steak night. Mac, the cook, does one hell of a fine marinated and bbq'd steak. There's no news today, because Saturday is happy hour in all the messes—hence no Ogroup. After supper, we watched a couple of movies then half our section played a great game of Trivial Pursuit (1980s version). There was a scare of losing our phone, but that passed. There was lots of painting and clean up going on today, but at a leisurely pace.

Sunday 23 Oct., Bruska Today we rotated with 3 Section to Donja Bruska. We sorted out our bunk spaces then myself, the medic—who arrived to make house calls—and Doug Peters from 3 Section, took a walk into the village. A 20-min visit turned into 3 hours, when the wine appeared. Drinking on patrol is the way it's done here. I'm told that beer is not sent to us because there is so much of the local wine available to us. I'm not sure I believe that, but there it is.

One of our section commanders, Sgt MacKinnon of 3 Section, appears to have been drinking a great deal of the time he was here. The boys in his section were pretty quiet about it, but you could see the strain it was putting on them. I guess as long as the section commander and the 2IC aren't drunk at the same time then things are covered, after all there's next to nothing to do here. Still, it doesn't impress me, or anyone else for that matter and it's just a matter of time before he gets caught.

Not much else to tell. While I'm here I hope to write many of my letters. George

Our new bunk spaces at Bruska

has to go into call sign 0 (Rastivic) to call his wife. Two days ago she was rushed into the hospital with acute appendicitis. The hospital immediately called the Battalion, and they in turn reached George very quickly. It seems she developed some complications and the doctor needed to talk to him. Everything appears to be all right now, but it gives me confidence to know that if Cat ever wound up in the hospital I'd know about it almost immediately.

Monday 24 Oct., Bruska I must have had some sort of reaction to the wine I had yesterday because I tossed and turned all night. At 3 A.M. I got up to do a patrol of the village with Jim, then I went back to bed. We were told the company commander and CSM were coming by, so we all dragged ourselves out of bed at 7:00 and cleaned ourselves up. I put in a quick appearance, and as it was raining out I went back to my bunk and lay down. At lunch I got up and made my bed again. The CSM never showed up.

At 4:00 I got up and stayed up until 3 AM, the end of my radio watch. After supper we drew names for a work party in Rastivic. I had a 2/7 chance in not going, and for once luck was on my side, and I didn't have to go (much to my relief). Bruce and David were given the task, and didn't seem to mind. All in all it was a pretty boring day.

> 24 Oct 94
> My Dearest Catherine
>
> I am writing this to you while sitting in a tent, in a town called Donja Bruska. This place has been nicknamed our "one-week leave center," because all we do here is sleep, eat, and when on patrol, drink wine with the locals. The locals love us here, and believe it or not bring the wine right to the gate in pots.
>
> There are two groups of people here, Serbs and Croats. Not a single Moslem to be seen. The three young couples in town are refugees, whom the Serb government has moved here. All the old people are Croatian and have lived here forever.
>
> This is a hard country, everything is made of rock, and it's a wonder there is any soil here at all. What soil there is, is augmented heavily with compost, and is red as P.E.I. mud. All the old people get up and drink wine or aracia (moonshine) right from breakfast till bedtime. It's only the young who drink coffee. The stuff is like Turkish coffee, served in a demi-tasse cup with walnuts in it. It's very sweet, but very good. The wine tastes a lot like our wild grape wine, but a lot more crude. Truth is, I won't touch much of it. When I first got here, I had half a litre of some of it, and I wound up sleeping most of the next day.
>
> I don't know when you will receive this letter; as yet I have not received yours, which quite annoys me. It's funny actually, I never would have thought that I would anticipate a letter from anyone as much as I do from you.
>
> I want very much to talk to you, but the phone has been down for the past week. By the time you get this letter though, I will have talked to you again. Sadly it will be a short call because we're told some PPCLI officer racked up a 100,000 DM phone bill. As a result we're told only 20% of the phone budget is left. This will result in us having only a five-minute call once a week until things change.
>
> We've been here 13 days and we've been given some idea of what's to come. On 15 November, myself and two others from the section are off to Budapest for a 96-hour leave. My intention is to take a HOT bath and sleep in a bed with sheets for a change instead of a cot and a sleeping bag. There's talk of sending us to Germany for a second 96-hour leave but we'll have to pay for hotels and transport. I have no intention of going if I have to pay. On the 14th of November one of our sections will be going to Knin for two weeks for security detail. Each section will rotate through once, that will leave one section here in Donja Bruska, one in Rodaljice, and one in Knin. For me this will be good. I won't be in one place long enough to get bored!
>
> I can't tell you how much I look forward to seeing you in England. I love you very much, and will write again soon.
>
> > Your loving husband
> > Kurt

Tuesday 25 Oct., Bruska   David and Bruce were up at 6:00 to be ready for 7:00, when the MLVW came to take them to Rastivic. They spent the morning moving rocks and building a defensive wall.

Jim and I took a walk today, while on patrol, up to the Camp Alpha gate. We've been told that the camp has stepped up training, and has about 1000 young men in it. We walked right up to the gate. I was in the lead with the radio, with Jim on the other side of the road and back a bit. Both of us could tell that the two young lads at the gatehouse were very nervous as we approached. We tried to keep things light, by smiling and shaking hands.

After we had introduced ourselves, we chatted, and I was surprised that they spoke simple but passable English. Certainly better than my Serbian! They're not supposed to talk to us at all, and when the conversation got too personal (or went too long, I don't know which) they told us to "leave now."

I recall as we walked away, that the younger of the two guards was sent into the shack to call in our visit. The rest of the patrol was as usual, uneventful. Later on in the afternoon I grabbed my sketchpad and Bruce and I went for a walk around the village, and I did some sketching. I feel frustrated because I'm not getting the kind of reproduction of the image that I want. What can I say, it's the artist in me.

Tonight Rodaljice called in two ShotReps. One of them was for 29 shots fired. The other was for MG burst with tracer. We overheard their reports being sent in over the radio. No word as to how things turned out.

In other news, Rodaljice (Yankee 1–3) lost their generator today. It's not that big a deal, but all the food is starting to defrost, which is somewhat inconvenient. Also we've had no end of problems with our vehicles. They've taken so much abuse over here it's unreal. Two of the carriers had to be towed to Rastivic to be repaired.

Finally, there was a dispute over wood in Rodaljice. A patrol was sent out to sort out the problem. Undoubtedly it will be brought up at the next town meeting when the resident Serbs, Croats, and UN reps sit down.

Oh yeah, MCpl Labell came up today with bunk beds for us, 9 frames and 5 mattresses. Once again the army supply system displays its powers. Well, I guess it beats sleeping on the floor.

A letter finally arrived from Catherine tonight. It was great to hear from her, but the letter was too short.

An interesting incident took place tonight that I should tell you about. We have a camp dog called Duchess. She was left by the PPCLI and looks like a rottweiler/shepherd cross. There's no way to tell for sure how old she is, but we guess it's about six months. She's very friendly, and some of the younger guys in the section have grown quite close to her—even going as far as to let her sleep on their beds with them.

The locals have been raising hell these past few days claiming that our Duchess has been sneaking out of camp and killing the chickens. The last section here received the same complaints but didn't believe them. The local Croat mayor stopped by again today and had a chat with George, complaining bitterly about the dog. George said he'd deal with it.

After supper tonight, when things got dark, I noticed George slip out of the tent, then come back to the door and signal me. When I joined him outside he quietly handed me two rounds and asked me to take the dog up the road for a walk. I knew instantly what he wanted.

I went back in and got dressed and headed for the door. Nobody noticed much until I picked up a piece of rope and slipped it around the dog's neck. Then all hell broke loose.

Robert led the charge with an incredibly spirited protestation against shooting the animal. Voices were raised, arms flailed and in the end the dog's life was spared. Strict orders were given to keep the animal on a leash, lest the locals find out she was still around.

I gave the rounds back to George, thankful that I didn't have to use them.

Wednesday 26 Oct., Bruska This morning's patrol took John and myself up to the Camp Alpha gate again. Once again the two young men on duty shook hands then politely but firmly asked us to leave. Their eyes gave them away. They were nervous as hell.

The patrol ended with a coffee at one of the refugee Serb places. The wife's name is Gordana. Her husband, Sveto, works in the kitchen in Rastivic. Twice the Serb government has moved them because of the war. We talked about her past and the effects of the war. All in all it was interesting stuff, and gave me pause to consider, as we walked back to the tent, how I'd deal with a similar situation.

Just after lunch we had a visit from one of the warrants. He passed on that it looks like 3 Platoon and 2 Platoon are going to trade places sometime in January. Nothing has been confirmed yet. But if it happens, we will come under the command of Charles Company. (Our JTF boys have used Charles Company as a base for black ops into the Zone of Separation—at least that's what the local rumour mill says.) It could be an interesting go.

On a funny note, Rastivic, or call sign "0", our strongest defended Canadian position, was broken into and shot up last night. Some drunken Serb cut through the wire and took an AK-47 and shot the place up, then ran away. No one was hurt but you gotta give the guy full marks for having balls. What's the bet the boys in Rastivic will be pulling extra guard duty for the next week?

Apparently the boys in 2 Platoon have had shots fired at them, mines go off, and generally been on their toes since taking their position at Pristeg in the zone of separation.

Back at our little camp, John and I tried to replace the end on our tent. We had requested a replacement for the one we have because it has a huge tear in it, and won't close properly. As it turns out, CQ sent us the wrong end piece. This, we discovered only after we took the existing end off and we were trying to string up the replacement. Strong militaristic language was heard as we struggled to put the original end back on the tent.

The rest of the evening was spent watching movies and playing the Game Boy that Jim brought along (one game of Tetris and you pass it on to the next guy). We're all getting pretty good at it. I went to bed about 10:00, then got up for the 1:00 to 3:00 A.M. radio watch. A quiet night.

Thursday 27 Oct., Bruska This morning's patrol had us handing out frozen chickens to the locals. We have so much food here it's insane. We have a freezer overflowing with meat, and the cook keeps sending more food to us. If we don't give it away, we'd have to throw it away.

Today's activities included a trip to the ranges to fire the C-6 and the .50 cal. The range lasted all of one hour and we were back in camp by noon. I have to admit that traveling inside the carriers has given me some trouble, namely motion sickness. If I'm not outside looking around, it becomes a problem for me when we travel over uneven ground, and trust me there is NO EVEN GROUND over here. One of these days I'm going to have my last meal come back for a chat.

Tonight was spent writing. One letter to the Reverend Doctor Andrew Stirling, to be read from the pulpit at Parkdale United Church in Ottawa, and one letter for Cat, to be read in bed.

27 Oct.
My Dearest Catherine;
  At long last your eagerly anticipated letter has arrived. It was genuinely good to hear from you.
  I've taken the liberty of using our home address to send letters to others. To date it has only been your dad, and Andrew, and I figure that seeing as how you were going to see them anyway . . . thanks.
  You asked what the people here are like. The young couples are no different than you or I in many ways. They just live in a war torn country in conditions that would try anyone's patience.
  I'm in Donja Bruska right now, and there are four Serb families who have been moved here. All are in their 20s and 30s. All have one or two children of preschool age. To be perfectly honest with you, I don't trust them. I like them, but I don't trust them. The old here are just that, old. Most are past retirement age and are still out in the fields working. They walk everywhere they go—there are no cars. That's not true, there are cars, just no gas. Besides, this is the equivalent of the backwoods. Things take longer to get out here.
  There are no middle-aged people here, just the young, the old, and abandoned houses.
  Just up the road from us is the gate for Camp Alpha. The Serbs are supposed to be training about 1000 new 18-year-old recruits. Whenever we approach their front gate, you can see whoever is on duty getting nervous. They're under direct orders not to talk to us. Even so, some will talk for a little bit in better English than my Serbian. If someone in the camp decided they wanted to overrun this place, we'd be toast. But that will never happen so please don't worry.
  Lately we've been having a great deal of trouble with our vehicles. For the past week we've been rotating vehicles through the maintenance pool trying to get everything up to snuff. It has been an inconvenience, especially when you consider that the vehicles have been worked hard up to this point, and the supply chain is fast running out of parts.
  I've been keeping my diary with details of what's been going on and I intend to bring it to England for you to read. These are some of the highlights from the first two weeks on the ground:
  —our foot patrol in Rodaljice, takes us past a house where 29 Croats were decapitated.
  —there's a church 100-m from our camp in Rodaljice. The roof is blown off and someone defecated on the altar—twice. The graveyard is a mess, graves opened, headstones broken, bones scattered, that sort of thing.
  —we drove past a school in the town of Ziminic on one of our patrols,

where children and teachers were lined up against a wall and shot. The bullet holes and bloodstains are still in evidence.

—there is a graveyard where the Serbs went in and dug up the graves, and scattered the bones.

Each day as we drive though the countryside, the evidence of ethnic cleansing is evident. Entire villages are destroyed. Other places (like Rodaljice) half the village is empty and ransacked, and the other half seems normal. It makes you shake your head.

But on to cheerier subjects. Most of our time here in Bruska is spent playing Game Boy, watching movies, playing Trivial Pursuits, or writing letters. There's a six-hour radio watch, between 2400–0600, which we split into two-hour blocks that everyone takes turns doing. During the day, we send out three two-man patrols. It's pretty much on a volunteer basis, but everyone does it. The truth is, we're bored to tears out here.

Since I've been here, I've managed to do some sketching, but not much (did I mention that in my last letter?).

I told you that on the 1st of November I'm going to Budapest. I'm looking forward to seeing what the city looks like.

We've figured out that it takes ten days each way for a letter to travel. So what I figure I'll do is once or twice a week, I'll write a letter to you describing what's been happening. I'll leave the detail description in the diary for you to read. For now, I'll wait until I get your next letter before I write again.

I miss you terribly. More and more I look forward to our time in England. I'll bring lots of pictures.

Love to all.
Your loving husband
Kurt

A final note about our vehicles. Our platoons total issue of vehicles includes, 1 Iltis, 1 MLVW, one box ambulance, a fuel pad and 4 carriers. After working on the Iltis for 2 days, the mechanics finally gave up hope. They spent one day replacing nearly everything on it that could be replaced. Brakes, rotors, springs, motor mounts, plugs, fuel injectors, filters, you name it. The second day they spent trying to get it going. Finally they figured it was contaminated gas that prevented it from starting, and they towed it away. I found out that after more than 2 years over here, our army still doesn't have enough spare parts here to do proper and regular maintenance on our vehicles. As a result, everything that's done amounts to a repair &/or recovery request after you've broken down on the road somewhere.

We also have just replaced the motor in the HQ track—for the second time since we've arrived. The first one went because it was overworked. The second because the oil cooler went and we burned out the motor. At this rate we'll need a new engine every week.

Friday 28 Oct., Bruska Today was the most ungodly boring day ever. The highlight was an evening patrol with NVGs (night vision goggles). Robert and I decided to pay a visit to the Camp Alpha gate. We are supposed to patrol using maximum white light, but Robert and I decided to turn our lights off and walk up the middle of the road, using the NVG to scope out the guardhouse, and see what the guards were up to. We moved to within 50 metres of their position but couldn't see them. Not wanting to get too close, and possibly get shot for trying to sneak up on them, we decided to turn on our flashlights.

As soon as we did, we could hear scuffling and someone came running out of the shack. We hadn't gone two paces further when he cried out "Stoy!" (Serbian for stop). We immediately called back "UN, UN," hoping that they wouldn't think we were one of their instructors trying to sneak up on them. Or worse still, the enemy, the REAL enemy, trying to sneak up and kill them.

Out of the dark came a panicked voice "You go now, you go now, go, go!" Hell, we were still 50 metres from this guy but he seemed so intent on not letting us get any closer, that we had no real choice but to leave.

Oh well, nothing like a little mischief to keep things interesting. Robert and I agreed not to tell anyone about our little incident. The fewer people who know, the less likelihood of us getting shit on. The rest of the patrol was uneventful. That is, if you call stumbling around in the dark uneventful.

Today was food day. Every second day we take yogurt and milk and hand it out to the locals. This practice however has become slightly skewed. Because we tend to spend more time visiting with the displaced Serb families, our food ration for them tends to be larger. Of course the fact that they have young children weighs heavily in this. Somehow it doesn't seem hard to justify giving a little extra to some of the families when children are involved.

When the Vandoos were here, there was a single Serb woman living in one of the houses. I don't know how it started, but one of the NCO's started trading blowjobs for food. The Vandoo was charged. The woman doesn't live here any more.

The village is populated predominantly with older people. One of them is an 80-year-old woman, whom the PPCLI have nicknamed the Peanut Butter Lady. She comes to the gate every couple of days and we give her food. She has no teeth so what we give her tends to be soft foods like peanut butter. Hence the name. It's our understanding that her son and daughter-in-law are trying to starve her to death. So on our foot patrols we pop in to see how she's doing. She lives in what used to be a sheep stall and manages to keep herself going on what little food she can gather. The other day Bruce and David came back off patrol absolutely beside themselves with anger. Here the son had gone in and cleaned out all the old lady's food and refused to feed her. They went back with whatever they could scrounge up, and tried to make her comfortable. Talk about a fucked-up people!

Saturday 29 Oct., Bruska Today is the last full day here. Thank God for that. We're all so bored that we're starting to engage in the most asinine, and animated arguments. They're all good fun, but the potential for someone getting insulted is really high, and there's still five and a half months left to go.

At long last we got some serious news from the outside. George went for an Ogroup today to get orders for the graveyard security duty we're supposed to do on the 31st of October. It would appear that the graveyard is in the zone of separation, at a place called Pristeg, and the local Serb Battalion commander has sworn that any Croat caught in the zone will be shot—UN or no UN. Sadly, I won't be with the section when we do the duty. At least I don't think I will be, I'm supposed to be in Budapest the next day.

I tried to switch leave with some of the guys, but no one took. I can't say as I blame them though. This is the first real excitement we've seen, and no one wants to give up on the opportunity. I'll just sit and wait until I find out for sure what's going on.

And now, the news from the front...

—Heavy equipment has been reported moving to the north of our position. As it happens there has been quite a lot of fighting, which has been reported near Brokov in northern Bosnia. While on vehicle patrol we've been asked (when we drive past arms caches and vehicle parks) to take note of anything unusual.

—Our CSM saw a platoon of Serbs in Zadar.

—Our first major accident just happened. A carrier from Bravo Company carrying four guys went off the road and down a 20-foot embankment and rolled over, while on patrol. The guy in the crew commander's hatch got away with a sprained wrist, but the others were worse off. One guy broke several ribs; one had a severely broken femur and the last guy had a badly banged up head. All were medivac'd out immediately. It's truly unfortunate. The Ogroup had warned us the night before about the slippery road conditions because of all the rain we've been having the past couple of days. The carriers have rubber pads on them that help reduce the damage to the road, and cushion the ride somewhat. The drawback with the pads is that it also reduces traction and control. These guys were simply going a little too fast and just skidded off the road.

Three guys back home will be packing their bags.

The side effect on us is that all the phones are down until next of kin can be notified, and a statement can be released to the press. I'm getting anxious to call Cat. All week I've been thinking about her. I've written two letters in the past couple of days and I'm sorely tempted to start another one. Each night before I go to bed I think of her. When I'm writing in this diary I look at her pictures. The guys here can't believe that I'm married to someone so beautiful. Sometimes I can't believe it myself. The local Serb women have asked me if I have children. I tell them that we can't. Part of the truth is, that in light of her current condition (MS) I would never ask her to over extend herself by having, or adopting a child. The stress would probably bring on a serious attack, and likely disable her.

It pains me greatly sometimes to think that she is alone at home, in that big old house, with the winter coming on, and I'm stuck out here on the other side of the world. I wonder sometimes if we shouldn't adopt. I look into the little kids faces, and it touches me somehow. It's terribly selfish of me, but I'm scared to death sometimes of waking up only to find that I'm alone and old. I wonder sometimes what I'd ever do without Cat. The six years we've been together have changed me so much.

Each night I hope and pray that some asshole doesn't run her off the road on her way home from teaching in Ottawa. She's all I have!

Sunday 30 Oct., Rodaljice Writing before we head out tomorrow.

0033 A.M., 01 Nov.
My dearest Sweet Catherine
Today your love letter of 22 Oct arrived. It was in with several others at the time, but I knew that this one was special. At first I did not know why, but then it came to me; as I raised the letter to my nose and inhaled the delicate scent which emanated from its folded pages, I was struck by an overwhelming image of you. Not a picture you understand, but the essence of you. So

powerful was it that when I closed my eyes, I had an uncontrollable urge to reach out and hold you close to me. Yet being alone, I was moved almost to tears for being without you.

As I write this, I am holding your note close to me, so that I might continue to be reminded of you in ways, which the written word cannot emulate.

Lying in bed prior to coming on shift, I needed once again to feel the length of your back pressing against me, the curve of your hip under my hand, the swell of your breast, the warmth of your leg against mine, and the scent of your hair. You are my North, my South, my East and West, my working day, and my Sunday rest. It is you who is responsible for who I am, and without you I am but a face in the crowd.

"How do I love thee?" I cannot even begin to count the ways. But, heaven forbid, should anything ever happen to me over here, know this, with all the certainty of the morrow's rising sun; that I shall walk through the very flames of hell itself to be by your side. When you are in the garden and a gentle breeze moves your dress, that will be me holding you close; when the sun warms your face, it will be my hand caressing you; and when you lay yourself down to sleep at night, I too shall lie with you, and watch over you, as you rest.

Sleep well my dearest.
Your ever-loving husband,
Kurt

The Trip to Budapest Our trip to Budapest began with Ray Labell, Ingersol, and myself piling into the back of an ML for the ride to Karin Slana. There we picked up others destined for Hungary and we headed for Rastivic.

We waited at Rastivic for several hours for the buses to arrive as people came in from the far reaches of the Battalion. This gave us a chance to visit the kit shop, pick up our duty-free, and chat with people we hadn't seen for a while. When the buses finally did arrive, we quickly loaded our kit, and piled onto whatever bus was closest, and our trip to Zadar began.

The one thing about these European buses is the fact that they're about three quarters the size of a North American bus. You can imagine the confusion created when sixty really big Canadians, loaded down with helmets, flack vests, weapons, and one carry-on bag each, try to cram into one of these tiny buses. There's nowhere to store anything. All of the overhead racks were taken up with weapons, helmets are under your seat, and the carry-on bag is left to find its own home.

Each bus has a set of double doors in the middle, not unlike a city transit bus. We solved our storage problem by carefully piling as much kit as possible into the well created by the steps, and hoped that the bus driver didn't accidentally hit the open button for the doors. What a fine mess that would make!

Resourcefulness is the middle name for us infanteers, and no sooner did the buses leave the gate of Rastivic, when the medics set a new high for the standard. We'd barely begun to move, when one of them began to make his way from the back of the bus passing out IV bags with drip lines and clamps attached. The contents of the IV bags came in two colours, red and clear. Everyone wondered what was up as the bags were evenly distributed amongst the passengers.

When the medic made it to the front of the bus, he began a lecture by following the tried and true method of instruction perfected by the military in thousands of lessons. He proceeded to give a parody of a weapons lecture pointing out the load and unload procedures for the IV bags complete with phrases like "watch to your front for a complete demonstration," and "check the back blast area," or "the IAs for a stoppage of the tube are.." (IAs means immediate actions). It all made perfect sense when you realized that the medics had replaced the contents of the bags with something more usable in preparation for the trip. The red bags were local wine, and the clear ones were aracia. At the appropriate point in the lecture the bags were dutifully clipped to the overhead racks and the drip lines were passed back and forth between three seats and their occupants. I can't speak for the other buses, but our trip started out with howls of laughter, and everyone took their turn at the spigot.

In a way we were fortunate, being on this trip. It breaks up the tour nicely into even chunks, but mostly because this trip is something of an experiment by higher. They've permitted us to drink on the bus before we get to Budapest, which I was kind of surprised to find out. I figure it will be only a matter of time, either the next trip or the one after, when someone will do something stupid, and all drinking on the buses will stop.

The trip to Budapest is expected to take something like 16 hours. As we drove up the coastal road to Zadar, it became clear that whoever built it didn't have any idea what a straight line was. There can't be more than 200 metres in a straight run anywhere along the road. It's all twists and curves. I suppose when you consider the level of drinking we participated in, it is surprising we didn't have anyone tossing their cookies.

About halfway to Zadar we were, however, forced to make a stop on the side of the road to relieve seriously extended bladders. The three women on the trip had to look for a convenient hill to hide behind, while the rest of us just lined up beside the road. Good thing the HASMAT boys didn't see that. They probably would have charged the lot of us for environmental damage.

When we finally pulled into Zadar, getting off the bus proved to be more interesting than getting on. A whole lot of stumbling around took place as we tried to empty our bus in something resembling an orderly fashion. With kit in hand, we were ushered to a long hallway on the second floor of one of the buildings, and told to change into civilian gear. So, nearly 180 men and women looked around for a four-foot square of the floor, and started to strip. Off came the flack vests, helmets, and combat boots, all to be stuffed into your mesh laundry bag. Your weapon was broken in two, and stowed along with the rest of the kit. Stripped to our underwear, we began the transformation into civilians. Suitably attired in comfortable clothes, we herded back downstairs to the buses where we were shuttled to the airport and a sea container in one of the protected areas. All of our kit was stored in the one container. I remember standing there, thinking that this was going to be a bloody dog's breakfast trying to sort things out when we came back.

Zadar marked a transition for us. In a very real way we were now out of the war zone, and it was a chance to leave the whole mess behind. Not only did we change clothes, we changed buses. Finally we were into a proper travelling coach. These ones even had TVs and a VCR. As soon as we hit the road, the bus driver plugged in the first tape, his "treat" for us. And thus the next six hours passed as we watched European hardcore porn movies, drank beer, and watched the countryside pass us by.

When we got off the bus after pulling into the hotel in Budapest, I have to say that I was honestly disappointed in the way some of the guys were dressed. While

The First Half of the Tour

most of us had donned fairly decent clothing (good jeans and a golf shirt, etc) some of them decided to put on old gym shorts, sandals and muscle shirts. "Is this the way you want the people of Hungary to see you?" I thought to myself. These guys were loud, badly dressed, and set a poor example of a Canadian in a foreign land. The worst part was they were older and of sufficient rank, so they should have known better. I was very disappointed.

Assigning our rooms was the next step, and two sergeants on permanent assignment here, who had made all the arrangements, met us at the door of the hotel. Because I had requested a single room, I was one of the last to be given a room. That was fine by me, I wasn't going anywhere tonight anyway, except into the shower, and then to bed. Many of the others however started to party in earnest.

You can imagine that I didn't get up too early the next morning. I did manage to get up before the bus left at 10:00 to do the tour of the town. We went around to some of the monuments, cathedrals, and local shops. It was a whirlwind tour designed to give you a quick lay of the land. We caught lunch on the fly, and in the afternoon we went to a place out in the country. It was kind of like a theme park. There were some old buildings, a horse show (riders in traditional costume showing us their stuff), and a ride around the area in a horse-drawn cart. You can imagine how impressed a bunch of soldiers would be being ferried around in a horse-drawn cart at two miles per hour.

There was a craft shop, an eating area, as well as stables and various outbuildings. It was interesting to see the old buildings with the thatched roofs and post and beam construction still being used.

At one point in the horse show several of the guys were brought forward and the horsemen demonstrated their ability with the bow whip by making the end of the whip wrap around various parts of the guy's body. Nobody got hurt, but it was plain to see that the guys on the receiving end of the whip were nervous.

The funny came when one of the horsemen offered a ride to one of our guys. The guy accepted, and promptly took the horse for a ride around the field at top speed while hanging on for dear life. The horseman was not impressed. I guess they don't get many takers and wasn't really expecting someone to ride off with his horse.

But the main attraction of the place was obviously the all-you-can-eat-all-you-can-drink meal that had been arranged for us, during which we ate-all-we-could-eat and drank-all-we-could-drink. The party was going along exceptionally well until two of the medics—a guy and a girl—decided to dance on a table, which provided great entertainment value. That is, until the table broke. Things got quiet after that and we all staggered out of the place rather sheepishly as the sergeants dealt with the damage.

Before we left I stopped into the little gift shop, and picked up a hand carved box for Catherine's dresser. Nice little piece, really. I hope she likes it.

Back on the buses, and back to the hotel for around five. A bunch of us decided to go out that night, so we crashed for a couple of hours to sleep off the afternoon's festivities. It's really interesting to see people's image of themselves. I was dressed in Dockers, topsiders, and a golf shirt and a sweater. Ray Labell came out in square toed biker boots, black jeans, a tight black Harley Davidson T-shirt, a leather vest and topped it all off with a bandanna and a black leather Harley ball cap. In his back pocket was a large billfold attached to his belt with a silver chain. The classic biker image.

Interesting, but the prize of the night had to go to Ingersol, the young black kid from the streets of Toronto. This guy was an unbelievable sight to see, and he drew comments from everywhere. From the ground up he was dressed in high topped sneakers, open and barely done up. He had on white sports socks with grey track pants. One leg of the track pants was tucked into one sock, and the other leg of the track pants was over the sock so they mismatched. The track pants only came up to his hip joint, which revealed his boxer shorts into which he had tucked his T-shirt. He had on a grey pullover with a hood and a pocket in the front. This is important because he wore the hood up and his hands stuffed into the pocket. He wore sunglasses and a blue bandanna on his head (his gang colours) under the hood.

And then there was the issue of jewellery. In his mouth he had three gold teeth— I shit you not— several gold earrings in each ear, and a massive gold box chain around his neck that had to weigh close to a pound. On his right hand he had one ring that was worn on three fingers. Any bigger and it could have been used as brass knuckles. And on his left hand he had four separate very large rings. To top it all off, he walked like his hip was broken, judging by the way he dragged one leg behind himself as he shuffled down the road. This kid was, for all intents and purposes, the personification of the "I'm so cool, don't mess with my black ass" kid from the Bronx that had been plucked right off the streets of New York, and cut loose in downtown Budapest. I felt sorry for the locals.

So there we were: the biker, the homey, and the hip-hop kid to hit the town. What an unusual sight we must have made. Talk about your odd bunch. We piled into the back of a Lada taxi and headed for where else but the best strip joint in town, The Citadel.

This place was amazing. It's a club that is situated inside a castle that was built in the 1200s. Behind the bar was a bank of 20-foot windows that ran for 100 or so feet, or the length of the bar. If you ever jumped out of one, it'd be three hundred feet before you hit the ground. This place was built on the edge of a cliff, and the view of Budapest was spectacular, the reflected image of the Parliament buildings sparkled in the waters of the Danube, as spotlights highlighted its Edwardian architecture. The Danube, now there's a word with history. It was an incredible image to behold from the heights at night.

The dance floor was in the middle of the room, and rising up on either side like an auditorium, were the tables and seats. Overlooking everything on a raised dance area 8 to 10 feet above the tables were the go-go dancers/waitresses, who danced in lingerie only. Very nice indeed. Nothing like teasing a room full of sex-starved soldiers. Like all bars the world over, the music was loud, the beer was expensive and the girls looked better towards closing time. Hell it wasn't even 10:00 and they looked pretty good to me.

Our little group, of course, weren't the only ones to hit this place, just one of the first to arrive. We partied long into the night, and it fell to me, who had remained comparatively sober, to get a large group of us, and some of the companions back to the hotel. Suffice it to say that it was an education to realize that everyone in this country gets a cut when you bring a working-girl home. Unless the girl comes from the hotel bar, the guy is obligated to pay a premium to the hotel where he is staying. Kind of like a permission fee. One of them had to borrow 100 DM from me to cover the additional expense. There's a lesson here for all you international travellers—but in the interest of protecting the indiscreet, I shall tactfully move the story along...

The next morning, Ray and I linked up for a quick breakfast, then grabbed a bus down to the trolley station. What a place! The bus stop we got out at was, I believe, on the south side of the Danube River. It was in a bit of a square, where the buses terminated and the electric trains picked up. As soon as we stepped off the bus gypsies surrounded us. They come in from the countryside to sell their crafts and things for whatever they can get. Mostly table linens and such, with really fine needlework was shown. But there was also an impressive collection of odds and sods available. Almost anything you could want, you could get here, everything from tools to trinkets. Sort of like an open air Canadian Tire outlet.

A group of us jumped a trolley and as soon as we crossed the river, we got off and started walking. And walk we did, for almost 14 hours. Noon found us outside the old train station, a very impressive building. It was built in the mid to late 1800s and sported all the Victorian trimmings, including a wing of the building that was framed in cast iron, not unlike a huge greenhouse. As a piece of architecture it was beautiful. Sadly, someone had converted the building into a McDonald's, and as soon as the group saw that, they were off like a shot. Ray and I just looked at it and said, "fuck that, I didn't travel half-way around the world to eat at a bloody McDonald's", so we left the others behind as we went in search of one of the many really nice restaurants in the area.

In retrospect, I suppose we should have taken a moment to go inside to see the architecture and what they had done to the place. But at the time I had no desire to go anywhere near the place.

Ray and I found a lovely restaurant within 100 feet of where we left the rest of the guys and went in to have some real food. This place was beautiful. Fifteen-foot ceilings decorated with plaster inlays, crown mouldings, interesting old oil paintings hung on the walls, and there were private booths with leather seats, a huge desert bar under glass, and in the background there was classical music playing. We ordered a good bottle of wine, and settled in. I ordered a venison stew and Ray ordered roast pheasant. This is why I came to Budapest.

Two hours later, after polishing off a full four-course meal and a bottle of wine for a ridiculously low price, we rose to walk off the meal. I honestly feel that the maitre d' was pleased to see us go. Ray's "leader of the local pack" impression seemed to trouble him somewhat, and I think he was worried that we might do something untoward.

For the next ten hours we walked the streets of Budapest, popping in out of the cold to grab a cappuccino, or cafe au lait at a convenient cafe. We saw the schloss on the hill overlooking the incredibly ornate parliament buildings on the other side of the Danube. We walked around the ongoing excavation of the original part of the castle. We had a coffee at the Howard Johnson's just down the cobblestone road from the schloss and later had a Guinness in a basement bar along the same road. We window-shopped, bought presents for our loved ones, and couldn't help staring at the bewildering array of beautiful women we kept running into. The women in this city have raised the fashion of knee high leather boots and mini skirts to a new high (no pun intended), and it was difficult to keep from snapping your head around whenever you passed one.

Around seven, we found ourselves back on the north side of the river, walking through one of the many parks in the city. Things were getting a little nippy and we were looking for a place to get out of the wind for a bit when we discovered an old train car that had been converted into a cafe. The Orient Express Cafe it was called, and we slipped inside to settle in for a meal and a beer.

What started out as a chance to get out of the cold, turned into a three-hour discussion about many things. We talked of architecture, ceiling plaster, biker gangs and kings. But mostly, with reverence we spoke of our wives, and our dependence upon them. Now, I know that soldiers are supposed to be tough, and not have such discussions or show their emotions. But in that three or so hours that we talked, more than once we were close to tears as we tried to express how we each felt about our wife. We discovered that we are both in awe of our wives, and agree that they are the stuff that makes us want to be better men. And, how utterly lost we'd be without them.

As the discussion wore on, we became more open with each other, as we trusted the other with a little bit more information about ourselves. When we finally rose to leave, I can honestly say that I felt closer to him than I did to anyone else on the tour.

Back out in the cold, it didn't take us long to grab a cab back to the hotel, where we quickly cruised the bar and then went up to our respective rooms for the night. We were both beat.

The next morning when we got up it was sunny and bright. Our trusty sergeants had laid on a last tour of the city if we wanted to go, so Ray and I jumped on the bus and headed into town. I'm glad we did. It gave us a chance to talk some more, do some last minute shopping, and see the sights again.

Once back in the hotel, we gathered everyone up, and headed back to Zadar. Looking around the bus it was clear there were some tired puppies. Three days of straight partying had taken it out of them, and people were planning to take advantage of the fact that we were going to be travelling through the night to get back.

Zadar was mayhem as expected. The sea container leaked and some of the kit was wet. Mine wasn't thank God. We all stood around as a couple of guys went through the pile bag by bag and called out names, then it was over to the barracks to change, and squeeze back into the tiny buses for the final leg of the journey back to Rastivic.

What I remember most about the trip back was that I was in the back seat sitting beside Ray, on a bench seat that should have held seven normal sized people, we could barely seat six big guys with flack vests on. For eight hours the six of us were squeezed in, shoulder-to-shoulder, tight enough that none of us could move comfortably. We made the best of it though. Guys were spread out everywhere there was space. Half a dozen or so managed to stretch out on the floor of the aisle, and one guy was small enough to squeeze into the overhead racks. And that's how we rode, all the way back. Each huddled in his flack vest like a turtle trying to get some sleep.

Saturday, 05 Nov., Rodaljice After an unbelievably long 15 hours on buses, Ray, Ingersol, and myself finally pulled into camp at Rodaljice. Budapest had been an incredibly good time. I figure I needed two or three more days to do everything I wanted to in the city. Ray and I spent the vast majority of our time together, and I've gained a new appreciation for bike gangs (he's heavy into being a biker) and a new friend in the process.

Meanwhile back at camp. It would appear that after a massive build-up, nothing happened. The boys came back to camp after the security detail genuinely disappointed. It's not that we're warmongers you understand, it's just that this is our job after all, and it would have been nice if someone (meaning the Serbs) had bothered to show up and give us a bit of a run for it.

2 Platoon, who have a camp in Pristeg, would appear to be the only ones who saw anything of interest. I am told that a section of Serbs pulled into the area near them carrying AK 47s and M80s, and took up positions in close proximity to them. Then they just sat there until it was all over, not a shot fired, not a word said.

A big part of the Yugoslav persona is bluff. They may cock their weapons, shake their fists, and scream bloody murder, but if you stand up to them and don't flinch, they'll back down.

As with all things in life, there are extremes. While our boys only heard shots being fired, and 2 Platoon actually saw the "enemy," things were pretty quiet. Meanwhile, two other missions were scrapped altogether, because the situation was too hot. You never really know what's going to happen.

Our mission, while not action packed, was a good exercise in preparation for battle. Everything from the orders and task assignment, to the rehearsals and execution, went off without a hitch. It's a clear demonstration of the level of professionalism found within the ranks of this platoon.

Relying on people outside your organization is what makes a mission dangerous. The Croats, for example, had assured us that they were 95% sure the cemetery was clear before our graveyard security duty (makes you wonder which 5% they weren't sure about). Faced with those odds, our engineers were called to clear several lanes out to the sentry posts at each corner of the cemetery. Even after being assured that the place was clear, our engineers found several mines, parts of mines, and discarded ammo. Good thing we checked the place first.

With everyone in position, the buses full of mourners arrived. Warrant Fuller told me of a guy who found his family grave opened. The guy called the warrant over to talk to him. As he approached, the guy bent down and picked up a skull, and thrust it into the warrants face, saying "this is my mama, you help me put her back."

The poor warrant was dumbstruck. Without moving his feet he nearly bent over backwards trying to get away from the skull being held so irreverently towards his face (which is kind of a funny image when you consider how big Fuller is). In the end the guy lowered the skull into the grave by wrapping a piece of wire around it and maneuvering it into position. Neat people eh?

While I was on leave, CNN reported that the UN had voted to lift the arms embargo on Bosnia. All that remains is for the Security Council to ratify the decision. At the same time the Bosnian Serbs had just lost a major battle for a town in their northern region somewhere. The Bosnian leader, Radovan Karadic (the guy with all the hair) has said that he will declare all out war against the Moslems and Croats as soon as the embargo is lifted. With all the troop movements going on around us, what we've been told about a potential spring offensive, and now this arms thing, I wonder what we're going to do when this whole thing explodes. Perhaps it's another bluff.

Finally, a word to be said about our fearless officers. It has been noted by higher, that our platoon has been starting rumours about a potential move into the Zone to replace 2 Platoon due to "morale problems." Lt Alec Reid of 2 Platoon, is acknowledged amongst the troops as wanting to win the VC on this tour (posthumously we hope). The going bet is that within six weeks of arrival he will get himself or someone under him killed. He has two weeks left.

Lt McConnell is competing with him for attention. It's gotten to the point where the warrant and the CSM nearly got into a fight about what's been said, or supposed to have been said by these two. It's stupid, asinine, and childish. Everyone is happy where they are, it's just the officers and CSM who are bored to tears, because we're all in a groove, and doing our jobs well. Sometimes I wish these kids would grow up. It's got everyone in the platoon talking.

Sunday, 06 Nov., Rodaljice Up this morning at 5:00 to get ready for a 6:00 shift at the gate and radio room. Doing the shift from 6:00 to 12:00 is a good way to start the day. I have the guys get me up at 0500 so I can get cleaned up and gave a cup or two of tea and a light snack before I go on duty.

My preference is to start the shift in the bunker at the gate (we've taken to calling it the Archie Bunker). This gives me four hours of uninterrupted writing time to get caught up on my letters and diary.

To tell the truth, Catherine occupies my mind a lot while I'm in here. She's sent me a love letter sprinkled with her perfume, and I can tell you that more than one person has caught me wearing the envelope on the end of my nose. Each time I inhale her scent, it conjures up images of us together. I swear at times I can actually feel her pressed up against me as I hold her in my arms. It's enough to drive a guy insane . . . and I love it.

My beautiful wife, Cat

Fitness is a big thing with us here. We have a weight room (actually it's a weight tent) that is fairly well stocked with free weights, and while everyone is expected to workout regularly, only about half the guys are serious about it. Lately I've tried to get in there every day, but I expect this will vary according to our work schedule.

Saturday night the boys at Zero laid on a barbecue. If you're not on duty you can come in for as many steaks as you can eat, and as much beer as you can drink. Last night some of the boys went in for the first time, and came back after midnight pretty wrecked. By then I'd already gone to bed. You see, I brought back a 26er of Lambs Navy Dark Rum from my 96er in Budapest. So while the boys were shellin' out 2 DM per beer at the mess, I was drinking heavily spiked hot chocolate for nothing back here. After all, I'm trying to save money.

Before we left Canada, the Battalion commander made it quite clear that the limit on beer would be 2 beer per man, per day, per haps. Because we are a platoon located away from headquarters, we are entitled to our own bar (damn decent of them, we thought). The day we hit the ground, the warrant changed the rules. "Boys" he said as he gathered us together, "you know your limit, but if someone behind the bar cuts you off, don't argue. And if anyone gets into a fight because he's been drinking, that's it. The camp goes dry." It's been a month now, and while there have been some great parties, there also have been no problems. This, in spite of the fact that we will go through six cases of beer in two nights (highboy beer cans—500 ml). I, of course, never partake of the evil liquid! Does anyone remember where my bunk is? I'm sure it was in this direction. . . .

Monday, 07 Nov., Rodaljice Ray and I took a run into Benkovac this morning to pick up our interpreter, a girl named Marilla. Benkovac is a town of several thousand people, and home to the main headquarters for the Serbs in the Krajina. It also houses a Battalion of Serb regulars. We pulled up in front of her house, and it was a bit unnerving to see all these guys walking around with camouflage fatigues, and the odd AK-47 slung over their shoulders, giving you the eye as you escort one of "their" women. The only solution is to keep your weapon ready, and scowl right back at them. Admittedly there is nothing to it all, aside from the realization that if they ever wanted to, they could take you out in the blink of an eye and you'd never know what hit you.

After we got back, I went for the best workout I've had since I've been here. It was so good, in fact that I had to lie down for a couple of hours to recover. Many more workouts like that and I'd be out like a light for the rest of the tour.

After supper, several of us were sitting around discussing all the troop movements and the war going on in Bosnia. As I understand it, there are four main factions (there are in fact 14 different factions but this is a simplified version). There is Serbia (the former republic of Yugoslavia—this is mostly a Serb population), Croatia (the Croatian), Krajina (a small province captured from Croatia and held by Serbs—this is where we are, and where much of the "ethnic cleansing" took place), and Bosnia. Inside Bosnia, there are Bosnian Serbs, Moslems and Croats. Here's how it plays out:

—The Serbs are Greek Orthodox, the Croats are Roman Catholics, and the Moslems, well, the Moslems are Balkanites who converted to the Moslem faith during the Turkish rule. But this is not a religious war. It's ethnic.

—The Bosnian Serbs are fighting the Bosnian Croats and Bosnian Moslems.

—Serbia is supporting the Bosnian Serbs, and Croatia is supporting the Bosnian Croats.

—The troop movements we've been hearing about have been the Croatians moving to support the Bosnian Croats.

—Croatia gets its arms from Germany, who we speculate are repaying a debt from the Second World War.

—The Americans are acting as go-betweens.

—The Russians are supporting the Serbs behind the scenes.

Now that you have the picture, imagine what will happen when the arms embargo is lifted on Bosnia. Let the games begin.

In other news, Mac the cook asked me to go with him as escort to Zero to pick up supplies last night. While I was there I ran into one of the cooks I had roomed with in Petawawa. He told me that last night for more than an hour he watched "fireworks" (read artillery, mortars, and machine gun tracers) going off to the west of the camp. The hot rumour at the time was, that we were watching a live fire exercise going on around Zadar, where Can Log Bat is located. We'll have to wait for an update on that.

Two things came down in orders tonight, which were of particular interest. The first was about two engineers thinking with their peepees. Apparently they had driven one of the local female cooks to her home after work and went inside to have a coffee, leaving their weapons in the foyer of her building. When they came out one of the weapons was missing (though why steal one unguarded weapon, when you could have two?). Both are in protective custody at Zero awaiting investigation. Although our people may imbibe with the locals, we at least keep our weapons in the same room with us.

The other thing of interest happened in the Zone. 2 Platoon were witness to a firefight between the Serbs and Croats in the town of Prestig. It only lasted a few minutes, but it provided entertainment, and a bladder control exercise for the boys watching.

Tuesday, 08 Nov., Rodaljice The 0600 to 1200 shift again today. I managed to get a lot of writing done. Today I received two letters from Cat. It is a curious thing that when I read her letters I always look for the line or two in which she describes her love for me. Lord knows that my letters are filled with them, and I hope they bring her as much pleasure as her lines do me.

After lunch Doc (now there's a novel name for a medic), myself, the lieutenant, and Sgt Macari took a bit of time to do some IV training. The lieutenant was into it big time, hoping to feel "the cool rush of the IV solution coursing through his veins." In an effort to satisfy the need, I stuck him twice (missing both times) and Doc stuck him once (and missed) before George stepped in to offer his arm as a pincushion. Alas the lieutenant was denied his IV high, but Doc was successful on the first try with George (more distended veins). The lieutenant was green with envy, as George teased him by describing the sensation of the IV solution moving up his arm. It was quite amusing to watch actually. After that, the needles started to fly, as Doc and I talked the lieutenant and George through the procedure of inserting needles into the vein, each of us acting as guinea pigs for the other two. On his second try the lieutenant stuck the needle a bit too far into my arm and struck a nerve in my wrist. My wrist was sore the rest of the day. I think he now has a new appreciation for the skill involved in inserting a needle.

The other night Mac and I took a run into Zero again; the latest name I've heard for the place is "Fraggle Rock." On the way we passed some Kenyans. It's come down in orders that these guys are selling fuel on the black market—right out of the back of their UN trucks, and people are lined up for it. The Kenyan battalion goes through more fuel in a month than we do in six. Now you've gotta ask yourself who knows, and who's getting a cut. The records will clearly show the difference between their actual needs and what they're "using." The black market price for diesel runs at one million DM per tanker truck (about the size of a Canadian milk truck)—someone has to be getting a shitload of money out of this.

Observations:

—WO Fuller brought up an interesting point. "There's no doubt in my mind that we're being patrolled against by Camp Alpha. We're being used as training aids to train their boys for the front." Kind of make you look up at the hills a little differently. I wonder when they will start to use us as self-indicating moving targets?

—Word came down that the Army has sent a 707 with a surgical team for the two guys involved in the carrier accident a while back. The guy with the banged up scull survived the crash because the frontal portion of his skull separated from the rest of the skull. This allowed the brain to swell unencumbered. The surgical team is on hand in case they run into problems during the flight home.

—I've noticed that since I started sitting in the kitchen to write my diary, more people are showing up with diaries of their own. Do we detect a trend?

—Bravo Company had six Shot Reps today—it's become a standing joke.

8 Nov.
My Dearest Catherine

It's 11:00 am, and I've been on duty since 0600. The vast majority of my time has been spent writing in my diary, and dashing off a letter to your mother, Meaghan, and Derek. I've saved writing to you for the last because it gives me the most pleasure.

Undoubtedly you've heard and been told about the fighting that's going on in Bosnia. Fear not my sweet, for I am quite safe. The fighting is in another country, and may as well be on the other side of the world for all the effect it has on us. We sit around at night and watch CNN to get the latest updates, then try to marry that up with what's coming down in orders. But like mushrooms we rarely get a glimpse of the big picture.

You asked me once where I lived. The truth is, I live in what's called an ISO trailer. This is just a fancy name for a sea container with windows and a door. There are four of us in our trailer, so things are a little crammed. We have two sets of bunk beds, a double locker, 12 barrack boxes, a rifle rack, four duffel bags and four rucksacks packed into an area the size of . . . well . . . a sea container. With all the kit packed inside, we all sleep on the ground outside the door. Just kidding, we really sleep on top of the trailer.

The routine around here is pretty straightforward. One week at Bruska, one week camp security in Rodaljice, and one week of patrolling. This is our week for patrolling, but because we aren't going to start patrolling until Thursday, we've taken over the 0600–1200 at the gate at Rodaljice. This is the second time this week I've pulled duty and frankly I don't mind. It forces me to get up early, and it gives me lots of time to write to people. In all honesty, I've written more letters in the past thirty days than I've written in the past thirty years. I think I've found a new hobby.

The compound we occupy is about half an acre. In one corner there is a two-storey schoolhouse. Our carriers and trailers are at the other end, with the workout tent in between. My description is woefully inadequate so to solve the problem I've taken pictures. We pause now for a tasking.

Back again. I just went with Doc to Bruska as his escort (we have to travel in pairs). We saw a dozen or so old people, handed out some medication, struggled with the language, drank a little wine, then came back.

  I've just received letters #6 and 7, letter #5 is conspicuous by its absence. Speaking of absence, is it not a curious thing that we miss each other now more than when we first got together? Why is it that each generation must rediscover the old saying "absence makes the heart grow fonder?" Alas, I must, and freely do, acknowledge the fact that you are the center of my life. At times I quite wonder what I would do without you. It pains me at times to think that you are all alone in that house without me to protect and serve you. Quite honestly I feel at times I've been incredibly selfish and abandoned you. My only consolation is that I'll now be able to offer you the honeymoon you should have had five years ago when I married you. It is with undisguised delight that I look forward to our trip to England, if for no other reason than to once again be near you. To again inhale the soft scent of your hair; to feel the warmth of your back pressing into my chest; to run my hand over the alluring curve of your hips. How's that for poetic prose? Hard to believe that under all this camouflage there beats the heart of a true romantic.

  I love you my sweet, unabashedly and shamelessly. You are my life, never forget that.

  Alas I find myself running short of space. In a day or two I will sit down and write to you again. But until then my love, fare thee well, and look after yourself.

Your ever loving husband,
Kurt

Wednesday, 9 Nov., Sveti Roc/Rodaljice This morning I took a trip with Mac and Ray over the mountains to get rations for the camp. It was, without doubt, one of the most beautiful trips I've had to date. We passed three places of particular interest.

  The landscape is incredibly harsh. When you get up on the side of one of the mountains and look down, all you see for miles and miles is rock. Rock scattered with scrub brush, and occasionally there will be a tiny patch of green where someone has laboured incredibly hard to make a farm work.

  Let me begin by saying that the place we went to is called Sveti Roc, affectionately know as Sweaty Rock to those who know and love the place. It was my understanding that this was one of the first places Canadians were stationed when hostilities broke out, and is considered part of the Medac Pocket where the PPCLI were engaged in three days of firefights. It's obvious this was an area of heavy fighting. Bomb craters and signs of fighting are everywhere. For the last ten miles into the base, every single house as far as you could see from the road, had been destroyed. The area must have been Croatian or Moslem because there ain't much left of it.

  The next thing of interest was a simple wall. I say simple because from a distance that's exactly what it looks like. Then it dawns on you that the wall is holding back a lake; then you see that the lake is above ground and if the wall ever broke it would flood the whole valley and quite a number of farms and villages with it. The wall, more of a dyke really, appears to have been there for an awful long time. Long enough anyway for farms to be built on the land below the dam. The darn thing is over a kilometre long and you gotta know that a shit load of work went into it. If it was built by hand, the whole thing is made of rock. One wonders where they got the idea to build a dyke and drain half a lake to create the farmland. I thought that was a Dutch idea.

The First Half of the Tour

Obrovac and the remains of a monastery

The last place we saw was a town in a valley. Nothing special really until you look at the valley. The walls were almost vertical, most of the valley floor was taken up by a river, and right in the middle was a hill with what was left of a monastery sitting on it. The town's name is Obervac, and it was Dukes Company's original tasking to be there, but the power plant they had picked for our HQ was pretty badly shot up and heavily contaminated with PCBs from broken transformers.

One other thing was rather interesting about the trip. That lake I mentioned seems to have been put to good use. On the drive up the ocean side of the mountains, you pass under a whopping great big pipe. From the other side of the valley it looks like some giant drilled a hole in the side of the mountain near the top, and ran a big cable all the way down the side into the valley. You don't get a sense of the scale until you stand under the thing. I swear you could drive an MLVW through the thing and not touch the sides. It has to be thirty feet across. Whoever did the engineering on this must have spent many a night without sleep. It's impressive as hell.

There was one more interesting incident I wanted to mention. The road in and out of the supply camp at Sveti Roc has been badly damaged by traffic, mortar shells during the fighting, and general abuse. Lately it's been raining here a lot, and that too has had an effect on the road conditions.

As we were leaving the camp we came around a corner leading to a straight section of the road. Mac, who was driving at the time, hit the brakes and our truck came to an abrupt stop. In the distance we could see four Serbs in uniform carrying weapons and daypacks making their way down the road away from us. We all leaned forward in our seats as we paused to considered the risks.

Since basic training we'd been told that the Serbs had a nasty habit of placing land mines in puddles so you couldn't see them. No one ever thinks a puddle is dangerous until you hit one of those things. Now stretched out before us was roughly one hundred yards of road filled more with puddles than pavement, some of which took up the whole width of the road. The presence of the Serbs had just thrown a new light on the situation.

The engine of the ML rumbled on in idle as the three of us watched the Serbs intensely. Time passed. The Serbs were walking away from us but were looking back over their shoulders in our direction. Was it my imagination or had they picked up their pace when we came around the corner?

After a bit, I broke the silence by offering to wade through the puddles ahead of the truck to see if I could find anything. Mac figured he could drive around all but the largest of the puddles and cover most of the distance. After some discussion Ray and I decided it would be safer to get out and walk up the road ahead of the vehicle just in case.

It took Mac nearly ten minutes to cover the short distance to the end of the road where Ray and I waited by the largest of the puddles. In places he drove right off the road and up onto the embankment to get around the holes in the road, and in other places he straddled the gaps with the tires. His arms were getting a workout as he slowly worked the big vehicle back and forth across the road.

Finally, Mac brought the big vehicle to a halt at the edge of the last and largest of the puddles and waited. Ray and I moved to the front of the vehicle and spreading ourselves out the same distance as the tires on the ML. We slowly worked our way through the water, carefully sweeping our feet back and forth trying to feel for anything that might resemble the 20kg mines that were commonly used against vehicles. It took a while, but when we made it to the other side we hadn't found anything, so we backed off a safe distance and watched Mac take his turn. Creeping forward slowly, he pushed the ML through the water working his way along at only a few metres per minute, trying to follow the path Ray and I had taken before him. It seemed to take forever but the big vehicle slowly emerged from the water unscathed. Once clear we loaded up and made our way down the road for home.

Looking back one might be tempted to ask if we were scared? No, I don't think so. We took all the necessary precautions and everything worked out in the end. Though I will admit to holding my breath as Mac worked his way though that last big puddle, but otherwise it was pretty much business as usual. We just had to take some extra precautions. It only occurs to me now that I did a real live impression of a Newfie mine detector.

That's pretty much the news for today. The only other thing I wanted to pass on were some stories the lieutenant related to us over beer tonight.

The first was a story about a young Lt in Bravo Company. He had been on the ground here only a couple of days when he paid a visit to the local Serb Battalion Commander (seems everyone around here is a Battalion Commander) one Captain Kadic. Upon arrival at his house, the lieutenant was invited into the front room where they sat to have coffee. Before the pleasantries were even complete, Capt. Kadic cut right to the chase. "Will that flack vest stop a 9mm bullet?" he asked pointedly.

"Yes, I believe it will" said the lieutenant somewhat guardedly, wondering what this guy was up to.

"Ah" said Kadic leaning back in his chair, "I will bet you that I have a weapon

The First Half of the Tour 107

which will go through that vest and take your life," he said. Then he turned to his assistant and nodded. The assistant disappeared from the room for a few moments, returning with a polished lacquered box. The box was dutifully laid before the Captain who opened it and removed the handgun. In one smooth motion he inserted the magazine, cocked it, rose to his feet and pointed the weapon across the table directly at the chest of the young Lt. All of this took but a second to execute. There was little time to react, and being new to the zone, the lieutenant fell back on his tried and true response. He just sat there (and no doubt squeezed his little butt cheeks together just as tightly as he could).

Tense moments passed. Neither protagonist wavered. Finally after what seemed like forever, the captain withdrew the weapon, and sliding the action to the rear, dropped the round onto the table.

"For a moment I held your life on the tip of my finger. I now give you your life," at which point he handed the round across the table to the lieutenant.

The coffee was served and the meeting passed as if nothing had happened. At the end, Captain Kadic read the young Lt's coffee grounds as if they were tealeaves. "Your girlfriend is cheating on you," he pronounced. "You must be strong and tell her you love her. She will come around."

And then, as abruptly as it had started, it was over. You gotta admit, it's one hell of a way to start the tour.

The other story I wanted to relate was about our own Platoon Commander, Lt McConnell.

Before I begin, you should know that Rodaljice has only a single road into and out of it. The road continues through the village and on through the hills, passing through Camp Alpha, and then down into Donja Bruska. The Serbs have closed the front gate to their camp as well as the back gate, thus forcing us to travel the long way around to get to Donja Bruska.

Two days after his arrival, Mr. McConnell was being given the grand tour by a sergeant from the PPCLI. Part of the tour included a run down the village road to the back gate of the Serb camp. It was a hot day, and the doors were off the Iltis. The sergeant was driving, and the lieutenant was riding in the passenger's seat. As they approached the back gate, a guard appeared out of the shack beside the gate. The Iltis rolled to a stop in front of the gate, and the guard approached on the lieutenant's side. "You go back now" he said somewhat agitatedly.

"Ya, ya," said the lieutenant as he looked around at the local terrain. He then looked at the sergeant inquiring with a glance what they were to do next. The guard solved the problem. Moving his weapon from the port position, he cocked it and placed the end of the barrel a few inches from the Mr. McConnell's nose. He had everybody's complete attention.

"You leave ... NOW!" he said forcibly.

Before the lieutenant could open his mouth the Iltis was moving backwards down the road. The lieutenant tells me that his first thoughts were "what the hell's this guy's problem?" It was only later that it dawned on him that he had a loaded AK-47 pointed at his face.

Both of these stories are true, and documented in the patrol reports (for those of you who think I'm making this up). I will only tell you that I have taken literary license in their description, not the actual facts of the story.

Bravo Company had three Shot Reps today (the joke continues)."

Thursday, 10 Nov., Patrolling Patrol day today, so things got off to a slower start. Breakfast first, then vehicle prep, orders, and final checks. All that's left to do then is fill your coffee cup and bugger off at the high port.

Today's patrol took us into the back 40 of our patrol area. We started out going past Karin Slana, home of Dukes Company HQ, otherwise known as Call Sign One, then looping back past Obervac then tootling around on the back roads up in the mountains.

If I haven't mentioned it before, let me say now, that Rodaljice has one of the worst of the desecrated cemeteries in the area. It's not so bad now because one of the locals is a stonemason and has taken the time to fix some of the damage, and return most of the bones to their resting-places.

About half an hour into our patrol, we passed the other of the really badly desecrated cemeteries. Nobody had bothered to fix this place up, so we got to see first hand exactly what's been done to the place.

I think it is difficult for most Canadians, most people for that matter, to understand the level of hatred required to go into another man's cemetery and dig up his dead. Standing in the middle of the cemetery surrounded by so much destruction, I was absolutely lost for words. Emotionally I'm not sure what I felt. The barbarism to which I had become witness was so foreign that I was at a loss for any response other than being dumbfounded. Every single crypt we saw (there had to be at least 75 or more) had been opened. You had to watch where you walked because bones had been scattered everywhere. There wasn't a headstone in the place left standing or intact. All had been destroyed.

In the middle of the graveyard was what was left of a small chapel. It had been so utterly destroyed that all that was left standing were the foundation stones and the floor. I don't ever want to even begin to understand this kind of hatred. None of us do.

Being soldiers, and the morbid bastards that we are, you can guess what happened next. Out came the cameras. Shortly thereafter the jokes about the half-life of polyester started, as there were several skeletons dressed up in suits that were in surprisingly good condition. What was left of one of the bodies was wearing white socks, and as we all stood there taking it in Robert lamented that he wished he could get his socks that white. A little graveside humour always helps to relieve the tension.

I had my picture taken while I knelt at the side of a repository for a large pile of bones that was located at the back of what was once the chapel. I'm told it is common practice to move the bones of the dead to an area inside the chapel so they rest in holy ground and perhaps this is what this was. I cannot tell you what I felt at the time, but I can tell you that I couldn't bring myself to smile. As you might imagine, things were pretty quiet for the next little while, as we each contemplated what we'd just seen.

I've mentioned before how I felt this was a hard land, populated by hard people. This patrol only reinforced that. Life is a tenuous thing at best, and it is interesting to observe how these people have made the best of a hard land.

The land is covered in rock, there's no getting away from that. But in the valleys there would appear to be less rock and more soil. I would surmise, that over the eons the soil has washed down off the hills, and collected in these valleys, exposing the voluminous amount of white-gray lava rock everywhere. A valley, I might point out, is anything from a depression in the ground to something larger that we might compare to North American standards.

The First Half of the Tour 109

The people have turned this phenomenon to their advantage, making the most of every little opportunity. There was one example that well illustrates this point. The patrol took us several hundred feet up into the mountains to cross over a saddle between two ridges. On the one side of the saddle, it was a gradual slope up to the crest. For the most part we passed through scrub brush and by most standards unusable land. But every now and then, even near the top of the saddle, there were walls, and small fields someone had put a great deal of effort into. As we crested the saddle, the ground fell away abruptly, and there, in a small horseshoe shaped valley was a cluster of houses. This place was totally isolated, save for the one road that wound it's way up from the lowland several kilometres away. There were rock walls of course, but also sheep and goats grazing, corn in the field, garden vegetables of all sorts, and about a dozen homes. In a total sea of gray rock and scrub brush, here was a patch of green.

This whole country is like that. It speaks highly of our ability as humans to survive; it's a shame we have to wreck it all the time by killing each other off.

The patrol lasted a total of six and a half hours, and I surprised myself by nodding off for a couple of kilometres about halfway through. I haven't told anyone, lest they start calling me "Grandpa" in earnest, and insisting I take my afternoon naps. The truth is all the noise, vibration, diesel fumes, and cold wind take a lot out of you, and a lot of getting used to, and right now I'm not fully up to it. Mind you, this being only our second patrol everyone was hurting when we got back.

Target practice on the .50 calibre on the range

The last part of the patrol involved a quick stop at one of the local ranges where the company was set up for heavy weapons practice. Karl Gustav and I just pulled up, grabbed our 60-mm mortar and the 84-mm anti-tank weapon and said "Hi, here we are, what do we shoot at?"

"Hello," they said, "step up to the line, here's your left of arc, here's your right of arc, the tank in the distance is 750 m, here's your ammo, carry on." This is how a range should be run.

Two of our boys in 1 Section, Peters and Newson, get the boner-of-the-day award. They managed to jam an 84-mm round into the tube the wrong way, and when I say jammed, I mean JAMMED. They managed to force the round in far enough that they could close the venturi. It's difficult to explain, but suffice to say, that it was most embarrassing when the round would neither go off, nor come out, so tightly was it wedged in place.

In orders tonight we were told of a change in the rotation plans. Where before we had one section in Bruska, one section patrolling, and one section as camp security in Rodaljice, we now will be sending our patrolling section to Knin to help 1 Platoon with the security duties there.

The task involves providing security for Headquarters Sector South. It's a duty that is rotated between each of the battalions in the sector. We apparently are taking over from the Jordanians. The warrant is going there tomorrow to do a recce for us, and find out what we're required to do.

My day ended with a call to Catherine. She's been feeling really tired lately and it's been of some concern to me. When I called tonight she told me she was experiencing some new numbness in her hands and that the doctor thinks it may be a new episode. He wants to see her again next Wednesday to be sure, but he remains encouraged with the improvement in her balance. She may have to go into the hospital for another course of steroid treatment regardless. In light of how she reacted to the last course, I can't help but think I made the wrong decision by coming over here. By rights, I should be there to look after her even though she seems to be holding her own. I only pray that our friends remain true, and come to her support if she really needs it.

No Shot Reps reported from Bravo Company today. Must be a relief to the boys over there.

Friday, 11 Nov., Remembrance Day Today was Remembrance Day, and, in keeping with tradition the world over, we held a parade. When I got up this morning though, it was pissing with rain and hail and when the thunderclouds clapped overhead, my trailer shook.

We had been given word yesterday that several of us would be attending the official parade at Zero, so with the rain pissing down, we all jumped into the back of the ML for the ride in, and we arrived just as the rain was letting up. We lucked in, and our early arrival meant that we weren't immediately needed, so the hunt for a decent cup of java began in earnest.

The parade itself was nothing special, but given our location and the destruction around us, it took on a special significance for me. About a hundred and fifty of us formed up in front of the three flags at the front gate, which acted as a cenotaph. The bad weather held off long enough for the padre to say his piece, then the CO got up and read the 23rd psalm—The Lord is my Shepherd, I shall not want. . . . We got the impression he was moved as he read the words. Perhaps it was the fact that we were in a war zone, or perhaps they had taken on special significance for him. Either way his voice wavered slightly as he read through the passage. When he'd finished, Mac fired up the pipes and stirred the heartstrings as the parade was handed back to the RSM. As he proceeded from his position at the right of the line to the cenotaph, an errant cameraman, who'd been filming the proceedings, chanced to stray in front of the oncoming RSM. "GET out of my way!" bellowed the RSM. The poor cameraman, not realizing he was in danger of cutting in front of the oncoming RSM, nearly jumped out of his combat boots. Sniggers rippled though the ranks.

The parade ended mercifully just as the rain started again, and it was a mad dash to the Junior Ranks Mess for our mandatory free issue of one beer.

We returned to Rodaljice for a late lunch and an afternoon's detail of sandbagging. The HASMAT (hazardous material) people had paid a visit to our location and gave very clear instructions about protecting the environment around two points in the compound. The first thing involves a 1500-gallon diesel tank that supplies fuel for our generator. The HASMAT people asked us to lay plastic under it to contain any possible spills, but they won't send us a crane so we can lift it up high enough to put the plastic down underneath it. We settled for building a short wall around both the generator and the tank, and lining it with plastic.

While work was proceeding on the modifications, it was brought up that HASMAT was aware that somebody in the past had dumped oil in the well that's in the compound. It's figured that it would take more than a million dollars to clean up the mess, but nobody can tell for sure how far the oil has spread in the local groundwater system.

The next area to tackle is where we fill up. There's a 500-gallon bowser of diesel fuel, and numerous 45-gallon barrels. They want us to move a layer of gravel, and lay down a layer of plastic, to prevent any drips from soaking into the soil, then replace the gravel. It's a task I'm not looking forward to. Of course, it seems a little odd that in the middle of a war zone, surrounded by burned out tanks, millions of mines, and destroyed homes that the Canadians are trying their best to protect the environment. Is it just me, or does anyone else see how bizarre this whole situation is?

And now for the news in brief:

—We've been told to reduce our number of foot patrols in Rodaljice, and Donja Bruska, from six per day to four. The joke is, that Rodaljice only gets four patrols per day anyway, one after every shift, and Bruska only gets three patrols. One all morning, one all afternoon, and one most of the evening. We all nodded dutifully when told of this development by the lieutenant in orders tonight. We're all convinced that the lieutenant has no idea how many patrols are really being done.

—Apparently a Canadian soldier threatened either the Serbs or Croats with air strikes. Air strikes for God's sake!! What the fuck was this idiot thinking? Anyway, surprise, surprise, we've been told not to threaten anyone anymore.

—The Americans have lifted the arms embargo on Bosnia. The British (we've been told) have announced they're pulling out of their sector. And thus the wheel of international politics spins round and round. There should be no immediate impact on the war because the Bosnians have been receiving arms by other means (according to CNN).

—If you will recall, some time ago the Serbs put an OP in the Zone and manned it. We were supposed to bulldoze it, but that fell through. It appears that high-level negotiations have been ongoing, and have just come to a conclusion of sorts. The Serb, Croat and Canadian generals sat down and hammered out an agreement whereby the Serbs could keep one or two people in the OP but the remainder would have to leave. The Serbs didn't want to lose face as they left, so they asked for civilian clothing to hide the fact that they were leaving. (We heard the request for clothing while we were on patrol, and wondered what the hell was going on). When the clothing arrived, it was rejected because of "poor quality." There's some heavy game-playing going on here.

—Today around suppertime I started to develop abdominal cramps. Trust me when I tell you that explosive diarrhea does not spell relief. The medic says I may be in for as much as two weeks of it. He thinks I managed to get some of the local water into me, which is what is causing the trots. He's given me Loperamide Hydrochloride, which is the same as Imodium to slow things down, but we'll have to see.

Saturday, 12 Nov., Bruska Today was our day to rotate to Donja Burska. It was also the first rotation of one of our sections to Knin. 1 Section had the honour of breaking ground in Knin for the platoon, and according to the warrant, the place we're staying in is a shit pit. He told us they had to bring in an ablution ISO to give us somewhere sanitary to clean up. Our turn comes on the 28th I think, and should be interesting.

Shortly after arriving in Bruska, John and I went for a quick patrol. Everyone seemed to be where they belonged, and nothing seemed to have changed so we headed back to camp, where I immediately went to bed. Just before lunch I went for a liquid shit, only to repeat it several hours later. I find if I lie down the cramps aren't so bad.

Each Saturday night is happy hour at Zero. All senior NCO's take a run in for a beer or two to get caught up on the latest news. George had left about 6:00, and wasn't expected back till past midnight. About 7:00 George pulled back into camp and all hell broke loose. The Croats had threatened to attack the Serbs, so the battalion responded by going to alert state orange.

State Orange means a lot of things. It means 50% stand-to; half-hour radio checks; permanent guard at the gate (in our case it meant someone in the carrier outside the tent manning the 50); .50 cals mounted on all vehicles; go everywhere with helmet, flack vest, and rifle—even to dinner or the can. There's more to it of course, but that's the gist of it.

Right after he got back, George took Kini and went to pull in the patrol that we sent out after supper. Now, one of the things about code orange is that all of your drivers are in camp and ready to go. You'll never guess where ours were. Yup, both Ted and Jim were on patrol. George had intended to be about half an hour. His "plan" was to find the patrol, have a glass of wine, let it drop that he had orders to give (so as not to alarm the locals), then leave, dragging the patrol with him. Two hours later the four of them staggered back into camp.

It's now one o'clock in the morning and I'm looking across the table at three of them (David went to bed). They're all asleep, and I would still be on duty if I didn't have to shit so badly. As it turned out Robert Nowlan was still awake and covered for me as I emptied my bowels yet again. We each have to pull a one-hour shift in the carrier, for as long as this thing lasts. I started my shift at 10:30 and didn't get off until 12:15, which is why I'm somewhat pissed at the boys for being asleep. The little shits were actually going to leave me out there till 01:00, before relieving me. Looking at their sorry state, I doubt they would have been able to wake up even if they wanted to, which means I'd still be out there freezin' my ass off.

I'm going on patrol now with Robert. We're going for a quick walk around the village before going to bed. It's been howling out there, and there's nothing I'm looking forward to more than warming up in my sleeping bag.

Sunday, 13 Nov., Bruska Not much to report today really. I was on guard from 0700 to 0800, and then again from 1400 to 1500. The rest of the day I slept.

When I got up this morning, I had terrible stomach cramps, so after I finished my duty, I decided to try and have a big breakfast. This seemed to help a bit more, and by supper I felt pretty normal, but was still plagued by occasional rumblings. I realize this doesn't constitute a good UN type discussion topic, but hey, it's on my mind.

We found out specifically why we went to state Orange. It would appear the Serbs of the Krajina were shelling the Bihac pocket from their side of the border (this whole country is so small you could almost fire an artillery shell across two countries before it came down). This is strictly illegal by the way, as the Krajina is a UN protected zone, and this type of activity is strictly verboten. The Croats said that if this continued, they would send troops through the Krajina into Bosnia, to support the Bosnian Croats there; no doubt taking pot shots at any Serb they saw along the way. We went on stand-by in case that happened. We've been told to expect 36 to 48 hours more of the same kind of guard duty.

Our battalion commander has put his foot down and told us to stop any heavy equipment movement in our area. We'll see what two little carriers can do against a bunch of tanks. They'll probably tell us to fuck off and roll right over us as we wave our UN flag. When in Bruska we have been told to stay in camp, and to only report on any movements in our area. There's not much a section can do against a company.

Speaking of companies, there's no doubt that the Serbs in Camp Alpha know Rodaljice has enough fuel to keep their company on the go for two weeks or more. We were told, by the warrant, that if they show up at the gate wanting to take it, we're to stand back and let them. Like the warrant says, no point in losing a life over a little gas. If they ask for our weapons and ammo, that's another issue.

In other news, George got his peepee slapped for reporting the anti-aircraft guns we saw on our patrol Thursday. Even though he said that he saw them in KENBAT's area, and mentioned that fact several times in his patrol report. I guess the higher ups thought he was lost because he specified a position outside our normal patrol area. The reason for which, was for us to reach the "back forty" I told you about, we had to cut through part of the Kenyans' patrol area, which is where we saw the guns.

Turns out the Kenyans had no idea the guns were there, which caused them great embarrassment at sector HQ. Fuck'em. If they did their jobs, instead of hiding in their over-heated trailers, this kind of thing wouldn't be a problem. The guns are now on the master trace as "new emplacements."

One of the local Serbs had a birthday today, and some of the boys in the section were dropping in for drinks while on patrol. I haven't traveled too far away from the bathroom.

There is some speculation that CANBAT One may be tasked with security in the Bihac pocket. It would mean thinning out the battalion to achieve the aim but smart money says we won't be affected. More to follow on this later.

Finally, Molson, the Bravo Company mascot-dog stepped on a mine and disappeared. Woof, woof. Poof. A moment of silence was observed, followed by comments about the red mist in the air. Morbid bastards aren't we?

Monday, 14 Nov., Bruska Today was distinguished by the change from state Orange to state Green. That meant that we could finally get back to something resembling a regular routine. This also means three or four patrols per day, lots of sleep, doing odd jobs, lots of sleep, nightly radio watch, ...and lots of sleep. Did I mention lots of sleep? Good, I wanted to be sure I got it down that we got lots of sleep!

To tell the truth, it was one hell of a boring day. The only real excitement came when Warrant Fuller, while on his way to Karin Slana, passed what could best be described as a "backyard special." It started out as a soviet M53/59 self propelled anti-aircraft gun, but had so much shit welded to it, and hanging off it, that it had to be called something else. Warrant Fuller called it in and I'm told that the platoon commander just about lost it. He sent Peters on a mad sprint to the corner by the main road to get a visual on the thing, while he climbed on top of the bunker at the gate to try and see it. By rights we're supposed to stop these things when we see them, but it was going so fast I doubt anybody could have stopped it. In the end, the sighting was called in and life returned to normal.

Ever since we went on this state Orange thing, wheeled vehicles have not been allowed to travel. This is strictly a company thing. Our fearless company commander appears to have flinched big time and ordered all movement to be in carriers only, and never alone but in pairs. The result, aside from a massive inconvenience for all, was that we didn't get our food re-supply or pay. Everything in fact stopped. It has been said that "lessons were learned." Thank God for that. I'd hate to think what they'd do if we went to state Red.

In other news, my cramping has subsided and my appetite is coming back to normal. My bowels, however, have yet to move.

You'll recall that a few weeks back I was asked to dispatch our dog because she was suspected of eating local chickens. You'll also recall that I never even made it out the door of the tent with her before the protesting started. Well, tonight, George took her out and did the deed. It appears she slipped her lead and one of the locals complained yet again about losing a chicken, leaving us with no option. No protests were heard this time as George tied the noose around the dog's neck and left the tent with David. Such is life in the UN. Save the children and shoot the dogs.

The night ended with a patrol and a stop for drinks with one of the locals. It's interesting to hear what they think of the overall situation. They believe (the Serbs that is) that there will be war soon. It will be interesting to see if they're right.

14 Nov.
My dearest Catherine,

Forgive me my love for I have been delinquent in my writing duties. These past five days have not been stressful in the least, other than to say that I have been overly concerned with the working state of my bowels. It would appear that I have contracted a mild form of dysentery, which has forced me to remain relatively inactive in order to relieve the stomach cramping. While I share in your laughter at the situation (who else would travel 8000 km for the experience of running to the potty at irregular and inconvenient moments?) I must assure you that it is not exactly pleasant wondering whether you are going to survive the shift without an accident. Rest assured that the Doc and I have conferred and all that can be done is being done, which, I might add, is precious little.

I trust that this letter finds you in better health, and that our newly acquired canine friend has not caused too much irretrievable damage. Being trained to go after small animals does not bode well for a house full of cats.

Last we spoke (Thursday, I believe) you had just come from a visit to the doctor. It pains me to think that I will be unable to nurse you back to health should it be required. It has become one of my more pleasant duties as husband and guardian of our humble kingdom, and while I do not look forward to its occurrence (for it means discomfort to you) it is a duty from which I do not shrink.

My platoon commander, Lt McConnell, has given me carte blanche to call you whenever I feel the need. It is truly a generous offer as we have been limited in our time on the phones as you well know. I am reluctant to make use of this offer for a couple of reasons. The first is while I love you very much, talking to you every day would take away from the pleasure I derive from writing to you. It is quite selfish I realize, but by spacing out our communiqués the anticipation of contact with you is heightened. It also preserves the privilege for times when it may truly be required. The other reason involves the other troops here. I would feel badly if I took phone time away from someone else if for no other reason than to hear your loving voice. I trust you understand.

As I told you on the phone, I am in Donja Bruska. Almost from the moment we arrived we have been in a heightened state of alert. Code orange it's called. It's most inconvenient, as we have broken into three groups and are rotating on eight-hour shifts, which of course affects our eating and sleeping habits. The reason no doubt, you are already aware of. Bosnia is in the midst of a war in what's called the Bihac pocket. It appears the Krajina Serbs have been shelling the Bosnian government troops from their side of the border. This is a no no as the Krajina is considered a UN protectorate. The Croats have said they will launch a counterstrike in support of the Bosnian Croats (confused yet?). In order for the Croats to get there from here, the Croatians have to go through our (the battalion's) positions. They also said they wouldn't mind taking pot shots at anyone in their way (that would be us). Be assured in the knowledge that I am quite safe. While we have orders to stop any heavy equipment moving in our area, our platoon tasking is only to observe, and continue to protect our two villages.

On the 28th of November my section is rotating to Knin for a security detail. One section is already there, with us in Donja Bruska and the section in Rodaljice. Every eight days we rotate, and if you follow it through you find that I will be spending Christmas in Donja Bruska.

I would tell you more, but I'm limiting the details so that it doesn't worry you needlessly (not that there's much to worry about anyway). It is one of the reasons I am keeping a diary. Sadly, I am running out of space here, and must bring this to a close. I love you my sweet, never forget that. It won't be long now until we will be together again.

Your loving husband,
Kurt

Tuesday, 15 Nov., Bruska This day marks the beginning of the UN leave blocks, and first up on the rotation is Newman. For this I am somewhat pleased. Ted and I are diametrically opposed. He is a simple soul and his entire life revolves around the military. He's a year younger than I am but you'd think he was in his forties by the way he acts and looks.

Don't get me wrong, Ted tells a good story, and he is a fine soldier, but he tends to be a blockhead sometimes, as no doubt we all are from time to time. It's just that he tends to be one more than most, and sometimes he doesn't pull his weight, which everyone is aware of. His big claim is that he has been in the military for thirteen years and intends to hide in the ranks for the remaining seven until his pension can provide for him. After 20 years in, he's outta here.

He refuses to take any leadership training, and doesn't mind kicking around as a Cpl. His worst habit however, comes when he's made up his mind on something. If he's decided he doesn't want to do something, even George has trouble convincing him. His argument is that he's been around long enough that he doesn't need to do any of the shit jobs any more, which extends to carrier maintenance, which as a driver, is more than a little odd. Those jobs are for the young guys with no experience. As you can imagine, it puts quite a strain on the section.

George and I have talked about it from time to time in private, and I know his assessment will reflect his attitude problem. Hell, he's already been pulled aside by the warrant on a couple of occasions and warned about it. The thing is, once you've been in the battalion for a while, everyone knows who you are and how you act, and they are less inclined to call you out on it, preferring instead to pass it off as Ted being Ted.

His going on leave means we don't have to put up with him or him with us. Life in the section should be easier for a while anyway. You can tell today was a boring day because I'm starting to talk about the guys in the section—it's never a good thing when this happens.

In other news, Robert and Jay went to Budapest today on their 96-hour leave. That brings the section down to seven people. Not many people to spread the work amongst.

This makes day six without mail. Everyone is starting to make comments about it. This is as far as I go for today because there's not much else to say.

Wednesday, 16 Nov., Bruska I have two funny stories to tell today; the first involves one of the locals whose name sounds an awful lot like "Bozo;" so that's what we'll call him. About 0800, Bozo's wife and another guy came to our gate and asked for our help. The old lady was crying and tugging at David's arm, so he grabbed his kit and the radio, and followed her back in to the village to her place. Being the advanced first-aid for the section, I was hauled out of bed to go and see what was up. Unfortunately David had already left, and in my rush to get out the door I forgot my glasses, so I wound up stumbling around in the general direction they went, before I finally found them.

After all the excitement died down, Bozo was diagnosed with a severe nosebleed complicated by thin blood, due to excessive drinking. It took two hours to get the medic there, a translator, and the guy diagnosed. I felt bad for Doc. When I had arrived, Bozo's breath was so bad I had to hold mine whenever I went near him. Doc spent 20 minutes kneeling in front of the guy, and you could see his face cringe every time Bozo said something to him. It's a wonder he didn't melt away. David and I just exchanged knowing glances and shared a good chuckle.

The other story deals with Ted and Sgt MacKinnon from 3 Section. Ted went in to Rodaljice a day early for his UN leave. Being fully packed, and with nothing to do last night, he started drinking in the schoolhouse. Sgt MacKinnon, who was on duty at the time, decided to join him. When the mess closed down at 2400, they both decided to go back to Sgt MacKinnon's ISO trailer and continue the party. Round about 0500 in the morning they decided to start playing basketball in the courtyard. When the warrant got up at 0600, he took one look at the two of them stumbling around the compound outside his trailer, then told them both, rather forcefully, to go to bed. He was not impressed. Leave it to Ted to get himself in shit just before he goes on leave.

When Doc came out this morning, Peters came with him as escort. While he and I were waiting outside, he told me of Sgt MacKinnon's drinking problem. It would appear he spends as much time in the village as he does in the camp when he comes to Bruska. This results in his being drunk most of the time. It also appears that he is not a very nice drunk. He berates his troops mercilessly, and threatens them constantly. This is not good. Judging by Peters's attitude and mannerisms, I'd say the whole section is under an awful lot of stress.

On a lighter note Bruce and David went for a little foray into Camp Alpha today. They took a circular route into the camp by walking through the abandoned part of this village at the bottom of the hill, and ended up at the top of the opposite hill overlooking the buildings inside their camp. From what they were saying, there's no way there could be 1000 people in there. If that's the case, we've been fed an awful big line of bunk since we arrived. I think at some point in the future I'm going to have a look for myself.

According to CNN, the Bosnians are trying to get the Bihac Pocket declared a UN exclusion zone. No word as to why, but it's probably because they're losing the war there. Politics again.

In conversation with one of the locals an interesting point was raised. CNN does not cover all the potential news here. For example; it was announced on Croatian television that the Krajina must rejoin Croatia by 28 November or there will be war. I think that's important, don't you? So why aren't CNN reporting this? And why haven't we been told about it in orders?

The local Serbs don't have a good feeling about the near future. I've been asked twice what I think UNPROFOR will do in the event of war. I tell them what I think. If there's a chance of war, UNPROFOR will pull out. You're on your own baby! We're just not equipped for an all out war. It's a tough line, but it's the truth.

The only visit we had today was from the paymaster. By my calculations I should have about $3,000 to spend on my trip to England. I'm really looking forward to this trip.

To conclude today's entry, I will tell you about Wilcox. You'll recall, back in training, he was the guy puking his guts out at the top of Passchendaele Hill during one of our runs, and the guy who had the huge blister on the bottom of his heel during the ten-mile march. Anyway, he was going to get married while on leave in Canada but wasn't going to tell anyone till he got back. The warrant got wind of it somehow, and using chains from the MLVW, had him tied to a chair. What followed was a merciless slagging of the poor guy. He was covered in ketchup, mustard, flour, beer, aracia, and wine, washed down with ice water, then warmed up with more beer. The poor lad went to bed a total wreck, and was justifiably excused from duty the next day. That will teach him to keep secrets from the guys.

Thursday, 17 Nov., Bruska This was another slow day in the thriving metropolis of Donja Bruska. I got a good arm and chest workout in the morning. In the afternoon Jim and I took a stroll up to the gate of Camp Alpha. For the first time the guard at the shack had on a maroon beret. Could it be that they've passed basic training? Speculation in the section runs rampant.

At long last I've received some mail—one card from Cat and a letter from Derek. The mail has slowed down considerably, almost to a trickle, and it's pissing everyone off. The Christmas rush is coming and hopefully things will get better.

This evening George, David and John went out on patrol around 6 p.m. and didn't get back till midnight. John was actually quite entertaining. As if watching him stumble around trying to get undressed wasn't funny enough, he actually fell asleep in one of the port-a-potties while trying to relieve himself before going to bed. We left him out there for 45 minutes or so, then brought him in and put him to bed.

These past few days Cat has been on my mind a lot. When I called last Thursday, she had been to see the doctor for her monthly checkup. She hadn't been feeling well and was experiencing new numbness. The doc said he'd let it go for another week before deciding whether to put her in hospital. Well, now the week has gone by, and I find myself wondering what the final outcome is. It pains me to think I can't be there for her.

CNN, once again, seems to be lacking in ability to get the full story. For example, they reported that someone tried to kill the Bosnian president. I'm sure with a little digging they could have expanded on the 10-second sound bite they put on the air. The Serbs here heard that and knew instantly that something was afoot. Why is that? What do they know that CNN doesn't? Or for that matter, what do they know that we don't?

The seesaw battle for the Bihac pocket continues. Just the usual shit on the TV.

Something happened in Rodaljice last night involving one of our patrols and a group of Serbs. I'm going to try to get to Rodaljice to find out what it was.

Friday, 18 Nov., Bruska Forty-two more days until Cat and I can be together. At first being away from her was hell, but lately it's not so bad. I wonder why that is? Maybe I'm just getting used to being away from her. It will be interesting to see if, as the time gets nearer to our reunion, I miss her more.

Tonight I got into Rodaljice to make a call to Cat. It took a couple of tries, but I finally got through and talked for 20 minutes. There's good news and there's bad news. The good news is that she's not going into hospital. The bad is that without a doubt, she's done it again, and taken on too much. She's taken in a dog that was bound for the knackers, if Cat didn't do something. It's not a small animal either, it's a German Shepherd cross named Molly, and she's been trained to attack small animals. It'll be interesting to see how many of our four cats are left when I get back. Two dogs are fine when I'm there, but not when she's alone in her current condition.

Today's big activity was the handout of UNHCR food allotments. The allotments are supposed to be for a one-month period. For example, one person is entitled to 14 kg of flour; .8 kg salt; 2 kg powdered milk; 3 kg lentil beans; one 500 ml can of corned beef; 7 cans of tuna; 1 litre of cooking oil; 1 small box of yeast; 2 boxes of detergent; and 1 box of frosted flakes (Tony the Tiger type for the sugar—mothers of the world take note). It's not a lot of food for one person to live on, which is probably why it's intended as a supplement. The truth is, from what we've seen these people don't need the extra food right now. We're in a farming district, and with all the animals around, there's plenty of fresh meat and root vegetables. That, of course, could change in the future.

The amount of food that we get to feed a section of 10 people for one week surpasses anything remotely resembling reality. We have so much food that we're throwing it out. For example, we'll get two 50-kg sacks of onions (one white, one red),

The boys weighing and handing out UNHCR food rations to the locals

one week and the next week receive an additional 25-kg of red onions. We're throwing out fresh veggies all over the place because no one is eating it. While we're here, we're mostly inactive, which in turn means we don't eat much. This doesn't seem to be taken into account when the rations are doled out.

I talked to the two guys involved in the incident at Rodaljice. Macmillan and Madison were called on to shadow 3 men and 2 women through the village as per SOPs. All the Serbs were wearing uniforms and carrying AKs. Our boys escorted them to the other side of the village from a discreet distance (they were headed to Camp Alpha). When our guys turned to return to our camp, they heard a rifle cock; they didn't turn; then a round was fired; still, our guys stayed in control and continued walking. This rates as a 9 on the pucker scale. The Serbs were obviously just trying to rattle them a little.

The warrant said to me today that the tone of the tour is, and will become, more aggressive. Why? That night, after our patrol was shot at, three mortar rounds went off close to the village (within a kilometre). Today the Kenyans up the road shot a Serb in the leg for trying to steal gas (pissed off that he was cutting into their black market money, no doubt). More and more, small incidents are taking place in areas where they shouldn't. I'm inclined to agree with the warrant.

Saturday, 19 Nov., Bruska This thing with Cat and the dogs has been bugging me. It's obvious that she's taken on too much again, and simply won't admit to it. Yesterday when I talked to her, I could tell by her voice that it was getting the better of her. It frustrates the hell out of me when she does things without stopping to think, but I know her heart is in the right place. To call and give her shit is no answer either; she doesn't need the added stress. My only recourse is to sit here and work on grinding another millimetre off my back teeth, until the urge passes. Odd how her inability to say no is one of the things I both love and hate about her. Ah! the bittersweet duality of it all, I guess you gotta see the humour.

The big highlight of today came with a visit by the General. Nothing special really, but we did go to the effort of cleaning up and polishing our boots. His entourage trailed in, gave their approval, were suitably impressed and then trailed out. Same old pre-programmed shit! All good morale boosting stuff—NOT! We sometimes wonder whose morale it's meant for.

Once the general was gone the OC, CSM, and Warrant Fuller stayed for coffee. Warrant Fuller quietly asked me how Cat was doing. I told him things were pretty tense for a while, but that things were getting back to normal, and that she was walking with a cane on bad days. He nodded and said he'd pass it along to the CSM.

The CSM gave us the lowdown on what actually happened to Molson the dog. As it turned out Molson accidentally wandered into the minefield where he received a "C4 assist to heaven." Talk was of giving a medal of bravery for clearing a path through the minefield for the boys. There's that army humour again.

Today I did two foot patrols. An afternoon patrol with John took us to an abandoned part of the village about a kilometre from our position on the far hill. We spent about an hour rooting around one of the houses, looking through what was left of it. The house itself was OK with just the insides having been ransacked. We found a couple of old wine barrels big enough to hold 500 litres each, stoves, beds etc, and two photographs. One in black and white and the other a colour Polaroid picture. It was kind of spooky looking at the people in the photographs, while being surrounded by their former belongings. While viewing the photographs, we received a radio call to return to the camp, so we cut our visit short. There are five more houses in this little group, so John and I made plans to make a return visit when we rotate back through Bruska.

The second patrol was with Henry and Jim. Our first stop was to drop off a tin of biscuits at one of the houses in the village. The old fella there has only one leg, and appears to be bedridden. When we showed up at the door, the lady all but dragged us in for a glass of wine. Two glasses later, we managed to make our way out the door. I gotta admit, that old lady (50 plus) had one hell of a handshake. She had a grip that would put most men to shame.

The patrol ended with us learning a new card game at Sveto and Gordana's. The game is called Tabliza (tab-lee-sza), and I can tell you that it's a lot of fun. We played a couple of games, and drank some more wine, then wandered home. It was a good time.

CNN has been reporting on the war in the Bihac pocket again. They said today that napalm and cluster bombs were used for the first time. What they didn't report was that gas has been used as well, something the CSM passed on in the discussion today. This means that the Bosnians are willing to escalate the situation—let's hope they don't have any nukes!

The UN Security Council sat today, and authorized the use of NATO air strikes against airbases to keep the Krajina (read Serbs) from attacking the Bihac pocket in support of the rebel forces.

These airbases are in our area (no one seems to know exactly where) and if any soldiers are killed in the air strikes, we can expect retaliations on the ground. All that remains is for NATO to approve the air strikes.

At this point, I'm looking forward to getting back to Rodaljice for some decent food and regular showers.

Sunday 20 Nov., Bruska Today was one of those days that fit into the category of max flex. We got up at 0800 to be ready for pick up at 0900. At 0600 this morning, the Battalion went to stage Orange. That meant that all movement had to be in carriers, so you can imagine things slowed down quite a bit. At 40 km/hr patience becomes a necessity and you cultivate an interest in the countryside. 11:30 saw the arrival of our replacement section and by 12:20 we were back in Rodaljice. No sooner had we arrived, than the warrant called us all in for a chat. NATO had approved the air strikes, (we knew that anyway from CNN); there were an increased number of Serb troops on the roads; and someone pointed a weapon at the warrant. Things are getting interesting out there.

We discussed the situation for a bit, then dealt with administrative issues. We placed orders for wine that the Regiment had made arrangements to purchase on our behalf at one of the bigger wineries in our area. I tried some of it, and it tasted terrible to me so I passed on buying any. Mail was handed out, and as we all got up to leave, the warrant smiled and said, "Oh! by the way, pack a barrack box boys, you're going to Knin" (dirty clothes and all). It turns out Peters stepped on his peepee in a big way. He went on shift at the gate at 0600 and was caught sleeping at 0615 by his 2IC, who'd just come back from a patrol. When he was awakened, he promptly told the 2IC to fuck-off and went back to sleep (or so the story goes). The warrant put it quite clearly: "he's going to jail; the question is for how long." The reason we're going to Knin is because Peters has to have his charge parade, so we're filling in for his section. There is a silver lining to all of this; I understand there's no time limit on phone calls where we're going. We trundled off to pack our things.

12:45—Ogroup. Start loading all your kit into the ML and be ready to move by 13:45.

12:55—All kit loaded and we're ready to move. George, David, and Jim are ready to go on their 96-hour leave. George's wife is waiting for him in Budapest at the hotel (he flew her over). He's very anxious.

13:05—Ogroup. Warrant Fuller gathers everyone in the camp (15 of us) for an impromptu meeting in the middle of the compound. "Boys," he started out, "in the next 24 hours we're going to state Red. As of now all leave is canceled; George, your section is going back to Bruska so offload all your kit and load up the carriers again—you leave at 1:30. Now listen closely. In state Red, the rules of engagement change. They shoot at you, you shoot back! If there's any doubt, cap'em! Don't bother yelling at them or firing warning shots. Shoot to kill." He paused for a moment, then continued "I hope you get a chance to do the thing that you been training for and hoped you could put into practice over here and I hope it's everything you thought it would be. Good luck boys. Carry on."

There was a stunned silence for a few moments, as people let what was happening sink in. Holy shit! This is no game! We're in a shootin' match. The hair on the back of my neck was standing up. We paused and then in true military fashion, we carried on.

13:20—We've gone to state Red.

13:25—Carriers are loaded, and we're moving out.

13:50—We're back in Donja Bruska.

The routine starts immediately. Two men on the .50 at all times. Keep your flack vests handy when in the tent, and wear it outside. No patrols. Weapons always to hand.

As I'm writing this, I'm sitting at the table, my rifle and helmet are beside me, and I'm wearing my flack vest. Looking around the tent, things are pretty quiet. The guys who were to go on leave are pretty bummed out. David looks like his puppy just died, and George is wishing he was with his wife. Now him I feel for.

20:30—status change: state Orange. David is bouncing off the ceiling. There's smiles all around. The ML comes to pick up the boys at 2100. Regular nightly routine starts. Tomorrow we leave for Knin—at 06:30.

Through all of this, my biggest concern has been to get to a phone. Lord knows what the people back home are seeing on the tube. Sadly, when the state goes to Orange the phones shut down, so with any luck we'll go back to state Green sometime soon so I can call Catherine.

Just a final note about Peters. What he did is inexcusable. At the time, there was only one other person in camp, a radio operator, who was awake. The day before, the Serbs had fired a shot near one of our patrols. Last night, he'd been out late drinking heavily, knowing full well that he was on duty this morning. His falling asleep at the gate meant that anyone could have walked right into the camp. There's no doubt that the OC will make an example of him and rightly so. What he did was just plain stupid, and can only be ascribed to the fact that he's barely twenty years old, and unable to control his emotions and desires. The warrant hinted that he may end up spending 30 days in Edmonton. Now there's a sobering thought. Edmonton is the home of the CF jail. It's so tough it makes Kingston look like a cakewalk.

Monday, 21 Nov., Knin At 06:30 the ML showed up to take us to Knin. While loading the truck I overheard the warrant talking to Henry, "we're going past the camp where the Kenyans shot that Serb for stealing gas" he said quietly, "if we take fire, tromp on it and drive through it." I can tell you that the whole trip to Knin, I kept my weapons VERY handy. Robert and Jay just slept—ignorance is bliss.

Last night I didn't get much sleep at all. I pulled the 0300–0400 shift and couldn't get back to sleep. As soon as we got here we went to state Red due to the air strikes on Udbina (they were canceled yesterday due to poor weather, which I'm told is why we went to state Orange). The UN is anticipating retaliation from the Serbs, but we just look at it as a pain in the ass.

Our job here in Knin is simple: camp security. This is the headquarters for Sector South. There are more than 35 countries represented here. The camp has three OPs around its perimeter. One is at the highest point in the camp beside the helipad and overlooking a mechanical target range built into the side of a hill. One is to the west by the Czech hospital and is called the FST (Forward Surgical Team). The other is the front gate. There are additional positions between them but they remain unmanned until there is a stand-to. Three sections are required to man the positions on a 24-hour basis. A fourth section is required to fill in as QRF, which is why we are here. With only three men required on duty at any one time, there are enough of us to allow for one or two of us to have a day off during our rotation here.

Essentially we keep the bad guys out, and make sure no one gets in without proper authorization. The Kenyans used to have the job, but it was taken away from them (so we're told). Here are two reasons why. The Kenyans only strung one roll of wire (about 3' high) around the camp. If they took a running start, any self-respecting kid could jump over it. Because the Kenyans have a reputation for not going out after dark, anyone could come and go as they pleased.

Because Knin is a major Serb stronghold, the camp was suffering at least one break-in per night. The other reason was that one of the Kenyan officers on duty at

The First Half of the Tour

night, sold the duty room computer out of the headquarters building, right over the fence to a Serb! No word of a lie. The Kenyans have not left people with a good impression of themselves as soldiers.

The Jordanians replaced them, and the first thing they did was erect wire three rolls high and two deep. Break-ins during their six-week stint dropped to less than one per week.

We've since replaced the Jordanians and we've built bunkers all over the place. 1 Section, (our guys who were first to be sent here) was responsible for the last two being built. The next thing we did was to crack down on the gate. The Kenyans were in the habit of giving their UN ID cards to one man and sending him on a shopping spree in Zagreb to buy things on their accounts. As it happened, the first day the Canadians took over 210 Kenyans showed up at the gate. 72 of them without ID cards. 72 of them found themselves outside the gate, standing around with hands in pockets wondering how they were going to get to their kit. This included two majors, several captains, and numerous lieutenants. This only happened a couple more times before they got the message, and started keeping their ID cards with them.

This used to be a JNA (Yugoslavian National Army) base. It's a little smaller than five city blocks long and maybe half a dozen wide in size and quite impressive. It's been split, more or less, in half, with the UN occupying the largest portion, and the Serbs in the other bit. From what I've been able to see of the Serb half, the base is loaded with equipment. APCs, tanks, trucks, artillery pieces. You name it—I suspect they've got it.

Two nights running now we've caught someone trying to get in through the wire. In one incident one of our Sergeants caught two guys halfway through the wire. When he shone the flashlight on them they froze. He just smiled and said "Dobordan" (hello) in a slow, musical voice while smiling from ear to ear while pointing his gun at them. They both froze face down until he turned the light off. Then, both of them got up, put their hands in their pockets and said "drunk, no problem" turned and walked away. Right buddy. You're drunk and I'm Santa Claus. Our record remains unblemished.

Shortly after we arrived here, we were given a tour of the place. When it was over, a couple of us were standing near the gate. It was sunny out, there was a cool breeze, the kind that can raise goose bumps on your arm, but out of the wind it was bordering on hot. I was wearing my flack vest, ball cap, sunglasses, and had my sleeves on my shirt rolled up. The Look Cool factor was definitely high as we looked around at the other country's soldiers and sized them up by their appearance. One of the Sergeants at the gate came over and asked if I would guide a truck up to the gas pumps to be refueled. This entailed my walking in front of the vehicle all the way to the filling station, watch it get filled, then walk it back to the gate. A simple enough task.

I was told that the pump was manned, but when I arrived there was no one to be seen. I started looking around and found this moving bundle of clothing bouncing around in a doorway. It took a moment to recognize him but, here was a Kenyan dressed in complete winter warfare kit; I mean he had everything. Mukluks, wind pants, big parka, a balaclava pulled down over his face, and a huge scarf wrapped around his neck. I just stared at him as I stood there in my short sleeves.

He removed his glove long enough to fill the tank as I watched, then went back to his corner and began bouncing around like a Mexican jumping bean trying to keep warm. "This," I thought, "is going to be an interesting visit," and went about my business.

One of our first tasks as a section was to secure the windows in our sleeping area. Once we'd each stowed our kit, we took to taping the windows with masking tape. When we were done each pane of every window had a taped X on it with a border of tape for good measure.

The food here is questionable. Your options are beef, beef, or beef. Let me explain. There's beef in mushroom sauce, beef in mystery sauce #1, and beef in mystery sauce #2. There's chicken noodle soup for variety, but the chicken looks and tastes suspiciously like beef. These menu options are offered for our dining pleasure at lunch and supper each and every day. Some of the guys have taken to eating frosted flakes in the shacks instead of going to the mess. I'll let you know how I fare. I will say this though. The bread here is excellent. It's the one thing they do really well.

Knin is a beautiful city from a distance. It appears to be untouched by the war, and is one of the largest cities in the Krajina. It's located about 18 km from the Bosnian border and as I understand it greatly desired by the Croats. The city itself is located in a valley and is overlooked by a large castle on top of a steeply sloped hill. In ancient times, the city was the hub of activity for an enormous area. There are three valleys that terminate here, and along each valley at regular intervals, are towers. I'm told that the towers were used as a system of communication, and that the people of the time were capable of sending a message several hundred kilometres up each valley by signaling from tower to tower. I, of course, took pictures.

The city looks to have a population of about ten thousand or so Serbs. If it weren't for the war, I would seriously consider visiting here. It is truly a beautiful place. I am reminded of the Black Forest in Germany, and Vancouver because of the surrounding mountains. The place drips with history.

I tried to call Catherine tonight, but the phones are all shut down because of the alert status. CNN reported that the "UN went on high alert." Sure we did. I was sun tanning on top of a hill, while filling sandbags. We heard the locals blowing off ammo in the city, but just kept working in our t-shirts. In state Red, we're supposed to go everywhere with helmets, weapons, and flack vest. It's a right proper pain in the ass, but everyone plays along. Well, at least the Canadians do. The rest of the camp acts as if nothing has changed, and walks around in their uniforms or sports gear, which makes us wonder more than a little.

Because our section is QRF, we're on immediate notice to move, 24 hours a day. That means sleeping in full uniform. I've cheated some, and have taken my boots off. My back is sore, and my body is tired. I have a watch from 0300 to 0400, so I'm going to try and rack. More to follow in the days to come.

Tuesday, 22 Nov., Knin Day two as QRF, which is another way of saying day two of general duties. Because we're used as reinforcements in the event of an emergency, and because we're mostly idle while on duty, we get tasked with doing all the odd jobs around camp. Like this morning, at 0800 we were called on to move four tank traps into position which block off the old roads leading from our camp to the Serb camp on the other side of the wire. They're not all that effective really. They're light enough that one man can roll them out of the way. They do, however, look imposing enough, standing well over 8' tall.

After laying the traps, we went up the hill to finish the C-6 bunker we started yesterday. The fine infantry art of making a simple job last forever as a way of avoiding extra work was in excellent practice here. Our intention was to make this job last long enough, so that we wouldn't have to start a second bunker somewhere else. It worked. We finished the bunker just before lunch, and Warrant Ferguson (1 Platoon warrant) decided it was too late to start a second bunker, so he had us come back after lunch and fill sandbags until the gravel ran out. This is when the previous theory works in reverse. Work as fast as you can, so as to maximize your time off. This too worked in good order, as we finished in less than an hour, filling some 300 sandbags between us.

There was a phone at the helipad where we were working, so as soon as I was finished I made a b-line for it. At lunch today we switched from state Red to state Orange and I was gambling that the lines would be opened. They were, and I got through to Cat on the first try.

Without a doubt, the hardest thing a man has to do in his life is listen to his wife cry on the other end of the phone. Cat came apart on me twice, and when it was all over, I was left with a lump in my stomach and I felt like I'd just had the shit kicked out of me. It's agony not being able to reach out and hold her. All of this just reinforces my belief that taking on the extra dog was indeed too much for her. I told her so. I also told her to get rid of it, not too forcefully I hope, and I think she agreed. For a fiercely independent woman, my being here is turning out to be a lot harder on her than we both imagined. It's become obvious to both of us that she relies on me a lot more than we both have realized. Only 37 days and a wakie, then we can recharge our mutual batteries.

The rest of the afternoon was pretty slack. We took the sandbags we filled, and used them to reinforce the gatehouse. The rest of the afternoon and evening was ours, so I engaged in two of the true pleasures available to me; a hot shower, and rack time. Lifting sandbags all day can take it out of you.

On my way to the shower, I discovered two things in the basement of the building. A Moslem mosque, and an ammo locker. Praise the Lord and pass the ammunition!? Both are Kenyan. The ammo locker is on an outside wall, which does not make me feel good. A stray artillery round or RPG rocket could set it off. Of course, by then no one would really care, because we'd be preoccupied trying to cover our collective asses.

In the news today, it was reported that two NATO Harriers had missiles fired at them while enforcing the no fly zone over Yugoslavia. It would appear the NATO air strikes yesterday had little or no effect on the Croats' will to fight. We'll have to see what will happen if the NATO jets are fired on again.

Under the category of Stupid Kenyan Stories we were again shown just what kind of troops we're working with. This morning we were given 15 Kenyans to man certain bunkers along the perimeter under our command . As they came up to our position, I saw them removing the plastic wrap off their flack vests. How long has this battalion been here? We Canadians go nowhere without flack vests and rifles. This once again reinforces the difference between the two armies. I've heard it said again today by a guy in the UNHCR, that the Canadians are considered among the elite of the UN armies. In spite of our problems, and judging by what I've seen, I'm starting to believe it. Though I'd put the British and French pretty high on the list as well.

Tonight I have radio watch from 0500 to 0700 and then I'm off till 1900, when I go on 12-hour shift at the gate.

Wednesday, 23 Nov., Knin I slept till noon. I needed it—if you'd dropped a bomb

I wouldn't have noticed. This morning's radio duty passed quickly, partly, I'm sure, because I never really woke up. After staggering to and from lunch, beef again, I just sort of laid around and watched TV, took a shower, had a shave, went for supper, then about 6:30 got ready for duty.

Tonight's duty runs 12 hours, from 1900 to 0700 at the front gate. This ranks up there as one of the most boring tasks ever assigned to a soldier. It's now 0300 and I've written three letters and called my brother Joel, and my Mom and Dad. I'm biding my time until I call Cat. I want to catch her when she gets home and surprise her. Otherwise there is absolutely fuck-all to do!

There are some things I simply must get on paper before I forget them. The Kenyans, my favorite army to punt about, originally had the task of camp security. They had 120 men for the detail with at least half of them on duty at any given time. As you know, they suffered one break-in per night. Aside from the computer incident, I heard today from Warrant Ferguson that a meat locker was raided during their watch. Not only did the culprits tear the door off the hinges and clean out a small transport truck's worth of beef, but no one on duty saw a thing!?!

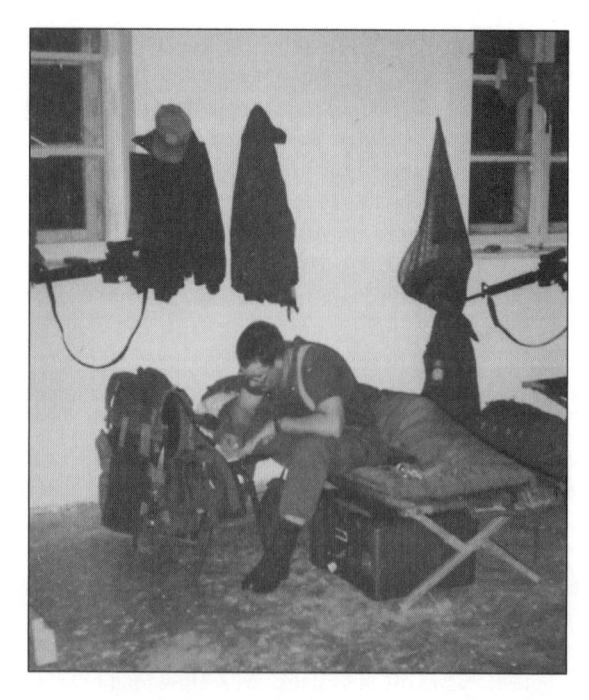

Passing time writing in Knin

I find it amusing to imagine a platoon of Serbs dodging and weaving through the shadows, each with a side of beef on their back, probably giggling like children, as they snuck back through the wire. Somebody somewhere had to be in on it.

The Jordanians took over and they improved the situation vastly. After erecting the wire, which is imposing though not installed the way we'd do it, the break-ins dropped to near zero. The Jordanians had a policy in their home country that when they heard a noise they would empty a mag in the general direction of the sound, then investigate. Camp policy was that they didn't put the mags on their weapons. There's a thought, camp security with no ammo. Anyway they brought 60 people to do the same job as the Kenyans, and did it better.

We, on the other hand—start the fanfare—brought only 30 people, have only 12 people on at any given time, and improved the defenses. All of this while carrying mags on the weapons. What can I say but "we're the best!" You want to open the door a little more, I can't get my head through. Thanks.

In the news today, NATO struck twice against Croatian artillery positions. Will these people ever learn? If this keeps up it's going to turn into a NATO war and we'll end up earning our pay.

Thursday, 24 Nov., Knin This morning, after I came off shift, the only thing I had in mind was to rack. Bruce and I must have broken the overland speed record going from the mess hall to the fart sack. The only good part about last night's duty (actually there were two) was that I got three letters written, and ate the most scrumptious, warm, fresh baked bun that we lifted from the bread man as he came through the gate this morning. It's something of a ritual actually; the bread guy has been in the habit of offering to those of us on duty, a fresh bun each when he comes through the gate. Everyone knows this, so the other two posts send a foot patrol along the perimeter to the gate, about the time he's due, to pick up their ration of buns. As you can imagine the gatehouse gets a little crowded as we all gather to await his arrival.

I got up around 1:30 in the afternoon simply because I couldn't sleep any more. I seem to be averaging 6 hours sleep a night. I'm not sure why, I just am.

The Canadians are situated on the main floor of a wing of this building. Everyone in the building is supposed to know that another army's lines are expressly off limits unless you are invited and escorted through. The shower (though to call it that is overly generous) is no exception. On my way back from my shower (we brought in specially equipped ISO trailers) I caught a Kenyan in our wing taking a shower. Trust me when I tell you that I wasted little time in telling him to leave. The reason is quite simple: never let troops you don't know within your lines without escort because kit will invariably go missing (presuming for argument's sake that a naked guy in your building isn't carrying a bomb).

No sooner had I tossed the first guy out, than I caught a second guy also taking a shower. This one decided to protest by saying he was an UNPROFOR soldier just like myself and what was my problem. I just looked at him and said the reason I wasn't tearing him a new asshole was because he was with UNPROFOR. I guess if I was back in Canada, this wouldn't be such a big deal. But over here, we've closed ranks, and truth be told, nobody here trusts these guys.

Shift started at 1900 and got off to a really slow start. Around midnight the officer, Lt Babcock, came down to the gate with the evening's Sit Rep.

SITREP 25 NOV 94

    A. 5 x SVK constructed bunker on SE side overlooking helipad
    B. Camp defensive construction continues
    C. Nil
    D. Nil
    E. Possible demonstration at camp gate this morning. Advise against sending any CANBAT ONE personnel to this location as access may be denied.

The officer gathered all the section commanders at the gate and gave them the lowdown. Word has reached the camp that there may be a demonstration at the gate around 0600-tomorrow morning. As a result our shift change has been bumped up to 0500 so we don't get caught in the middle of a shift change during a demonstration, and we're sending the guys going on 96-hour leave out of camp at the same time to guarantee their departures. This we thought was decidedly odd because it would make more sense to simply keep the two shifts on for the duration, thus doubling the number of people at the gate until the disturbance had passed.

During the Ogroup, I asked the lieutenant if he was considering deploying marksmen in an over-watch position for security. This was something the PPCLI had done during their tour. Teams of two marksmen were deployed in over-watch positions when the need arouse. I'd read about it in the Infantry Journal prior to coming over, and it seemed like a good idea. Yet the response I got back really bugged me. The lieutenant just looked at me as if I were some kind of clown. Then he berated me for even considering the possibility. "The battalion commander has to deploy the snipers," was his argument.

Of course the battalion commander has to deploy the snipers! I was asking if we would be deploying two marksmen, to provide over-watch security for the guys at the gate. The reasoning is pretty sound. The roof of the building we're staying in offers a clear view in both directions of the road in front of the camp. By putting two people up top with rifles and a spotting scope, they can quickly identify anybody planning to do something that you normally wouldn't see from ground level. It seemed like a reasonable question, but the lieutenant clearly saw it as something else.

I'd heard, through the grapevine, that this guy wasn't at all liked by his troops, and now I can see why. He treated me like a piece of shit, instead of dealing with the question as a viable option. When morale is low, you have to look to the leadership for the reason. 'Nuf said.

The SITREP mentions an SVK trench being built on the southeast side overlooking the helipad. This is just a game with them. They were pissed that we built the trench on the helipad in the first place, and because our trench overlooks their base, they didn't want to be outdone.

In the news today, it was reported that 55 Canadian soldiers are being held hostage in central Bosnia. This is crap! It was explained to us, in no uncertain terms, that they are not hostages. What's happened is the SVK have surrounded the area, and have stopped all UN movement. Those boys are a long way from being hostages. The restricted movement however means the Bangladeshi troops can't be resupplied, which is bad for them because we understand they are running low on food. The fighting in the Bihac has intensified.

Friday (0000-24000), 25 Nov., Knin The shift that started out boring ended with a bang—literally.

INCIDENT REPORT

A. 25 Nov 94 0310 A.M.
B. Front gate, Camp Knin.
C. Sighting of two paraflares followed by what seemed to be an RPG explosion.
D. Nil.

The First Half of the Tour

E. Reported to C/S 58. Received Sit Reps from Oscar 2 & 3. Patrolled engineering stores (in area of explosion) found nothing.
F. Concluded
G. Cpl Ryerson
H. Felt concussion at front gate as well as the smell of powder. Approximate range when reported was 400 m but believed to be closer.

What happened was this. Bruce, Cpl Ryerson from 1 Platoon, and myself were in the gatehouse on duty. At about 0310, two paraflares went off. We heard the pop of the flare igniting, and watched them through one of the windows, as they floated down. The flares were followed by someone shooting an RPG in our direction, from the field in front of our position. I had my back to the wall at the time, as I sat on one of the tables. The explosion was loud enough, and close enough, that it shook the floor and knocked dust off the stone walls inside the shack. There was a pause as we realized what was happening, then we started to move. The adrenalin was pumping through us, but rather than becoming unhinged it produced a calm in all of us and it was obvious what had to be done. Bruce immediately got on the radio with the duty officer (C/S 58), then started fielding calls from Oscar 2 and 3 (our two outposts along the perimeter). I grabbed the rifle with the Kike night vision scope, and started for the door to do a recce. Cpl Ryerson, who was technically in charge of the gate because he was highest ranking of the three of us, was standing in the corner dazed and confused trying to figure out what to do next. On my way out the door I told him to grab his rifle and follow. The poor guy was still a little confused as he grabbed his rifle and followed, but at least he could provide local security while I scanned the area.

Across the street from us, there are two large buildings. One houses a generator, the other some telephones. We were in no real danger from the incoming round since the buildings acted as an effective shield, unless whoever fired at us could clear these two buildings with the RPG round. Continuing away from the gate on the other side of the buildings is an open area about the length of a football field, half as wide, and ten feet lower than the road. We kept extra engineering stores there. The ground drops away again to a large field, about 700 metres across, which on the far side, has a road running along its edge. With Ryerson trailing, I found a spot in the darkest shadows of one of the buildings and took up a solid fire position, turned on the Kike sight, readied my weapon and started to scan the area.

There wasn't much to see. It was a cool night and the ground fog was pretty thick. Whoever fired the round was either long gone, or far enough into the fog that I couldn't see him.

What we suspect is that a couple of Serbs got drunk, sent up a pair of paraflares so they could see what they were shooting at, then loosed an RPG round in our direction. What they hadn't counted on was the ground fog obscuring their vision (or the fact that we were nearly a kilometre away). The grenade fell short and ran into the berm below the engineering stores, exploding harmlessly. It got our attention, but no one was rattled by it.

Speculation was that it was a range finding exercise so they knew where to aim during the protest this morning, but I don't put much stock in that.

The rest of the shift passed quickly and we were relieved at 0500 hrs. In spite of the potential for a protest and lots of fun, I went to bed—albeit fully dressed.

There was no protest. All the precautions turned out to be a waste. I got up around noon and went for lunch, then came back and watched the tube for a while. Around three o'clock, George David and Jim came back off leave and bless their furry assholes, they brought mail. I thought I had done well with one package and three letters. Bruce beat everyone, he got 7 packages and 27 letters. I think even he was surprised. They say the way to a man's heart is through his stomach. If this is true then Bruce is lost. His girlfriend has sent him nothing but Christmas baking. The poor guy is in danger of becoming a diabetic. The sugar alone in the baking has to weigh ten pounds.

This evening's shift at the FST started out peacefully enough. The Serbs were back in town getting drunk. We could hear them easily, they were singing marching songs at the top of their lungs, and the sound carried nicely across the valley, about a kilometre from our position. Every now and then someone would cock a rifle and let off a burst of 10 or 20 rounds. This went on till past midnight.

Around 8:30 things got real interesting. It started when, from the other side of the valley, we spotted what looked like paraflares going off. We knew we were wrong when the "flares" just kept going up. After a moment, it dawned on us that what we were watching was anti-aircraft fire in the form of rockets, because they went up quite high and then exploded. Closer to the ground, there were streams of tracer fire running horizontally from a point part way up one of the mountains. This we figured was ZSU 57U anti-aircraft fire. For a few minutes there, it looked like Baghdad by night during the Gulf war, just like watching a fireworks show!

As it turned out, CNN and SKY NEWS both reported that NATO had made a reconnaissance run over the Bihac pocket. And, that they had missiles and anti-aircraft fire directed at them, but that all aircraft had returned untouched.

We had been witnesses to some of that fire. Admittedly it was at the other end of the valley, about four kilometres away, but "I was there when....."

The only other thing that happened tonight really pissed me off. I broke the blade off my pocketknife. And worst of all, it was the blade that had been engraved by Catherine for me. It had "Kurt, always Cat" inscribed on it. I had grown found of that knife. I was in the habit of stroking the blade each time I took it out. I felt sick after I broke it. Holding the pieces in my hand, I just wanted to put it back in my pocket and pretend it never happened. I don't know what I'm going to tell Cat. It was a gift from her, and she worked so hard to get it right. I feel like shit!

Finally, word came down about Peters. Fourteen days CB, and extra duties. He was given the option of two weeks in jail or two weeks of warrant punishment. He chose the latter and the bugger doesn't know how lucky he is. If this was the Turkish army, he would have been shot for what he did.

Saturday, 26 Nov., Knin The remainder of the shift passed uneventfully other than my being dogged by feelings of guilt each time I fingered the knife in my pocket. I've kept the blade and put it in my camera pouch. I don't think I have the nerve to throw it away yet. The highlight of the shift, after last night's excitement, was the arrival of the bread man. Fresh buns have a way of perking you up after a long cold night.

I have today and tonight off. I'm rotating to day shift and have to skip a shift to get my sleeping pattern sorted out. That's fine with me because I haven't had a beer in what feels like weeks, and this will allow me to go to the CAN-DO mess for a couple of barley sandwiches.

I must have been overtired when I hit the sack this morning, because my eyes

The First Half of the Tour 131

didn't open until 1:30. David was out of it till 3:00, and at 4:30 I went and woke up George.

I had been looking forward to a Barbecue that the Canadian staff had laid on for tonight, but found out just before supper that it had been shifted to tomorrow night. Great! Another meal of this crap they call food. Tonight it was fish cooked in butter that tastes like lard, dry rice, and shredded cabbage. A true culinary masterpiece. I finished about half of it before my gag reflex kicked in. At six, I hit the mess and sat to enjoy the first of my "true Canadian taste experiences." I then pulled out my diary and started to get caught up on my entries. By 7:30, the boys started showing up off shift, and the real drinking started. It was here that I came across another of those "stupid Kenyan stories" that make you shake your head and wonder why they're here.

It turns out that Monday, the day we arrived and went to state Red, Lt Babcock had approached a Kenyan Major about deploying the Kenyan OTR 64s parked in the compound. (Note: the OTR 64 is an 8-wheeled armoured troop carrier, with a .50 calibre machine gun mounted on top in a turret. The Czechs had donated them to the UN, and the ones on base were assigned to the Kenyans). At first the Major didn't know who owned the vehicles, that is until the junior lieutenant with him told him that, yes indeed, the vehicles were under his command. Lt Babcock then inquired about moving them to a position in support of the gate, and was informed that the Kenyans had no drivers for them.

"Could we at least turn the turrets so that they cover the gate?" he continued.

"Why? We don't have any ammunition for the guns," responded the junior lieutenant.

Lt Babcock just shook his head and walked away.

It was getting on to 9:30 at the bar and I was down to what I figured would be my last beer, so I could hit the sack early. I had a pretty good buzz on and was looking forward to stretching out in my nice warm sleeping bag. I'd just come back from the washroom, and sat down at our table, when WHAM! Everyone in the bar paused and listened, the music thumped on. Then . . . WHAM!

Two explosions went off just outside the door of the bar.

In short order the music was shut off, and, like idiots, people started filing outside to see what happened, of course led by the senior officers in the bar at the time. If whoever fired at us, had waited thirty seconds and fired another round, they could have taken out the entire upper command staff of Sector South with one round. They were all outside the bar trying to look official and officer-like.

We infanteering types just kept drinking our beer. The walls are two feet thick and made of stone—why go outside?

Bruce was behind me coming back from the washroom and was near the door when the rounds went off, so he stuck his head out and reported that the explosions were caused when someone lobbed two rifle-grenades into the parking lot outside the washrooms, from whence we'd just returned.

As soon as he said it, an MP captain contradicted him saying it was the gas pipes on the shitter trailer exploding. That explanation lasted about two seconds, when Sgt Graham walked up to him, took one look at the damage and called the officer a "stupid fuck" right to his face. "How do you expect my boys to react if you don't tell them the truth?" The officer didn't have a comeback.

"Stand to, Stand to, Stand to." The bar emptied. Down the hill we flew, into the building to grab out kit, then back up the hill. Going down was no problem for me, I couldn't feel my legs. Coming back was another matter. Loaded down with helmet, flack vest and weapon, I had my hands full trying to stagger up the hill. About halfway to our intended position, I hit a flat spot on the road and met up with Robert, who also had his hands full trying to walk a straight line. Bruce caught up to us here and passed on that we were to man the OP on top of the building we were standing beside, so mercifully our uphill stagger was cut short.

Standing on top of a building on a cool evening with the wind blowing is no fun when you're sober, and have the proper clothing, let alone when you've had too much to drink and don't. In all the hubbub I had forgotten to grab my gortex jacket off the end of my bed, and was dressed only in my sweat pants and sweatshirt, so that after the adrenalin wore off, I started to freeze my knackers off. Ten minutes of animated discussion and speculation followed our arrival on the rooftop, then I said fuck it and crawled inside the bunker to get out of the wind and try and stay warm.

Finally, one hour and ten minutes after the first explosion, the order to stand down came. I'm sure I set a new standard for going from OP to the sack. The last thing I remember before passing out was that maybe I should take some aspirin and drink some water before I go to sleep. . . .

The view from the OP at the heliport at Knin

Sunday, 27 Nov., Knin I should have. This morning I woke up with the worst headache I've ever had. To top it off, the power went out and I couldn't shave, shower or shit, so I settled for brushing my teeth (with the help of a paint-scraper for my tongue). God I felt terrible, even with three aspirin and breakfast, the headache didn't subside until 9:30 or so.

I'm at the heliport today. It's up high so you get a great view of the city of Knin. Looking through the binos, you get a pretty good idea of what the place is like. Lovely from afar, but far from lovely. Aside from the lovely surroundings, this place reminds me of an English industrial town out of the 1800s, without the neat architecture. There are some modern buildings, but even they look old.

A Canadian colonel came up for a visit this morning. He wanted to know where the grenades were fired from, so we pointed out the bunker the Serbs built and told him it was suspected that's where they came from. Ballistics confirmed that two rifle grenades had been fired, but the report was still pending on where exactly they were fired from. Universally, everyone (soldiers that is) admires the guys who did the shooting. I say guys, because the time lapse between explosions would indicate a well-practiced team. Also both rounds landed within ten metres of each other, which also indicates a well-practiced marksman. Of course, with three years of war, one tends to get a lot of live fire practice time.

Fortunately little damage was done. Both rounds landed close to 300 m from where they were fired (the limit of their range) and hit an area that the shooter could not see because of our position blocking his line of sight. If they could have seen their target, I'm sure we would have had casualties.

While we admire the shooter's skill, we pretty much agree that he was a coward. Had he stuck around for one minute after the first two rounds, and sent another two on their way, he could have taken out a whole passel of officers and men. Our luck, his loss.

The current contingent of the RCMP is rotating back to Canada tomorrow. Bruce's uncle is one of them. Tonight they opened the bar at the CAN-DO mess and picked up the tab for everyone, while the Canadian soldiers supplied the steaks and black forest cake. The result was the best meal I've had since arriving here. The steaks were thick and juicy, and pulled apart without needing a knife, and the beer went down like water. What a party!

In talking to several people (mostly RCMP), I learned all kinds of interesting facts about this place. For example:

—80% of the policemen sent from other countries to the UNCIVPOL are functionally useless on the job. The RCMP, the Irish, the Czechs, and Norwegians do the bulk of the work.

—the #4 man in the Bangladeshi state police (45 years old) cannot drive, type, operate a computer, or fill out reports. He was caught by his RCMP counterpart, sitting in the front seat of a Land Rover, making the sounds and motions of driving (screeching tires, car noises, like a four year old) while waiting for his partner to return.

—The Canadian army has the highest reputation for being tough, professional, and incorruptible.

—the Canadian army is the ONLY army not to be accused of black marketeering.

—the average Kenyan soldier gets $15 US per month of his $1300 US UN pay. The remainder goes back to the Kenyan defence department. The Kenyan officers get their entire allotment.

—the Czechs make six times their annual salary while on UN duty. Frequently a nurse with 15 or more years experience will fill a Med-A's position. Top administrators have been known to fill driver's positions.

—Two Russian policemen were sent to UNCIVPOL; one was a plastic surgeon, the other a nuclear warhead programmer. Both are making more money here as drivers.

—most "chief inspectors" from third world countries cannot drive, or operate a computer.

—most policemen sent to UNCIVPOL only work for the police department, and have no formal training, i.e. commissionaires, surgeons, photographers, etc.

—the Canadian RCMP are looked upon as something akin to gods, and a constable usually ends up running the detachment he's assigned to.

It was an illuminating evening. As a closing note, the three grenades fired in the past three days, is the most fire the base has taken since the UN has arrived. It is understood that the tight security provided by the Canadians and Jordanians is pissing off the local Serbs.

Funny Kenyan Story number 406. The base deputy commander's car was stolen from INSIDE the compound during their watch. It has yet to be recovered.

Col. Morgan (the top Canadian officer here) didn't know what the Kenyans do here. Neither did his # 2 man.

The E.C. observers drive Land Rovers that weigh 4000 lbs and are capable of stopping a .50 cal bullet. Each costs $1 million Canadian, and most of them end up sitting in the compound, because no one knows how to drive them.

What a place!

Monday, 28 Nov., Knin-Rodaljice This morning Henry, Bruce, and myself went back up to the heliport for our regular shift. We were expecting to be relieved in position around 9:00 so we could head back to Rodaljice. Our relief did not come around till 2:00 in the afternoon!

This morning, the Serb camp commander came up to visit us and check out the bunker that his boys built overlooking the heliport. Yesterday, the Serbian general came by to assess the situation and have a look for himself. It was negotiated that the Serbs would come by today and dismantle the thing. But last night was a different matter. We were given clear instructions for engagement if we saw anyone in and around the bunker. Step one was to call Sunray (platoon commander) and Sunray minor (platoon warrant) to let them know what we had. They in turn would contact the Serbs and try to have the men removed. Step two was to fire a warning shot. If that didn't work, we were to open up with the .50 cal and level the area.

To make sure everything was working Bruce and I took the Karl-G out and bore sighted it behind some buildings so the Serbs wouldn't see us. Henry stripped and cleaned the .50.

To help us in our night observations, we have three pieces of equipment which do the job to varying degrees. The first is the KIKE sight. It's a scope mounted on a standard service rifle, which uses passive light to illuminate the target. This is a good piece of kit, far better in fact than the starlight scope. It's amazing what you can see with it.

The second piece is called the NOD (Night Observation Device). This thing straps to your head and works the same way as the KIKE sight, gathering and intensifying passive light. It does, however, have the added advantage of being able to pick up an infrared laser beam, which has been mounted to your rifle. You see these things in the movies all the time, the little beam of light coming from the end of the rifle, and landing on the target. All very Hollywood, but effective as hell.

The last piece of kit weighs in at $250,000, stands on a reinforced tripod, and is called the NODLR (Night Observation Device Long-Range). This baby works off heat instead of light, and with the 8X lens engaged, you too can watch rabbits playing at 300 yards in the dark of the night. In fact, last night when we turned it on, we watched a rabbit amble through the woods, and disappear into its hole more than 300 yards away.

Looking through it is like looking at a screen with varying shades of fluorescent green. It's really cool, sort of makes you feel like the Terminator. So much for professionalism. Oh well we're all just big boys anyway, with really neat toys to play with!!!

The night shift was geared up for action in light of our orders, and was greatly disappointed when nothing happened. The only real action happened to Lt Babcock coming back from his Ogroup at C/S Zero. Two cars sped past him and then cut him off. One guy got out and started waving a pistol around. The lieutenant and the boys all cocked their weapons and waited. After some negotiations, the lieutenant went on his way. No doubt much relieved.

The RCD's barracks in Visoco took a direct hit from an RPG round last night. Fortunately everyone was sleeping in a different area of the building, and no one was hurt.

Rations are running low. Last week the ration run got blocked coming into the country, and much of the fresh food was spoiled. Some of the companies are starting on hard rations because they've run out of fresh, and had no reserves built up. Mac in Rodaljice is doing OK. He's low on some items but otherwise fine.

Our road-move back to Rodaljice was uneventful. We were told that we might run into resistance in one of the towns but didn't see a thing. The warrant cocked his pistol for nothing. The boys have gone off to Bruska and I've been left behind to do the laundry. It should take me till noon tomorrow or so to finish. I don't mind really, at least I'll be able to get my laundry done and fire a few bottles of beer downrange in the process.

I sat in with Sgt Goldsmith's sections for orders tonight. Speculation from higher, is that the HV (Croatian army) are getting ready for a push. More and more soldiers are being seen and equipment is being massed in various areas. At this point it's all intuition and speculation. I don't intend to get excited until I see the tanks rolling down the road.

And finally, the dentist rolled into the village today to work on the locals. There was an opening in the schedule, so I had a filling replaced in one of my upper molars today. Without thinking I decided to have it done just before supper, so you can imagine what it was like trying to eat with half your mouth frozen. I will say though, that these boys are real good. Their setup is on the back of an MLVW, and though cramped, it's very efficiently laid out. I was in and out in 45 minutes, and most of the time was spent waiting for the x-ray. The hygienist and the Doc made a great comedy team, and it was really hard to keep from breaking up during the operation. Aside from a little soreness as the numbness wore off, I'm good to go. Easily my best dental experience ever!

Tuesday, 29 Nov., Rodaljice This morning I was awakened at 0500 by the dulcet tones of Sgt Goldsmith giving drill to Peters. Warrant's punishment means he's pretty much under house arrest for the full period, except when he's on duty or being tasked. It also means a 0430 rising for pack drill, by your bed kit inspections, and doing every little job the warrant can think of.

This morning I looked out the door to see Peters in the pushup position, pack on, and helmet under his chest with both hands on top of it, struggling to get a last pushup. When he could do no more, he was stood to attention and was marched over to a large pile of gravel. Where he was made to march up, over, around, and through the pile for ten minutes with arms swinging breast pocket high and executing turns on the march in fine military fashion. We're not supposed to watch or comment upon anything that happens to Peters while it's happening, lest we end up joining him. Still, while it's going on you can't help but think "better him than me."

A very slack day today. I did laundry all morning then took a nap in the afternoon. This evening I loaded up all the laundry and what I needed for Bruska. I drove into Karin Slana for orders with the warrant. Afterwards, I was dropped off at Bruska to settle in for the duration.

An interesting thing happened while I was at Karin Slana. Three of us were waiting on the warrant when a black guy walked past us. Turns out, this fella is from UNCIVPOL and is now living there. Apparently the Serbs told the UNCIVPOL at Obervac that if they came back (they left when they went to state Red last Monday) they would be shot. They have not returned.

(Note; in state Red, all UNCIVPOL must make their way to the nearest base. For Obervac, Karin Slana is the closest place where the police feel safe. There is a closer Kenyan base, but for some reason no one went there.)

In orders tonight it was again mentioned that the Croats are prepping for some kind of action. The timing seems to be right, and apparently some of the signs are there. For me it's still speculation. I would point out that one of the targets has to be Camp Alpha, the other is Knin, because it's the capital of Krajina (something I didn't know till tonight). Both places I could be at when the balloon goes up. . . .

On a lighter note, if the schedule holds, I should be spending Christmas at Rodaljice, which means that we'll be eating well and drinking hard.

This next bit we're not supposed to know yet. Lately we've been told that we may be switching our position with someone else. It's supposed to be a morale thing, so the troops don't get bored by being in the same place too long. The fact that none of the troops want to move doesn't seem to be a factor. Mind you, if the OC and CSM say move, we say when and where to? All the speculation and rumours are affecting morale alright—the wrong way!

It was revealed tonight that there are several options in the works. A move to Bosnia is one option, and a move home is another. It's possible we won't go anywhere, but one of the most likely options is we'll end up going to CS Zero and form a QRF/patrolling company, meaning we'd abandon our current positions in the villages, and only patrol through them on a daily basis. If you get the impression no one really knows what's going on, you're right. This, and any other army runs on speculation and rumour, and believe me it's quite amazing some of the shit that comes down the line.

In other news, the 400 UN peacekeepers being held in various places in Bosnia have been allowed to travel freely. This is false, of course. No one is going anywhere.

Wednesday, 30 Nov., Bruska Thinking back over it, today was a fairly busy day, but by no means strenuous. It started about 10:00 when the platoon commander came by with Doc. For the most part everyone was still in bed when they arrived. The lieutenant and the platoon driver headed off into the village, and Doc stayed behind while we got ourselves sorted out.

How do you know something is going to happen in the next little while? When they tell you to make sure you life insurance is in order, and they give you medical refresher training, that's how. We spent about an hour around a table talking about various medical situations, and brushing up on our general first aid knowledge.

Our food re-supply finally arrived today around noon. Mostly fresh stuff and meat. No canned goods. We had told some of the Serbs we were low on food, and what we had run out of, and they offered to feed us until we were re-supplied. And when I say feed, I mean full meals for nine men twice a day. Makes you wonder if they have that much food, why we are giving them supplements?

John came off his 96, and out to us on the re-supply run, then four of us mounted up and went to C/S Zero for haircuts. This is the second haircut I've had since arriving in country. For 2 DM (about a dollar), I get a #4 clipper on top, #2 on the sides, and a taper on the back. It doesn't matter if the cut doesn't suit you, everyone else looks the same.

This evening we sat around and talked a bit about Knin. The one thing everyone agreed on was that 1 Platoon has no morale at all. They have little or no respect for their superiors, and there is no cohesiveness in their sections. It's a sad thing to say, but we all couldn't wait to get out of there, and we don't look forward to going back.

The local Serbs have told us to be careful when we go to Benkovac to pick up bread. In spite of orders from their president not to touch the UNPROFOR people, there are Serbs out there who, when drinking, may take pot shots at us. The word is they're pissed about the air strikes, and don't differentiate between NATO and UNPROFOR thinking that we're as responsible for the air strikes as NATO is. Local propaganda said that NATO dropped a bomb on a house with six kids and a pregnant woman, killing them all. This is shit of course, but what can you do?

Finally, eight of the boys who picked up working girls in Budapest, appear not to have practiced safe sex. The result of which is that they now have the clap big time. That will teach them not to wrap their peepees when they take 'em out to play.

Thursday, 01 Dec., Bruska This morning I took a walk up to the Camp Alpha gate with John, and was pleasantly surprised when the young lad at the gate called out in English, and used my name (it's on my flack vest). We'd been told that the camp commander likes us, (he should, we're giving him free dental work next week) and that must have been translated to his troops. In all, we chatted for about 15 minutes about nothing in particular, then we went on our way.

Our satellite TV link has been screwed up these past few days, so our news from the outside has been limited. The lieutenant came out again today to fill us in.

Bhutros Bhutros-Ghali, the UN Secretary General, has asked for US help to get the UN out of Bosnia. If things get hot the RCD will come to us. Whether it happens or not is another issue.

My favourite army (the Kenyans) had some mortar rounds dropped in front of their position. Makes you wonder who they pissed off this time.

C/S 1 had a drive-by shooting yesterday, just like downtown Toronto! Hey! Who says America doesn't have an influence over here (no one was hurt).

One of the things, which really piss me off about being over here, is the news media. They appear to be extremely selective in what they report. But worst of all, their reporting is indiscriminate. I worry sometimes that Catherine is getting the wrong impression of what is going on over here. Yes, there is fighting in the Bihac, but that's miles away from any of us (about 60 actually). I worry that she and everyone else back home are getting all worked up over nothing. It's not fair to them and it's not fair to us.

This bit in the news about the peacekeepers being held "hostage" is a good example. The truth of the matter is that the Bosnian Serbs stopped all movement in the country. Now, if someone came to your door and said you couldn't go to work this morning, I'd hardly think you would consider yourself a hostage. It's more like being under house arrest. You're not being held at gunpoint, and you're still free to defend yourself. But just try and tell that to the media. Pretty much everyone feels that way and it's beginning to piss us all off. Some of the guys have actually stopped watching the news because of it.

Friday, 02 Dec.Bruska Around 10:00 this morning we got a call on the radio that the CSM was on his way with a set of swings for the local kids. He's big on the "hearts and minds" thing and wanted to personally ensure that the swing set was delivered and installed. Painted a charming UN blue, it stands out nicely against the green grass. The kids love it. A seesaw is being built now and will be delivered soon.

After the swing was installed we all were invited into Gordana's for a glass of aracia, and coffee. This business of drinking in the morning is for the birds. Diplomacy and tradition are one thing but I gotta start cutting back.

After the CSM left, David, Jim, and I spent an hour moving wood for Gordana. We were just about to sit down for lunch, when we got called back to camp. Fortunately David and I weren't needed, so with Robert in tow, we headed back for a free meal. On the way down, one of the Croats stopped us and insisted we drink with him. Instead of a container of water to refresh him while working, this guy had a pot of wine. We all faked drinking by bringing the glass to our lips, but not actually drinking—the wine was almost rancid. It was funny, because we hadn't said a word beforehand, yet we all did the same thing. Lunch lasted till six, with lots of conversation. I went to bed early.

Saturday, 03 Dec., Bruska I slept poorly last night, getting up several times to go to the washroom. The only consolation was the shower I had this morning. The routine is as follows; start the immersion heater and wait for the water in the 45-gallon drum to warm up. Take the jerry can with the showerhead, and fill it up from the immersion heater with a pot, being careful not to spill too much on yourself. Adjust the temperature of the water by adding cold water from the jerry cans filled at the well. Carry the can inside, and fight with it to get it in the overhead rack in the makeshift shower stall. Get undressed, and stand in the tub below the jerry can. Release the clamp on the hose attached to the jerry can and get wet. Squat down to get the top half of your body wet. Soap up. Squat down and rinse off. Freeze while you try and dry off. Shaving today was like pulling hair. I only have a dull razor to shave with, and it hurts like hell.

All day we've been watching vapour trails in the sky. We've been told they were American AWAC's painting all the Serb and Croatian radar sights. Another indication that something is afoot.

Orders today revealed that the entire zone is very quiet. Unusually so. People are starting to notice. The only exception was JORBAT, where a jeep was hijacked. Calm before the storm?

It also came down in orders, that our government has released a new white paper. We had a long talk about how it affected the army. We all figure the air force and navies are going to get the shaft this time around.

After orders, the platoon commander took me aside and asked me to quietly help Sgt Macari with an article he had written. It appears his first submission has been rejected out of hand and he wanted me to lend my literary skill (limited though it may be) to the writing of a new draft. It turns out the joke was on the officer, because George caught on before we had finished talking. It made for a good laugh all around.

Tonight we had a big mail run. Packages were everywhere, and it was just like Christmas. While the young guys got chips, gummy bears, junk food, and porn mags, I got one of my mother's famous Christmas cakes (which I looked forward to—because it's heavily spiked with rum) and a Chatelaine magazine from my parents. Christ! Here I am 8000 miles from my wife, everyone's getting the latest porn magazines, and mom and dad send me a goddamn women's magazine. You gotta see the humour.

Most of today (and the last three days for that matter) have been spent writing letters. I've written to nearly everyone but my wife. Which is what I'm going to do right now!

Sunday, 04 Dec., Bruska/Rodaljice Only 25 days and a wakie, and I'll be with Catherine. That says it all!!!!!

I was on the 0600–0800 shift this morning. I was going to go to bed again but decided to watch Jurassic Park for the umpteenth time. That's a pastime with us here. We watch bad movies twice and good movies at least four times, and if you're on shift, you get to see them all again uninterrupted. What I'm saying, there's not much to do here!

This morning the dentist showed up to work on the locals. The opportunity was too good to pass up so I had my teeth cleaned and fluoride treated. Once again it was a chore to keep a straight face while sitting in the chair. Following much friendly banter, I shook hands with the Doc. He's someone I could really get to like (in spite of his handicap of being an officer).

I mentioned yesterday that I've done a fair bit of writing these past few days. All told, I've written about a dozen letters to various people. I'm telling you this because the person I've written to the most is Terri. I should tell you that I've known Terri for fifteen years now. We met when I was 19 and she was 16. Our relationship has been on-again, off-again throughout the ten years leading up to my marriage to Catherine. In fact, I had at one point intended to ask Terri to marry me, but she went off and married someone else. A lot of baggage there.

I received a letter from her when I was in Knin, and for four days I laboured to write a suitable letter in return. I've longed for meaningful conversation with this lady for so long, that now that she's ready to talk, I'm going to exploit the opportunity. I want to say that I don't feel guilty about writing to her, but the truth is I do. It's kind of like cheating on Catherine, though in reality we're not. We talk candidly about issues that normally only a husband and wife would talk about (or very, very close friends). Catherine means so much to me, and yet, so does Terri, though I'd never leave one for the other.

HOLY SHIT!! I just got out of an Ogroup where the platoon commander had a chat with us. Our OC has just been FIRED! He'll be on an airplane tomorrow for Canada. The company 2IC will take his place for a couple of weeks until a replacement can be found. I feel sorry for the guy. Everyone thought he was a bit of a dweeb, but now his career is over. Stay tuned, I'll bet there'll be more to follow on this one.

Oh yeah. I'm in Rodaljice now. 1 Section needed some help, so John and I volunteered to come and do some of the shifts. It's nice to take a real shower and shit on a regular toilet. Ah the simple pleasures of the infanteer!!!

The gatehouse at Rodaljice

04 Dec.
My dearest Catherine

Forgive me, my darling, for not having written to you sooner. It has been a week now since last we spoke, and I long for the opportunity to converse with you. Sadly our phone has been temporarily removed from Rodaljice, and I don't know when it will be replaced. Therefore I am using this written form to communicate with you.

Your latest letter of 29 Nov arrived this morning not five days after it's writing. It feels good to be less than a week behind in your news.

Please continue to sprinkle your perfume on the letters. Though I have been caught many times with the envelopes hanging off my nose I gladly suffer the ribbing the guys give me for it transports me instantly back to your side. I too, think of our dancing around the kitchen and my singing in your ear. Though I will say that I am shocked and taken aback by your questioning of my considerable vocal talents!

I continue to write daily in my diary, and in doing so lay your pictures out on the table before me. I have been smiled at many times for doing it but no one ever says anything for, to a man, they are envious as hell of me for having a wife as beautiful as you. The other night, for example, I brought your pictures on patrol with me. In spite of my telling the Serb women we visit regularly how attractive you were, everyone who saw the pictures simply could not believe what they saw. The Serb women huddled for a while around the photos, and were genuinely envious. The men just drooled. One guy who sat beside me couldn't take his eyes off you for the hour we were there.

It made me very proud to be married to you, but I did try my best to be humble. NOT!

I am sitting in the dining hall in Rodaljice right now, and am surrounded by all the letters you have written to me during November. Your perfume gently rises from the written page to permeate the air around me, and I need but to inhale to be again by our side. I can feel your hand in mine as we walk together side by side, the press of your body against me, the smell of your hair, the sweet tenderness of your lips. I need only look at the pictures before me to again be reminded how truly fortunate I am to have you as my wife.

These past few days have seen the arrival of many letters. Joyce, Winnie, your father and mother, and my mom and dad. In fact, yesterday I received a box containing mom's extra potent Christmas cake. I'm saving it for a special occasion, but am extra careful to keep it away from open flames as the alcohol content is so high.

I have dutifully dispatched letters to all of your students who have written to me, and have just sent a letter to Daphne and David. Forgive me, but I told them that you had assumed the role of social director for the trip, and that all plans should be made through you. I trust your judgement completely and will willingly go along with whatever you choose for us to do on our honeymoon.

As to the matter of Molly the dog. You must follow your heart and do what you feel is best. As always my concern is for your health. Otherwise you have my complete support.

Sadly my sweet, I am running out of space and must bid you farewell. I would remind you that there are but 25 days and a wakie before we can again feel our lips press together.

I love you my sweet.
Your loving husband,
Kurt.

Monday, 05 Dec., Rodaljice 12 hour shift today, 0600 to 1800. Nine hours of which was spent at the gate. We've been told that we can't read out here anymore. This sucks, because aside from writing, there is absolutely fuck all to do out here except stare out of the windows all shift. (I know that sounds vaguely like doing my job, but it still sucks).

Orders tonight revealed a little more about the out-going OC. It seems he broke a directive issued by the CO by drinking on the 96-hour leave buses. It appears, after the duty sergeant stood at the front of each bus and expressly forbade drinking on the trip to Budapest, the Major stood up and reversed the order. This was just plain stupid on his part, but at the same time, it's been said that he pissed a lot of people off by sticking up for Dukes Coy. Who's to say for sure?

As you might guess, we've been warned about drinking. It's been pretty slack around here, with the occasional party lasting into the wee hours. For the time being, anyway, that will stop.

JORBAT had 40 some Shot Reps, KENBAT 30 some. CANBAT ONE (us) had less than ten. Things in our sector are pretty quiet all around. I never thought I'd hear myself say this, but I miss CNN. I feel like I'm in a vacuum not knowing what's happening over here. Even if the reporting is inaccurate.

Tuesday, 06 Dec., Rodaljice The company 2IC, now temporary OC, came by to talk to us and dispel any rumours. He told us that the outgoing OC got on a plane today for Canada. When he gets home he'll be posted out of 1RCR, so that he's not around when we get back. Talk about bringing a promising career to a screeching halt. This year he was slated to go to Col's school in England, and also this year he was supposed to be offered his unlimited contract to take him till he was 55 or so (he's 38 now). Neither of these things is likely to happen. He will be lucky to finish off his four years to make his "20 years in" pension.

He was given an "administrative reproof," which back home is nothing really, but in directly breaking one of the CO's stated policies, the CO had "lost faith in his ability to carry out orders, specifically the CO's orders." By being relieved of command during a tour, you can bet his career is so far in the dumpster that it's irretrievable. I can't help but think there's a little more to it than that. The rumour about the major pissing people off keeps coming back.

These last two days there's been a suicide watch on him. I can't say as I blame them. If I had a promising career cut short like that, I'd be emotionally distraught, and likely suicidal as well.

After the OC left, John floated a rumour that he heard at Karin Slana today about Warrant Fuller. He said some people told him the warrant is in hot water because he pisses people off, and that he's going to get hung out to dry. Maybe, but if it happened, they'd start a bloody revolution in this platoon. I don't know about the others, but in spite of his failings, I like the guy. Fuller went in early to see the CSM today, I guess we'll just have to wait and see if anything comes of it.

I escorted Doc into Rodaljice today, and as I sat outside one of the houses I was struck by the fact that these people live in squalor. They have no self-pride at all. Their houses are garbage pits, they drink constantly, they smell for lack of washing, and yet they have electric appliances, TV, radios, and the ability to make things pretty decent for themselves.

I am told these people have no concept of buying and selling land, and that mortgages are virtually unheard of. Land is handed from generation to generation, and people live in the same houses their great great grandparents did. Going out into the country is like walking back in time. People still have smokehouses, and use horse drawn carts. It's amazing, if they put some effort into cleaning up their yards, and picking up the garbage, it wouldn't be so bad, but this place is like the slums. Geese, turkeys, and chickens run free, and there's sheep shit everywhere, so you can imagine what the place smells like. It's gotten to the point that in Rodaljice, I keep my patrols as short as possible, and I refuse to go into any of the houses. Like the smell of death, I expect the stench of this place will follow me the rest of my life.

Now that I've thoroughly lambasted the country folk, let me just say that the city folk are only a little better. Their standard of living is higher than in the country, and the towns and cities are cleaner, but there still remains a primitiveness about these communities that is tangible.

A lamb will be slaughtered in the street and cooked in a large Barbecue beside a pub. Then there are the ever-present rock walls, and everything is small. The cars, the lots, the apartments, and the houses. One day on patrol I stopped into an old house, and when I went to leave I had to duck to go through the door. Unfortunately I didn't duck far enough and promptly whacked my head on the top of the doorframe. It would have been funnier if it didn't hurt so much.

My biggest problem is that most of us wonder what it is we're doing here. The UN, as far as I can see, serves no useful purpose here. For example, in the two villages where we're stationed, we've been given no clear mandate. We are told to protect the local Croats, but we haven't been given enough people to do it, or allowed to do it properly. We just sit in our camp, and every couple of hours or so wander the streets. Some protection!

Humanitarian aid you ask? These people don't need our help. They've been farmers all their lives and you can't tell me their larders aren't full, war or no war. Lord knows their wine barrels are. How else would the local Serbs be able to offer to feed a section of us two meals a day? The food we do give them is not enough to feed one person for two weeks, let alone for a month; and if they did depend on it, they'd starve because its distribution is so irregular.

I have yet to see a single homeless or starving person. The farmers are doing well, and the city folk are holding their own. Life goes on. For a country under a fuel embargo, there are a remarkable number of vehicles on the road. Chaos theory says that life will always find a way to survive, and this is a good example of that.

Wednesday, 07 Dec., Rodaljice I got volunteered last night to be part of a work party that will be used to reduce the size of the compound at Karin Slana (C/S One). The UN is paying $10,000 US per month to rent all the buildings in the compound, and most of them are sitting empty. The original plan was for a company (124 people) to occupy the location, but right now there's less than a platoon in position. The purpose of the work party was to bring the perimeter in closer thus eliminating many of the buildings from the compound, and bringing down the rental cost. Besides, from a security point of view it makes the compound more manageable.

Last night I went for a workout, and worked my shoulders, biceps, traps, and abs. If I had known I was going to lift sandbags all day, I would have worked something else, because those are all the muscles needed to move sandbags.

Four of us were responsible for moving between 1000 and 1500 sandbags in six hours. We had to dismantle a bunker and stockpile the bags. This involved moving the bags from the roof of a one-storey building onto the back of an ML (read: stand at the edge of the roof, and throw the bags in the back of the truck ten feet below). Then move the truck to a spot inside the new perimeter, and off-load the bags. Each bag weighed in between 40 and 60 lbs, with some as much as 90 or 100 lbs, depending on how wet the clay inside was.

My arms feel like they're 10 feet long, and it's painful to straighten them. My back, surprisingly, is OK. At the end of the shift we were pretty tired. I've got the midnight shift tonight so I won't have to go again tomorrow—thank God, because I don't think I could handle it.

At lunch I took the time to call Cat. It took half an hour to get through and when I did I was shocked. Cat was in the throes of one of her bouts of laryngitis, and I could hardly hear her. In spite of her support network, she was alone at home with no help. I can't tell you how pissed off I was. It was all I could do to contain myself.

The doc told her she has to cut back even more on her teaching schedule. I guess she's working a 46-hour workweek not including her extra stuff. That means the pressure is that much more on me to "bring home the bacon." I'm sorely tempted to toss in the towel right now and just go home. I know that the longer I wait the harder it will be to find work at my old position with the Post Office, or anywhere else for that matter.

Cat needs me to be at home with her especially with this cold she's got. She becomes completely dependent when she's sick, and with no one there to help her, I feel like I've let her down. It's hard enough listening to her weep on the phone, but to barely hear her because she's sick and can hardly talk is almost intolerable. I worry sometimes if I'll have a wife to come home to.

In other news, the Croats and Serbs have signed an economic agreement for road access to the coast, power, and trade. Of course, neither army has agreed to anything, so I guess nothing will change.

Rumours are still flying around that we may be stuck here an additional three months if the UN decides to pull out. Pulling out is a 6-month process, and it wouldn't be worth it for the UN to send replacements for us if the decision were made to leave. That would mean we'd be here for a total of nine months. There's been a lot of brave talk by the guys about demanding a "2" for their medals, indicating that you have done two tours. Nine months is a long time in one place, especially this place. We're told the decision is to be made in January sometime.

I suppose if I think things are bad now, they can only get worse. PS: We got our UN blue toques tonight. Whoohoo!

0315 A.M., 07 Dec.
My dearest Sweet Catherine
    I take pen(cil) in hand this evening in an attempt to cheer you up. My hope is that when you read this, some of the burden of your sickness will be lifted from your lovely shoulders, and a smile may again grace the face I so dearly love.

    Our conversation this afternoon distressed me greatly. When I heard your voice labouring so painfully to reach out to me, I knew instantly that you were tired beyond words. With every fiber of my being, I wanted to rush to your side to hold and protect you as you recover, but in looking at my clothes and my surroundings, I can only be with you in spirit. The disappointment angered me.

    My love for you, my sweet, seems boundless, and with each passing day I feel your absence more keenly. In spite of your insistence, the longer I am over here, the more firmly I believe I have done you a disservice by leaving you. My place is by your side, more so now than ever before. I long to see you smile, and feel your arms around me. I miss our walks together and our quiet chats at our favorite coffeehouse. But most of all, I miss touching you. The softness of your skin, the smell of your hair, the gentleness of your smile. This separation has been hard on both of us.

Upon my return, we shall together purchase a cappuccino machine. I can think of nothing more pleasurable, than to sit on our porch, cappuccino in hand, my favorite girl by my side, and our zoo in attendance. This truly is the definition of living well.

Take heart my dear, at this writing there are but a scant three weeks until we meet in England. When you read this, there will be less than two weeks.

When we meet in the airport, you will run to me, and I shall envelop you in my arms and protect you from the world. Then, lovingly, tenderly, I shall give you a kiss that will reach into the very center of your being, and caress you. It matters not who is watching, for in our world, there is just you and I and no one else, which is as it should be.

I hope I have been at least partially successful in achieving my stated aim. When we meet in England we shall create many new memories together.

My love to you always
Kurt

Thursday, 08 Dec., Rodaljice Three shifts today, 0000–600, 1600–1800, and 0000–0600. The middle shift I volunteered for. It was a bit of an odd situation with us being short-handed because of the work party to Karin Slana. I told George I'd put in a couple of hours to give David and Bruce a bit of a break.

After shift this morning, I went to bed but only got about four hours of sleep. I simply kept waking up. I wanted to do a workout this afternoon, but I was too sore from yesterday's ordeal to really get into it, so I didn't bother. When I come off shift tomorrow, I'll do a quick one before I turn in.

The boys left on their UN leave this morning, and Ted came back. The second leave block has started, which means there's less than three weeks before I see Cat in England.

Ogroups these past two days have concentrated on Reg Force courses for when we get back, which just goes to shows how deep into the routine we are.

Friday, 09 Dec., Rodaljice This morning Ted, Jim, and I were on from midnight to six. I really wasn't looking forward to sitting for two hours in the guard shack with Ted, but was pleasantly surprised to find we were quite civil to each other. Perhaps the break from each other was what we needed to sort ourselves out.

The other day I wrote a letter to Andrew and I'm beginning to feel it might have been a mistake. What I wrote him was a load of pious, pontificating, bombastic crap that should have been tossed in the can right after it was written. I hope he has the good sense to edit it instead of reading it as it is written.

Padre Rembaldie popped by today and was kind enough to ask after Catherine's health. I filled him in briefly. Nice of him to remember to ask.

Not much in the Ogroup today. I've been told I'm attending the medal ceremony with General Vance sometime in January. That's nice. The Bihac was quiet today. That's odd.

It is a curious thing to note how incredibly anticipatory the whole platoon has become of the daily mail run. Though we jokingly ask if there was mail today, the lack of it is keenly felt. Lately we've been receiving Christmas packages with lots of home cooking and presents. There is a tremendous feeling of being left out when it is perceived that everyone except you gets a package or letter. The frustration is heightened when there is certain knowledge that there are indeed letters and parcels "on the way," but have yet to arrive.

One way of thwarting some of the frustration is to open one of the cards addressed to "any peace keeper." "Thank-you for your part in world peace" one person wrote. We'd all love to do something for world peace, but in light of our situation, or better, lack of situation, one is left to feel like a eunuch in a harem. One knows how, is very willing, but not a damned thing is happening.

As for myself, I find that I'm rereading Catherine's letters time and again. She has anointed the letters with her perfume, and each time I open the envelope, I pause to inhale her scent. Without fault, it generates a Pavlovian response in me, and my body begins to react as I recall some of our times together.

The keeping of this diary has afforded me the opportunity to both vent some frustration as well as record what daily life is really like. I have noticed also that I've become somewhat softer and more intellectual in my approach to things lately. I'm not sure why that is. My gut feeling is that it's a reaction to the lack of intellectualism I find around here. That's not to say that the men here are not smart, quite the contrary in fact. But I do get tired of off colour remarks, and derogatory comments about women.

Some of it's an act, which is partly why I don't say much, but some of it isn't. And alas, to be truthful, I too, am guilty of participating to some extent in the verbal assaults on various ethnic, or sexual groups.

I find I'm longing for good, honest verbal discourse with someone who doesn't hold a redneck, extremist, or aggressive attitude about the topic of discussion. The sort of give and take that normal people have when having a discussion, rather than the constant verbal assaults and defenses that are so common here. No doubt when I return to the sane world, I shall revert to "army" mode as a defense against all the Yuppie and bleeding heart attitudes which so pervade civilian life.

In this environ I am considered by many to be a very intelligent man. Probably because I am capable of articulating thoughts in greater than monosyllabic verbiage (even though I can't spell to save my life). I have no idea how the civilians I encounter at home perceive me on the other side of the fence.

What I do know is, that within the army, I grow tired of the extremist viewpoints held by some of its members, and outside of it I am increasingly intolerant of the "bleeding heart liberal" approach to problems that is so prevalent in our society. I'm finding I'm firmer in my beliefs, more forceful in their articulation, and less tolerant of objection. In short, I'm becoming that which I have just spent the past ten minutes railing against. So much for intellectual discourse.

For now, anyway, I will try to be content with lifting weights, doing my job, sharing a few brews with the boys, and recording my observations in this diary.

When I return things will be different. Where before I was wishy-washy about my career, I am now resigned to the fact that I must continue in the role of consultant, at least for the next five years. My intended goal is to pay off the mortgage, and put some money by so that Catherine need not ever worry about finances again.

I have decided also, to start wearing better clothes. I opened my passport the other day and was genuinely embarrassed by the photo I found there. Strong words, and noble intentions indeed. We shall see.

Saturday, 10 Dec., Rodaljice Today's shift was from 0600 to 1200. Rather than change around with Jim halfway through the shift, as is customary, I chose to do the

The First Half of the Tour

entire six hours in the guard shack. Lately I've found solace in being out there alone. It allows me time to think and put my idle thoughts down on paper, or get caught up on my letter writing. Either way, I don't take too kindly to interruptions.

In reading yesterday's entry, I find there's one more point I need to cover. It involves the internal struggle I have with myself. I've always been a tolerant sort of fellow, but since I've come to 1 RCR, I've had to struggle with my own self image and beliefs. Tolerance is perceived as a kind of weakness that is preyed upon in the army, and since my arrival I've felt like I've done nothing but dance internally in an effort to avoid having the hammer come down on my foot. There are times I feel like saying "fuck you all," and take a stance on a particular subject, be it right or wrong (and more frequently in opposition to the popular view). My problem is with the lack of understanding some of these guys exhibit, and my fight is whether or not to say anything at all, because I know as soon as I open my mouth, I'll get verbally jumped. I don't relish the type of verbal sniping that goes on here. In fact I try to avoid it by being the exact opposite, calm and articulate. I am reminded of the character Charles Emerson Winchester the third, from MASH, and can identify with the revulsion, love, and frustration he feels for his situation (my level of frustration is currently at 6 on the Dewy Dicky scale of 1–10), perhaps there's a lesson there.

For supper tonight, Mac cooked up something special. Steak and lobster. The steak was overdone, and the lobster was dry, but hey, this is a war zone, and it was good of him to make the effort.

These past two days I've been on a painting frenzy. I've completed a four-foot Canadian flag, and the bulk of the Dukes Company emblem. It's hard work, and it's all done free hand so it's a bit time consuming. Looks good though, and is good for morale.

Finally, we moved the gym into the schoolhouse today as the tent had too many leaks. It's nice to have a dry place to work out.

The schoolhouse at Rodaljice

Sunday, 11 Dec., Rodaljice I don't believe I did this. I got up at 0500 to go on shift at 0600, only to find I'm not due to start work until 1200!!! The only indication I had that something was wrong was that they didn't come to wake me, and it never occurred to me that I had already completed two days on the 6 A.M. shift. So here I sit in the mess trailer, tea in hand. I'm going to complete this entry and go to bed for a couple of hours.

Up out of the depths of despair we rise to greet the season in all its finery. Yes ladies and gentlemen, the silly season has begun in earnest. Last night a warrant officer from welfare lost it big time. Scheduled to depart for his three-week UN leave, he arrived at the airport in Split only to find his specially arranged direct flight with an unsanctioned carrier had been canceled. With no way home, and nowhere to stay, he was sent back to his home base in Rastivic. Not wanting to disobey the CO's orders about drinking on the bus, he remained sober on the ride back. However, upon his arrival he felt he should drown his sorrows by dispatching his duty free, and so off he went in search of mix.

His quest lead him to the camp Sergeants' and WO's mess, where, upon making his request known to the bartender, was promptly denied (for reasons unknown). This greatly perturbed the warrant, who then began to verbally bludgeon the unsuspecting bartender. At this point a sergeant major stepped into the fray, seeking to control and defuse the situation. It was to be his first and biggest mistake, for as soon as he made his appearance on the scene, the door literally came off the hinges, and the warrant officer took to physically assaulting the sergeant major for his efforts. This continued long enough for the duty officer, a major, to put in an appearance on the scene, where upon he promptly had a few choice pokes directed at his person. This proved to be the limit, as the warrant officer was immediately set upon by the assembled masses in the mess, and subsequently subdued.

The warrant officer for all his efforts went straight to jail, did not pass go, or collect 200 dollars. The sergeant major is recovering very nicely thank you, after a visit to the MIR to straighten his nose. The Major is writing up the charge report. The RSM . . . is NOT amused.

Speculation runs hot and heavy as to the type and length of the upcoming penalty. However, I have it on good authority that a phone call was made to the offending party advising him to plead temporary insanity based on a delayed "post traumatic stress syndrome" reaction to his experiences in Somalia. If the presiding officer accepts this version of the events, then he will likely get off with a fine, and be able to retain his rank. If not, the smart money says he will be busted to Private and do some jail time. This will be unfortunate, as he has only four more years on his contract, and as your pension is based on your last six years of service, this will most certainly affect his retirement pocketbook.

Like all good spectators, we await the referee's decision. Updates will be forthcoming in the days to come. Yes folks first the OC, now a warrant officer. At this rate, speculation is that around next Thursday some Cpl/Pte type will be next up on the charge parade. I'll keep you posted.

As for the remainder of my day, after settling into a comfortable sleep following my early morning error, I was rudely awakened and told I was to go to Karin Slana to move sandbags for a large portion of the day. Unexpectedly, this did not bother me, and I took to the task gladly hoping to get a good arm workout. This was duly achieved along with three other things.

The first occurred during lunch. With 45 minutes on my hands, I slipped off to the gym, and got a good back and triceps workout on their new pulldown machine. Then off I went to place a call to Catherine, where lo and behold, I got through on the first try. I'm pleased to report she so doing much better, and is over her cold for the most part. Sadly because the call went long, I was late reporting back to work and was taken aside by MCpl Constanteneau who was in charge of the work party. When he tried to give me shit for being late, I immediately admitted I was wrong and that I wouldn't let it happen again. The result of this little admission was quite astounding, the poor MCpl was completely befuddled. When he tried to come on to me again, I repeated my admission, which had the effect of leaving him speechless, whereupon I returned to work, having clearly won the verbal battle between us.

The final thing which occurred involved an MLVW and a pile of sandbags. While I was ground guiding Jim in the ML back towards our offloading point, I misjudged the distance from the tailgate to the sandbag pile, thus allowing him to come in contact with them. Remembering that force is equal to mass times acceleration, the result was a bent tailgate. So much so, that it took six of us to get it to close again. Nothing has been said of the incident, but for now I'm keeping my head down, lest the scheduled date for the Cpl/Pte-type going to jail be made sooner.

The day ended with my doing a three-hour shift to cover for John, who did my 12 to 6 shift while I was at Karin Slana. Just before going on shift, George took me aside and gave me my two-month assessment. He has been surprisingly generous in his assessment of my skills, saying things such as "he knows his job well and obviously enjoys his work." My only bad point is that I know too much, and tend to jump in with the answers, which "causes friction" with other members of the section (that would likely be Ted). In the end though, he told me he is, and would be in the future, glad to have me in the section. This concludes a very good day.

Monday, 12 Dec., Rodaljice Last night before retiring for the evening, I had the opportunity to chat with Lt McConnell. We talked of many things, and were eventually joined by others. In the end it was a succession of war stories told between friends, and there was much laughter, and good times.

But, in the beginning, we talked about his new orders. It appears that for once we actually have a withdrawal plan. One which uses back roads and trails that will link us up with Bruska, Karin Slana, and then on to Rastivic. From there, we're to cross the Zone, with our asses being covered by NATO (read the Americans). When we cross the Zone, off comes the blue beanie, and on goes the green beret and, most importantly, off come those damned rules of engagement taped to the butt of our rifles. Anything goes after that.

At long last we have some bite behind the bark. This was clearly demonstrated by tonight's Ogroup. The Americans have expressed the desire for UNPROFOR to remain in place. They in turn will increase their logistical support. That makes us the pointy end of the stick.

Another thing, which reinforced the upgrading of policy (and perhaps the new OC's priorities), was the arrival of the FAC boys today. FAC stands for Forward Air Controller. They are the artillery officer and NCOs who act as FOOs (Forward Observation Officers) and in concert with artillery and naval guns (which we have at our disposal now) can direct artillery barrages onto the target by acting as the eyes on the ground for the gunners.

Their visit today was to scope out an OP overlooking Camp Alpha, and to get a feel for the land. It's all quite hush-hush because neither side is supposed to know that a) the FAC boys are here in the Krajina, and b) that they're conducting recces on various locations to pre-designate targets if the shit hits the fan.

What's left of the church in Rodaljice

The news in brief. For the most part it's pretty quiet all around. A Bangladeshi troop carrier got hit by a wire-guided-flying-what's-it yesterday but no one was hurt, lucky for them. And of course there are the usual plethora of Shot Reps reported all over, but otherwise things are slow.

The Bihac has slowed right down due to resupplying problems. Seems there's some freezing rain falling in the mountains, and they can't get in with the extra ammo they need. I'd hate to see how they'd handle a Canadian winter. They'd probably shut right down and wait for spring.

Ray got nabbed for speeding this morning. A Kenyan and Czech police officer pulled him over for going 10 km over the limit. The problem was the limit is not posted for that area (now there's an original excuse). Also, there is a difference between battalion policy, and UNPROFOR policy when it comes to speed limits, which means what is 10 km below battalion speeds, turns out to be 10 km above UNPROFOR speeds, hence our dilemma.

Ray was understandably pissed. He refused to sign the ticket, much to the surprise of the two cops, and he tried to get the badge numbers from both of them—also to their surprise. The Czech reacted poorly by refusing to give him anything, the Kenyan gave him everything but the back seat out of their Rover. The matter is being looked into. A speeding ticket in a war zone! God, what will they think of next, littering charges during a firefight?

The other thing we did today was mine refresher training. The Engineers came by with their traveling road show and ran through the various mines that we might encounter. It was good refresher training, and it was interesting to handle the live ordnance. As a bonus, they'd brought along a cluster bomblet, and an air deployed anti-personnel mine. The cluster bomblet looked like a green softball, but weighed about 7 lbs, and is a whole lot more dangerous. I found out as well, that in the two months since our arrival we've not had a single landmine incident—with the sad exception, of course, of Molson the dog. By comparison we've only cleared 50 km of routes to the PPCLI's 600 km, and there have been a few close calls, but we still have all our people in one piece. Lets hope it stays that way.

Finally, I did some more work on the company crest tonight. I have to admit it really looks good. Unfortunately I destroyed the only half-inch brush I had which made doing the fine work next to impossible, but nonetheless it still looks great, and gets a lot of admiring stares. Now that I think of it, George mentioned in my assessment that my "artistic talent was good for the platoon morale."

Speculation is that the Vandoos, upon their arrival, will paint a fleur-de-lis over the Canadian flag, and a Montreal Canadians "CH" over the Toronto Maple Leaf. Their choice I guess.

Personal observation: I've noticed lately how much I am anticipating my upcoming trip to England. I don't know if it's because I'm tired of this place and I'm anxious to get away, or because I long to see Catherine. Probably both. Either way, I'm thinking of her a lot more lately.

12 Dec.
My Dearest Catherine

A short ditty to thank you for sending the new diary for me. It is the same as the one I am currently using. The addition of the Wooden Boat magazine and the Lee Valley flyer were an unexpected bonus. I can tell you that each article in Wooden Boat has been read dutifully twice, and the Lee Valley catalogue has been scanned to glean every detail from its pages. Nothing like a tool catalogue to make a handyman happy. Thank-you, thank-you, and again thank-you.

Two days hence I shall again go into the breach to suffer the indignities of long shifts, poor platoon morale and incompetent soldiers, in the worst hell hole in the Krajina-Knin. My only consolation is that I shall have access to a phone where I may call you more often than usual.

I have decided that this will be the last written communiqué I shall have with you before we meet in England. By the time you read this, it will be on or about Christmas, and there will be but a few short days left until we get together.

To help pass the time here, I have been diligently going to the gym for workouts. It seems to be paying off, because yesterday I bench-pressed slightly more than my own body weight, 215 lbs. I think you'll like what you see.

For Christmas I'll be back in Bruska. On the 24th at noon, all the troops will be gathering at Rodaljice to have a big Christmas dinner and drunken blowout. On the 25th at noon I'll be back in Bruska to recover. I'll let you know how things go.

It seems strange to be so close to Christmas and not see snow or hear Christmas carols. But what I miss most is the cooking. I really enjoy all the preparation that goes into a traditional dinner. Standing in the kitchen with wine in hand and the smells of turkey, apple pie, spices and you by my side. Nothing could be finer.

What do you say to taking a double-decker bus from Norbury to Manchester? Or perhaps the train? I don't feel good about asking Daphne to drive all that way down then all the way back again. Give it some thought and we'll talk in England.

I'm arranging to bring two bottles of Crown Royal as gifts. One for Graham, and one for Daphne and David. I also feel we should put some money into re-supplying David's wine cave during our visit. It just seems unkind to drink the man out of house and home and not replenish at least some of his wine. We'll talk.

My love to you always, my sweet. Just a few short days now.

Your man in the blue beanie.
Kurt

Tuesday, 13 Dec., Rodaljice This morning I went on shift at 0600. At 7:30 Warrant Fuller relieved me at the gate so I could go to Rastivic and sort out my pay for my upcoming trip. For the trip to England, I'll be bringing $2200 US and 400 DM with me. I'll keep the DM, and what I don't use in Germany, I'll bring back and use here. The remaining US funds I'll give to Catherine to take home.

I also took the time to pop into the kit shop and picked a UN teddybear for Cat, and two UN ball caps.

When we finished in Rastivic, we loaded up with some firewood and headed back to Rodaljice, and by 10:30 I found myself on radio watch till noon. Since we've moved the gym indoors, and it being just outside the door of the radio room, I took the opportunity to do a real heavy workout while keeping one ear cocked for the radio. By the time I finished my shift, I felt so tired that I had to lay down for the afternoon to recoup some energy.

The rest of the day was pretty uneventful. I did a bit more touch-up work on the crest, but I've decided to leave it until I get some small brushes when in England. No one is supposed to know this, but Ray told me today that our platoon is not moving from our position. There will be some shuffling within the battalion, but nothing that affects us apparently. This is part of the reason I've chosen to leave the crest until after my leave.

Ray and John went on a Christmas tree hunt today, and came back with a real nice one. To hear John tell it, they were bombing down the road when he spotted a likely tree about 50 metres off the road to their right. Ray brought the ML to screeching halt and John hit the ground running with axe in hand. After he had cleared the first rock wall, he recalls Ray yelling after him "don't step on a land mine, I hate paper work and

I'd have a hard time trying to explain it." Needless to say John became more cautious about his route to the tree.

Not wanting to get caught stealing from private property, the two of them brought the tree down in the most expedient fashion possible—short of using explosives—and stuffed it into the back of the ML, before anyone could catch them in the act. Fortunately no one did, and I'm pleased to say that the trophy is on proud display in the corner between the Toronto Maple Leaf symbol and the Dukes Company crest. In retrospect though, it must have been something to see two grown men loaded to the teeth with weapons and ammo, running with a rifle in one hand and a tree over their shoulder giggling like children. Makes me smile just to think of it. Nothing like a daylight raid to keep the adrenaline running.

This type of activity speaks to the level of morale found in 3 Platoon. I've been told that the new OC remarked on our high morale, and that he considered it the best within the company, and possibly the battalion. That's a little out of my range, so I won't comment on that. Suffice it to say that I truly feel lucky to be a member of the fighting studs of combat two, and proud to be part of the "third herd." Our section is not only tight, but smart as well, and we've had some really good discussions. In fact we've coined a new phrase—"intellectual odiferocity"—to describe some of our more intellectual discussions. This not only passes time, but helps preserve sanity over the long term.

The mail run tonight was again nonexistent, with one notable exception. The wives in Petawawa got together and sent everyone in the battalion a gym bag full of little ditties. I chose a blue one and will be taking it to England as my carry on bag. It was fun to see everyone sitting around in the common room rifling through their bags to see what kind of goodies they got, not unlike Christmas morning beside the tree.

That's about it for now. There wasn't anything interesting in the Ogroup tonight, so there's nothing to report there. I'm on duty now (2400–0600) with the lieutenant and Jim. When it's over, our section is going to Knin for our final tour of the place. Thank God.

Before I go, it occurs to me that I forgot to record an incident that took place at Karin Slana the other day. Believe it or not, while loading sandbags on the truck, we were approached by a young fellow selling drugs. Grass and coke to be precise. We couldn't believe it. Broad daylight and this kid is trying to sell dope to UN soldiers. What more can I say?

Wednesday, 14 Dec., Rodaljice-Knin This morning's shift was relatively uneventful. Jim, the lieutenant, and myself were on from 0000–0600. Working with the lieutenant was a real head shaker, one of those "ya gotta wonder" kind of deals. Most of us look at coming onto shift as something akin to going to the dentist, yet here was this young Lt (he's maybe 24), who was keen as shit to do his shift. It was like sitting with a hyper kid the whole two hours he was with me. He kept quizzing me on different things. "What would you do if you saw someone in the wire? Who would you call if . . . ?" and on and on. I humoured him by playing his silly little game, and tactfully changed the subject to something marginally more interesting whenever I could.

When you are on at the gate, you're supposed to get out and walk the fence line around the compound, once an hour. Most of us don't even bother to do it once during the shift, let alone once every hour. It hardly seems worth it, you can see almost all the way around the compound without getting out of your chair. But, no, the lieutenant was into it big time, and watching him walk around the wire, you'd think he was on a stalking exercise or something. There he was, rifle at the ready, sneaking up on the walls, then pouncing to peer over them. Like I said, it was a real head shaker, but I suppose you gotta see the humour.

After shift I snagged a couple hours' sleep before packing for Knin.

The truck ride to Knin was its usual bumpy, windy, uncomfortable self. The temperature has been dropping lately, so things were more than a tad nippy for the hour or so we were on the road. As we came into the city, some young guy in a car with his girlfriend, started following us ridiculously closely. Ted was driving at the time and didn't know they were behind him when he slammed on his brakes to make a turn. We were all watching out the back and got a great laugh when the girl screamed and the guy turned white as he tried to avoid the back end of the truck. Light entertainment, what can I say?

After we arrived and got ourselves sorted out, I put in a call to Catherine. We managed to talk for twenty minutes before being cut off. It was good to hear her so healthy. It gives me hope for the trip.

With nothing else to do, Jim and I headed for a quick supper then off to the CAN-DO mess for a few wobbly-pops. At 7:30, David, Bruce, and George joined us after coming off their shift.

It was understood that this will be the last chance to drink for some time, so, not wanting to pass up the opportunity, we started pounding them back. I tried to moderate myself, but David was like a pig in shit when he discovered that Slivovitz was free at the bar, so as you might guess more than one round appeared on our table.

We staggered home around 11:30 after being thrown out of the bar. George and I heard that the Czech mess was open, so we headed over to check it out—no pun intended (it's at the other end of our building so it wasn't too far to stagger). We only stayed a short while, as there was little going on, and we were all getting real tired. This time when I hit the sack, I had the foresight to drink a litre of water. Hopefully it will make a difference.

Thursday, 15 Dec., Knin Other than feeling somewhat more tired than usual, I really wasn't feeling that bad when I got up this morning. I went to the ablution ISO and locked myself in and took a 25-minute hot shower. God that felt good!!!

The bane of all infanteers is to be assigned to sandbag duty. If you're using sand to fill the bags, it's not so bad. But if you're dealing with rock and clay, as we were, it becomes a right proper pain in the back. Tim, David, Jim and myself were assigned a pile of dirt out by the Czech hospital, and told to have a go at it. We got off to a slow start but in the end, settled down to a reasonable pace and filled about two hundred bags between us. When the last bag was full, we thought that would be it until tomorrow, when we would be moving the bags to their final resting-place. What happened next was a clear demonstration of why morale is so bad in 1 Platoon.

Warrant Ferguson inspected our work and told George that we should go back and fill the sandbags more because "it's a waste not to fill them up all the way." So what if you couldn't pick the things up because the damn things weighed so much. So the crew were duly dragged out of bed, and dutifully led back to the dirt pile to finish the job. After doing a cursory examination of the situation, George summed it up nicely by saying, "Hey, I'll have none of those common sense looks around here." We laboured for two more hours in the dark to finish the job. This is the definition of "more cock," a popular expression used by everyone in the battalion when they perceive a slight against them by higher.

The high point of today came after we got back to the shack the second time. The mail run came in loaded down with parcels. I received cards from Catherine and Josie, and a box full of cookies and baking from Joyce and Winnie. It's like Christmas around here with all the candy and baking kicking around. Morale has definitely picked up.

Friday, 16 Dec., Knin Today was not a day for the weak of back. Not only were the sandbags we filled last night frozen, but also they weighed in at 80 pounds plus each. Some of them took two of us to lift into the back of the ML.

Our first, and we thought only, task of the day was to put a third layer of sandbags on the C-6 bunker we'd previously built. This necessitated our dropping the sandbags out of the ML onto the road, to break up the contents so they would be more malleable when placed. We took our time and managed to achieve the task in less than an hour, then we broke for lunch.

After lunch it was passed on that the officer wanted another layer of sandbags put on two more bunkers. Fine, we thought, this shouldn't take too long if we put our minds to it; besides there will be lots of time left to put in a workout. NOT!

The first bunker we came to was at the heliport. It was quickly determined that the support beams for the roof could not withstand the extra weight. The telltale sagging in the middle of the beams was our first clue. So a call was put in to the officer, and off we went to complete the second bunker.

It turned out that not only did we have to put another layer of bags on the roof, but also we had to take the roof off and replace the beams and then put the roof back on. "By the way," said the officer as he turned to leave, "we need four guys to help unload two UNHCR tractor trailers." Morale hit an all time low.

When we arrived to unload the boxes from the flatbeds, we discovered that, according to the packaging, each one weighed in at 32 kg. It would have defeated us if we hadn't come across a Scotsman we met while drinking in the mess last night. When we explained the situation to him, he told us to hang on and he went and fetched a forklift. If he hadn't, we would still be there to this day doing the job by hand. Between the smell, the food, living conditions, and the shit jobs, the bad morale of 1 Platoon is rubbing off on all of us.

On an upbeat note, we had another mail run today. Parcels and letters were flying everywhere. I'm told by Warrant Ferguson that there are 1000 bags of mail left to be sorted out. Tonight I received a parcel from someone I've never heard of. They sent me a jar of peanut butter brittle, and two boxes of Kraft dinner, always a hot commodity. The card they sent was one of those singing jobbies, and in it they explained that they got my name from a list that the battalion had generated and given to interested groups. It was really very nice of them to write.

Believe it or not, one of the packages I received was an autographed photo from Bobby Hull, addressed to "Cpl Grant." I was both surprised and impressed. One of the officers back at the Unit works with him, and he must have put him up to it. I think it's great. A real keepsake. I'll have to have it framed when I get home.

Tonight we're going to a camp meet and greet. It costs us 5 DM to get in and the money is going for the "socially endangered" children of the area. This should make some NGO feel good about us being over here.

To end on a funny note I have to tell you about the Kenyans. Let me pause here, to tell you that I'm really not trying to pick on these guys, but this is priceless. We discovered tonight that the Kenyans just burned down their headquarters building, mess, and some of their sleeping trailers. This was achieved when they jury-rigged their main electrical panel, bypassing the circuit breakers in an effort to increase the number of heaters available to each trailer. Each heater draws so much power that when you put two of them in a trailer, it throws the circuit breaker. The fuse panel finally let go and started a fire. For a day now trucks have been going out of the gate with replacement trailers and food.

I don't know whether to feel sorry for these guys, or split a gut laughing; at the very least you gotta see the humour in it. Poor guys!

Saturday, 17 Dec., Knin Last night's do was quite nice. There was lots of food and plenty of people to talk to. The only problem was, our section was still on QRF, so there was no drinking for us. I hooked up with the ALO (air liaison officer) for Sector South. Both of us being helicopter pilots, we talked contracts to come over here to work. It was most informative, and he agreed to dig up some information for me.

This one guy stood out at the party. Let me paint a picture. He was black, about 5' 8", was VERY big around the middle, well dressed in a white cotton suit with an open necked shirt, and wore a large plantation style hat. Get the picture? I asked who he was, and was told that he was the top Kenyan officer on the ground. Talk about stereo typing, he looked like something out of a bad movie.

Today was for the most part uneventful. I slept in, had lunch, went for a workout, then Jim and I went to the Can-Do mess. In a replay of what happened the other night, the beer started to go down quickly. The boys coming off shift joined in and as usual we closed down the mess. I had a really good time.

We all left the mess in high spirits, and were singing, and talking quite loudly completely oblivious to our surroundings. That is, until we met George. He met us halfway between the mess and the barracks, and told us in no uncertain terms, that we were to keep our mouths shut! He was on duty at the gate and had heard us coming down the hill, and made a beeline for us. Seems we were making just a bit too much noise, and he didn't want us to get in shit.

It's amazing how poor the morale is here. We were drinking with one of the guys from 1 Platoon, and he was telling us that most of the boys in 1 Platoon are jealous of 3 Platoon. And would probably give their left nut to come over to us. That's sad. All I can say is that our entire section looks forward to the day we leave as soon as we get here.

Sunday, 18 Dec., Knin I slept in this morning till about 10:00, then I got up and went for a buffet style lunch. I must be getting better at drinking because I woke up with only a mild headache. I have to comment on the food here. IT'S THE SHITS!! Each time I go into the mess the smell makes me gag. It's a wonder I can eat anything at all for all the grease the food is floating in. My intake is always cut way back when I'm here, but my energy output remains the same. A hell of a way to diet!

I called Catherine again today. We talked for twenty minutes before getting cut off. It was nice. I also called Winnie, and I think I made her day. She has a leg problem, and is pretty much bedridden right now, so it felt nice to be able to cheer her up.

Tonight I'm on the gate. There really isn't much to do here but write letters and listen to the locals fire off their weapons in the night. Fortunately we have nine people in our section, which means there will be 24 hours off between shifts instead of just 12. My next shift isn't until the day after tomorrow. No doubt tomorrow will be a lazy day.

Another note about the Kenyans. While on duty, we are obligated to walk the wire every now and then, just to confirm that no one has broken in. Several weeks ago, while I was at the gate, I went on my usual rounds and found that some Kenyans had killed a couple of goats, and skinned them, leaving the skins on the wire by their barracks. Tonight while on patrol, I found that the skins hadn't been removed. Very different culture, or maybe they just forgot about them.

Monday, 19 Dec., Knin I cannot believe how pissed I am. This morning I went to bed right after shift, and woke up at noon, when John came into the room and started unpacking a box of gifts his parents sent him. As I lay there in a doze, I overheard John and Gaetz talking. It seems that 3 Platoon missed out on the best go of the tour by a hair. Orders had been passed down to prep all vehicles for escort duty—we're going to the Bihac Pocket as convoy escort. We were to leave this morning, but it got shut down at the highest possible levels, and given to OP CAVALERE—CANBAT 2.

All the work had been done (admittedly without our section being there to help) and at the last possible second we get yanked out. To top it off we are now pulling out of our two villages and will be redeployed to Rastivic some time in February. This means no booze, no fun, camp security, no fun, sandbag detail, and infinite opportunities to step on your dick. You want a definition of "the Rod" as in "we're getting the rod," now you have it. I feel like a racehorse that's been brought to the track and given sideline seats. I'd like to be philosophical about it all, and say that there will be other opportunities, but the way I feel right now, I really don't believe it.

Our villages are being handed over to UNCIVPOL, which should really cheer up the Croats.

The rest of the day was uneventful, but my back is starting to bug me again. I think it's because of the cot. Whoever the hell invented these damn things must be a masochist at heart.

Tuesday, 20 Dec., Knin I went on shift this morning with Robert and George. We were on duty at the FST which is no fun at all. When it's dry, it's simply boring. When it's wet, like it was today, it's not only boring, but it's cold, wet, muddy, and miserable. The ground up there is all clay. And one spends a fair amount of one's time trying to keep the buildup on one's boots to a minimum. After a day up there, you begin to understand what it must have been like to go through the First World War trenches.

Only two things of interest to report today. We were told that there will be one planeload (707) of mail per day for the next seven days, delivered to the troops over here. I've already received three letters from school kids, and the packages I mentioned earlier. We'll all have lots of writing to do.

The other thing involved the locals. All day, and most nights, we listen to the locals firing off rounds, for whatever reason. Tonight some wing nut decided to fire a

The Forward Surgical Team photographed from the helicopter pad overlooking the camp. Note the OP at top left

The Observation Post at the Forward Surgical Team

couple of bursts off directly overhead of our front gate. We had been treated to an unusual amount of firing in the city about half an hour earlier this evening, complete with tracers, but thought nothing of it. When these rounds went off, they couldn't have been fired from more than 100 yards away. John and I slipped outside to see what was going on, but there was nothing to see.

This is the capital city of an emerging republic. One would think that a certain amount of pride and the locals would exercise restraint, in an effort to receive the world recognition they so desperately want. Instead what I see, and hear, is a people who don't have any restraint, who claim that before the war the standard of living was better than Canada's—a statement that completely baffles me—and who live in bloody awful conditions, war or no.

As individuals, they're not bad people. But what can you say about a race, or group of people who willingly shell their own women and children to get the attention of CNN and who appear to have never heard of dental hygiene, and who refuse to leave a man alone because of an arbitrary label (Serb, Croat, Moslem).

Given the long and sordid history of Yugoslavia, and the fact that so many different groups have overrun it, one has to question the purity of any ethnic group. The concept of a "greater Serbia" cannot possibly work, short of every Serb moving to one area of Yugoslavia, the same way the Jews did in Israel. This is hard if not impossible for anyone who is tied to the land the way people here appear to be.

Moving is unworkable also because of all the intermarriages and lack of tolerance found throughout Yugoslavia. Can it be that these people will never find peace? It appears to the outsider that hatred here is a way of life, not unlike it is in Ireland.

How these people can still claim there is a difference between ethnic groups is quite beyond me. Until they come to grips with that one point, the UN will never be doing anything other than "fattening the calf for slaughter" (Mackenzie).

My final point is directed at our own government. It appears the government can't make up its mind between reaping the rewards nationally and internationally for sending us abroad and making it look like Canada actually gives a damn, and facing the flack back home if some of us come home in body bags. Peacekeeping, or more accurately peacemaking, is not a game, and when you play with live ammo the chances are pretty good Johnny is going to lose more than an eye. When faced with such indecision, and constantly changing mandates, can you blame the field commanders for changing the priority from mission to troop safety. I think not. In the end it makes a lot of us wonder WHAT THE FUCK ARE WE DOING HERE if we can't do our jobs the way we can and should!?!

Wednesday, 21 Dec., Knin My back is killing me, and it's because of these damn cots. Just to get out of bed and put on my socks is a major operation. Last night I went for a workout and did some leg raises. The pain started in the middle of my back and went down to the back of my knees. I wound up spending a lot of time just stretching. If this keeps up I'm going to Rastivic to have it looked at. For now I'll wait until I get to Bruska and spend a night or two on a real bed and keep up with my stretching, if that doesn't make a difference, I'll go to Rastivic for sure.

These past few days I've been in something of a funk. I'm pretty sure it's a combination of the weather, this place, being away from home, and putting up with the locals. I've been thinking a lot about Catherine lately, and right about now all I want to do is crawl under the covers and cuddle up with her. Instead we soldier on.

Shift starts at 1900 and runs till 0700 tomorrow morning. Tomorrow it's off to Bruska. I'll finish this entry when I come off shift.

What can I say about night shift on the highest point in the camp, with a howling wind, in the sleet, rain and snow, on the coldest night thus far? Well, how about that it is a fine military tradition dating back thousands of years and is one of the things infanteers all over the world have in common. It was shitty, cold, wet, and uncomfortable, and the warmest spot was in the fire barrel. Unfortunately the closest we could get to it was around the edge, which had the effect of leaving us smelling like we'd spent a week in a smokehouse.

The worst part was the boredom. There wasn't much to see because of the low cloud, snow and ever present watering eyes due to the smoke. I recall at one point thinking as I watched the snowflakes appear out of the darkness of the night, that if a Roman soldier were to walk out of the mist and ask to warm himself by the our fire, I wouldn't be at all surprised. The sense of history in this place is almost palatable at times. It's not much of a stretch to think that at some point in the distant past there probably were Roman soldiers on this very hill, standing by a fire trying to keep warm, and cursing their luck that they were chosen to stay up all night. It really brings home the point that the game of soldiering hasn't changed that much down through the years.

Tonight, George and I decided to break things up a bit by letting Robert and Jay sleep in the back of the carrier for three hours, then we hit the sack for the next three.

Truly one of the greatest pleasures experienced by any soldier has to be the hot shower at the end of the shift. Standing under the hot spray and feeling the blood return to my extremities let me know that some things are really worth waiting for. Hitting the sack after that was NOT a problem.

Thursday, 22 Dec., Knin-Bruska To bed at 08:00 and up at noon, surprisingly well rested. When I got back from lunch our replacements had arrived, and they brought news of a potential move to the Bihac. This got everyone's attention, and the speculation started to fly. There was a bit of time to kill so we talked aimlessly around the topic until it was time to go. My primary concern involved my leave. We're supposed to be leaving right after Christmas for a three-week tour, right about the time yours truly is on his way to England.

The trip to Bruska was made via Rodaljice. We stopped in long enough to drop off our laundry and Robert to do it for us, and for the remainder of us to sort out our kit and load up our ML. More tidbits of info were picked up regarding the Bihac. It seems each company will be spending about three weeks in the area, and Fuller and McConnell were both in to Rastivic getting orders. We'll likely get the lowdown tonight.

I'm getting an uneasy feeling about this.

Bruska Nothing has changed at Bruska, other than someone has brought us a pile of used pallets for us to use as floorboards in the tent to keep us up out of the mud. Things are a little slippery right now with all the snow (about 3 inches have fallen in the past day or two) and when it melts this place will become a mud pit. Labell for whatever reason has not delivered enough wood to keep the stove going, so Jay and myself patrolled down to Zoran's and asked if we could have enough to get us through the night. We came back with a wheelbarrow full of wood.

A few thoughts about Knin. It was an interesting place to visit, but I wouldn't want to live there, certainly 16 days was more than enough.

Before I left, I sent two letters to Andrew expressing my total disgust with the Canadian government and the people of Knin. I was angry when I wrote them and I know full well that it came across in the letters. My experiences with 1 Platoon, their officer, the Kenyans, and the mess hall, all left me with a bad taste in my mouth about the place. One of the things I shall never forget is the ever-present smell of burning coal used to heat the city. It brought back memories of Germany, when they used to do the same thing in the late sixties and early seventies. While my memories of Germany are very pleasant, they have been supplanted by this place, and next time, the smell of burning coal will evoke a very different memory for me. The place had such a gloom about it, it's hard to describe, perhaps because I choose to see the bad side. I don't know. We certainly had some good times there. The Can-Do mess is glad to see our section leave. We partied so hard there that they had to throw us out six nights in a row. There were some stimulating conversations on OP duty, but what will remain with me is the mind numbing boredom we were all forced to endure. I don't believe there is anyone in the world that has anything good to say about 12 hours on and 12 hours off guard duty.

Two final stories about the Kenyans. I had lunch with a Sergeant from the MP section. He was the investigating officer for the fire that took out the Kenyan HQ buildings a few days back. His report laid the blame squarely on the shoulders of the Kenyans. This of course meant that the Kenyan government would have to pay for all the damages instead of the UN. They were not pleased!

The other story involved one of the Kenyan OPs in the Zone of Separation. It seems the Kenyan soldiers were "co-habiting" with some Serb soldiers. The fact that the Serbs were in the Zone at all was a violation of the separation agreement, but to have them living in the same house as the UN troops that are supposed to keep them out of the zone, that is inexplicable.

The UNMO, an RCMP officer, who discovered the situation, walked in on a Kenyan private huddled in front of the fire, wearing a Serb trench coat. The Serb soldier who owned the coat, was found upstairs with a spotting scope scanning the Croatian side of the Zone. What an incredible sight THAT must have made.

No doubt I shall remember Knin as one of those things I'm glad I did, but wouldn't want to repeat.

Under the category of "humour where you find it," Jim got the weenie of the week award for using the ramp of the carrier as a bulldozer blade in Knin. He was at the MST at the time, and was supposed to take the carrier down to the front gate. So, he fired up the carrier and started to back up, completely forgetting to raise the ramp. He managed to dig a trench 100 yards long before someone finally caught up to him and made him stop. Embarrassment was the emotion of the hour as he laboured to dig the dirt out of the back of the carrier.

Situation Update—We're going to the Bihac! All personnel going on leave, except George, will go on leave as scheduled. The remainder will pack rucks and follow on kit in duffel bags. All carriers are to be outfitted with grousers, and all weapons are to be cleaned and test fired. More to follow.

Those of us going on leave are pissed about being left behind. The Bihac represents the only true test we've had, and likely will have on this tour, and fate has decreed that some of us are to be "away on vacation" while it's ongoing. We are not amused.

The platoon tasking as I understand it, is to do vehicle patrols and food convoy escort to supply the 400,000 people trapped in the city there.

Friday, 23 Dec., Bruska All morning we made preparations. I cleaned up the morning's dishes while the others worked on the carrier, then I helped John clean the .50. When that was done I made lunch for the guys. Everyone was either cleaning their weapons, or putting grousers on the tracks (grousers are like snow spikes for a tracked vehicle. They give extra traction on snow. The Bihac is located up in the mountains and apparently there is quite a bit of snow up there now). All morning I felt like an extra wheel, with nothing specific to do, so I busied myself by doing what I could to support the section while they worked on the kit.

The emotion I feel about not going on this tasking surprises me. Whenever I think about not going, it just wells up inside of me and I have to fight it back. It's hard to believe I feel so passionate about it all. These are my guys. My buddies, I should be there with them. Odd as that sounds, there it is.

The work completed, I slept the afternoon away, then got up to find that it had begun to snow pretty hard outside. With nothing much to do I cooked supper for everyone. Zoran, Denitza and their daughter Tatiana stopped by around 7:00. Their truck got stuck on the road and they walked through the blizzard to our camp. We brought them in, gave them something warm to drink, then went and towed their truck into the village with the carrier. When that was done, we asked them to stay for supper. Zoran produced a bottle of the best liqueur I've had in a long while. He explained that to make it, you had to start with a bushel of green walnuts (when they're soft) in a barrel. Add enough water to cover them, then add sugar. Put them in the sun for 30 or so days to ferment. Drain off the juice, and mix with aracia to taste, add sugar to sweeten. The result is quit surprising. Remarkably smooth and flavourful.

We've just received word over the radio that our Christmas party is on for tomorrow. That will be a good excuse for us to drink too much and forget about what's outside the schoolhouse walls. We'll see what happens.

Saturday, 24 Dec., Bruska/Rodaljice Christmas Eve and all is well. It's snowing outside and this morning I got mail.

We received another Ogroup this morning dealing with the Bihac. We're not to leave before January 1st for the area. As usual opinions are divided on whether we're going or not. Higher seems to think we are, lower are not so optimistic. As for myself, I'm hoping it gets delayed for two weeks. That way at least I'll get my vacation and then be able to join the platoon. It's a selfish notion, I know, but we have to aggressively pursue those things that we want in life, and right now I want a great vacation, followed by a real challenge.

Ultimately it will be up to the Canadian government whether we go or not, which doesn't inspire anyone here at all.

When we go back to Rodaljice we'll be packing our rucks and follow-on kit, before the drinking starts in earnest. With all the snow on the ground, no doubt there will be a good old-fashioned snowball fight. The mood around here is decidedly jovial. The anticipation of tonight's party and the nervous energy generated by the upcoming mission has put smiles on the faces of all. It's going to be a good night.

02:45

Tonight's party was a real blast. Mac cooked up a traditional Christmas dinner fit for a king. The OC and the CSM stopped by to help with the serving. There is a tradition in the army of the junior ranks trading uniforms with the command staff. Jay Palmer was the youngest man in the platoon (18?) so he was granted the honour of wearing the OC's shirt, and being the oldest fart in the platoon, I switched shirts with the CSM (which turned out to be WAY too small).

We all pitched in to clean up, then the serious drinking started. Wilcox couldn't seem to keep his pants up the whole evening. Every chance he got he dropped them, much to the amused dismay of all and sundry. We finally put off his need for exhibitionism to a British mannerism and left it at that.

Around 11:00 George sent us a garbled "Santa Rep" from Bruska. The radio room was located just outside the party/eating area, so everyone gathered outside the door to listen. As soon as the report finished, someone observed that George had used the incorrect format to report his sighting, stating that the proper format should have been an "overflight report" instead of a "situation report." This information was passed to George who responded by acknowledging his error, then resent his message using the appropriate format.

At midnight everyone gathered in the radio room again, and sang a single chorus of "We Wish You a Merry Christmas" (because we were too drunk and nobody could remember the second verse). It was broadcast over the airwaves to the two lonely sergeants and one officer left behind at Bruska who were covering for us. Proper radio procedure was, of course, observed.

The party finally broke up around 02:30. It was a genuinely good time. Mac got drunk and tried to pick a fight, which ended with him being escorted back to his ISO by two of the guys as directed by the warrant. But otherwise everyone had a lot of fun and a lot of beer.

By unanimous decision, "the Grinch that Stole Christmas" won out over the Grey Cup final, as the entertainment of choice during the meal. Now what does that tell you about the INFANTRY?

Sunday, Christmas Day, 25 Dec "Wasn't that a party . . . " (goes the song by the Irish Rovers). This place is as quiet as a church on a Monday morning.

> *It was the morning of Christmas*
> *and all through the camp,*
> *not a creature was stirring*
> *Not even the camp dog,*
> *Who was sleeping off an alcoholic haze.*

When I passed the poor little guy this morning, he was still passed out and snoring up a storm having ingested massive amounts of beer provided by last night's partygoers.

Ray showed up in my ISO at 08:35 and asked if I would co-drive him to Bruska to pick up a sergeant who had to go back to the main camp. We'd picked up a sergeant and an officer from HQ Company to fill in for us while we celebrated until we could return to our posts. S.O.P. requires a minimum of three people in an observation post by night, and only two by day. I had to get up to take a leak anyway, so I agreed. Besides aside from one or two stalwart individuals on duty, there really wasn't anyone else who could have done it, everyone else in camp was still asleep.

On the way out the door I grabbed my camera, and after dropping the sergeant off in the base, I asked Ray if we could make a detour on the way back to camp and swing by the cemetery we had visited on one of our patrols.

We rolled to a stop at the side of the road below the cemetery, the engine of the Iltis spluttering to a halt as Ray and I threw open the doors and stepped out into the cool air of Christmas morning. Rifles in hand, we skirted the perimeter wall that marked the boundary for the hallowed ground, and made our way up the small rise towards the gate. We came to a pile of rubble that had once been a bell tower outside the main entrance, then passed through what remained of the gate, where we came to a stop and just stared.

The sky was overcast and lowering. In the distance across the valley, the clouds came down to meet the tops of the blue green hills. On the ground lay the remains of two or three inches of snow that had fallen a few days before.

The air was heavy with the smell of moisture, yet everything was incredibly still and quiet, the kind of deafening quiet that you get when you are standing in the woods just after a snowstorm and nothing has had a chance to start moving yet, not even the air. It seemed appropriate for this holiest of mornings. And yet, despite the stillness you could hear everything. Ray was standing ten feet from me when he whispered an exclamation at what he saw, and the sound carried as if he were standing beside me talking aloud.

Spread out before us, lay the destruction wrought by a vengeful people.

We began to move by picking our way between the open graves and scattered human remains as we worked our way towards the center of the graveyard, conscious that someone might have paid a recent visit and left a booby trap behind, and that we could very easily add our own bodies to the remains of those scattered about us. There would be no one to call for help. Nobody knew we were here. We moved slowly.

As we walked I took several pictures to record for posterity what I was seeing. I needn't have bothered. What I saw there on that morning will remain with me the rest of my life.

Wordlessly we moved towards the middle of the graveyard and what had once been its most prominent landmark, the chapel. All that was left of the structure was its outline, all four walls were no higher than two feet above the foundation. It was obvious that someone had used powerful explosives to destroy it, because the rubble radiated out from the center of what was left of the building, and seemed to cover the entire area of the cemetery.

At one end of the chapel, to the left of what had once been its entrance, there was a hole in the floor that was filled with bones. The cover had been broken and pushed aside exposing the bones to the elements. There was no way of telling how many bodies had been piled on top of each other. As I knelt beside the opening, looking down at the collection of bones, I felt a cold shiver run up my back and all the hair on my neck stand on end. It was a nightmarish experience to look into the tangled mass of bones and see the empty eye sockets of a skull looking back at you.

We continued on, weaving our way through the rubble, looking in open graves and side stepping bones. All the time stunned at what we were seeing. Time seemed to stand still as we moved about, each of us on his own journey through the graveyard until Ray looked at his watch and made a sign that we should be getting back.

As with most important experiences in life, it is only in retrospect that the true magnitude, or significance of what you've just been through hits you. I had focused on

The First Half of the Tour

being a good observer, recording what I saw as we moved about through the graveyard and it is only now, as I write this, that I feel the full weight of what I was doing on Christmas morning 1994.

While I stood surrounded by the evidence of so much hatred, other than shaking my head in disbelief, I was not overly moved. Perhaps it was more than my senses could take in, I don't know, but as we drove away from the graveyard, I felt an overwhelming urge to apologize to the dead, both for what had been done to them, and for my adding to the insult by taking pictures. I wanted to say a prayer of some sort, but not really being experienced at that, I sort of composed it, jumbled in with snippets of distracted thoughts, and left it unsaid.

We had been in the area for only half an hour or so, and as we wandered around pointing to things we found, neither of us had said a word. What could you say? What kind of logic drives a man to kill someone out of hatred, then continue on to that person's most sacred of places and commit this kind of crime? The thinking that would lead someone to commit this level of desecration was utterly alien to both of us. Perhaps that's a good thing.

When we climbed back into the Iltis and drove off towards camp, we didn't look at each other, we didn't comment on what we'd seen, and we haven't mentioned it since, but it was clear we'd both been moved in ways we couldn't express.

As I sit here in my ISO trailer, I am reminded of a poem by William Blake that seems to sum up my feelings of the morning's experience:

> *Oh for a voice like thunder, and a tongue to drown the voice of war,*
> *When the soul is driven to madness, who can stand?*
> *When the souls of the oppressed fight in the troubled air that rages,*
> *Who can stand?*
> *When the whirlwind of fury comes from the throne of God,*
> *When the frowns of his countenance drive the nations together,*
> *Who can stand?*
> *When Sin claps his broad wings over the battle,*
> *and sails rejoicing in the flood of death,*
> *When the souls are torn to everlasting fire, and fiends of Hell rejoice upon the strain,*
> *Oh who can stand?*
> *Oh who has caused this?*
> *Oh who can answer at the throne of God?*
> *The Kings and the Nobles of the land have done it,*
> *Hear it not Heaven, thy ministers have done it!*

Once out of the area our mood lightened, and we came back to camp to have a steak and egg breakfast that Mac had laid on for everyone. By 1300, people were still crawling out of the sack, so I went with Ray again to Bruska to pick up the Serb kids and parents for the Christmas party we'd laid on for them.

For some reason I didn't much feel like sticking around for it. Partly I think because I'd developed a splitting headache from the Serb cigarettes (which stank

"The sky was overcast and lowering. In the distance across the valley, the clouds came down to meet the tops of the blue-green hills. Spread out before us lay the destruction wrought by a vengeful people"

"While I stood surrounded by the evidence of so much hatred, other than shaking my head in disbelief, I was not overly moved. Perhaps it was more than my senses could take in . . . as we drove away from the graveyard, I felt an overwhelming urge to apologize to the dead, both for what had been done to them and for my adding to the insult by taking pictures"

like burning sheep shit), but mostly because of what I'd witnessed this morning. It somehow seemed hypocritical to be with these people: whether they were guilty or not of any crimes it was what they represented that turned me off. So I went back to my trailer and packed my kit in preparation to return to Bruska, then lay down for a bit.

We returned to Bruska in fine form, and sat down for a while to watch a movie and pig out on Christmas sweets. Zoran wanted to speak to George, so Jim, Robert and myself accompanied him on patrol. Jim and I went to Gordana and Svetoe's, and had something to eat. George and Robert came by after their talk with Zoran. It seems that Zoran wanted food for a trip to Belgrade. He's going there to pick up a passport for his family. Gutsy move considering he's in the Serb army (all Serb males are considered to be in the army I understand) and if he leaves the country it's tantamount to desertion.

Since we've arrived he's surreptitiously asked questions about emigrating to Canada, and several times asked to borrow 10,000 DM to get his family out. It was starting to get on our nerves, and had become something of a standing joke with us (the Serbs are at the door and they want something else . . .). But now that he's put his money where his mouth is, I am gaining a small amount of respect for him. I have the time of day for any man who is willing to risk life and limb to improve the lot of his family.

During the Christmas party at Rodaljice, the CO and RSM stopped by for a visit and to update the warrant and Mr. McConnell on the Bihac move. Parliament will not be sitting until 15 Jan to debate sending us in, add a week or two to sort things out, and it looks like around the end of Jan we'll be going (if we go at all). Should this happen, we'll be there for the rest of the tour. If not, in mid to end Feb, our platoon will pack up and head to Rastivic.

I am greatly relieved now that there is a real chance of joining my platoon if we go. I don't have any qualms about going into that area at all. I don't expect it will be much different from what we're doing now on patrol, just more intense. The only thing stopping us now is Parliament, and God only knows what they'll do. I guess it's just back to the wait and see game.

Monday, 26 Dec., Rodaljice A fine sunny day today. The wind is calm and there's nary a cloud in the sky. I was up at 6:30 for shift until 8:00 but decided to let Jay, who was to replace me, sleep an extra hour, electing instead to finish some journal entries.

Just before noon the section was asked for volunteers to fill in for Scarth and Ingersol from 1 Section, who were both down with the flu. Jay and I jumped at the chance because it allowed us to get back to Rodaljice a couple of days early and sort out our kit for the Bihac—and our upcoming leave—in a relatively uncrowded ISO trailer.

A quick trip to Rastivic had been laid on for some of the guys who wanted to use the phone. I elected to go but not to use the phone. Instead I went to the pay office and confirmed my pay was ready and in order. I'm bringing to England 450 DM, and $2250 US in travelers' checks. I hope to not spend it all, but it's there if we need it.

Our visit to Rastivic was short but productive, and we arrived back at Rodaljice with time enough for Jay and I to make up our beds, sort ourselves out a little and grab a quick bite to eat before going on shift at the gate for six hours.

This was the first time Jay and I had been thrown together for shift work, and I must say that it was a very pleasant experience. We talked for the whole six hours about our wives (he's 19 and has been married 7 months); the army, life; and his little problem (Jay was replacing me on shift at 0200 one morning, and quietly explained that he had a problem. Seems he picked up a working girl in Budapest, and now three days later, it appears he contracted something. The poor guy was at his wits end as to what to do. I calmed him down and made arrangements with the warrant to have him taken care of. The next morning he was into the hospital and left with a full course of antibiotics).

He told me how grateful he was that I had listened and helped him without passing judgment. Frankly I was just glad he thought he could trust me enough to take me into his confidence.

The real revelation of the night was that we both felt both the section and the platoon had passed a kind of emotional speed bump.

There's a certain synergy about the section now that is hard to put into words. For myself I can say that I feel like I've adapted to the battalion environment well, but in truth it's tough to make the transition from civilian to military life.

At the Christmas party, Ted pulled me aside and told me that both he and George greatly appreciate the "extra leadership" I provided for the section, which kind of surprised me at the time, because he was sober when he said it. In spite of our initial problems, Ted and I seem to have developed some common ground between us and we even verbally gang up on others sometimes. Surprising, but nice.

Jay said he felt we were a family—I look at it more as a marriage. For better or worse, we're stuck together, and we're making the best of it. We each know the others weaknesses and strengths and are protective of each other. Love is blind they say, but friendship merely closes its eyes. I think the latter has begun to take place between all of us.

Tuesday, 27 Dec., Rodaljice Last night Jay and I talked of many things, one of which I had forgotten about until today. It involved Jay and Robert and the first day we arrived at Knin. Both had been put on duty at the heliport. The shift had gone slowly for them, and they were eager to get out of there, and back to the shack. It was dark out, and while they were waiting for their replacements, they were privileged to overhear two Danish policemen talking as they returned to their rooms after supper. The first Dane seemed to be explaining the lay of the land to the second, who clearly was new to the area.

"Before," said the first guy "when the Kenyans were doing security for the camp, nobody felt comfortable. There were break-ins every night, and people simply didn't feel protected. When the Jordanians came, things improved a little. Then the Canadians came, and things really changed. They took charge, and really improved everything. They built all the bunkers you see around here and began patrolling the perimeter. These guys are really professional, and everyone now feels very safe. Our only regret is that they will be leaving soon, because everyone wishes they would stay."

I've gone on at length in the past, about how I and others feel about our work here, but it is always nice to know that other people have faith in the way we do things. It's a real boost to morale and the ego, to know other countries hold us in high regard.

Today's main activity was the arrival of 1 Platoon from Knin on their way to Karin Slana. They stopped into our position for about twenty minutes to have a pee break, and let their hearing return somewhat before finishing the last leg of the journey. In spite of their denial, it was clear to me anyway, that they were genuinely pleased to get out of Knin. Everyone wore smiles and they were eager to start the Christmas party that had been laid on for them. Undoubtedly it will be as big a blowout as ours was.

Here's something I should have told you about, but didn't. On our last visit to Knin, we found out that the 1 Platoon commander did something that not everyone agrees with. You will recall that the day before our first visit, two Serbs were caught trying to sneak into the camp by crawling through the wire. Lt Babcock has recommended the two sentries who caught them for the CLFCC (Commander Land Forces Command Commendation). What stumps us is why someone would be recommended for a commendation for doing his job. Rushing a machine gun position we understand, but patrolling along the wire and catching intruders having fun? Give me a break. One theory is that it's an attempt to improve 1 Platoon's morale. It may be true, who knows?

In other news, Carter (the former US president) has negotiated a cease-fire agreement for the Bihac pocket, which appears to be holding. While this may be good news for the residents of the Bihac, the pessimist in me thinks the Serbs are probably using it as an excuse to conserve ammunition and improve their supplies. Beside, I don't know how much of a victory Carter can claim, things had pretty much ground to a halt because of the weather. The Serbs, if nothing else, are a practical people.

Our advanced recce party will leave for the area tomorrow to scope out the places where we can set up our camps. We'll be living in modular tents and eating hard rations. We've been told if we go it will be for the rest of the tour. Talk about a change in mandate. All my kit is packed and ready to go.

Wednesday, 28 Dec., Rodaljice Just a wakie now! We're down to counting hours now before we leave. It feels great! Everyone who's going (there are nine of us) is walking around with an extra bounce in his step, and a smile on his face. It shows in other ways too, like Ray's driving. He asked me to be his co-driver as he ran some errands. This was fine by me so off we went. In all my military career, I have never had the privilege of really driving in a two and a half ton MLVW. It was a wild experience and a shit load of fun. We took the back route to Karin Slana, our first stop, and there were times on the winding and pock-marked dirt road, that I KNOW all six wheels weren't on the ground. Particularly when we crested some of the hills. In the corners, it was more common than not, that only three wheels were on the ground. With no seat belts to keep us in place, it was a good thing everything else was bolted down, otherwise it would have ended up on the road somewhere. As it was I had to have one foot braced on the dashboard, and I hung on to the windows, door, and parts of the roof to keep myself from being tossed around. It was more fun than a roller coaster. Ray later admitted he had a latent desire to drive a big support truck in the Baja 12000 rally run. Lord knows he's training hard for it.

Our errands were quickly completed and we paused for lunch at Karin. The CSM found me and inquired if I was going to get my hair cut before I left. Missing the hint, I told him I didn't think I had the time to get one. He then strongly suggested that if I didn't, I would be doing 21 extras upon my return. Fortunately one of the guys in our camp has a set of clippers, otherwise I'd be reduced to looking for a Boy Scout with a sharp pocketknife.

Briggs is on his way over—that'll make four from our Regiment. I got the word today that he will be attached to our HQ group as a driver. Good for him I say. He has a weight problem and had all kinds of trouble with the PT, which is why he was left behind on standby. He always had a good attitude about things, and I feel he deserves a break.

Ray has received a promotion of sorts. He's been moved to Coy CQ. He'll stay there for a year, then get his Sergeant's. It's been a long time coming, and he deserves it.

Drinking among those going on leave, as you might imagine, has reached an all time high. I abstained for the most part (that's my story) choosing instead to remain sober to avoid a hangover during tomorrow's trip.

Anticipation is peaking.

Thursday, 29 Dec., The long ride out Can you believe it? Eight guys from Charles Company were charged for fighting during the Christmas party last night. We're told one guy, for no apparent reason, walked up behind one of the Reservist and pounded him in the back of the head. The Reservists fought back—of course—and all hell broke loose. This would not have been a big problem, but for the fact that the RSM and CO were visiting at the time. Guess who just bought themselves a ride to the crowbar hotel without passing GO, or collecting $200?

Speaking of jail, you will recall the warrant who got into a fight before Christmas? Rumor has it he too is on his way to jail—in Edmonton. Smart money says it will be as a corporal. Yes folks, the silly season is truly upon us.

Before I tell you about the trip out, I want to pause to comment upon the military travel arrangements. This has to be the only organization that regularly subjects its members to endurance tests to get them to various places in the world. The amount of waiting around we do is enough to break any seasoned traveler, and the conditions under which we travel sometimes, would never be tolerated by anyone outside the military. There really is no life like it. But much to their credit, the military does ensure you get where you are going, even if you have to ride in the back of a truck to do it.

Leg One—We're off! Up at 0700 to shit, shave, shower, and shampoo, and do the final pack. With everything put away we loaded up in the back of the ML for the first leg of the journey which took us to Karin Slana. As we left the compound Jack, the camp dog, followed us down the road, so we stopped and put him in the back with us. With only two weight lifting benches and our kit to sit on, there wasn't much floor space for the little guy to sit, but we managed. The little guy had never ridden in the back of a truck before, and it became quickly evident he was developing a case of motion sickness. He started to slobber all over the place and kept trying to bury his head in Mac's lap. We all watched our kit, and tried to figure out which direction the flow would go if the little guy lost his breakfast.

As it happened, Jack survived the trip to Karin Slana, with little more than a puddle of drool between his front paws, much to our relief.

At Karin Slana, the only thing we had to do was pick up our leave passes, then load up to go to Rastivic. We arrived at 9:35 or so, but stood around until 10:30 before they handed out the passes. To help pass the time, we took up a collection for a 100/100 draw (winner takes all), and Ray, the lucky bugger, won 100 DM for the trip out.

The military mind is a clever and witty thing at times, and here's a good example. One of the warrants looked at his watch and figured out that we had ten minutes before we had to form up, so he said, "OK everyone, ten minute coffee break." Whereupon someone quietly pointed out that to be on time is to arrive five minutes early, ergo we only had a five-minute coffee break. It was then pointed out that one must always arrive fifteen minutes early for orders so we can mark up our maps, therefore we should have arrived five minutes ago with coffee in hand. Smiles all around. The warrant just shook his head and walked away.

Do we need to get out of here or what?

Leg Two—Karin Slana to Rastivic. This is a short trip taking about fifteen minutes by ML. Everyone loaded up including Jack, and down the road we went followed by a column of dust. As soon as we started moving Jack started to get woozy, and everyone kept a close eye on their kit. We thought he was going to make it, when 100 metres short of our final stop, breakfast made a reappearance on the scene. Thankfully the quantity was small, and confined to a tiny area away from the kit near the tailgate. As a safety precaution we moved some of the kit around for fear the ML's motion might cause a migration of the contents into the "danger close" zone around the kit.

As you can imagine, laughter and black humour about the contents of Jack's breakfast accompanied its appearance on the scene. Fortunately the ML is EXTREMELY well ventilated, so smell was not a problem. When we stopped, everyone grabbed their kit and ran in an attempt to get out of sight before someone got assigned the task of cleaning up the mess. I was nearest the back so I got out first, kit in hand, and disappeared. Something to be said for age and experience.

The military has a fixation with arriving early to avoid complications. Our arrival at 1100 on the ground was in keeping with this as our busses were not due to arrive until 1330. When you are motivated (as we all were) one tends to do things with dispatch and efficiency, so when they said form up here, and lay your kit out there, it was done in record time, which resulted in us standing around wondering what to do next.

It was getting on to 1130 when they decided to give us a briefing which stressed the alcohol policy. In no uncertain terms, drinking was forbidden on the buses. We were then given our bus numbers and cut free for lunch, 1300 being the next timing. It took forever to arrive, particularly when we were forced to eat cool watery spaghetti with greasy meat sauce and cold garlic bread. Oh well, this is the army, and real food is just 24 hours away.

At 1300 we gathered by our kit as were told, but nothing happened. This is normal in the army and one comes to expect it. By 1330 people were getting antsy. Word finally filtered down that the buses were delayed an hour and wouldn't be in until 1430. This didn't bother us too much as we'd almost expected a delay of some sort.

When the buses finally did arrive, the CSM stood up and said "right lads, give the boys on the buses a chance to get their kit off and clear the area." So, when the word was given to mount up. we all but ran to our assigned buses and dutifully waited in line before stowing our kit and climbing aboard.

Trust me when I tell you that the loading and boarding were done in record time. But this didn't help matters as we sat until 1500 before we left.

Leg Three—Rastivic to Sibenic. An audible sigh of relief could be heard from all as the buses began to move. The journey out was on in earnest, and we were finally on our way home.

I don't remember much about the trip other than the exercise of crossing the Zone. It's kind of like a ritual. We all sit on the bus with our flack vest on, weapons between our legs, and helmets under our seats. When we approach the border, we stop about 100 m short, pause to remove ball caps and put on helmets, load and move weapons to a more accessible position, then we move on. No one says anything and I've noticed that we all became very quiet during the short trip through the Zone from one side to the other. Upon arriving on the other side, everyone lets out their breath, removes their helmet and flack vest, stows the weapons, and carries on.

The first time through we were all in awe of the situation, and never said much during the whole trip. This time we were more relaxed but then, nobody missed a thing either. The next couple of hours to Sibenic were nothing special and I slept for a part of the trip.

One thing I did notice, was that on the Croatian side, things were obviously better. Pleasure boats were in the harbors, houses were in excellent repair, and greenhouses were full of green vegetation. The war clearly had little effect here.

Upon arrival in Sibenic, we debused and were told to change into civilian dress in a maintenance hanger. There was, however, only enough room for about fifty people inside, what with all the tools and parts strewn about. So 100 of us were left to stand under the stars and strip to our undies. What a picture that must have made.

Leg Four—Sibenic to Split. This was a short trip of a couple of hours. I slept for part of it, so I didn't see much. The big scare upon arrival was the booze. I had three bottles and wasn't the only one to be over the limit—we were permitted only two. The thought of having to pay duty had people talking, until we realized that while in Europe, movement between countries is unrestricted and not a problem, it's only upon return to Canada that one must pay the extra. Some of us were greatly relieved to hear that. Customs wasn't a problem, as we simply showed our passports and boat tickets and carried on.

Ray and I were supposed to get a room together, but the bugger hooked up with George and I was left on my own to find a roommate. In the end Ryerson and I (my roommate from Pet) hooked up and wound up in the hold of the ship. Small comfort if the boat rolls over, but not if it goes straight down (I have this thing about being on a boat in the open ocean – gives me the willies just thinking about it).

Leg Five—Split to Ancona, Italy. We'd been told to gather in the bar at the front of the boat to collect our airplane tickets, after we'd found our rooms and stowed our kit. There should be a rule about bars and infanteers. As soon as we got there, everyone forgot about the tickets and formed a line at the bar. George, two of his friends, Jim, Jay, Ray, and myself, got into a game of liar's dice. This lasted several hours as the beer flowed freely. I collected my tickets some time during the game but I'm not exactly sure what time it was. Few of us were familiar with the exchange rate for the Lira and DM, so as the night progressed, people kept eyeing the bartenders suspiciously feeling that they were getting the short end of the stick when money changed hands. I'm sure things would have gotten out of hand some time in the wee hours, if we hadn't drunk the bar dry some time around 1:00. Nonetheless, I'm pretty certain the bartenders took home more than a pocket full of change on this trip.

Jim and I decided to explore the ship and wound up getting the boot from the crew quarters after a wrong turn. We finally made our way onto the aft deck, and I had my breath taken away by the sight of the stars and the foam from the wake of the ship. I'd always thought I'd be scared shitless to be on a ship out of the sight of land, and I'll admit the adrenaline was running there for a while, but for the most part I didn't feel too bad. It's quite an experience to be on the open ocean at night. The sight and sound of the sea is quite intoxicating, not that I needed any help with intoxication at the time.

It was a relief to finally be out of the country and back into civilian clothing. They feel softer somehow. I could feel the tension draining away from me and I felt like a real human being again, back in my own element.

I finally stumbled into my room sometime around 1:30 AM.

Leg Six—Ancona to Rome. In keeping with fine military tradition, 0600 A.M. was given as our report time on deck. I was expecting to get up around 5:30, dress, wash quickly, then report on deck with time to spare. Ryerson had other ideas.

At 5:00 o'clock sharp, his bloody alarm clock went off, scaring the holy bejesus out of me. I sat bolt upright and because I was on the top bunk in a small room, promptly whacked my head on the ceiling. A suitable exclamation was muttered as I sagged back down to the mattress. The bed being too short for me, I soundly thumped the back of my head against the headboard of the bunk. Another exclamation was uttered and I rolled over to the right. In the dark I had not noticed how close to the wall I was, so when I rolled, my face made immediate contact with the wall, which had the effect of redirecting my nose towards my left ear.

At this point, I thought it prudent to pause and gain my bearings. The pain on the surface of my scalp was compounded by the pain on the inside of the scalp due to last night's festivities, and the fact that I was totally dehydrated. Movement was both slow and painful to put it mildly.

We gathered on deck, turned in our room keys, and collected our passports, then sat and waited. The boat had not yet docked, in fact, it was still an hour out of port. Ya gotta love that military timing thing.

I am grateful for one thing. Our army, while subjecting us to endurance tests from time to time, does in fact look after us quite well. Last night we came across another contingent of UN soldiers who were forced to sleep in deck chairs on one of the back decks because no one in their organization had booked rooms on the ship for them. They were then left standing on the hot dock, as we drove off in air-conditioned buses.

The trip to Rome was a trip of scenic diversity. In Ancona where we docked, the Canadian Army had dug in during the Second World War and spent the winter there before advancing further north. Some of the bloodiest fighting of the Italian campaign took place in these hills, and driving through the countryside one could develop a real quick appreciation for the hardships our boys faced nearly fifty years ago.

We started on the coast and began to climb up into the mountains, then down the other side to the coast again. Looking out the window, Italy struck me as a place that was well looked after. Lots of farming and industry, quite different form Yugoslavia, more soil for one thing, and olive groves everywhere. I'm sure it would be quite beautiful if it weren't the middle of winter, and so wet and dreary.

We arrived at the Rome airport an hour late, so when I checked in, the checking agent told me to run because my flight was boarding.

As luck would have it, the gate I needed was at the other end of the airport, and I was forced to cut to the front of the customs line, then run the length of the airport with two heavy bags. Like something out of a movie, about 100 metres from my gate, I zigged when I should have zagged, and made contact with a slow moving passenger. My folder containing traveler's checks, passport, leave pass, and damn near everything that was of any importance went sailing off into mid air. It took precious minutes to collect everything and get on the move again.

How nice of British Airways to wait for me! I was the last one on and no sooner had I taken my seat than the airplane started to taxi. I could go on at this point, but suffice it to say the trip to London felt very short, and was made all the shorter through anticipation. There is no doubt this will be a trip to remember.

Cat and I at Heathrow Airport. If a photo is worth a thousand words . . . 'nuff said

THE SECOND HALF OF THE TOUR PART FOUR

Thursday, 19 Jan. 1995 Planes, trains, and automobiles was the theme for the return trip from England to Yugoslavia. If you reversed the out-bound trip, you get a fair idea of what we had to go through to get back. A noticeable difference, however, was the level of talking that went on. On the trip out, nobody would shut up. On the way back, nobody would say anything.

On the ferry, the bar was nearly empty by 10:30. The five of us—Ray, Jay, Jim, George, and myself—stayed up past midnight playing liar's dice. There was little else to do, and we were all in a good mood, if somewhat more low key than when we left.

On the bus the following morning, where previously everyone had been jovial, I looked up to find the whole bus had gone to sleep. When we changed into uniform at Sibenik, it too was done quietly, and in the gentle rain, as there was still not enough room for everyone to change under the shelter. When we slowed to make the final turn to go up the hill into Rastivic off the main highway, someone uttered a deadpan "welcome home," which was responded to with an equally deadpan, and dejected "yee haw." There can be nothing worse for your morale than to come home to a sea of mud on an overcast, wet, cold, and rainy day. What a way to start the second half of the tour.

I knew shortly after I got off the bus, that I wasn't going to the Bihac. A look across a sea of mud revealed that my ISO trailer, with my kit in it, was sitting amongst all the other 3 Platoon trailers that had been moved two at a time on a flatbed from Rodaljice. One of the guys from the platoon was passing as I was collecting my kit from under the bus, and told me that the tasking had been "shit-canned" right after we left on leave. So much for the grand adventure!

The bases at Rodaljice and Donja Bruska don't exist any more. The routine has changed again. We're doing standing patrols from the carriers in each location, on a 12 on, 12 off, basis and four men in each location. That leaves one section on QRF in Rastivic, and the other section patrolling.

Trying to get into my trailer proved to be something of an adventure. After an hour of searching for a non-existent key, I found a technician with a hammer and crowbar, and gained access in short order, at the expense of being able to close and lock the door. A new door is in the works, but in the meantime, we've rigged a bungee cord to hold the door closed.

They've shuffled us around a bit as well. Where before we were four to a trailer, we're now three and we're not all from the same section. It's not a bad idea really. At least I won't get stuck looking at the same faces for the entire tour.

They moved Robert and Jay out, and Virk in. I see he's made himself at home already. The walls at his end of the trailer are plastered with pictures of his newborn, and his wife.

John is still in with me. He's been my bunkmate from the beginning of the tour, and I have no problem with that. We get along well, and can talk about most things easily.

After a little cleaning, this will be home for the next three months

After I got into the trailer and dumped my kit, Henry came by and gave me two hours to reorganize myself for my 12-hour shift at Rodaljice, so that kept me busy till supper.

Lots happened while I was on leave, as is wont to happen. Here's what I've heard so far:

Just after New Year's Day, Serbs shot up two of our boys from Charles Company pretty badly after they ran a roadblock. They had been told by higher up not to stop for any Serb checkpoints, as these were strictly illegal. The two had just gone out to run an errand, when they came across, then drove through a Serb roadblock. I'm told they heard the Serb weapons being cocked as they drove past so they tromped on it. The driver was saved from becoming a paraplegic when the radio slowed a bullet enough to only do minor damage to his lower back. He did however get hit in the right shoulder, and had to drive and shift the Iltis using his left arm only. His passenger, a reservist from the 48th Highlanders, got the worst of it, taking several rounds to the head and upper body. In all, the driver had to drive 16 km on only

The remains of the ILTIS, shot up just after New Years'. There are 59 bullet holes in the back. It is now on display at the Canadian War Museum as part of the Peacekeepers exhibit

two good tires. Both right side tires had been shot out and were down to the rims. Both are back in Canada and are recovering.

The best comment I've heard about the bravery demonstrated by the driver came from the commander of BRITBAT. Originally directed at his troops for bravery in the face of fire, it applies here. "Let no man tell me that the youth of today are not as brave as the youth of the past." Enough said.

A Serb in Rodaljice stoned an old Croatian lady. She apparently caught him stealing her firewood, and when she tried to stop him he started throwing a few of the inexhaustible supply of rocks at her. She took a couple of direct hits and was pretty bruised, but otherwise she's fine. The local Croatians were understandably upset, and one or two of them came into the now abandoned schoolhouse for protection. There simply has to be some kind of social commentary on a stoning in this day and age, but I'm just too tired to make it.

Here's something on the Q.T. I found out that Sgt MacKinnon and a few boys from his section celebrated quite a bit on New Year's Eve. Apparently they went down to Sveto and Gordanna's and took an ammo can of 5.56 rounds with them. Most of the section, Sveto and his dad gathered on a balcony and proceeded to fire off the spare ammo. Gordanna's father, a WWII vet, produced an old German submachine gun and they all took turns target plinking.

I have no idea who else knows about this, but it strikes me that if higher found out about it, the good Sergeant would find himself in the Crowbar Motel in one stink of a hurry. Why would anyone want to take that kind of chance with their career?

Word is that the Airborne is to replace us. The Vandoos are needed somewhere else because they speak French. The rumour goes on that their recce has been delayed and possibly cancelled because of the Croatians' demand to have the UN cleared out. It's looking more and more like we're to be the last mission and we'll be here until June.

The 20th of January is the end of the cease-fire between Croatia and Krajina. There's lots of vehicle traffic all around and we're just waiting to see if the bullets will start flying. Definitely more to follow on this.

You know you're good at your job when the Serbs don't want us to go to the Bihac because we're too professional. Recall that the Canadians are the only Battalion over here not to engage in the black market (or at least not to get caught). We're told that the Serbs are worried that the local economy will fall apart if we go. Our friendly neighbourhood Kenyans are in there now, which is probably why the black market is doing so well.

I received my block leave dates today. They're from 5 April to 1 May. They've extended our contracts until 1 June to clear up some Battalion stuff. What stuff they're talking about remains a mystery.

Sgt William Goldsmith left for home early. He was scheduled to do his 6B, or warrant's course, but his wife was involved in an accident. She apparently was driving along a road when a guy stepped out from behind a car, and she ran smack into him, killing him instantly. She was quite broken up about it so he was granted compassionate leave and allowed to go home early and sort things out before he starts his course. A good friend of George from the Airborne, Sgt Gray, is replacing him.

That's just the short list of things that happened while I was away. I was thankfully absent from the teardown of Bruska and Rodaljice. As well, I missed the arguments about surplus food with the local Serb women. All I know for sure is that for the next two weeks I'm doing 12 on, 12 off until we start patrolling full-time.

It's either the weather or the shock of coming back, but right now I do not care much for this place.

Friday, 20 Jan., Rastivic Last night was pretty quiet. It was eerie to come back to a place you called home, only to find it totally abandoned. Walking into the schoolhouse, my footsteps echoed through the empty building. Where before it was full of life, now there was only silence, the paintings on the wall a mute testament to the good times that were had here only a few short weeks ago. The compound too, seemed strangely silent. Once filled with trailers, vehicles, and people milling about, all that was left was a cold concrete slab and the barbed wire that defined the compound.

It was dark when we arrived so we set up a quick shift list and hit the hay. The night came and went, and each of us (Ted, Jim, Jay and myself) pulled two one-hour shifts listening to the radio, and keeping a general eye out.

Our replacements showed up at 0600 and we went back to Rastivic for breakfast and more rack. In spite of the pseudo-sleep of last night, I find that I'm still tired from all the travel.

Today's Ogroup was pretty interesting. The Airborne replacements have been cancelled. The speculation is that we're going to be here for an extra three months. It's not official yet, so we can't tell anyone at home anything about it, but it doesn't look promising. Rumours within the platoon run rampant.

One of our OPs took some fire last night, but didn't return fire. They say they were between the two groups doing the shooting, which is why they didn't return fire. How do you miss seeing an OP that's lit up like a Christmas tree at night, and claim to be shooting at someone else? Sounds a bit odd, doesn't it?

Bihac Pocket is tense so basically no change in situation.

John tells me that on the 6th of Jan (Serb Christmas Eve—Orthodox Christian), 157 explosions were recorded around Rodaljice. They appeared to be artillery rounds by the sound and weight of the explosions. Several thousand small arms tracers lighting up the sky also accompanied them. The Serbs can afford to waste that much ammo? Good fire discipline boys.

These past few days have seen me in an emotional quandary. I feel a strong need to be with Catherine, yet am honour bound to complete my contract, and not let her condition affect my performance for fear of endangering someone. The strain of keeping my emotions in check has worn me down to the point that I sometimes just want to close the door of my ISO and hide in isolation from the world. But even that is denied to me until they fix the bloody door.

As with all things, some days are better than others, but I've noticed that my moods seem to be tied to the weather. When it rains, I feel like hell, and when it's sunny, I feel fine. Sitting in an OP for 12 hours is anything but interesting if you don't have a book, mostly because no one wants to talk about anything. And because at this point in the tour, the blush has worn off, and nobody gives a damn anymore. They just want to do their time and go home. I've noticed this kind of attitude before. It's the beginning of phase three of a three-phase degeneration in one's attitude. You go from let's go over there and help those people to holy shit, it's us vs them, to it's just me against the world now. Everyone is different in the way they deal with things, and it'll take them a different amount of time to go through the phases, but we all do it.

Right now I'm in us vs them mode, as are most of the guys. Nic is the obvious exception. He seems to be in a perpetual me against the world, no matter where he is. Having him along with us always seems to put a damper on things.

Making the shift back to the military way of thinking after living with civilians for three weeks is hard on all of us; both for the guys coming back, and for those who have to put up with you when you get back. We all go through it, and there seems to be an unspoken acknowledgement of the fact, and a tolerance for the people returning. I'm just having trouble getting my mind back into army mode again, for thoughts of Cat.

For now, I shall treat myself with the universal cure to life's many ailments: a medicine called sleep.

Saturday, 21 Jan., Bruska I have to be more careful around Ted. Last night at Bruska I made one suggestion too many, and he started to "come aboard me." He was in a crabby mood anyway, and I should have seen it coming. It wasn't a pleasant exchange, and it damn near ended in a fistfight. I really have to get back into an army frame of mind.

The evening was uneventful, and I spent the night in the track on one of the benches. I woke up a little stiff but otherwise none the worse for wear.

This morning just after we'd pulled into our lines there was an incident that woke us all up. The regular routine is that we pull in, park the vehicles, make our way to the unload bay where we all unload our personal weapons and then trundle off to our trailers. We'd completed the unloading and were on our way to our trailers, when we heard a machine gun burst go off immediately to our right. Seems 3 Section had been preparing to leave on patrol, when Peters handed his C-9 up to Newson so he could climb into the vehicle unencumbered by the gun. Newson had grabbed the weapon by the pistol grip and pulled the trigger and fired off a burst of five or six rounds before letting go. It caught everyone off guard.

There are a couple of things you need to know here. First, that to load a weapon, you insert a magazine, or in the case of a machine gun, lay in a belt of ammunition. The weapon will not fire if you pull the trigger. To make a weapon ready to fire, you need to cock the action, then the only thing that is stopping it from firing is the safety catch. As a policy, we always leave the compounds with loaded weapons, but never with our weapons at the ready, unless it's been deemed that there is imminent danger, and the order has been given to ready weapons. When we are inside our compounds, we always have our weapons unloaded. The first thing we do is to load when we leave, and unload when we enter a compound.

I'm telling you this because Peters had loaded, then readied his machine gun, and not applied the safety. There had been no call to do so. So when Newson squeezed the trigger, the weapon fired. And everyone shit himself or herself. Our returning patrol was caught out in the open and we were in the direct line of fire. What saved us was the fact that the barrel of the C-9 just happened to be pointing at the ground at the time. Had it been raised another 20 or so degrees, the rounds would have gone straight through the shitter ISO, and into my trailer.

When the rounds went off, John and I were only a few feet from our door, and we stopped dead in our tracks, both assessing the situation, then quickly realizing how lucky we were. When I opened the door to our trailer, Virk was stretched out on the bed at the end of the trailer looking at the both of us, and enquired what the commotion was all about. I have little doubt that he would have been hit had the rounds taken a slightly higher trajectory.

Both Peters and Newson are up on charges for accidental discharge. One because he pulled the trigger, the other because his weapon was at the ready, when it shouldn't have been.

The standard charge for this offence is 14 days in jail, and a $1000 Cdn fine, plus loss of pay for the two weeks you're sitting in the can. Debate rages as to whether they'll get sent home as well, but we just don't know for sure. This late in the tour it's hard to say what they'll do. You'll hear more soon.

After racking in the morning, then going for lunch, I went out for a workout. I'm way out of shape. My work's cut out for me, that's clear enough.

Nothing happened in the Ogroup today. They're toying with the reservists' contracts again. No details yet, but it looks like it's been extended to June 01 if we go home in April as planned.

The Airborne is in the hot seat again. A video of one of their hazings, and some shots of Somalia were released to the media and played nationally. Speculation is the Regiment is not long for this world.

I called Cat today. Things are fine at home, but man it was hard to hear her voice. She told me again how much she loves me and how much she enjoyed our honeymoon. I'm glad I could fulfil her dream of returning to England.

As I left the phones and made my way back to my trailer, it occurred to me that I've become really worried at the idea of having an invalid for a wife. I've always been very healthy and there was a time Catherine could keep up. But now she can't keep up as well, and I recognize I had some of the same feelings I had when I was with Derek last year for his trip to England. After ten days of poking around with him, I found myself becoming short with his inability to keep up. The situation is nowhere near as bad with Cat, thank God, but I still recognize the symptoms in me. It's compounded by the thought that this disease could very well take Catherine away from me by the time she's 50. The despair increases when I realize that I love this woman beyond all else, and that I need her in my life. The longer I'm away from her the worse it gets. This trip to England showed me how badly the disease has affected her, and how much I'm truly needed at home, which of course makes coming back here all the harder.

Reality check: Two guys burned themselves on OP last night while cleaning a small heater called a Yukon stove. It seems someone put naphtha into one of the jerry cans and clearly marked it. The guys grabbed the can without looking, thinking they were using water to scour the outside of the stove. The resulting fire singed their hair and burned them slightly, and they were treated for smoke inhalation, but otherwise they're recovering well. Embarrassed and accusing looks abound.

Sunday, 22 Jan., Bruska Last night at Bruska was kind of mild so it was nice to sit by the fire and just think. I spent a lot of time just reflecting, and eventually fell asleep in the warm embrace of the burning glow of the fire. In the morning we drove the carrier back to Rastivic, where, because I didn't have to work, I took the day off.

After cleaning up, I lay down for a bit. When I woke up, the search began for my glasses. They're the only ones I have, aside from my prescription sunglasses, so you can understand the importance of finding them.

For two hours I searched frantically, retracing my steps and exploring every possibility. By 11:00 I had formulated a theory. There were three possibilities. Either one of the cleaning ladies had picked up the glasses for sale on the black market (something we had been warned about); I left them in Bruska; or one of our guys found them and picked them up. I went door to door along our lines asking if anyone had found the glasses. In the end, Jeff Baker had indeed picked them up after I had left them in the ablution trailer. I was greatly relieved, but didn't know whether to hug him, or hit him for picking them up for me. I eventually just said thank you and left.

After lunch I went for a workout, then read a book for a while, thus passing a quiet afternoon and evening. Tonight's Ogroup was a bit of a shocker. Sgt MacKinnon of 1 Section has been thrown in jail for alcohol abuse. He was put on a verbal warning a couple of days ago, and tonight he got caught drinking again. He went straight to jail.

It's hard to say what they'll do with him. We're on the wrong side of the pond for a spin dry course (alcohol detox), and they can't afford to lose any of their section commanders. I think they'll move him out of the section, but it's hard to say where to.

I expect the boys in that section are relieved. It was something none of them wanted to talk about but it was clear to see his drinking was really tough on them.

Monday, 23 Jan., Patrolling Today we put in a full day's work before 1300. Up at 0530 and on the road before 0700 for six hours of patrolling. We've been tasked with covering the Charles Company patrol routes because they are occupied with OP duty, and don't have the people to spare. This is fine by me, it'll be good to get out and see a different part of the country, and get the hell away from the bloody HQ weenies.

We drove through some high hills overlooking the Adriatic Sea on the Croat side of the Zone, and talked to some Serbs in OPs on their side of the Zone. Then we went into the lowlands and through some farmland, where I saw the largest field of cabbages

I've ever seen, there had to be at least 20 acres of the things. The air was fresh with the smell of them. We stopped for twenty minutes, and talked to a Croat in a small OP by a stream, then motored off.

The only bad thing about the trip was the constant beating one takes when going over rough ground. Thank God I was wearing a helmet, because I whacked the back of my head off the hatch cover about two dozen times. The flack vest, which is fairly thick, protected my ribs. It wasn't as bad as it could have been; after all, the whole trip could have been on rough ground.

They say shit flows downhill and gathers momentum. We've been here three days and we've had three people charged with weapons offences, and a section commander removed from duty for alcohol abuse. On the discharge thing, they got the owner of the weapon, the guy who pulled the trigger and the MCpl in charge of the patrol for not supervising his troops closely enough—if you can believe it. They tried to get the section commander, but they already had him on alcohol related charges, so that was a no go. And they tried to get Warrant Fuller and the platoon commander (who's on leave right now), but for some reason they weren't charged.

The fun continued when higher tried to go after Warrant Fuller for a second time, for not doing his job and keeping a bad section commander in place, but he produced documentation showing a pattern and listing all the warnings he'd given MacKinnon, so he got off the hook.

All these charges feel like it's a witch-hunt. By going after everyone in the chain of command up to the warrant and platoon commander, they are creating an air of paranoia within the Regiment. As I see it, it's an issue of responsibility. The charges should have stopped with the two involved as they made the mistake and they should be dealt with. Instead, higher tried to blame everyone under the sun for a simple mistake. Granted, a negligent discharge is not a simple mistake, but charging everyone who came in contact with them makes no sense. As a result of these charges, there has been a change in policy. We now have to have supervised personal weapons cleaning, and we can't touch the .50 without a Sergeant or a W.O. being present. This flies in the face of everyone here, and there is more than a little grumbling going on because of it, in fact it's the closest I've seen the guys to getting violent about something. The military has spent millions training everyone here in how to do their jobs. The infantry's stated role is to close with and destroy the enemy and weapons handling is a huge part of that. As infanteers we consider it insulting in the extreme to be subjected to a supervised weapons cleaning, especially when we work with our weapons daily and can effect repairs in the dark, with our eyes closed and one arm tied behind our backs. To us, it's a tool, not unlike a shovel (which is about how useful it is when you run out of ammunition) and, being a military obsessed with safety, we live, eat, and breathe weapons handling and safety. We understand the need to punish those who made the mistake. What they did was pretty dumb. But why would you punish the entire Regiment for it?

In the immortal words of the man who said it first, "This is a crock of shit, and it stinketh." But as usual we shall soldier on. It's times likes these that really test one's morale.

Tuesday, 24 Jan., Rodaljice I started this diary as an emotional outrigger. The problem is that I am starting to feel like the damn boat is sinking.

Today, in thirty words or less: Up at 04:15; clean up; carrier ride to Rodaljice;

standing patrol all day; first half in sleet, second half in sun and blue sky; return to Rastivic.

The only two things of interest today were visits. The first was from a couple of local Croats. They were asking about all the artillery that's been happening these past few days. We told them the Serbs were practising. That seemed to answer their question, so they left. We of course had no idea who was doing the shooting but it seemed a plausible enough answer.

What they were talking about was the anti-tank range we've been told the Serbs have been running. The local Serb commander figures he can hold the Krajina against anything the Croats can throw at them. Brave words.

The other visit was from the OC and CSM. They showed up at 14:00 and stayed for twenty minutes or so, then buggered off. Before they left, the OC told us that the Airborne had been disbanded! Their colours are laid up and they are no more, by direct order of the Prime Minister himself. Wow! That'll piss a few people off. There's going to be a lot of people crying in their beer over this one.

Of course what they don't tell you in the media, is that the army is either going to form a new Regiment called the 1st Canadian Para Regiment, or some suitable opposite acronym. They are going to go back to the old jump companies they used to have before the Airborne Regiment was formed.

What I mean is, you can't just willy-nilly get rid of the Airborne. They fulfil an important role in the infantry's grand scheme of things and getting rid of them is harder than just disbanding a Regiment.

They also said there was going to be a new enquiry into the Airborne/Somalia thing, but instead of slagging the boys at the bottom, they're starting at the top. It's about time.

Tonight's Ogroup was interesting. The court-martial of the warrant who struck a superior officer is going long, so Peters and Newson's charge parade has been postponed till tomorrow. There's a chance they may get off lightly because both are in Sgt MacKinnon's section and he's going up on charges tomorrow morning. They figure stress may have played a factor in the mistake that led to the discharge, so higher is trying to deal with things in order. Sgt MacKinnon has left his quarters in the platoon lines, and is now in transient shacks. Speculation is he'll be heading home as soon as the trial is over.

David got pulled in on this one too. He was the one on patrol with the Sergeant when he got drunk (oh yes, did I mention: no drinking with the locals anymore). He was temporarily assigned to that section to fill in when the guys from our section were on leave. It'll be a good experience for him to go through a charge parade. Everyone should have to be charged at least once in his career, it means you're pushing the limit and using your initiative. That or you did something truly stupid and you need a kick in the ass to straighten you up. God, I sound like an old man here. Grantpaw indeed!

With the Airborne out of the way, 2nd Vandoo are back on the front burner. No word yet if they're actually coming, but we're told their recce people will be here next week.

Warrant Fuller is worried about morale. Is it any fucking wonder? We're here in Rastivic five days and we've had more charges than we've had in four months, eight if you go back to June.

This place is emotionally draining. There's no routine (we're always in flux), the place is a hole, and there's no place for the platoon to hang out as a group. Is it any wonder there's a morale problem?

I've said it before, and I'll say it again. Right now, this place really grates. The morale is the shits right now, and everyone is grumpy and snapping at each other. But each day is a new day, and maybe tomorrow will be better. Life, they say, is never so bad that it can't get worse. I wrote Catherine three letters today. At least that took my mind off things for a while.

Wednesday, 25 Jan., Rodaljice Back out to Rodaljice today. We spent about an hour picking through the leftover hard rations to get something to eat. We leave so early in the morning that the kitchen isn't open, thus we are left with box lunches and French army rations out of the carrier. The box lunches are their usual exciting fare of two sandwiches (two slabs of bread slathered in lard which is being passed off as butter, and a piece of cheese or meat—so exciting I could shit). In addition there are two drinking boxes, and maybe an Euro-Twinky (the nickname we've given to this chocolate covered fluffy thing in a bright yellow wrapper).

The French army rations aren't terrible, but they're awful close. One box is supposed to last one man the whole day but somehow I doubt it. There simply isn't enough food in them for an average man to keep himself going. And if it's cold, there are nowhere near enough calories in them. You'd have to eat at least two per day just to keep up your energy. There is supposed to be a small bottle of wine with each ration, but we've never seen any of it. Somewhere between leaving France and getting to us, some bastard stole it all. Someone in the UN supply chain got a cut, you can bet on it. The price of doing business I guess.

After eating, we started to tear down what was left of the wire surrounding the old compound. The top layer of wire was fairly easy to remove, but the bottom was something else again. It had been there so long that the brambles and blackberry bushes had grown up through the wire and made it impossible to save. In the end, we just hooked a cargo strap to one end of the wire, and used the carrier to pull it out. It made for a hell of a tangle of wire, but there really wasn't any choice. That took most of the day.

While we were working on dismantling the wire, we had a visit from three of the local kids. The visit was odd really, because as a rule you don't often see the kids except when they are on their way to or from somewhere, never just hanging around. And yet it was their demeanour that caught my eye. They acted as if they were much older even though I'd put the oldest at no more than 12 or 13. All three were smoking cigarettes, which isn't really that strange since damn near everyone and their dog smoke in this place. One of them wore a trench coat that made him look like a miniature Serb soldier. It was the way they stood and the way they talked to us, but mostly the way they just sat and watched us, the false bravado of these . . . children. You'd think you were looking at forty-year-old men in children's bodies. It was most unsettling to watch them watching us. I was left with the impression that these were people—children or not—that you simply didn't trust. They were entirely too old for their physical ages. If ever there was a social comment upon the effects of this war, these children were the manifestation of it.

When our replacements came there were only three of them, so I volunteered to stay for 24 hours because our section was short-staffed and someone had to stay behind. With their arrival came news of the charge parade with Peters, Newson, and Perez.

Perez, the MCpl in charge of the patrol, was fined $1500 CDN because of lack of supervision, and it was his second charge within a year. That had to hurt, he has just had a little girl, and you know money is tight.

Newson received a $900 CDN fine for firing the weapon. And Peters went to jail for two weeks. The only reason he didn't go home was because there is no one left at home to replace him, or so we're told. The trial of Sgt MacKinnon is on for tomorrow.

All of this has resulted in paranoia within the platoon. Orders were passed that we can't unload, or load our weapons in camp without being supervised by a MCpl or higher, and all weapons cleaning must be supervised. Outside the camp it's another matter. Within our section, it's understood that away from camp we'll continue with the regular routine, provided there are no prying eyes about. The same applies to the other sections. Everyone recognizes what a crock of shit this order is, and we're hoping that given enough time it'll just fade away and we'll carry on doing what we always do.

I think what really burns my toast is, instead of charging only those responsible in this incident, this Regiment tried to hit everyone from the platoon commander down. So much for accepting responsibility for your actions and higher having faith in "trained" troops. This trial amounts to an insult to all of us and the effect on morale is tangible.

Thursday, 26 Jan., Rodaljice Spent the night at Rodaljice and came into camp early. We used the carriers to switch around between positions because each carrier stays with the section and our next standing patrol was at Bruska. We drove over to Bruska where we left the carrier, then caught a ride back to camp with 3 Section.

I had breakfast then hit the sack for the morning. When I got to the ISO, John had left me a note telling me of a mousetrap he set in amongst my kit. He had already caught one mouse and wanted me to check if he'd caught another. I checked, he hadn't, so the trap remains in place.

When I woke for lunch the warrant gathered us for a quick briefing. Sgt MacKinnon is now MCpl MacKinnon, and he now has a severe reprimand on his record for the next three years. He's staying, but has been moved back to CQ into his old job.

David, who was drinking with him, has 21 extras to be served in the next 7 days. We've moved him to night shift and we'll cover for him so at least he can get some rest.

Because of this, we're down to doing 24 hours on and 12 off. Tonight I have to go back out for 24 hours. Last night David and I went for a patrol of Rodaljice. As it happened we went back to the same house where he and the Sergeant got drunk. On the way up the road we found two full bottles of wine they had stashed on the way back into our patrol base. It was remarkably good wine, but in light of the current situation, we opted to dump it all. Though I have to admit it was tempting to keep it for later.

The people we visited were very nice. One brother was in the Serb army and was adamant that they could defend against Croatia. The other brother and his wife, whose house it was, I know little about. David did most of the talking. On his last visit with them he had agreed to do a trade with the guy, so for a can of silicone we both received Serb army belts, which are very hot items amongst our guys. I've been looking for one of those things since I got here, but they've been hard as hell to get hold of. Nice bit of serendipity there!

My attitude has improved in the last 24 hours. I choose to see the humour in the hoops we have to jump through, and with the sending of the letters to Cat, I feel better.

It was really tough to make the adjustment when I came back off leave. It's such a different world here, and it requires a different mindset from the civilian world. The job itself isn't really hard; the problem is keeping a positive attitude. Talking with the guys helps a lot, and writing in this diary also helps. Workouts are a big help, but more than anything a regular routine makes all the difference. It gives one a chance to plan your spare time, and it gives you the feeling that you have at least a modicum of control over your life. I would also say writing letters helps, but that requires such a shift in thinking that at times it is extremely hard to motivate yourself to talk in terms people on the outside can understand—especially when they have no military experience. What can you tell them? How much must you explain? After a while your letters take on a very simplistic tone with everyone but your closest friends with whom you can speak frankly, or who at least who understand what you're talking about.

Anyway, I think I have it back under control, as I sit here by the fire in Bruska. I'm on for the next 24 hours so hopefully I'm not struck dead by boredom.

Friday, 27 Jan., Bruska A quiet night last night, calm, it was nice to sit by the fire for a couple of hours (0200–0400). Bruska Camp is just a flat slab of gravel now, surrounded by barbed wire and wide open to the elements. The generator, tents, and ISO trailer are all gone now, and the carrier and porta potty are the only structures left. We've set up the section tent for sleeping space and another place to get out of the wind.

Just as my shift ended it started to drizzle. Henry, who was to replace me, was in his sleeping bag on the other bench in the carrier, and didn't even bother to get up. We were both in the carrier at the time so it really didn't matter, all we had to do was listen for the radio, and we had the volume up so high that had a message been received, it would have awakened the dead.

For the shift change at 0600 I just stayed in bed, I figured I wasn't going anywhere anyway so I just lay there and listened to the Ogroup being held on the ramp of the carrier.

The Bihac has lost its interest for us, so we skimmed over it. Shot Reps are so common that most of the time we just ignore them unless there's something special about them. If they come from other Companies we pretty much ignore them also. So I guess the only interesting thing from this morning's Ogroup involved the jerry cans on the back of the carriers. It started with an attempted highjacking of one of our fuel convoys. It seems the fuel embargo is starting to affect the Serbs. A couple of days ago, while one of the carriers was working its way up a steep slope (at about 5 km/h) just outside Rastivic, two Serbs jumped out from behind some bushes and tried to cut the jerry cans off the back of the carrier, unsuccessfully I might add. Because the carrier was moving so slowly, they thought they could just run out behind us and snag the cans. They must think we're particularly stupid. No sooner had they stood up, than our guys saw what they were up to, and told them to back off.

It all ends with the whole battalion having to remove the jerry cans from the backs of the carriers. Removing the temptation as it were. Of course, we now have the damn things inside the carrier with gas slopping around in a confined area that already doesn't have enough room to move around in.

The day started out mild enough, then the wind shifted, the temperature dropped, and it started to snow and rain. Then it cleared up and the wind picked up. By the end of the day the wind stopped and the sun came out again. The Met Rep—from Trenton no less—called for a high of 12 degrees Celsius and cloudy skies. Yeah right. Try again, boys. I guess it isn't so easy predicting the weather from halfway around the world.

By 10:00 I was back in the bag in an effort to stay warm. I read till 2 P.M. then lay down to give my eyes a rest. Nick, Robert and Jay had already gone to ground around 12:00 and were resting comfortably. Nick and I were on the benches in the carrier, and Jay and Robert in the section tent we set up.

Around 3:00 I was reclining comfortably and enjoying a good read, when I heard an Iltis pull up. I was the first out of the bag to see who it was. As soon as I stuck my head out of the carrier I immediately swung around and got Nick up, the bloody CO and RSM had come for an unannounced visit. You've never seen four guys move so quickly in your life.

CO: How are things boys?
US: Fine sir. [We were all standing there shivering]
CO: When was your last patrol sent out?
Nick: The last one went out just before noon, Sir, [glances at his watch] and the next one is due to leave in about half an hour, Sir. [We hadn't sent any patrols out at all today]
RSM: [brief silence] What you need out here, lads, is a Mod tent for shelter. Where's yours?
US: They took it away when we cleared the location, Sir!
CO: Don't worry. I think we can arrange for one to be sent to you, I have some pull with the guy who runs this outfit. You'll have a tent out here tomorrow. [Smiles all around]

That'll be a nice change. When they packed up, they took everything. All that was left was a blue rocket and a four-foot table. When the wind picked up the only place to hide was in the carrier.

The CO and RSM stayed for another ten or so minutes, then left. Much to our relief. With the adrenaline still running high, we cleaned up a bit, got a fire going, sent Jay and Robert on patrol, and waited for our relief to arrive. It's truly amazing what a visit from 9er can do to motivation.

Robert and Jay stayed on patrol for over an hour, so when they came back Nic came aboard them for staying out too long. At one point I thought it would come to blows, but things calmed down. I feel that the young guys are playing fast and loose with the rules, particularly Robert who seems to have little discipline in this area, and they need reigning in some. Because I agreed with Nic, I let him have at them and didn't say anything. They lack experience, and under the current situation we can't afford any mistakes. Drinking with the locals, even if it's coffee, is forbidden now and they seem to have forgotten that, instead letting the friendship they've formed with the locals override the need for discipline and an understanding of the big picture.

Our replacements arrived right on time. I got back and went for a workout and shower, then sat in on tonight's Ogroup.

I was given the dates for my 2nd 96-hour leave, but it was my return dates at the tour's end that I was most interested in. All unnecessary kit leaves on the 2nd of March, and I leave with advance party on 4 April. My leave dates are from 5 April to 1 May, then I return to Petawawa for two weeks or so and then I'm finished.

Catherine will be so pleased to hear that. Tomorrow's our anniversary and today I received a beautiful card from her. It's one of those schmaltzy ones, and it must have been hard for her to pick it out. It's really beautiful and I was quite moved. I'll call her tomorrow and give her the good news that it arrived.

Saturday, 28 Jan., Wedding Anniversary, Rastivic This morning started with a wake up at 04:45, for a 06:00–08:00 shift at the main gate to Camp Rastivic. Watching the sun come up over the mountains was the perfect way to start the day, that and thoughts of home and Catherine. What wouldn't I give to wake up beside her and spend one of our Saturdays together just shopping and going for coffee at our favourite bistro. But alas, the constant interruptions of people coming and going from the camp keeps bringing me back to reality. And reality is that after the 6–8 shift, I had a 10–11:30. Between shifts I had breakfast and then got a haircut.

David had relieved me at 8:00, so I decided to cut him some slack and show up a bit early for my shift at 10. He still had a bunch of the extras to work off, so any down time we could give him was a help. When I arrived, he was in the process of writing up another statement. Poor David, he was beside himself with angst thinking about having to go back up in front of the CO.

This statement involved Sveto Draca, one of the Serbs who lives in Bruska and who works at the kitchen here. While John and David were on patrol in Bruska a few nights back, it came up in conversation that if UNPROFOR were to withdraw in the face of a Croatian advance, the Krajina Serbs would be: A) less than impressed with UNPROFOR, and B) they may try to keep us from leaving.

David and John listened politely to this and took it for what it was. The next day it happened to come up in a conversation with George, who then mentioned it to Warrant Fuller, and so on up the chain. Eventually it wound up on the CO's desk. He apparently got so pissed that he decided then and there to get statements from everyone involved, and fire Sveto for threatening UN personnel.

Now let me stop here and just say that I don't particularly care for Sveto, his wife, or any other Serb in the village. I simply don't trust them. But doing the right thing in life is always the hardest thing to do, and I couldn't just stand by and watch him get fired because information was passed incorrectly.

Sunrise over Rastevic, Croatia. A nice start to our 5th wedding anniversary

What he said has been said a dozen times before by everyone in the village. The Krajina Serbs were pissed that the French and Kenyans pulled out of the area the first time, and they will be disappointed if UNPROFOR does the same again. Whether the Serbs will detain us is pure speculation, and I feel what David and John passed on has been grossly misinterpreted and distorted.

Sveto for his part should know better. He's still in the Serb army part-time, and he's working in a UN installation, therefore he should watch his step a little more and be careful in what he says. The warrant says he suspects Sveto of passing information to the Serb army, which is not entirely inconceivable. If he were fired for passing information, then that's fine, it's no different than getting a battlefield wound, but don't fire him because someone twisted his words. After all, the man's only trying to look after his family.

Enough of that, I'll tell you if anything more comes of it.

I called Catherine today and wished her happy anniversary, and then I gave her the dates of my return. I know I made her day. She was so happy to know when I was coming home, she can hardly wait.

Remember the two guys who were burned by pouring naphtha on the stove? Well on the medals parade the other day, the RSM had the perfect retort; "We're all tigers and no donkeys here," he said, "and I don't want to hear of any of you donkeys putting naphtha in unauthorized containers any more." Snickers rippled through the ranks.

Sunday, 29 Jan., Rastivic On the gate again this morning with David as my mid-morning replacement. Around 11:00 one of the MPs and the duty Sergeant escorted Sveto to the gate and told him not to return. It was obvious that Sveto had been taken off guard by the sudden dismissal. He was in a good mood this morning when he came through the gate to go to work and he suspected nothing.

After the MPs left, he and I chatted for a bit about what had happened, and I tried to answer his questions. One of the MPs I knew from my advanced first aid course, so when I asked the reason Sveto was being let go he said it was because he had "uttered threats against a Canadian soldier" and the CO's policy on that was crystal clear.

I didn't feel good about it, but was just as glad to be free of him. There is really nothing I can do about this anyway.

At shift end, when I grabbed my rifle, I didn't look at it other than to go through the motions of clearing it before walking across camp. When I got back to my ISO I realized I had the wrong rifle. My first instinct was to check with David to see if he had perhaps grabbed mine by mistake. Wrong! I then went back to the gate, after changing to check the weapons list for transient visitors. Nothing.

My next guess was that I had grabbed John's rifle in the dark (we share a weapons locker) so I waited for his return off patrol. In the meantime I went for a workout.

John got back sometime just after supper, but again I was wrong. What to do next? I went to our section Ogroup and told Henry what the situation was and that I was on top of it, after all I'm going on my 96-hour leave tomorrow, and I didn't want to be wasting any of it looking for my rifle.

I pondered my next move for a while then I hit upon an idea, and walked over to HQ. After finding the clerk and explaining my situation, he produced exactly what I was looking for. Before I left my ISO I had recorded the rifle and sight numbers from the weapon I had mistakenly grabbed. What the clerk did was pull up a file on the computer of everyone in the battalion and the serial numbers of their rifles. We kept the sight number as a cross-reference in case the rifle number had been incorrectly put into the database. It was likely that one of the numbers on file had been incorrectly inputted, but not both.

In a matter of seconds, the search of the records produced the name, company, platoon, and section of the person whose rifle I had.

As it turned out, I had the rifle of the guy who had relieved me yesterday. When I realized this, I felt kind of stupid for not having checked my rifle sooner. That's one little fact that won't get out any time soon.

Speaking of feeling stupid, while the clerk stepped out to look for something, in stepped the captain responsible for all civilian employees on the base and the one who fired Sveto. What an opportunity I thought. After introducing myself, and asking permission to speak freely, I explained the real situation with Sveto and how it had come about. He didn't feel too good when I was finished, but I told him I'd prefer if he simply let it drop as there was little he could do now, so he agreed and thanked me for filling him in.

I feel somewhat relieved having spoken to both ends of the chain in this matter. I at least feel I've cleared my conscience on this situation and am content to let it lie.

I want to pause here to comment on Warrant Fuller. To this point in the tour I have neither known him long enough, nor been close enough to him to evaluate his performance. In fact, it is difficult to get past the sheer size of the man let alone his sometimes gruff sometimes easygoing manner. However, this past incident, and several others, have exposed him as one who tends to overreact or overstate a situation. The boys in fact have lost considerable respect for him because of this. For my part, I am undecided. I will follow him without hesitation in a military situation, but I find that he is less than I thought he was. Twice, when we were at Rodaljice he insulted me personally during animated group discussions we've had, and I've watched him do it to others. This tells me he is incapable of defending some of his redneck positions without the use of intimidation, or verbally threatening his opponent. It has become such a part of his way of doing things that he probably doesn't realize he's doing it. After all, who's going to tell a guy that big that he's wrong? In spite of this, I still like the guy.

In a sense it's kind of funny to watch him. Some of his viewpoints, I'm sure his wife would never let him get away with if he ever expressed them at home, she'd have his balls for it. But in the army, he can get away with it. The army is truly the one place where boys remain boys.

Monday, 30 Jan., Rastivic, 96-hour leave Ahhhhhh, the joys of time off! While those around me scurry about coming and going at ungodly hours, I lay snuggled contentedly in my sleeping bag reading a book. Totally ISO-lated I am not though. I have chosen to continue to frequent the section Ogroups, as well as stay in close contact with everyone in the section, that way I'm not completely lost when I come back.

Last night was Super Bowl Sunday, and no matter how hard I tried, I simply couldn't get into it. A pool had been started back when the playoffs began, and now it was down to five guys. Jeff Baker, who never watches or follows football, wound up winning because he said that San Fran would beat the Chargers by 21 points or more, which they did. Much to everyone's chagrin, he walked off with 190 DM for his trip to Budapest, and an ear-to-ear grin.

With time off, I thought I'd take the opportunity to put in a nice long workout. After half an hour on the Stairmaster I got off and sat down to cool off. I decided then and there to end the workout. These past few days I've been fighting a minor cold, cough, sniffles, that sort of thing, and today it caught up with me in the form of dehydration. It was a chore just to move around. Thank God I decided not to bother drinking at the mess. Where everyone else gets bombed on this leave period (Virk and I picked John up off the floor and put him under the covers one night), I decided not to bother. Instead, I curled up with a good book and read till the wee hours.

Tonight's Ogroup had little of interest in it. The Bihac, as usual, is hot—what's new? They stressed again that we have to remove jerry cans from the back of the carriers before going on patrol. And beware children. It seems that the company 2IC had his windshield broken by kids throwing rocks at him as he drove past a school. Ungrateful little shits! The OC has threatened to remove the school supplies we provide, if the teachers can't get a grip on things. It also appears that kids are firing BBs at passing patrols. How long till they start using AKs?

In the mess I chatted with a guy from 1 Platoon. These were the guys who were stationed in Knin. Do you know why the Kenyans don't patrol at night? Well doesn't everyone know? There are ghosts out there in the night.

Tuesday, 31 Jan., Rastivic, 96-hour leave The second day of a relaxing break was bright and sunny, a nice day—if you could stand up! The wind here was gusting to over 70 miles per hour, and never dropped below 50 mph the whole day. To keep things from blowing away, we've taken to parking trucks on the windward side of all the trailers to act as a windbreak. Even with the trucks in place, my ISO shook to the point I thought something was going to break. A couple of weeks back, during a similar blow, two of the ISOs on the base had their walls punched in and were totally destroyed. Since then the policy with the trucks seems to have made a difference.

Today at noon, Camp Rastivic and Charles Company went to state Orange. That is to say, state plaid. Plaid, because some of the companies are still at state Green; so we're having a little fun with trying to name our state of readiness. It's sort of like semi-tactical. You get all cammed up, but use white light instead of red in the patrol hide.

All of this came about as a result of something the CO did. Back on New Year's Day, the Serbs in a roadblock shot up two of our boys. The men who controlled the roadblock were under the command of the Serb battalion commander. When our CO asked what had happened, he got the runaround, with no explanation forthcoming, or apologies offered. The standoff lasted about a month, with the CO badgering for answers, and the Serbs doing everything to avoid the questions. Then the brigade commander invited the CO to come to a local celebration. The CO's response, was to write him a letter in which he called him every name in the book, including unprofessional, rebels, uncultured, etc, etc. You get the picture.

Of course the battalion commander was pissed and retaliated by saying he'd have his men kill a few Canadians for good measure. Hence the state Orange.

The moral here: "Don't back down; meet force with force, meet bluff with threat." These are blockheads we're dealing with. The concept of compromise is foreign.

Another warning about kids in today's Ogroup. Seems now they have expended and discarded weapons to play with, and to point at us. The M80 looks like our M72 anti-tank weapon. After being fired, all that's left is the fibreglass tube. The kids apparently have found some of these, and are pointing them at us. Kinda like a Serb version of cowboys and Indians. Maybe the real thing is closer than we figured. With all the

Home for 3 Platoon in Rastevic

weapons being taken home from the front, who knows what can happen.

With time on my hands to think, and listen to the constant nightly rattle of machine-gun fire, I've had opportunity to finish Richard Bach's book *Bridge Across Forever*, otherwise titled *The Quest for Your Soul mate*. It's an interesting read, and has given me pause for thought.

"How do you know you've met your soul mate?" the book asks. "Look for a love affair that gets better with time, admiration brightening, trust that grows through storms," is the answer. Can it be that I've found my soul mate with Catherine? All the signs appear to be there. Our love affair has done nothing but grow. Our trust and faith in each other has improved with each year together. And our need to be with each other has continually increased. We mesh well, we compliment each other, and we've become good friends.

It didn't start that way though. When I married Cat, I did it because a little voice inside me said it was the right thing to do, and she was the one for me. Since then, she's shown me the true value of love. She is far more spiritual than I am, and where once I used to smile at her intuitive knowledge of something, I now find myself wondering if maybe I should be paying more attention.

Maybe she is my soul mate. She seems to know things about me that I never told her. She'll know how I'm feeling, or what's on my mind without my saying a word.

This book seems to have been dropped into my lap at this particular time because I was in need of it. Though I've read Bach (*Jonathan Livingston Seagull*) and Og Mandino (*The Tower*) in the past, their message of "love is all that counts "seemed a bit too simplistic or flower-childish for me.

In reviewing this diary, it occurs to me that what I miss most about Catherine is our intimacy. In England we had some wonderful discussions on all types of subjects, and I find myself longing for that kind of interaction again, based as it is on respect, love, appreciation, and a genuine need to listen. Because we're so different, we have worked hard to find those things we have in common. And we've done it, too. Antiques, old homes, music, gardening, cuisine, and our pets are but a few of the loves we share.

Our relationship is also marked by physical contact. Wherever we go, we are always holding on to each other. A hand here, and arm there, perhaps a stolen kiss in a quiet moment. Or, as we did in England, dancing together on top of a turret in a 12th century castle in Conway. The more intimate I get with her, the less desirous I am of being with other women.

Catherine is always telling me she is a plain person who looks great with a bit of makeup. To her this may be true. But to me she is beautiful with or without makeup. But in my opinion, she looks her best when she wakes first thing in the morning. Is she my soul mate? From the evidence it would appear that, yes, she is.

This past year has been a tough one for us. But it is not without its rewards. I have spent far too much time away from Catherine and now it's time to rebuild our intimacy, love, and trust in one another that once we had, only better.

In my journey through life, my quest to know and learn about God and myself has slowed to a snail's pace of late, and this tour represents an opportunity to do some mental housekeeping as it were. Perhaps by opening myself up to Catherine more, we can grow together in ways we never dreamed possible.

Wednesday, 01 Feb., Rastivic, 96-hour leave Day three of my leave, and little of interest happened to me today. The day itself was beautiful, with clear blue skies, high of 15 degrees C, and crisp clean air. I took a couple of barrack boxes outside with a chair, and did some writing while working on my suntan. I'd been out there about half an hour when the CSM came by looking for people for a work party.

He was going to tag me, but before he said anything, I threw my hands in the air and said "sorry sir, I'm actually in Budapest right now and can't help you." This has become the standard response everyone on leave has been using in this situation, and it's become something of a standing joke. "OK," he replied, "you hide before I put you to work."

It didn't take much to convince me, so everything was packed up in record time and inside I went for the rest of the morning. Then in the afternoon I went for a good workout.

The fourth of February is a big day in these parts. I think it's the celebration of the start of the war, but don't quote me on that. It came down in orders that we're to keep a sharp eye out when patrolling. Who knows what some drunk will do?

There was also a minor change to our rules of engagement as well today. If our equipment or property is being shot at, then we may not engage the enemy. Only if we are being shot at can we return fire. Interesting. What if they're trying to steal our equipment off the carrier? Can we shoot them then? (Two warning shots to the chest and one killing shot in the air perhaps?). I'm told it's being looked into.

This thing with disbanding the Airborne has ruffled a lot of feathers around here. People have been sending us clippings out of various newspapers, and it's amazing how far off the media can be at times. Suffice it to say that the guys in 2 Commando, the western boys, have really done a number on the Regiment.

I'm not sure what's driving it but the locals have come to expect much more than we're willing to give them. At this month's town hall meeting in Rodaljice, the Croats nit-picked about nearly everything we did, until the OC just stood up and left. Sad to see such a blatant case of biting the hand that feeds you. These people have no grace at all sometimes.

Thursday, 02 Feb., Rastivic Today was another extraordinary day. Bright clear sky, cool crisp air, simply beautiful.

Jay had a bit of excitement last night out at Bruska. Seems he was sitting by the fire when he heard a dog barking by the wire. When he shone his flashlight at the noise, he found two Serbs in fatigues just outside the wire watching him. As soon as he picked up his rifle, they buggered off. A SITREP was called in, but nothing more happened.

In tonight's Ogroup we were briefed on our new tasking. We're to start four days of patrolling, then two days at Pristeg, and two days as QRF. This will go on till the end of the tour. Finally! Some solid routine to sink our teeth into. Because of the local celebrations coming up, we've cancelled night patrols, and there's two-vehicle movement at night if you have to go anywhere. The CO isn't taking any chances.

Still no word whether the Croats will extend the UN mandate. If they do then we're out of here on schedule, if they don't then who knows what'll happen. The Bihac, as usual, is heating up again. Heavy casualties are being reported.

This morning and this afternoon for several hours, I found a quiet place in the mess and started writing. When it was over, I'd written seven letters.

On a whim, I called Catherine today. As soon as she answered I knew she was sick. Sunday she lost grip in her right hand. Monday she was into see the neurologist. He was not impressed with the relapse of the same area of the brain, only six months after her first episode. It hasn't been Cat's fault; she followed the rules to the letter. This damn disease is the cause. It's so unpredictable. The only hope he held out was that it should be cured within ten years. That will probably turn into twenty years, if we're lucky. Even so, as a precaution, the Doc put her on another course of steroids. This won't be easy for her.

The one good thing about all of this is that our friends have come through with flying colours. Many of them have altered their schedules to help Cat manage while she's on the steroids. There is someone with her 24 hours a day, and they're helping her manage with the side effects. It is an enormous comfort to know that she is well looked after. I know this episode will pass, but it gives me such a good feeling to know that our friends have not abandoned us, but rather come to the fore to help us in our time of need. I've decided that upon my return I shall throw a party and invite those who have supported us and try to thank them. What more can I do?

Catherine said it again—and I know it's her darkest fear—she doesn't want to end up in a wheelchair. I think it would destroy her. She needs so much to be mobile. I, too, would hate to see that happen to her. I think it would destroy me as well. But we'll deal with that kind of possibility if and when the time comes.

A curious thing happens to me from time to time. I get these snippets of film, which run through my mind. I see things as they might possibly turn out. While I was writing about Catherine and the wheelchair, I had an image of her funeral. In it I had to leave during the eulogy because I couldn't take it any more. At the door I turned and said something about saying farewell to Catherine and I'd be just outside. The image instantly brought tears to my eyes and I had to fight hard to control myself because Virk was in the trailer at the time (No weakness. All tigers, no donkeys ... it's a guy thing).

I have no control over these flashes, and no way of predicting when they'll come. Sometimes I wonder if someone is trying to give me a glimpse of what is to come. I hope they're wrong.

Virk and I just had a chat about missing our wives. I stepped outside for a moment, and when I came back, Virk looked terrible. He looked like his puppy just died or something. His shoulders were slumped forward, and I never noticed it before, but he had bags under his eyes and he looked like he hadn't slept in a week.

We've all got it bad. The other day when I was coming back from the phones, I passed the platoon commander and the warrant. The lieutenant asked what was on my mind and I looked up from the ground and responded, "my wife." They both just nodded and understood. This tour is really taking its toll on all of us, it's not the activity that's killing us, it's the boredom! It gives us too much time to think and wish we were somewhere else. With any luck the increased pace of patrolling will make time pass faster.

Friday, 03 Feb., QRF The first day back to work and it was both a good day, and a bad day. It got off to a reasonable enough start with gate duty from 6–8 and again from 10–11:30. I woke up this morning with a tent in my sleeping bag after having an erotic dream about Catherine again. I had to lie in bed for ten minutes before I could get up. Damned uncomfortable it was.

Morning duty went fast enough, then after lunch our section got tagged for another work party. We had to put up some modular tents, and load a few trucks.

One of the CQ staff took me away from tent building and asked me to build some shelves for him in the CQ stores area. We scrounged around for wood for about half an hour, I then sat down and did up a rough design using what we'd found. Dimensioned lumber is a scarce commodity here and part of getting it involves who you know, because most of it is off-limits. We finally settled on a plan, and he will look into getting the extras I need to complete it. Some time in the next couple of days I'll have to change hats and become a carpenter. I don't mind that at all. It's a chance to work with my hands and do something productive.

Around 2:30, I asked if I could call my wife, and was given permission to leave. Before turning to go, I also asked if I was needed for anything else. When I was told I wasn't, it essentially gave me the rest of the day off, while the other guys continued to work on the tent. What can I say? Old age and treachery win out again.

My call to Catherine was a good one. We're only supposed to have one call lasting 10 minutes, but I've gotten into the habit of calling back after we're cut off so each call actually lasts about twenty minutes. Quite frankly I don't care if I get caught. Catherine's illness is the perfect cover, and I don't think anyone would dare to challenge me on it. The platoon commander has encouraged me to call as often as possible, and I always feel better after talking to her. In fact, my spirits have been up these past few days for having had our talks. I'll probably start spacing the calls out to once every four days shortly, but for now I call every chance I get.

One of the things we've talked about is her staying at home more often. She can teach a dozen or so students from home, and start writing the book she's been talking about. It's time for a change we think, and this might prove to be the opportunity. I certainly would feel better if she worked at home and had to travel less.

Good workout this afternoon. The food here is SO laced with fat, that I'm certain I've put on at least ten pounds. If I can keep this routine up, hopefully I can trim down by the time I go home. Certainly my back isn't bothering me as much since I started stretching and exercising again.

In tonight's Ogroup, we found out that the twenty Marks we each put into buying wine seems to have gone missing. No one has a record of it. Somewhere between Gaetz, who collected it and the warrant who was making the arrangements, all the money has gone missing. That's it for me, I was going to get a couple of bottles, but we all feel ripped off so I'm not going to bother. If they can't have better control of the funds than that why should I give them money so they can lose it?

Here's a typical army situation. We are the patrolling section, but we can't patrol for some reason because 2 Platoon is patrolling. So we do work parties. Tomorrow for instance, we are going to Karin Slana, and on Sunday every free man in Rastivic will be used to build a series of bomb shelters just outside the trailer lines. Yet, because we're designated the patrolling section, we're not permitted to drink. Welcome to 1 RCR.

The laundry people have lost my laundry. I've lost a uniform, undies, sweatshirts, socks and t-shirts. Clearly someone dropped off their stuff, and picked up mine by accident. I wish people would be more careful.

Can you believe it? Do you remember the two guys who burned themselves by pouring naphtha on the stove? Well, their supervisor, one MCpl Weir, is up on charge parade tomorrow for failing to "supervise his troops properly." Don't you just love this place?

Good news! While at the mess tonight, a guy pulled me over and asked if I was missing some laundry. Seems my guess was right and he grabbed the wrong bag by accident. At least now I have clean undies to wear again.

Story—actually more of a rumour: I heard today that the UN has been so disappointed with the Kenyans' performance that they've not been asked back. I suspect their racketeering had something to do with it.

Fact—did you know that HQ Sector South in Knin has Serbs working the Operations centre, an area where Canadians can't even gain access? What's the bet that the Serb army knows everything there is to know about our positions, strengths, capabilities, and whereabouts? Kind of gives you faith in the old UN doesn't it? NOT!!!

Saturday, 04 Feb., QRF Today was a slack day. Hardest thing about it was getting, then keeping, myself motivated. My only line of defence against just sitting down and quitting are such motivating sayings as "you can't get out of it, so you might as well get into it," and the ever-popular "make work your friend." Both of these helped to keep me going as I walked around collecting wood, then cutting it, for the shelves in QM.

After rooting through QM stores and coming up empty-handed, I walked over to the carpenters in the hope that I could borrow a skill-saw to speed things along. No joy. So the remainder of the afternoon was spent doing things the good-old-fashioned way, with the aid of a dull old handsaw.

Around 3:00, Warrant Fuller pulled the platoon together in the conference room for a briefing. He gave us a quick run down on what's been going on generally, and touching on our tasking change, which has now been moved to the 9th of Feb. Then he paused and started to tell us about a letter that some General back in Canada had written to the media. The letter, it seems, had a major impact. So much so, that the CO has called in the company commanders and asked that all platoon commanders poll the troops for reactions.

What did the revealing letter contain, you ask? In a nutshell, it said this: the troops are tired, they're overworked, and they're away from home for too long. And while the pay is good, it doesn't compensate for the hardship. Case in point: this tour has produced seven divorces so far, with the number possibly to run as high as 30 by the time we get back.

Let me just make a point. Nobody's griping about doing 12 on and 12 off, sleeping in swamps, or patrolling at all hours of the night and day. That's what the job's about and we accept that. The tiredness comes from over-tasking. For example, if you thought this tour was the only separation this year for the troops, you'd be wrong. After spending six months away from home, the boys will go back to a three-week vacation, then it's on to summer training and courses, both of which will keep a soldier away from home for up to 16 weeks. This year is RV year (Rendez-Vous, a semi-annual gathering for brigade-level exercises in Wainwright, Alberta). So, as soon as training is over, ramp-up for RV starts, and then it's out to Wainwright for three months. No summer leave. Then back to CFB Pet for post-ex drills and the start of winter phase training. Christmas will see a three-week break, then back to the grind again.

Each Regiment could expect to go on tour every 24 months for six months. That's been bumped up to every 18 months, now that the Airborne has been disbanded.

When I think of the people like Jay Palmer, who's been married a year in May, and has spent only three months in one—and two-week stints over the year actually with his wife, is it any wonder that there are so many releases after tours? Any wonder there's such high alcoholism, and a divorce rate ten times that of the civilian population?

So how's morale? "This tour's been good, sir, but I'm starting to get tired." That's the answer we're supposed to give to the *Globe and Mail* reporter who will be with us tomorrow, and the rest of the week, as well as anyone else who asks. With any luck someone back home will listen.

I've always believed that the Canadian public fully supports its troops when it comes to peacekeeping. I sometimes wonder, though, if they really realize the price we pay to do the job as well as we do. There's no doubt in my mind that we're among the best in the world at what we do. And there's no doubt in my mind that we could do more if permitted. The question is, whether our role as an army is going to change enough to allow us to continue to do our job properly, and expand enough to give us the break we need to remember what our wives and children look like. These matters need to be addressed before the army wears itself out. There have been too many cutbacks, resulting in over-work for the remainder. Something has to give.

This afternoon's conference started with a joke about Lt Alec Reid, (the 2 Platoon commander). It appears he was in the Zone today, and as we started our conference, he was confiscating a video camera from a Serb soldier—something, by the way, not permitted in the Zone according to the agreement. By the end of our meeting he was surrounded by 14 Serb soldiers packing weapons and was in a shouting match with the Serb commander.

Then the call came in for the QRF to prepare to move. We had been at 60 minutes' notice to this point, and now it was down to 5 minutes. As you can imagine it was all assholes and chinstraps as we tried to get the 50s in place, the kit stowed, the vehicles marshalled, and everyone loaded up, only to be stood down ten minutes later.

We were told later that both sides had agreed to stand down their troops, and call in UNCIVPOL, who viewed the tape and deemed it to have "no military content." The tape was given back.

This incident was typical of what happens around here every couple of days, but it was the first time we'd been involved from the QRF side, and we learned that our reaction time was good. The OC was impressed. Eleven minutes from the word go to being ready to roll out the gate. Of course, the fact that the fight that might have ensued in this case would have been over by the time we got there is beside the point.

Tonight was steak night at the mess. Because we were on an hour's notice to move, Warrant Fuller told us we could drink, but not get drunk. That didn't stop the others who weren't in the QRF. The pure volume of beer that the JR's mess goes through on any given week is enough to make any bar owner green with envy.

The longer we're here, the greater the amount consumed by each person per night. It's kind of sad, but I was thinking the other day how incredibly fragile our grasp on reality truly is. There is next to nothing for people to do here except workout, read, watch movies, or drink. And while there are some really big boys walking around, the number of people that actually workout regularly can't amount to more that 25% of the base's complement of about 100 people. The number of people who drink is, as you can imagine, quite a bit higher.

The boredom is such that all it takes is something stupid, like missing laundry, for people to "lose it." David, for example, is even touchier than usual because he's done two days' more duties than the seven that were awarded him. It's being looked into. The slightest thing touches him off, and he snaps and snipes at people. Fortunately, cooler heads prevail when this happens, and we let it pass.

The higher-ups aren't helping matters. They have us running around like chickens with our heads cut off. It becomes a self-fulfilling prophecy. By enforcing supervised everything, they run on the assumption that the troops don't have a head on their shoulders or a brain to think with, and need to be watched all the time. But if they'd let us get on with our jobs, and leave us alone during our downtime, things would be a lot smoother. I guess it's like carrying a heavy pack on a long march. After a while, the weariness begins to show, and people start getting tired of being micro-managed. The weariness is compounded by the fact that people miss their loved ones, and worry about how things are back home. God knows I miss my wife. As always, we soldier on, making the best of things.

Sunday, 05 Feb., QRF Today got off to something of an unusual start. George came and got John and I out of bed around 8:30 and had us report to the mess for 9:30. The Canadian Armed Forces Stress Management team was in camp and we had to answer a questionnaire. These people are called the "Care Bears," much to our amusement. I don't know if it's their real name or something someone floated, but we had fun with it. In spite of the nickname they take themselves pretty seriously. John and I arrived at the appointed hour to find ourselves part of a larger group made up of a cross-section of everyone in camp.

They sat us down and asked us to complete a questionnaire that covered a surprising range of topics, some of the questions were clearly aimed at senior NCOs and higher-ups, and others were more relevant to us in the ranks. Responses could only be from "0," doesn't bug me, up to "5," bugs me a lot. Do you feel like you're being treated like a child? That's easy: "5" points. I don't know anyone who wouldn't answer that one with a 5. Do you feel you are being micro-managed? "4" points on the scale. Is there something going on at home that you wish you could be there to help with? "5!" Can I put in a higher number?

Other questions were a little bit out there. Do you cry a lot? Do I cry a lot? Am I a donkey or a tiger? I wrote "0," of course. I only cry at good cat-food commercials. Has anyone offered to physically comfort you? Uh, that'll be a "0" as in not without getting the shit kicked out of him. Most of the questions simply dealt with doing your job and being over here. For example, do you worry about being shot? "0." Do you worry about hitting a land mine? "1."

The way I look at it, we signed on to do this tour. It's only six months long, so I'm willing to live with others in cramped quarters until it's over, and deal with problems as they arise. It's not so much the work that bugs us, I believe it's been the lack of routine, which prevents us from having and controlling our own spare time. Max Flex is OK for a while, but not for the whole tour. When we get tired like we are now, three things happen: it's hard to keep morale up; it's hard to motivate yourself; and the fine martial art of hiding gets practiced more and more. It's quite amazing actually, how quickly people disappear when they're cut free. Some of us poor sods took longer to cotton on than others, and as a result got dinged for doing more work (I'm pleased to tell you that my skills in this area can be ranked among the best now). Why, just this afternoon, after putting in only two hours on the work party at QM, I mysteriously disappeared, not to be seen again until just before supper.

Where was I you might enquire? Well, I snuck off to call my dear ailing wife, of course, who is home sick in bed taking medication for that nasty illness as she is tended to night and day by our closest friends. She needs to hear from me as often as possible so that her spirits don't flag (she's probably at home drinking up a storm with her friends, and spending all my hard earned money). Yup, that excuse hasn't failed me yet.

The only thing about this call was that Kathleen answered and the conversation lasted about 30 seconds before her end went silent—crying—then when the phone was passed to Catherine she was crying too, so almost half of the ten minute time limit was wasted by listening to two grown women blubber at the end of a phone line halfway around the world. It was a happy sound, though, and a good call in any case.

Around 4:00 the warrant put the word out that "something was happening" and that we were to get our kit ready to go out to the OPs for the night. As we waited for the truck, two stories surfaced as to why we're manning our positions at full strength.

The first involves the celebration that the Serbs are having. Apparently all the guns in Benkovac have been uncovered and are pointed at Rastivic Camp, and there are more troops than usual around. That sounds probable.

The second story is more dubious, and the way things are going, more probable. It seems that a new family has appeared in one of the abandoned houses in Rodaljice—and we didn't know about it for days. This in not good, considering that it was Warrant Fuller, accompanying the DCO at the time, on a random patrol of the village who discovered them. This told the warrant that we hadn't been patrolling the way we were supposed to for at least the last eight days (that's how long the family have been in place). This of course got passed up the line, and the result is all of us are now sitting on OP. After all, "if four people can't do the job properly, then we'll send them all out there." At least that's the gospel according to Ted, who always knows what the real story is. All I know is that it's dark at 1800 and there is nothing to do in the dark without my wife, except sleep. So that's what I'll do.

Update: Lt Reid incident yesterday. Warrant Fuller told us before we shipped out, that during the flare up, our people on the ground had their weapons charged and targets assigned. Lt Reid says, "it's the closest I've come to things getting completely out of hand." Ooohhh, close one. Maybe it's time for somebody to take a break.

Monday, 06 Feb., Rodaljice Another day of boredom in Rodaljice. This morning the wrath of Ted finally got directed my way. Last night during my shift I tried to get the Coleman stove going, but couldn't because it was too dark and I couldn't see clearly what was wrong to fix it. When Ted replaced me in the middle of the night, I passed on that the stove wasn't working. He just said, "that doesn't surprise me," and left the room.

This morning when I woke up, Jim had the stove going and Ted was starting to lose it. He went on about how he couldn't trust me/us anymore, and that he would have to check everything we did from now on so that he wouldn't end up looking like a fool.

I tried to tell him, calmly, that maybe if he'd stuck around, that he would have found out what I wanted to tell him, namely that the stove was probably flooded and that I planned to clean it in the morning. But no, Ted lost it and off he went again. I then tried to explain that maybe he should put some of his much-touted experience to use and try teaching or showing us the right way to do things. That was it. Off the deep end he went. I just lay back down and smiled at him, which pissed him off even more, and he stormed out of the room. He remained quiet the rest of the morning, in fact I think it was well into the afternoon before we heard him say anything at all.

This brings up a point; fully half the section is prepared to take Ted out back and pound him into the dirt. David, John, Jay, Robert, and I think Bruce also, are very close to the line. I've gone to Henry about this but he feels powerless to do anything about it. "Ted is in a world of his own," is his standard response, but he refuses to say anything to Ted.

The boredom is starting to drive us nuts. We heard on the radio this afternoon that 1 Section is on five-minutes' notice to move (they're QRF), but exactly why, I can't tell you. This is the classic case of Militareous Mushroomeous. Maybe more will come down later.

Finally some clarity! At 1900 we were relieved and moved to Bruska. The reason we had to have the full section here was because the tasking called for a section right from the beginning. It was the OC (looking out for the troops) who reduced the number from ten to four (50% strength, 4 on duty, four off, two on leave). When the CO and RSM stopped by Bruska a while back, they figured it out and changed it back. Once again the troops get screwed.

Tuesday, 07 Feb., Bruska Last night was another cool clear evening, with no clouds and wonderful starlight. I did two patrols during the night. One at 2300, and one at 0300. I recall thinking during the last patrol how incredibly clean and fresh the air smelled and what a relief it was not to be constantly assaulted by the ever present stench of sheep shit. The dew hung in the air like a fog, and gave everything the aroma of fresh water. Very pleasant.

Scott was on the second patrol with me, and had trouble getting up. He'd developed quite a migraine headache and he really wasn't feeling well. In fact, it was so bad that we had to call STARLIGHT (Harmen Wells, the medic), to come and get him.

They arrived and pumped Jim full of IV fluid and gave him some heavy duty Tylenol and then took him back to Rastivic. Harmen suspects greatly that this is a classic case of Gameboy headache, brought on by obsessive playing and staring at the 2" X 2" Gameboy screen. Thus accused, Jim quietly got into the ambulance. Smiles all around.

While the medics were taking care of Jim, John and I were dispatched to draw a map of the village for Lt Reid's people. It seems that during the big teardown, our information book containing the names of the villagers, a map indicating which houses they lived in, and any other pertinent information, was left in Rastivic, so we had to come up with a map for quick reference.

Just as John and I were finishing up the patrol, Warrant Fuller pulled up ahead of the ML, which carried 4 gabions for us to put up. Gabions are like wire-mesh boxes, open at the top and bottom. They're 3' x 3' x 5' and fold out to make 9 attached boxes about 30 feet long. The object is to open them out in place, and fill them with rock, sand, or sandbags to create an instant wall. They're usually used to provide protection for modular tenting, against a blast of some kind-mortars, artillery, or grenades, that sort of thing.

The arrival of these gabions has been something of a source of amusement for us. After removing virtually everything from our camp here, higher have now started to bring things back. Two sections of modular tent are now up, with a third on the way. The gabions are now here, and a generator has also been brought to us. Today, also, a beaver-tail full of sandbags arrived so that we can build a bunker. There's a lot of work to be done, and to tell the truth, no one wants to do it. We're being relieved of this duty on the 12th now, and our section at least won't be here to move all the rock required to fill the gabions or build the bunker. The warrant told us to take our time doing the work, and we're making that go as far as possible. It's not fair to the incoming troops of course but, hey, every man for himself at this point.

The warrant was some pissed when he showed up today. It seems Reid is dragging his feet big time in the hope that he won't have to take over our tasking. What really got the warrant going happened while Lt Reid went on a patrol of Rodaljice. During the patrol he went past the upper part of the village where the abandoned houses are. He asked his guide, if we ever went into any of the buildings. The Cpl explained that we didn't because the engineers have not cleared any of the buildings, and therefore they were considered unsafe and off limits. In light of some of the ethnic cleansing that took place in the area and some of the booby traps found in the buildings when we got here, it was a safe bet to stay the hell away from them.

So what does Reid do? He walks right into one of the buildings and starts rooting around. The Cpl just about shit when he heard things being thrown around. The warrant wants to kill Reid. There are other reasons why the warrant remains pissed at this guy, the details of which I am not privy to. But from what I can gather Reid is simply being an asshole about the change-over process, and people are tired of it, and him.

Just before noon the VanDoo Col who will be leading our replacement mission, along with our CO, OC, and various staff toadies, showed up to get the low-down on the village. Jay, who was pre-warned by the warrant, put on his French hat and swung into high gear giving his prepared routine completely in fluent French, much to the surprise and delight of the VanDoo Col. The visit lasted about twenty minutes, then the assembled officers piled into their Iltis and headed off in a cloud of dust leaving us to continue filling the gabions.

We broke for lunch and started up a game of horseshoes. It was a beautiful day and no one really felt like working anyway, so the game generated lots of interest. Around 2:30 we started back to work. We had just begun when the ML showed up again with UNHCR flour and lentil beans for us to distribute. After John, David, and I unloaded the truck (while the rest of the boys stood around and talked) I decided I'd had enough of the flour so I went back to moving rock. I figured the rest of the guys can get themselves covered with flour, I at least wasn't going to look like a ghost and have to spend the next two days cleaning myself off. As it is, I can hardly stand my own smell. I've been out here for three days without washing or changing, and to say I'm starting to get a little ripe is only just beginning to describe it.

Ted and I were the only two in the section to work on the gabions; the rest were busy talking and playing around with the food distribution. We both filled two squares each, using rock from walls inside the compound, and then we called it a night. The fact that we were the only two working was "duly noted."

Since the start of this shift, I've eaten next to nothing. Aside from the fact that there's very little for us to eat, aside from hard rations if we want them—but no one does—I really haven't felt all that hungry. It's a hell of a way to lose weight, I know, but if you're not hungry why eat?

It's another clear evening and it promises to be a cold one, but as I finish this entry, the stars are out and it's nice and warm by the fire. Home weighs heavily on my mind.

Wednesday, 08 Feb., Bruska Today was something of a slower day, if that's at all possible. Instead of getting up at 6:30, we all got up around 8:00. The only major task of the day was to unload the beaver tail that had been dropped off yesterday, and stack the sandbags outside the wire. We were going to wait for Lt Reid to show up around 9:00 before we started, but when it became obvious he was going to be late we started working.

Again it was Ted and I who did the bulk of the work. No matter, when Reid showed up an hour late, we used it as an excuse to take a break and talk to his driver, Tim Drew.

Tim's a Cape Bretoner, and he's known far and wide for his stories, and rumour control. He's the man you want to go to find out about anything that's going on in the Regiment.

According to Tim, higher is trying to charge Lt Reid for that incident I mentioned yesterday. "Yes lads, another brilliant career down the drain," as Tim put it. A statement delivered with more than a liberal amount of sarcasm. Well we do it to ourselves I guess. In this case nobody seems surprised.

It also seems that the reason Reid has been dragging his feet on the change-over, has to do with the amount of work we've put into our camps, or more accurately, the lack of work. He's not pleased with our progress and doesn't want his boys to be stuck doing all the work of rebuilding the defences. They're leaving the camp at Pristeg in good working order and figure we should do the same. What's overlooked here is that Pristeg is in the Zone, and higher on the priority list to get defensive stores. We've only just received ours, and haven't even started work yet. Still, 2 Platoon feels it's getting the shaft, and to be honest I can't say I blame them.

Henry took the lieutenant for a walk around the village, and gave him the rundown on things as the rest of us worked on unloading the beaver tail.

By noon Reid had left, the beaver tail was empty, and we were relaxing. David, Robert, and Jay were supposed to leave during the afternoon some time. Jay and

Robert to Budapest for their second 96er, and David back to Canada for his block leave. We received a radio message that told us the pickup was delayed till later tonight. Now today was David's 21st birthday, and he had been in a good mood all day, jovial in fact. But as soon as he learned that the pickup time might be changed, he went from happy and friendly, to black and snapping at people. It was amazing. Then five minutes later we heard that the truck was on the way, he changed back to jovial again. It's almost scary to watch. I've never seen anyone change like that. And it's not just this time. Every day you can see examples of violent mood swings in him. It's very much like watching a child when he doesn't get his way. When he gets what he wants, he's happy. When he has to work extra, or do something he doesn't want to do, he gets angry and snaps at people. The best policy has been to ignore him, but he's starting to get on people's nerves.

What he's exhibiting, of course, are the classic stress symptoms. Violent mood swings, easily irritable, becomes quiet and reserved at times, it goes on and on. Some of it, I think, is because he's young and doesn't know how to deal with the strain of the job, and the pressures of life back in Canada. He has a promising pro football career waiting for him back home, and I know it occupies his mind a lot. I've tried to talk to him from time to time, but he won't open up to me. Harmen appears to be the only one he will talk to. This is fine of course, as long as he's talking. Hopefully when he returns off leave, he'll be a little easier to deal with.

Later in the afternoon Reid and a VanDoo company commander came by and Henry and I took him and assembled entourage for a tour of the village. Why this guy was here is a little beyond us. The villages are not in his area of responsibility (AOR). Reid did bring his platoon warrant with him on this trip and we gave him a rundown on the set-up and what to expect in the area. He too was not very pleased with the state of the defences, but at least he understood why things hadn't been done.

With all the reccees out of the way, and David, Jay and Robert on their way back to camp, Ted, John, Henry and I sat around the fire and waited to be relieved. We've adopted, or more accurately we've been adopted by, two small puppies ('tis the season, there's small things running around all over the place).

One, who's obviously the runt, is more long than high, so we've nicknamed him "Nick Cofare," as "Bobby the Rookie" (from the Beasty Boy video). The other, who's more tall than long, we call Webster. The two have staked out our camp as home, and bark at anyone who comes near; in return we give them food from our rations. I guess they know a good thing when they've got one.

Webster (foreground) and Nic Cofare resting by the fire in Bruska

Relief showed up at 2000 in a track, so we had to drive it back to Rastivic. That was OK. It was a nice night for a tank drive in the country anyway.

My shower was from 9:15 to 9:35 and man did it feel good!

Thursday, 09 Feb., Patrolling Today started out slow, then shifted into overdrive and went long, hard and wet. It was our turn to be patrolling section today, and last night before we went to bed, we confirmed our departure time as 10:30 A.M. With everything geared to that departure time, I woke up late and had a leisurely breakfast, followed by a chat with Jeff Baker about sports psychology. He's trying to get himself ready for the upcoming Ironman competition back in Petawawa, but doesn't know how to go about mentally preparing. I've had some experience with sports psychology through my shooting so I offered some pointers. Right in the middle of the conversation the door burst open and John, who was staying behind today to be on medals parade, looked at me and said, "get ready to go now! You guys were supposed to be out patrolling three hours ago." It was 8:55.

At exactly 9:03 we were loaded up and starting to move towards the gate on our way to Charles Company for the first leg of our 8-hour patrol. In the past couple of days there has been a new track route introduced which takes us around the town limits of Benkovac, and it now takes about an hour to get to Charles from Rastivic. The old route took 20 minutes but took us through the town, and by a Serb radio installation. Well, someone complained, and we now take the scenic route over hill and dale to get our orders for the day. So much for the UN having free access to travel any portion of the countryside!

Little of interest happened during the day. We did our patrol route and made the requisite stops to check for new work on old bunkers, but otherwise it was pretty much routine.

Patrolling is pretty straightforward stuff. We have two of the three patrol routes given to us first thing in the morning. There are bunkers and troop positions we're supposed to check, and we're always on the lookout for extra activity or vehicle/equipment movement. Essentially you're looking to see if anything has changed from the last time. After you get to know an area, you can tell at a glance if anything's up.

Our patrol time is set at eight hours, though truth be told, we could fly through the routes in under 5 hours, so somewhere along the line we have to kill three hours. This is usually done by stopping at some of our OPs for coffee, or along the route to suntan (weather permitting of course) while we overwatch an area. The point is that we must be in the Zone for the full eight hours.

Today was a bit of a pisser. Not only did we get off to a slow start, which meant we couldn't take any breaks, it was raining when we left. Fortunately it stopped about an hour into the patrol but by then you were wet and the constant wind of the moving carrier made you cold.

I've likened an eight-hour patrol to being in a 13-ton vibrating food processor machine. The vibrations come from the track pads slapping the pavement at 30 or 40 miles per hour, sending the millions of tiny shocks right through your body. The food processor part comes from the off road stuff. Like a giant piece of bread dough, you get bounced around in the hatch opening as the carrier jumps and slides around on the uneven ground. At one point in today's patrol, the carrier hit a rock and jumped sideways. At the time my knee was locked and I swear I felt it pop out sideways then back into place. It was uncomfortable for a while but otherwise fine.

The patrol was, as I said, pretty quiet up until about 2:30, when two things happened. First it started to rain again, and second, we got a call from Charles HQ that a "backhoe" was reported in their area and that we were to take our time coming back, but to find and track it. In the time it took us to get back to the Charles Company lines, any self respecting backhoe operator could have travelled to Zagreb and back, but this didn't seem to bother the boys in Charles HQ. They couldn't provide us with a grid reference for this thing so they had no idea where it was either. They were however worried that it might be engaged in digging activities in the restricted area near the Zone. "Don't worry sir, we'll find it," Henry assured them.

Trying to find this thing was next to impossible, if not completely out of the question without at least a starting point, which no one could provide for us. But like the dutiful troopies we are, we spent an hour tootling around in search of the "backhoe."

When the call first came in we took a moment to understand just what it was we were looking for. We all understood that a backhoe was like a tractor with a bucket on the front, and a shovel arm on the back and rode around on tires. The kind of thing you see working on street repairs and such. As we covered the final 500 metres to the front gate of Charles Company we passed the shovel that we passed on the way down the road that morning. A quick glance revealed that it had not moved from its location when we passed this way earlier today. We were all geared up to look for a backhoe, yet here was this shovel sitting there (a shovel is a tracked vehicle used for serious excavation, and has one really big arm on the front of it). As we drove past, we all just looked at one another for a second then shook our heads. It couldn't be. If you stood on the gatehouse at the front gate of Charles Company you could see this thing sitting there. Why would they send us on a wild goose chase to find something that could be seen with the naked eye from inside their own compound? It was just too obvious.

We'd pulled into Charles to make our patrol report around 1600. The race was on a bit, because it gets dark between 1730–1800, and we still had an hour's drive to put in before we pulled into Rastivic. After dark we can only move in pairs, so if we didn't get a jag on, things were going to get complicated real fast.

Ted was starting to peak because he wanted to get back and not have to wait around for another vehicle to escort us. Jim and I were just plain cold, wet, and tired.

Henry went off to do his report, which should have taken about 15 minutes, while we sat with the engine running ready to roll out. The longer Henry took, the worse Ted got. After fifteen minutes the engine was shut off, and Ted started to complain. After thirty minutes, he was out of his driver's seat and pacing the top of the carrier getting more irate by the minute. By 45 minutes he was doing everything but stomping his feet. All Jim and I could do was laugh internally at him or nod and agree with what he was saying. We did both.

Finally, after 50 minutes, Henry showed up. It turns out the "backhoe" they were so keen to find was the shovel we'd spotted in the morning and was still in plain view of the front gate. Henry had a hell of a time convincing them but when he dragged them outside to look for themselves it put an end to their protests. He said later that they felt pretty stupid when they found out where the thing was parked.

By this point we were all pissed off, but especially Ted, and he was driving. What followed was more fun than any ride at the CNE. My back road Baja run with Ray had nothing on this ride.

I can honestly say that it was quite an experience to feel 13 tons of tank slllllliiiiii-ddddddeeeeng through a corner at 40 miles an hour while watching the rocks roll down the hill into the ravine below. We missed two turns in our rush to get home, which only served to piss Ted off even more, and were forced to backtrack. I'd always heard you could spin a carrier, but I'd never experienced it until now. Jim is our regular driver, and every time I looked back he was hanging on for dear life and shaking his head in disbelief.

By my watch, the route should have taken an hour and fifteen minutes to drive. But 43 minutes after we left the front gate at Charles Company we pulled into Rastivic. Now that's what I call a ride.

I recall cataloging my ailments as I stepped from the back door of the carrier. My feet were numb from the vibration and cold, my back was killing me from standing for eight hours, my ribs were sore from being bounced around, and I could hardly move my hands from the wet and cold. This, dear friends, is what we in the army call FUN!!??

PS: a final note before I close out today's entry. MCpl Weir went up on orders parade today. He was charged as the supervisor for the two guys who poured naphtha on the stove and started the fire. He was found guilty and given a reprimand and told to supervise more closely. No loss of pay.

Friday, 10 Feb., Patrolling After yesterday's patrol and last night's beer (or two), I took my time getting up and going to breakfast. I knew last night that I wasn't going on patrol today, because we have six guys in the section, and only four are needed on patrol, so Jim and I stayed back.

I was in my ISO after breakfast, quietly writing in my diary, when MCpl Parry came in and said I was needed for a work party at CQ. Despite my protestations that today was my day off, I was met with the standard RCR line, "too bad bud, you're it." I'm going to have to learn to hide better!

After taking my time to get into my uniform and wander over to CQ, I discovered that they wanted me to move boxes so that I could put up the shelves. With a little bit of artful dodging and a "slightly" exaggerated need to go do some personal admin at the pay office, I managed to get myself out of a morning's work cleaning up the stores room with the promise to return after lunch and install the shelving.

With the morning off, I grabbed my diary and Cat's plane ticket and headed for the pay office to settle my pay claim, then to find a better hiding place so I could finish yesterday's entries.

With the storeroom cleaned up, it took only an hour or so to nail together, then wedge in place the shelving system I'd designed. And then, *quelle catastrophe*! I ran out of wood. Sadly, I was forced to stop. Damn—and I was so looking forward to working all afternoon too. Oh well, soldier on. *Smile*

With the afternoon off, the sun shining and a good book in hand, I headed off to find a new hiding place and enjoy the sun.

Around 4:00 I came back to our lines and struck up a conversation with George, who was sitting outside his ISO writing up reports and returns. He's been filling in as platoon warrant while Fuller did the lieutenant's job, and the lieutenant was on vacation. McConnell's now back, but Fuller's gone on vacation, so George stays where he is for the next three weeks.

With George you can always tell how stressed he is by the number of satirical comments he makes in any one-minute period. Today he must have been particularly stressed, because the satire was non-stop. We talked for about half an hour about his job, and various things, and there seemed to be a never-ending litany of biting, and off-colour remarks accompanying everything he talked about.

When we were done, I went to pack my kit for my upcoming trip to Rodaljice and our last shift on OP there before we start patrolling in earnest.

The boys hadn't come back from patrol by 5:00 so I went off to have supper and was shocked to find the food actually tasted good. A couple of days ago there was an officer from HQ standing outside the door to the mess asking people how the food was, and what they thought. Boy did he get an earful. I have it on pretty good authority that the CO had the KO up in front of him, and gave him the jacking up of the tour. The KO was told in no uncertain terms to improve the quality of the food or he was toasting (no pun intended). The KO appears to have reacted. I noticed tonight that the MCpls were doing the bulk of the cooking, instead of sitting back and supervising the hired help the way they had been in the past. This is a good thing, because they have all the experience, and are far better cooks than the local women. We'll have to see how long this will last, but for now it's made a difference in the way things taste and are presented.

After supper our platoon signaller came and asked me to suit up and go along as a co-driver for him, while we drove to Charles Company to escort Lt Reid back to Rastivic. It seems that Lt Reid got himself nearly shot again today. In talking to their driver for the escapade, we got the lowdown from the front seat of an Iltis on the scene; here's what happened.

Lt McConnell and Reid were in the Charles Company AOR looking for evidence of defensive digging. They found one place with no one around, but evidence of fresh digging. After reporting it, they started looking for more digging in the same area, and they found it. Spotting fresh digging in the tree line off one of the main routes, they stopped to check it out. They drove up to the sight but stopped short, as the officers wanted to walk the remaining ground. As McConnell and Reid approached the trees on foot, a Serb soldier stepped out from behind a mound and told them to "Stop" and "Leave." They both paused for a moment, and decided that it probably was best to leave. They turned to leave, walking a few paces back towards the Iltis, and then Reid spins around and starts walking towards the soldier. The soldier unslings his AK-47, cocks it, and points it right at Reid's face telling him to "LEAVE! NOW!" It happened so fast that McConnell was left standing in the middle of the road with no weapon to hand and the driver was scrambling to get his rifle out of the rack in the Iltis and cock it.

"Leave, now!" is always good advice when you have a weapon pointed in your face, and for once in his life Reid finally decided to listen.

Twenty minutes after leaving the area an UNMO was shot at from the same point in the tree line. Clearly someone didn't want the UN to see what was happening in that little section of the wood.

With the shooting, 3-9er (OC Charles Company) was sent by higher to negotiate with the local brigade commander. As a precaution all wheeled vehicles in the Charles AOR have to move in pairs. This is why we had to send the extra Iltis to escort Reid and his vehicle back to Rastivic.

We arrived at 5:30 and didn't leave until well after 7:00. Reid was in the Ops room the whole time filling in reports. We were in the TV room watching *The Simpsons*. There's something appropriate about that parallel.

Finally just as we pulled into Rastivic, the boys in the section were pulling out of the gate on their way to Rodaljice. It was decided that I'd catch up to them tomorrow, so I dumped my kit and headed for the mess but on the way there I stopped to call Catherine.

She's in the third week of her medication, and she's not much improved. What they did was give her a massive dose of steroids by IV, and are gradually weaning her off them by using steroid pills and gradually reducing the dosage. She's still weak, and the medication affects her vision, so she can't drive. She's been forced to take this entire month off because of the side effects of the medication, and I expect she'll need another week or two to get her bearings back before she can start working again. This week she will be at home alone, which only adds to my concern. I understand the neurologist is not overly pleased with her progress, which worries me that much more. When I get back we'll have to have a long talk about what she should do for a living. I feel strongly that she should do something that doesn't force her to leave the house that often, and I'd really like to see her take up writing seriously. Lord knows she has both the talent and the mind for it.

I met Henry in the mess and over a couple of beers I told him about Catherine's latest episode, and my feelings about it. I find it difficult to describe my feelings for Catherine and not get misty eyed about it. When talking to Henry I had to fight with myself from time to time to keep my emotions in check; even so I think Henry noticed. After discussing the matter for a while, Henry suggested that I talk to the lieutenant about getting a compassionate leave back home to be with Cat. This was an option I'd always kept in the back of my mind but never really seriously considered. We decided that before I went out to Rodaljice tomorrow I'd drop in to see the lieutenant and discuss the matter.

We walked back to our company lines and who should we run into but Mr McConnell. Now I didn't want to talk to him tonight because I'd had one beer too many and was lightheaded. I hadn't fully formulated my plan of attack, and wanted more time to think about it. As it was I wasn't fully convinced this was the route I wanted to take. Also, because I was lightheaded my main concern was that I might say something stupid I might regret later. With that in mind I tried to make an appointment for tomorrow. No dice, tonight or nothing, he was otherwise engaged tomorrow and wouldn't have the time. So off to his ISO we went.

I started telling him of Catherine's latest episode and how she and everyone at home were handling it. I remember listening to myself prattle on about how bad things were at home, and wondering to myself if he really gave a damn. Then, I just stopped talking. I looked down at him sitting on the end of his bed, and I made my decision. "Sir, this is her third episode in three months. If it happens again, I'm going to ask for a compassionate leave to return home." The silence hung in the air for an incredibly long moment. Then he looked at me and said, "Of course," and he offered to take it to higher when the time came.

I don't think it's so much that she needs me, but rather that I don't want to stand by and let her suffer without my being there to help her through it. I believe I've proven myself here, and that I've done a good job despite the burden of the troubles at home. But Catherine is my responsibility, and I will not let her down. In this I stand firm.

Saturday, 11 Feb., Rodaljice Well, I finally made it out to Rodaljice. I got here about 11:00 AM and it's now 11:00 PM, and that about describes the day. We cleaned up the compound a bit, John and I went for a longish patrol, and the rest of the day we slept, ate, read, or just talked. Peter Juneau from 1 Section is with us today to bring us up to six (Ted, Jim John, and Tim), and myself. It's pretty quiet here.

After rereading last night's entry, I have to say that there's a part of me that feels like I'm wimping out by leaving before the end of the tour. Like the Yin and Yang, I wage a constant battle between the various parts of my psyche. There's no doubt which argument will win this battle, but the fact that I have to think about it at all troubles me. I've always been kind of slow at times trying to figure out what to do in various situations. I have an enormous capacity for compassion and understanding all sides of the story, but I don't feel myself smart enough to always make the right decision. It makes me feel like a bloody idiot some times.

Fortunately it's not as bad as it used to be. I'm tending to stick more to the facts and less to emotion. Maybe I'm actually learning something in this lifetime! Stranger things have been known to happen I guess.

Here's the funny of the day. It comes to us from 2 Platoon while they were in Pristeg the other day. It seems that a herd of 70 Croat sheep, while being grazed in the Zone by a Croat shepherd, wandered over to the Serb side while the shepherd was dozing in the sun (probably drunk at the time). When the sheep arrived in the village the Serbs quickly established that they were Croatian sheep, and divided the herd up in record time among the local villagers. The shepherd, upon waking and finding his sheep missing, quickly tracked the herd far enough to realize where they were headed, then rather than go after them he returned to his side of the Zone before he got shot. The gravity of the situation thus realized, he quickly went to the local commander and relayed the situation. As the sheep were more or less headed in the direction of 2 Platoon's position, he probably hoped that they had corralled the sheep and were holding them. So up the chain of command on the Croatian side the request went. Within an hour a radio call was placed to 2 Platoon asking to talk to Sunray. Lt Reid was found and brought to the radio. With the radio room packed with listeners, the lieutenant listened as the guy on the other end tried to explain the situation. Finally he was asked, "do you have any sheep in your compound?" As the lieutenant began to talk, everyone in the radio room broke into sheep noises. The lieutenant tried to cover the mike so that only his voice was heard, but to no avail, for he sounded like he was broadcasting from the middle of a herd of sheep. A good laugh was had by all.

Sunday, 12 Feb., Rodaljice Last night was kind of interesting. While sitting around reading we heard Bruska call in and report a T54/55 rolling up the road to Camp Alpha. That, I suppose, is one way to get the attention of the local Croats.

Meanwhile back at Rodaljice, 2 Platoon is replacing us today, and I got nominated to stay behind and show them the patrol route through the village. Kind of a walk-and-talk as part of the handover. Fair is fair, I came out late so I don't mind coming in late. 2 Platoon arrived shortly after 8:00 and by 8:30 the section 2IC, myself, and one other were walking down the road on a guided tour of the local abodes, while the remainder of the section off loaded gabions, and began filling them with sandbags.

Upon our return I removed my flack vest and coat, and offered to pitch in to help work on the gabions with the rest of the new section. The offer died as soon as it was uttered, for the sergeant simply turned to me and said, "No! You go off and do whatever it is you 3 Platoon people do!" (". . . I don't want you anywhere near me"). I knew there was some animosity towards us, Lt Reid had not been pleased with the state of the defences here or at Bruska, but holy shit this was a bit much. Though sorely tempted, I chose not to push the issue. Instead I walked away and used the time to do some letter writing.

I know some of the guys in the platoon, so when I got my anger back under control, and out of sight of the sergeant, I grabbed one of the guys I knew and quietly asked what was up. 2 Platoon are quite angry with us for not handing over completed and stocked positions the way they did for us. As a private there was nothing I could have done about that, it's a matter for platoon warrants and commanders to sort out. Each time the sergeant came in during the morning, he would make snide comments to his men about the work 3 Platoon hadn't done, or how things could be done better than they were. I listened politely, but refused to rise to the bait. I kept thinking how terribly disappointed I was with this man. Here was a sergeant who was insulting fellow sergeants in his own company, in front of his troops no less. I felt like I was being blamed for everything that our platoon had done wrong, yet I knew if I opened my mouth I would have been eaten alive by this guy so I said nothing and kept writing. I felt it was the only way to deal with someone who was simply venting his frustration with the situation.

Relief couldn't come soon enough, and showed up at 11:30. By 12:30 I was in the mess eating a decent meal, then I grabbed my diary and letters and headed for the JRs to hide and write, happy that the morning's misadventure was behind me.

Freedom, they say is the feeling you get when you have discharged all your responsibilities. At long last I managed to sit down and write the kids in class 4N, one of my wife's music student classes. They had asked many questions in their last letter, and I had been putting them off until I could find time to deal with them. The following is the letter I sent:

12 Feb 94
To the class of 4N

Greetings from Croatia! Thank you so much for writing to me at Christmas. It was really nice to hear from home at a time when it is important to be with the ones you love.

You all asked so many questions that what I've decided to do is write to you as a class so that you can all hear the answers to the questions you asked.

Let me begin by saying that I am due to come home some time in early April and that I very much look forward to meeting all of you in person. When I get back I'll arrange to come to your school and you can ask all the questions you want.

What is the weather like here? Well, it's not like home. On Christmas day I was sun tanning in front of my bunker, while it was thirty below where you were. We're very close to the Adriatic Sea here, so it is quite warm year round. If I had to compare the climate to any place in Canada, it would have to be Vancouver, but not as pretty. There's snow in the mountains and rain where we are, and where there's rain there's mud. And here there's lots of it, so things can get messy.

Do I have much spare time? Not really, otherwise I would have written to you sooner. Right now we're in the process of changing jobs so things are a little confusing. This will change as we develop a routine and learn our jobs better.

Is it a lot of work? It can be. When we move to a new location we have to build a place to live, and protect it with sandbags, and while we're doing that, we still have our regular job to do as well. When we're finished building though, we have time to write letters or read, and things get easier.

Where do we live? I live in two places. For four days I live with nine other guys in a big tent. We eat, sleep, and watch TV, play cards all inside the tent. We patrol several times a day on foot around the village, but mostly we stay in the compound. The other place I live is in an ISO trailer with two other guys. An ISO trailer looks like a sea container with windows and a door. There is a heater, lights, a locker to hangs things, and three beds. It's not very big but we call it home. Every four days we rotate jobs. Two of the jobs leave from our main base so I live in my ISO for eight days then live in the tent for four days.

What made me join the Army? That's a tough one, but I will try to give you an honest answer. My dad was in the military, and I grew up believing that words like love, honour, respect, and loyalty actually meant more than the words themselves. Too many people say they respect or love something when they really don't. This is called paying lip service to something. It is easy to do, and we are all guilty of doing it. But, if we are going to make a difference in the world, it's important that we try hard to do the right thing all the time. This means that if you believe in something, you must stand up for it, or act upon it. Many people believed in the idea of Israel and they moved there to make that belief a reality. I believe in Canada, and I believe that to make a difference in the world we must reach out to help some way. Being in the Army is something I liked to do, so it was easy for me to sign up and come here to try to make a difference. Only history will tell if we all made the right decision. Nonetheless I did it because I didn't want pay lip service to the things I believed in.

I have to go now, but I hope you will think about what I have just written and maybe the class can write back with more questions. My love to all of you and I'll see you when I get back.

Your UN soldier in Croatia
Kurt

Tonight's Ogroup, the first in over a week, was interesting. Lots of stuff about not sending souvenirs home, things like bombs, rifles, pieces of kit, road signs, you know, the usual stuff. Then there were the stories; some guy tried to send a sheep crossing sign back in his barrack box, and another tried to send an unexploded land mine back—no shit! Zero tolerance, tough inspections, the usual crap.

A couple of good points though. The Krajina Serbs have all but declared war on Croatia. They've gone to the highest possible state of preparation without actually mobilizing. This is partly evidenced by the number of VCFA's (Violations of the Cease-fire Agreement) reported each day. At the beginning of the tour there were less than ten per day throughout the Zone. Now we're over twenty per day and climbing. We've been told that if we catch Serbs in the zone with weapons, to try and take them away, but if we can't, to escort them out of the Zone. Nothing like UN backbone. "I'm going to take your gun from you." "No!" "OK, then, we'll walk you home."

There have been reports of fake trip-wires across patrol routes, so we've been told not to become complacent. As if there was ever any danger of that happening! Patrolling has become the hot tasking to have. Charles Company tried to fob off some of its OPs on us so they could do it. We told them thanks but no thanks.

Can you believe it? The military is sending around a questionnaire on racism. With a section populated with a Frog, a Spick, a couple of WOPs, a couple of WASPs, some character from the Rock who managed to sneak in, and a section commander who loves the Aryan race, we're going to have a ball with this one. Racism? There ain't no racism here! Now where's that damn Newfy anyway?

Under the old-things-die-hard category, postings this spring to the Airborne Regiment are still on, as soon as they find a Regiment to sent them to.

Finally, in the "you must be joking" column, some guy lost it big time. Today being Sunday and with no one in Foxtrot Company working Sundays, the boys last night were having a few. I understand a clerk, with only a week left to go, got a Dear John letter. He got drunk and went back to his ISO. When his buddies showed up, he had his weapon loaded and cocked, and he pointed it at them telling them to get out or he'd shoot. Guess who just bought himself a stay at the Crowbar Hotel.

Did he have cause to get drunk? Hell ya. Were his actions justifiable? Not a hope in hell! I think I can relate to how he feels. I've been in a shit mood all day because of this thing with Catherine. But the thought of using my weapon hasn't even entered my mind, being as it's so small and all (my mind, that is). With me, her problem is like background music. Sometimes you listen, sometimes you don't, and today I did. But that's no reason to play with the pointy end of a loaded gun.

Life is never so bad that it can't get worse. This guy lost touch because of alcohol and pulled a boner. Now he'll pay the price.

Monday, 13 Feb., Patrolling Today, without doubt, we earned our pay. At last night's Ogroup, we were told to be ready to go at 0800 for a patrol that was to last till 1300. The QRF section has been tasked this week with picking up one of the patrol routes. This is a good thing, because it gets us out of the eye of the CSM and his make-work parties.

Around 2100 Henry comes around and tells everyone to be up and ready to go for 0700, the tasking has been bumped up. 2230 rolls around and Henry comes around again and tells us to get up at 0530, and to be at the track for 0615, we've been tasked to the engineers to provide security while they clear a roadblock and route. We're expected back at 1300. Cool, finally something interesting to do. Maybe we'll learn something about booby traps and mines.

0615—We're all ready to roll. Rendez-vous has been delayed to 0700. We all run to the mess to try and grab a bite of breakfast.

0700—At the back gate of Rastivic, talking to the engineers and medics about the upcoming task. The team is assembled.

0710—We're on the road and moving.

0720—While rounding a corner en route, a loud CLANK is heard, followed by a rapid deceleration accompanied by the sound of grinding. The carrier is pulled off to the side of the route in a clearing to allow others to pass. Ted jumps out, so does Henry. Bruce and I hang over the edge looking at the track on the right side of the carrier. Something is definitely wrong; the tracks are not straight. Closer inspection shows that not one, but three SETS, six road wheels, have self-destructed. There are bent rims, pieces of metal and dislodged track. This is going to be a LONG day.

0723—What to do? The engineers are chomping at the bit—they still have a roadblock to clear. John and I grab the C-9s and along with Ted, load up in their carrier and head out. Jim, Tim, and Henry stay behind to figure out the extent of the damage.

What's left of the road wheels

0730—Arrive at roadblock. Roadblock absent. We found evidence of where it was, but obviously someone removed it. Looks like someone ran a landline across the road and covered it. An old woman living a short distance away opens her gate and fifty chickens run out. Henceforth she's known as "the chicken lady." False alarm blamed on her.

0750—Back at our carrier, unload, wave good-bye to engineer, spit out the dust as they drive away, prepare for a long day's work.

0800—It's decided, we need Bluebell support (REMEs). We have a bent rear shock; seven road wheels need replacing, and a new track because of bent teeth.

0815—Bluebell denied; they're tied up with too much work. As soon as they find them they'll send the road wheels, and a jack. I'm getting a pain in my lower abdomen.

0900—Wave hello, then good-bye as Engineers speed by. Spit out dust. Someone put the roadblock back after we left. Chicken lady suspected. Pain in belly bad now, recognize symptoms, take paper towel and start looking for a convenient bush without a mine attached.

0920—Return to track. Much relieved.

0945—Engineers and medics fly by covering us with dust. They're smiling at us—bastards. Shake fist in defiance. Break out the rations, grab some rays, and have a meal. Wait for parts.

1245—Labell comes by with parts. Give him shit for destroying our track last night (he drove it last). He smiles, waves then leaves. More dust. Shake fist again. The work begins.

1500—"One Three Bravo. This is Three, send SITREP, over."

"One Three Bravo. We should be able to leave this position in figures 60 minutes, over."

"Three. What position is that? Over."

"One Three Bravo. We haven't moved all day. Over."

"Three. Rodger that. Out."

1600—Halleluja!!! We're on the road again. Track vibrates badly due to bent teeth. Everyone crosses fingers hoping to get home without breaking down. Maybe we'll get supper.

1620—Pull into Rastivic and park. Tell George the track needs to be worked on tomorrow, needs new tracks and parts. Expect a long day tomorrow. Time for supper and a shower. REMEs come over for a look. Carrier's grounded.

1824—George tells CSM about carrier. CSM pissed, goes to Bluebell. Argument ensues.

1900—"Get out of the shower, you're breaking track tonight." All parts and new tracks waiting for us at maintenance. "It shouldn't be too bad, boys," CSM says, "it should only take you five or six hours." He smiles. We're not impressed. Want to shake fist, but don't; grumble instead.

1920—Arrive at maintenance hangar, break into two teams, John, Tim, and I build new tracks from fresh parts right out of the crate. Robert, Jay, Jim, Henry, Ted, break track and change rear shock. One maintenance guy to help direct traffic. It could be worse, I guess; it could be raining and we could be up to our asses in mud. Take off shirt and turn up tunes. Led Zeppelin. "Let's have at "er."

(Note: How to assemble a track. Two boxes with five pieces of 7 connected pads each. Lay pieces on side and connect each piece using sledgehammer to drive end connectors in place. Watch fingers. Each track 64 or 65 pads long, depending. Each track assembled on side in big coil, then flipped over to put on end connectors on other side. Track weighs 800 or so pounds, and takes at least four guys with crowbars to flip. Track uncoiled, put on side, then each end connector is loosened, hammered into place, then torqued. Remove old track by disconnecting two end connectors and driving off the track. Old track is removed and carrier backed up. New track laid in line with the wheels then carrier is driven onto it. Wrap remaining track around wheels and connect using end connectors, sledge hammers, and a liberal amount of militaristic explanitudes).

2220—Skinned knuckles, sore back, two broken sledgehammers, and sweat-covered bodies. Second track assembled and torqued. John, Tim, and I take a break and wait for second track to be removed from vehicle. We're ahead of schedule.

2315—New tracks attached and working, clean up starts. Everyone's moving slower.

2400—Job done. George shows up and takes picture. Then drops a great bombshell. The CO at Primiston has been fired for being caught in a "gay liaison." Apparently there's quite the circle down there. Sergeant from the MPs has been sent down to investigate. CSM sends compliments, sleep in tomorrow.

I fall asleep as soon as my head hits the pillow; it's been a long day. Maybe I'll skip breakfast tomorrow.

24 VCFA's today. Things are heating up. Nobody cares.

Tuesday, 14 Feb., Rastivic A nice relaxing day today. In the morning I went to the mess and wrote a couple of letters and worked on the diary, then had lunch.

In the afternoon, I worked on packing all my UAB (unaccompanied baggage). It felt good to get that monkey off my back. It's supposed to be done by the 25th of the month, but I wanted to get it out of the way early. I recall in August how, when we sent our UAB off, we all had a feeling of anticipation. The anticipation isn't quite as high this time, but there certainly is a feeling that something's on the move. The end is starting to come into sight.

Here are a couple of interesting bits of news. Remember the warrant that was charged for hitting the CSM around Christmas? He was reduced in rank to sergeant and allowed to stay.

Major General Vernon, Commander of LFCA who introduced the Warrior training program, was fired today. Reasons to follow.

The guy who tried to kill himself a couple of days ago is in the Crowbar Hotel for his own protection. He had only seven days left before going home, and they've got him on suicide watch. Some of the MPs think he should be kept somewhere else (Zagreb or Split. Less stressful). But for now he stays where he is.

Do you recall me telling you about the sergeant in Knin who caught the Serbs in the wire? On medals parade the other day he received a plaque from the General. What more can I say?

WARNING ORDER

Situation: Security tasking tomorrow.

Mission: 3 Platoon will provide security for Croatians visiting graves in Zone to remember start of the hostilities.

General: No orders tonight. Frag orders issued at Charles Company before departure.

Timings: Recce departs 6:15 AM. Main body departs 7:30 AM.

RV: RV at Charles Company HQ at 0800 AM.

This is a section tasking that exploded into a platoon tasking. Consensus is that Charles Company OC is flinching again. Then again you never know.

14 Feb 95.
My dearest Darling Catherine
  It's raining outside, Dire Straits are playing on the stereo and I've just completed packing two barrack boxes worth of kit I'll be sending back home at the end of this month by sea container.
  It's Valentines Day today, and as I write this, there are but forty-nine days until I come home to you. I can hardly wait, can you? I've discovered something about you when we're separated. You're always with me. Kind of like background music, sometimes I listen sometimes I don't. But, everywhere I go I can always pass the time by turning up the volume and returning to you at Maplelawn. It gives me a great deal of pleasure and comfort to know that you will be there for me to come home to. Happy Valentine's Day my love!
   Yesterday was a tough day. We started the day at 0630 to provide security for the Engineers as they cleared a roadblock. Unfortunately, on the way to the tasking, our carrier blew a track and destroyed six road wheels (I'll show

you pictures when I get back). It took us nine hours to get the parts and make the carrier workable enough so it could be driven home, where it was grounded for need of two new tracks.

The CSM was kind enough to arrange for all the necessary parts and ordered us to do the work after supper. We were planning to do the work today, so the order to do the work after supper caught us all off guard. We were NOT impressed, but we soldiered on. We started at 1920 and four hours of sweat, skinned knuckles, blisters, and sore backs later we drove the carrier out of the maintenance bay with the new tracks installed. We had this morning off.

Coming to Rastivic has not been a lot of fun. Since leaving our villages, we've had to take down two complete camps (then rebuild them because the order to dismantle was given too early, and we could have left much of the stuff in place). Four people have been charged in our platoon (six in the company), one guy went to jail for two weeks. We've taken on new patrol taskings, which force us to spend eight to ten hours standing in a carrier no matter the weather. It's kind of like being in a giant vibrating food-processing machine. You get vibrated into a stupor and like a giant piece of flour dough you're beaten around in the hatch. Coming off one patrol I remember cataloguing my ailments. My feet were numb from the vibrations, one knee was sore because it popped when we hit a rock, and my lower back was in agony because of all the standing. My traps were white with pain because they were wet and cold (it had been raining). Walking, for that matter getting out of the vehicle, was a chore. And to think I call this shit fun, if I wasn't wearing my flack vest I'm sure I'd have broken ribs.

The one advantage is that the time goes that much faster. I've hardly noticed this past week go by, and with any luck the next seven days will go just as fast.

I sometimes wonder if thinking of you so much is natural, but just talking to some of the other guys tells me that I'm not the only one who misses home. Now that I think about it, hardly a day goes by when we don't have a discussion about how much we hate this place, or how much we miss home. Sadly the blush has gone and many of us see this tour for what it truly is, a waste of time. We can't see that we're making a tangible difference. Maybe time and history will help with that.

Like many veterans of wars, I'm glad that I came but I have no willingness to repeat the experience, and in light of your condition I sometimes wonder if it was worth coming at all. No doubt the tour's had its effect on me, thought I'm not sure about how much real growth has taken place. Maybe you can fill me in on that point.

I will end by telling you that I love you and am counting the days until we can be together again.

My love to you always.
Your man in blue
Kurt

Wednesday, 15 Feb., Rastivic Just when you think things are going to get interesting, the bottom falls out of it all. 0730 saw us mounted up and on our way to Charles Company where we sat around for an hour drinking coffee and waiting to get orders.

When they finally came, we all mounted up and headed to SC 50 (Pristeg in the Zone) to wait as the QRF. We'd been there maybe ten minutes when it was passed on the radio that the mission was off and we were to go home. It was 0915.

Back in Rastivic, we took the opportunity to get a shit load of work done on the carrier. Henry and I did a serialised kit check, and Jim and John helped the EME's work on the carrier. By the end of the day we figured we put as much as $50,000 (including the tracks we put on Monday) into our vehicle. There were two new final drives, fan belts, fan tower, bushings for the ramp, road wheels, and some other things I don't know about.

Not everyone worked on the vehicle though. Ted disappeared (to nobody's surprise) and Bruce and I worked on cleaning the C-6 in the HQ carrier most of the afternoon. It was in such bad shape that the carbon from the last firing (in December I think) had started to turn green. A chargeable offence under any circumstance, HQ was supposed to have cleaned it since it was theirs, but hadn't, so we were covering their asses in a sense. Good thing no one higher found out about it.

After cleaning the gun, Bruce disappeared, and I went over to our carrier to help out with the repairs. I had been working for about half an hour, and had just crawled out from under the carrier. I had my hat on backwards to keep the rim out of the way, when I looked up and spotted the CSM in PT gear sneaking up on me. When I saw him he came onto me. "You wear that goddamn ball cap properly Cpl Grant, and you muckel onto that soldier there MCpl Wyatt or I'll be coming onto you as well."

Clearly the CSM has nothing better to do than raise the pucker-factor of the troops. After he left, we agreed to ignore him and carry on.

By suppertime we were finished the repairs, and our baby was purring like a kitten. Tomorrow is the acid test, when we take her out on patrol. Hopefully nothing else will break.

If it seems like we've put a lot o f work into our carrier, it's because we have. They were never designed to take the kind of abuse and mileage we put on them. They vibrate and beat themselves to death, and trying to keep up on maintenance is next to impossible with our schedules. This is why we occasionally have to come to a full stop, and do the major overhauls.

After supper and a shower I decided to go over and place a call to Catherine. My timing was fortuitous, for as I arrived at the phones, I ran into Padre Rembaldie. What followed was a very interesting hour-long chat during which we talked of many things.

I began by talking about Catherine and the effect the additional strain of her illness has had on me. We've both noticed things about ourselves that we hadn't anticipated. For instance, for me this tour started out as an adventure, and a quest to determine whether I would have been able to actually cut it in the army. My pat answer for those who ask why am I here is, "I didn't want to be 55, and say I wish I had."

It has become so much more than that. Militarily, I've learned the nuances of battalion operations, and how things are really done in the regs. I now know I can cut it in the regs. Had I joined when the opportunity had first presented itself, I would have done extremely well. The adventure was something of a flop. It's still interesting, just not what I had expected.

The "more" part came with my writing to Catherine and Terri. My down time allowed me to explore and express my true feelings to these special ladies, and help put into perspective exactly what they mean to me. It has been a time of establishing contact with relatives, and seeing them for the first time as adults, and being seen as an adult. It was to acknowledge, vividly, the cycle of life, and to accept my rightful place in it. I've learned to deal with long-term stress and observe how others deal with it. Some well, some not so well.

Probably the most important point has been a certain solidification of who I am, and what I feel. I've become harder, and more capable of redirecting emotions, but mostly I will come away from this with some very clear goals for the short and long term.

I am reminded of a book Pierre Burton wrote about the "96 gold rush to the Yukon. The pictures at the beginning of the book of those about to embark on their great adventure reflect youth and exuberance, an immortal type spirit. All shot in studios, with false backdrops and props, the pictures show the anticipation of the adventure.

The pictures at the back of the book tell a different story. No smiles, or clean props here. The faces depict the months of hard work it took to cross Canada by wagon train, and the toll it took on them. Each face shows the 1000-mile stare of dealing with the harsh reality of pioneer life. It is in these pictures that I see the parallel with what we are doing here. Once we too were full of piss and vinegar, anticipatory of the coming adventure. Now our humour is black, and cynical at times. Dealing daily with the elements, the nightly machinegun fire, and the ever-present threat of bombs dropping into our compound, or stepping on a land mine takes its toll. Oddly, I feel somehow connected to every infanteer that had to suffer the indignities of army life. Standing by the fire in Knin on that cold snowy night of our last watch, I would not have been surprised to see a Roman legionnaire step out of the mist to warm himself by our fire. The implements have changed, but the game is the same.

There is no doubt in my mind that this is a young man's game, and perhaps I am too old to be playing it, certainly it gets harder each year to stay ahead of the pack. The padre remarked that I would likely be happier as an officer. Perhaps he's right, it certainly suits my mentality better.

Our conversation dwelled on stress quite a bit. On how each man has his breaking point (reference the guy in jail), and how there are no "no duff" time-outs over here. The mines are real, the bullets are real, and the guy pointing the AK at your face is for real. But that's just operations, add the bullshit of infighting between companies—QRF has been renamed "Quick Run Find Dukes for shit jobs"—and the strain of long patrols, and boring OPs. The causes of stress over here are too many to list; each of us sees the shadows of our personal demons in different places. For example, the PPCLI Cpl who dropped the grenade down his flack vest is still a colourful addition on the walls of the OP where he did himself in. Anyone having to look at that day in and day out would naturally begin to contemplate their own mortality.

The additional burden of separation from family, and in my case Catherine's new illness, probably has the greatest effect on people. It shows in the drinking and violent outbursts when things are slightly askew.

Dukes is particularly bad since coming to Rastivic. There's been no routine till now, and we've been shit upon quite a bit. Morale has faltered. Nobody talks about staying longer than necessary, even though it's still a real possibility. We've all forgotten about it in the mad dash to get today's work out of the way.

But in the end, things aren't really as bad as all that. I've learned to deal with this place a little bit at a time. I focus on the work at hand, and try to keep myself occupied by writing, or volunteering for work. I've always been task oriented, it's just that now it's much more important for my sanity. They say the sanest people are those who question their sanity. If that's the case then we all must be very sane people here, because hardly a day goes by when we wonder what the hell drove us to come here in the first place. I'm sure old Sigmund would have something to say about that one.

Bragging rights have lost their value. This tour has been about dealing with a different kind of reality, one that hasn't been seen since Korea. Sadly, with little to do, and no power to do it, we are self-destructing out of boredom, monotony, and the inability to do anything concrete. Not unlike the racehorse brought to the track and not permitted to run.

Infighting story—2IC Charles Company accused Dukes Company of not doing their jobs and not driving the entire patrol routes. Dukes Company CSM collected all mileage from all tracks to prove we do indeed drive the routes and do our job. This is your fine Canadian Army at work!

In a way it's kind of fun to see how much shit you can put up with before your attitude goes to hell in a hand basket. I figure I still have quite a bit of reserve left. The end is not clearly in sight yet, but it is getting closer.

Thursday, 16 Feb., Patrolling It's amazing how quickly the weather changes around here. This morning was sunny and calm, but by lunch it was raining steadily.

Henry took our carrier and started the patrol route at 1300, Ted, Robert, Tim, and I met them at Charles Company for supper, and then we both headed out to complete the patrol routes.

What can I tell you about patrolling in the dark when it's pissing rain out? It's wet; damn wet; wet and cold, but with a good rain suit and bandanna it's tolerable. I wear the bandanna wrapped around my face El Bandito style, to keep from inhaling all the dust, or rain. It acts like an extension of the collar of the coat and helps to keep me warm. By pulling the rim of the helmet down close to the top of my glasses, I can keep them reasonably clear of the rain. Dressed like this I'm good for a couple of hours. Much longer, and no matter what you do it's no help. Thankfully we were out only for a few hours otherwise it would have been bloody uncomfortable. By 2300 we were back in Rastivic, and after a quick cleanup, I was in bed by 2330. No beer tonight for this puppy, the soft billowy folds of my sleeping bag were calling, and nothing was going to get in my way, or stop me from letting it wrap its cuddly arms around me and whisk me off to la la land.

This is the first day of our new and improved rotation schedule. Charles Company OC felt that a four-day rotation wouldn't allow us to get to know the area of SC 50 well enough so they upped our stay to seven days.

This has its good and bad points. Bad is that instead of eight days before we return it's now 14 days. Actually, I'm not quite clear as to the need for us to be really up on things. We spend the entire time inside the compound only patrolling on request of Charles Company. So a longer stay in the Zone really makes little difference.

The good point of being on base is that we're near a gym for 14 days at a time. At least some sort of routine can be maintained for two weeks at a go. Of course, the major draw back is that we're now within eyesight of the CSM, so the old game of dodging, weaving, and making effective use of local cover has to be played. We've gotten so good at it that George has resorted to putting pieces of plastic with a grease pencil on each door because he could never find any of us. The object being that when we leave we're supposed put down where we're going, so that higher can find us for such joyous things as work parties. We play along of course, dutifully putting down where we're going. Occasionally, of course, we forget to put something down, or don't end up where we said we would be. Are we to blame if we are in a hurry? Or if plans changed after we left the Company lines? What can I say?

Upon ruminating about last night's discussion with the padre, it occurs to me that it would be terribly interesting to sit down with him, myself, and Padre Gregson from my unit—the Vietnam vet—and compare notes about stress in the field. It would be good to have Catherine in on something like that as well. A perspective from the home front, so to speak.

Speaking of home fronts and perspectives. It's amazing how many people receive letters that have the line "come home in one piece" somewhere in it.

While it is true, that some wacko may take a pot shot at us on something resembling a regular basis, the bulk of our work is no more dangerous than life back home. Perhaps it's just my familiarity with the situation, or perhaps it's because we trained so hard before coming over here, but we all feel that putting ourselves in harm's way is what we all signed on the dotted line for. If we are going to make a real difference in this country, the Canadian public will have to accept that some of us might get hurt. Whether we come home in one piece or not is something I, nor any of us, has little control over. What we don't need is someone back home who doesn't understand that and adds to my stress by making these kinds of annoying comments. Of course we want to come home in one piece, we just don't want to be constantly reminded of it.

I blame the media for the false perception the public has of what we do over here. In their quest for "news "they have bastardized the situation to the point that it is almost unrecognizable from reality. To hear them tell it, you'd think we're all in a shooting war every day over here. I would like some time to talk to Lewis Mackenzie on this issue to get his perspective.

This kind of reporting, as some of us see it, has an effect on our morale here and at home. Not so much here, because we don't get enough of the news to really pay attention. And when we do hear something, it's usually so far from our reality that it is dismissed out of hand.

Back home it's another story. People see pictures of the fighting in the Bihac and automatically assume that the whole country is like that. I know I've gone on about the media before, but occasionally they really piss me off, and I have to say something. It's usually because they've missed the real story.

By the way General Vernon was dismissed, I understand, for misappropriation of funds. Something to do with office furniture I think.

It's a crazy world we live in, this military. Sadly, it is completely misunderstood by the civilian world, and that perspective I don't think will ever change unless we work side by side for a while.

Friday, 17 Feb., Patrolling Today was a glorious day. As we came off patrol last night, the clouds parted and the moon was visible. This morning there wasn't a cloud in the sky, the wind had dropped to near zero, and it was wonderfully warm.

We had the morning off, so I put in a workout. Then after lunch the section gathered at the carriers to do our regular maintenance, and clean the guns. It had rained so much last night that we were worried that despite our precautions the guns would be rusty this morning. Because the .50 is my responsibility, I've taken to carrying a can of WD 40 with me on each patrol. Every time we made a stop I'd give the gun a good spray with the stuff. This was necessary because after an hour in the driving rain, there generally isn't any oil left on the outside of the gun to protect it. Some of the other gunners have been in the habit of applying a liberal coat of 10W30 motor oil to the exterior, which seems to work well at rappelling the rain. It does pick up every little bit of dirt in the air, which makes the gun a pig to clean the next morning. Retrieving the gun from the inside of the carrier revealed that little if any rust had formed and all that was really required was a good wipe down and reapplication of oil.

Tonight's patrol was nippy. The later it got the cooler it got, and the ground fog got pretty thick. Tomorrow I think I'll wear longjohns.

The routes we'd been given tonight were the two shortest of the three, so we had two or three hours we had to kill to complete the eight-hour shift in the Zone. Our first stop was to check out a bunker, so Tim, Robert, Henry, and Jay dismounted and walked off into the distance, while the rest of us waited for their return. We had been sitting there maybe ten minutes, when the local Serb militia started to come out of the woodwork. After twenty minutes a bottle appeared along with a glass, as they tried to give us wine. We resisted at first, but eventually we had a small glass we shared between the four of us. By now the foot patrol was back and the Serbs kept insisting we drink. I happened to have the glass in my hand when we fired up the carriers and started to move, and I didn't have time to return it. About a hundred yards down the road, and out of sight of the Serbs, it went over the side.

Our next stop was SC 50, where Ray Labell and the boys from 3 Section are. We arrived and for an hour we played liar's dice and watched porn movies. Nothing like driving around with a lump in your pants for distraction.

When we left SC 50 we drove through what was left of the town of Prestig. It was kind of eerie as we rumbled down the road in our carriers, the moonlight reflecting off the fields of grape vines, and the destroyed buildings ghosting by, a silent homage to Croat vs Serb.

Ah yes, the wind in your hair, the roar of the engine, the freedom of the road—and the mud in your eye as you follow the carrier in front of you. Sounds like a motorcycle commercial. Truth is it's kind of fun rolling down the road at night under a full moon, and clear skies. It's a very different perspective on life.

Our next stop was SC 56. This place is an OP located on a hilltop with a commanding view of both sides of the Zone. The OP took more than a month to build, and needed a superstructure of 8 x 8 logs, surrounded by an estimated 10,000 sandbags piled three deep all the way up the 60 foot structure. Each sandbag is filled with pea gravel, and had to be hand carried the 100 or so metres to the OP, then carried up a ladder, situated, and packed—using an axe handle—into its final resting place.

As you walk up to the tents near the base of the OP, you get the feeling that you are approaching a medieval watchtower. In the moonlight the white sandbags of the tower almost make the structure glow giving it an eerie feeling.

You approach the OP by walking up a short rise along a path that has had steps cut into the rock. The tower rises nearly three storeys above you as you duck to go through a tiny door at the base, then climb a ladder on the inside to get to the belvedere with a balcony at the top. It's surprisingly warm up there, and with the NODLR you can see quite a distance at night.

The room at the top is probably 10 x 10, and because this was the first time any of our guys had been to this OP, we had all climbed the ladder to see what it was like. All eight of us, plus the two guys on duty were packed into a tiny room trying to see the countryside and chat with the guys on duty.

SC 56. A medieval tower of sandbags where everything is tied down to keep it from blowing away

Back down on the ground, there are two modular tents set up, each surrounded with rock filled gabions, and each securely tied down. We hadn't noticed it at first, but Robert pointed out that the shitter had four ropes wrapped over it and was tied to metal stakes pounded into the rock. When we asked one of the guys who lived there about all the tie downs, he smiled. It appears that shortly after they had arrived for their first duty, one of the platoon commanders had stopped by for a visit. The wind had been blowing pretty hard when the officer made a run to the shitter. He hadn't been in there all that long, when a violent gust of wind knocked the shitter over and it rolled down a ten foot embankment before coming to rest. The officer was not amused. Everyone else of course, was rolling on the ground with laughter. The shitter has since been secured, and judging by the strength of the tie downs it would take an artillery shell to move it.

We stayed for 45 minutes or so and chatted with the guys on duty, then hit the road again. Around 0045 we pulled back into SC 50 and had a quick drink of something hot and a chat then headed for Charles Company.

We pulled in at Charles, and Henry jumped out and went to do his patrol report, while the rest of us had gone to fill up the tracks when it happened. We'd just finished filling up the second carrier, when it refused to start. For the next hour and a half, two confused drivers tried to get the beast started. A slave cable was acquired, and every possibility under the moon was tried. Finally we gave up, and simply towed the damn thing out of the way and everyone loaded up into the one working carrier for the ride home.

The night patrol has taken its toll. We arrived back at 0330 and in the time it took me to go and wash my hands and face, John went to bed and passed out. He told me later that he heard me leave but not come back.

I wasn't long for the living either. Though I recognize the need for night patrols, they take it out of you in ways you hadn't expected. Disrupted sleep patterns, calories burned staying warm, and the wear and tear of riding around for eight hours in the dark.

Anti-armour (AAP), Recce, and ourselves conduct these patrols on a 24-hour cycle, and it would appear they're paying off. New positions in the Zone are found within eight hours of their creation, and are plotted using a handheld GPS. The Croatians have been seen doing section attacks and patrolling training, and increasing numbers of convoys have been spotted in and around the area. Some would argue that we patrol too much. For myself, I'd much rather patrol than go and sit on a hilltop somewhere. It's something one develops a tolerance for. I've noticed a difference between the first patrol and how much it took out of me, and how I handled last night's patrol. I'm not nearly as sore and tired, and am in reasonably good spirits.

In the end, the important point is that time flies by. The more we have to do the faster the days go. I've likened this six week cycle to that of Knin. With definite blocks to work through, it makes things a great deal easier to handle.

Now if I could just keep away from the bloody CSM.

Note: we found out that the Charles Company OC had a bird after they figured the carrier wouldn't start because the batteries were low. This they said was lack of driver maintenance. When we heard this everyone in Dukes shook their heads and said "bullshit." The next day we found a loose wire behind one of the panels, which was the cause of it failing to start. The batteries were low because we spent an hour and a half trying to get it going.

Saturday, 18 Feb., Patrolling God, what a headache! I woke up at 1030 with a start as George opened the door to give us our mail. I just lay there for a while, completely dehydrated, with head throbbing. The door opened again a short time later, and I heard "get up, I have a sandbagging detail for you."

I lay there for another second or two, then it struck me, "wait a minute, we're a patrolling section, we're not supposed to have to do this shit, where's the QRF section? That's their job."

"They're off changing a track on one of their vehicles so you're it, budz," came the reply.

Oh well, it could be raining. I opened the door and you'll never guess what it's doing? Sandbagging in the rain. God I love the army! (And don't give me any of that it builds character shit. If that were true I'd have enough character to last ten lifetimes).

Alas, easy come easy go. Several of us arrived at the appointed RV site—one Very Large Pile of SandBags—only to find that there was no beaver-tail to load them on. Twenty minutes later it was discovered that someone had made off with our beaver tail for use on another job. Oh darn. And we were so looking forward to working in the rain. Maybe now I can get a shave, some aspirin, and some food into me before we do our 100% stock taking at 1300 hrs.

I have to admit the CSM appears to have little if anything to do so he invents things for us to work on. Like building a gym that no one uses because the base gym is better equipped. Or build a TV and Games room, which also no one uses because there's a big screen TV set up in the JR's mess. The guy has his own ISO, TV & VCR, complete with satellite hook up (when some of the boys in the field don't even have a TV). He wanders around looking for people to jack up, and spends much of his time

The Second Half of the Tour

in PT strip. Hard to respect a man like that when he's coming onto you about your hat being on backwards.

The afternoon's stock-taking of our vehicle only took a short time, and we were finished by 1340.

Tonight's patrol can best be described as an endurance test. It rained most of the afternoon, and continued almost until midnight so going out we tried to prepare for it. I wore two pair of wool socks, rain pants, fleece, shirt, gortex jacket, rain suit complete, and two bandanas around my neck and face. Despite the preparation, I was soaked down my front, and my gloves had to be wrung out several times during the patrol.

It was by far the hardest patrol we've had to do. The temperature dropped, and the rain turned hard—almost freezing—and as you rode along, your face got pelted pretty badly. When we pulled into SC 46 we were genuinely surprised that it was only 2100, and that we'd only been on the road for 3 hours. That's probably the best indication of how tough it was, we were three-quarters finished the first of the two routes and it felt like we'd been out there forever.

After spending half an hour at SC 46 to allow the blood to return to our extremities, we mounted up and ploughed on through the rain. For an hour we flew down roads, over fields, and through mud holes deep enough to hide a car in, not once stopping to check any of the bunkers we were supposed to.

The Serbs aren't fools. In this kind of weather they hole up with a bottle of wine and wait it out. Even the checkpoints into the Zone were unmanned. It was Saturday night, and the Serbs usually relax a little and party on these nights. One bunker on a hill we stopped at evidenced this. The boys were getting into the party mood, and when we produced a North American skin mag for them, they were absolutely beside themselves. They had a collection of posters on the wall of the bunker we'd noticed on a previous visit, and in the spirit of détente, we decided to add to the collection. Soldiers the worlds over have certain things in common don't "cha know.

Finally we pulled into SC 50, where some of the boys from 3 Section were. It was 2230, and we simply said "Fuck-it," and chose to stay put until around 0100. It was just too damn cold out there, and we were too wet and uncomfortable to really continue effectively, not that we could see anything anyway. Too much time was spent trying to stay warm and protected instead of looking around.

For two and a half hours we huddled around the heaters, drank hot chocolate and sorta watched a movie that was on. When the movie finished, a porn movie got slipped into the VCR, but I was more concerned with trying to dry my gloves (that's my story and I'm sticking to it!).

During our break, the rain stopped and the wind picked up, so much so that the tent damn near blew away. The tent leaks in several places, so the boys have strung plastic up on the inside like an inside liner. With all the wind, the plastic kept falling out of place, so every five minutes or so someone had to go around and tuck it all back into place lest all the sleeping area get wet. I can just see that staying here is going to be loads of fun.

At 0045 we mounted up, dryer, but still uncomfortable. The wind was so high that in climbing up into the hatch, I nearly got blown off the side of the carrier. Well, at least it wasn't raining.

A fast 15 minutes to Charles Company, to refuel and do a patrol report. Then back on the road to Rastivic. 2:30 saw me in my ISO, weapons sprayed down with oil, cloths hanging to dry, and me tucked in the bag, waiting for sleep to overtake me. I didn't have to wait long.

Nights like these no one likes. There's an old army saying that rainy weather is perfect patrolling weather, because you make less noise when moving about, and it's easier to sneak up on the enemy because he's working harder on staying dry than doing his job. That may be true, but I'm sure the Recce boys we passed along one of the back roads would have something to say about that. They were tilting into the wind as bad as we were. This, my friends, is the stuff of war stories.

Sunday, 19 Feb., Patrolling Boy did I need that rest. John and I hit the hay at 0230 and it wasn't until 1100 that either of us moved to get up. Thankfully, no one had bothered us all morning, so we rested undisturbed. Even so, I woke up feeling dehydrated and a little slow.

It's amazing the recuperative powers a hot shower, shave, and a litre of water can have. By lunch I was pretty much back to normal, and cleaning the gun was no trouble at all.

Each day there are little indicators of things being prepared for departure. UAB lists made, stock taking, and today, a list of what the section wants to take home from the duty free shop. The end still isn't clearly in sight, but we're nearly down to six weeks left, and that feels good. The big thing to look forward to right now is the Partiburg dinner on March 2. It's the first RCR battle honour, and every year there is a blow out party. This year, each man gets two beers and half a litre of wine free, and then you buy your drinks. We've been dry for I can't remember how long, so it's a good thing we don't have to report until 1300 the next day.

This afternoon was pretty much free after we finished the carrier maintenance, so I slipped away to call Catherine again. This is the second day I've called her in a row, and it was good to hear her voice.

She tells me she's rearranging the house, but was kind enough to leave the bed in the same place. This last point is something of an inside joke with us. It comes from a story dad tells about when he was working night shift, and came home late one night. Not wanting to disturb the household, he took his shoes off at the door, and quietly got undressed in the bedroom without turning any lights on. When he went to get into bed, he promptly fell flat on his butt. Here mom had rearranged the whole bedroom without telling him, and the bed was clear across the room. I guess he let out a series of expletives that woke the whole house, and defeated the purpose of sneaking around. We still smile about it.

She sounds like she's in good spirits, and the closer my return date gets, the happier she sounds.

Yesterday I received the first letter from her in a while that was hand written. She's been forced to use a typewriter lately because her handwriting had degenerated so much that it was hard to read. Catherine felt the need to clearly demonstrate what effect the MS has had on her.

Reading her "chicken scratch" was both painful and joyous. Painful because I remember how powerful her writing used to be, and to have to reread sentences because they're not written clearly is hard. It was joyous because she, like me, believes that we're soul mates. She was quite right to say that I had to get away to truly appreciate our exceptional rapport, our friends, and especially our elegance of lifestyle. All of these points have been driven home very clearly in comparison to the people I'm

The Second Half of the Tour 227

surrounded by. We have it good, without doubt, and I have no need to pay lip service to the saying "living well is the best revenge." I will continue to work hard to give Catherine the better things in life, if for no other reason than to provide her with as much dignity as possible to deal with her/our illness. And rightly so, she is after all the woman I intend to spend the rest of my life with, and it follows that I should do everything I can for her.

On to other things.... The JTF are in town. They were out on a recce in the same area we were last night, and apparently they got "stuck." Four highly trained MCpls in an Iltis got stuck!?! As Hamlet said "something sticks in Denmark." Speculation has it that they were in Charles Company AOR to scope out a hit on a local troublemaker. There's no way we could ever confirm anything, but it's neat to speculate about "black" ops and what these guys might be up to.

Charles Company, a former hotel, taken from outside the gate

Tonight's patrol was actually very pleasant. It was again a very clear cold evening, with lots of stars in the sky. I prepared for this one by putting on my long johns and wearing my gortex parka (Note: the army, in a typical display of pinpoint timing, issued us winter parkas after the really cold weather was over). Best decision I ever made. For once I was actually comfortable as we drove over hill and dale checking out positions.

Our patrol route was again modified so as not to disturb the locals. This happens from time to time and just adds to the aggravation. To us, it feels like higher has no balls and is giving in to the locals. This of course is completely unreasonable, but I'm just telling you what we feel.

Our feeling seem justified when, like last night, we found fresh digging when we checked the route from the other side. When we stopped to check it out, the locals appeared out of the dark and asked if there was any problem. They were drinking but to me they appeared a bit worried as well. Our SITREP dutifully called in and we carried on with the patrol.

Tonight we were on routes two and three, so our first stop was to SC 50 after about an hour on the road. Twenty-five minutes later we were back on the road again after having been subjected to only a brief viewing of porn on the TV.

The next stop was SC 56, on the number three route. We only stayed for ten minutes or so, enough to stretch our legs and get our hearing back.

At 2310 we were coming down the hill again and zipping past E-Company of KENBAT, which is located just off the main road below SC 56. In our camps people are up 24 hours a day, but this place always looks deserted with no lights on. Must be that ghost thing again...

Tonight we took a different turn in the road and took a run down the opposite side of the valley from SC 56. There wasn't much to look at over there. Farmland, some destroyed houses and churches, graveyards, the usual stuff left over after a war. When we got to the end of the road we turned around and came back.

We hit the main road in a town that has been totally destroyed. It's odd driving through these places, and seeing a village that would usually support two to four hundred people, with only one or two houses with lights on. Makes you wonder who these people knew to have their building saved from destruction, when the rest of the place has been wiped out.

Another quick pop into SC 50, then on the road again at 0100 back to Charles. The usual routine of refuelling, doing the patrol report, and having a coffee lasted only twenty or so minutes, and then we headed for home. By 0220 I was in the sack.

In all, it wasn't that bad a patrol. My back was sore and my feet were cold, but otherwise I was fine. Some of the almond trees are in bloom right now, and as we zipped by at night the tiny flowers look like someone strung popcorn in the branches. There's a thought. Put popcorn in the trees with a backdrop of a destroyed stone house. I must be losing it.

I'm told that the people of Pembroke, Petawawa, and the base have been holding rallies in support of the Airborne. Support has been coming in from England, the USA, and all over Canada. It seems in the face of so much support, all postings out of the Regiment have been put on hold. Interesting.

Monday, 20 Feb., Patrolling This morning I was awakened with a slap on the shoulder from George. "Kurt" he said, "I'm sorry to have to wake you, but I have the EME here and he's going to fix your door." What could I say?

I lay in bed listening for a while as this guy pounded and drilled my door, as he removed the old and installed a new door handle and lock. I got up and headed for the ablution trailer to clean up.

When we pulled into SC 50 the first time last night, we got a call to check the serial numbers on our Nags and laser dot sights. By the time we pulled into Rastivic at 0200, George was still up and took Henry aside for a chat. I found out this morning that our Company HQ boys had misplaced two NVGs and two laser dot sights. George spent most of the evening trying to trace them down, even going as far as calling Warrant Fuller in Canada, to try to get a fix on them. They were finally traced to an unlocked sea container belonging to CQ. As you can imagine today's brief Ogroup stressed the need for us to keep a grip on our serialised kit. It wasn't our fault that the kit went missing in the first place, but we got warned about it anyway.

The Second Half of the Tour 229

After that brief get-together, it was over to the carrier to do a clean up on the gun and some general maintenance. It was another great day, so I laid the gun out on the ground and started to clean it. No sooner had I stripped the thing, than Henry showed up and said to put it back together so that I could help out filling a beaver tail (the one that went missing a couple of days ago) with sandbags.

It was the strangest thing; the gun just wouldn't go together as fast as it came apart. And all those parts needed to be wiped down, as well as my personal weapon, which was quite dusty. Yup, by the time the .50 was back together and I was on my way to the beavertail, all the guys were walking back, the job was done. Oh well, you can't be everywhere I guess. *Wink*

On the way over to the mess to do some writing, I ran into Padre Rembaldie. We had another good chat and he wound up telling me a very interesting story. You will recall on 31 December, two lads from Charles Company were pretty badly shot up when they ran a Serb roadblock. A couple of weeks later Bravo Company got a call to pick up a couple of dead Serb bodies that had been found in their AOR.

When they showed up, they found two young Serb men in civi dress, both had been shot. One of them was missing an ear, and there was the clear imprint of a Croatian army boot beside one of the bodies (Croatia buys its boots from Adidas, and the tread is distinctive). One would think that the locals would be up in arms about two of their boys being shot. But the opposite was the case. No one seemed to care, despite the evidence seemingly pointing to the Croatians having done the deed.

A little digging by higher revealed the following. The Croats knew nothing about the incident. The locals were extremely pissed off with their own army for shooting up a UN jeep, especially a Canadian one. The lack of reaction by locals is suspected as being acceptance of the fact that these two were the ones responsible for the shooting. Killing them was a payback of sorts, and a way to instil discipline on the ranks. This is what happens if. . . .

The missing ear is probably proof that the hit was completed, and it's likely hanging in a mess somewhere. These are tough and independent people. Their reaction to many things tends to be very simplistic, and this is a good example of it. It has all the hallmarks of a bad Mafia movie, which is kind of scary when you think about it.

• • • • • •

Here are some thoughts about why carrier maintenance is so important. Our carriers were built in 1964, and they were designed to do about 1800 miles per year, after which they went in for overhaul. These carriers have been here for two and a half years. They do an average of 900 miles per week when we're patrolling. On an average rotation within the platoon, we may do two weeks of patrolling per month, which means in any given month, we do a year's worth of driving. Is it any wonder they break down so often?

This evening's patrol was a bit more interesting than previous ones. It started when Robert pissed me off while we were at Ljuben stand (that's the bunker on the hill where we left the skin magazine for the troops a while back). The track route only goes halfway up the hill, and we have to dismount and walk the rest of the way to get to the bunker. Robert and I got out to check the place out, and took our time to get to the top of the hill. Robert has a propensity for gabbing with all and sundry, particularly when he should be working. We arrived at the top of the hill and found a guy who spoke English. Robert went into action. I listened for a few minutes, then stepped outside the bunker and did a walk around of the entire installation on top of the hill. This took about ten minutes. When I got back he was still at it. The wine appeared and he reluctantly accepted though he didn't resist too much. I refused. A few more minutes of talk, and I was ready to leave, so I quietly told Robert to sum up. He was not impressed. More talk, and another hint to leave. He kept going. I got up and waited outside.

On the walk down we had a short, sharp, discussion about why we'd left earlier than he wanted to. I drove home the point that it's not our job to socialise with these people, but to ensure they aren't trying to get away with anything. He was having none of it. At one point he stuck his chest out at me and I laughed at him. It didn't come to blows, but it very well could have. I left him standing on the hill and continued down to our carriers. That pretty much set the tone of the evening. We didn't talk much after that.

The next incident happened at Popivich stand. A log blocked our usual access route across the road. The possibility existed that the road was mined so we stopped and called it in. Higher directed us to drive around and go in through the town, which we did. At the actual stand there was nothing new to report. As usual we were denied access to the building so we called in our SITREP and carried on.

In the valley—where the cabbages are—there is a Croat position at a junction in some roads that we've nicknamed The Arrowhead. Usually there are men at the roadblock, but tonight there wasn't anyone visible. About a thousand metres up the left arm of the arrowhead, is another bunker we regularly check out. It's very near the Zone, and usually unmanned, but for our last two visits it has been occupied. Tonight was no exception. When we pulled up the first thing we noticed was a fire barrel, and about six guys standing around clutching their AKs. Henry dismounted to chat with them and check things out. This bunker is so near the Zone that it's debatable whether it's actually in it or not. We know they're allowed to be there so we don't push the issue at all. Tonight it was obvious they'd been drinking, and the way they were carrying their weapons showed they weren't in the mood to even talk about giving them up.

After a brief discussion we mounted up and left, merely noting what we'd seen for inclusion in the final report. After five hours of bombing around in the open, it was getting pretty cold. At 2300 we pulled into SC 50 after having completed all of routes one and two—conveniently missing a couple of bunkers to speed things up.

At SC 50, we watched "Other People's Money" and had some hot chocolate to warm things up. At 0100 we were on the road again, and by 0220 I was in the bag. Tomorrow's going to be a short one and I'm looking forward to having a beer for a change.

Tuesday, 21 Feb., Patrolling This day dawned another beautiful day. The third in a row in fact, but it looks like rain is coming.

I was late out of the sack around 1030, and after cleaning up I sat around and chatted with the boys until it was time for lunch. After lunch, I worked on my diary a bit, then went and spent an hour working on the .50 and my personal weapon. The timing of this activity is important, because the CSM usually looks for people for work parties about the same time we work on the carrier. After the work parties are assigned, we quickly finish up what we're working on, and bugger off until its time to go on patrol.

This afternoon's workout activity for me was a run. 6.6 km, or three times around the inside of the camp, to be exact, and surprisingly it didn't hurt. I guess all the work on the Stairmaster is paying off. I think for my next run I'm going to wear my combat boots instead of runners. The ground is too rocky to risk twisting an ankle or jabbing your foot on a sharp stone.

The first crew left on patrol at 1245 to begin the first of the routes, and we'll rendezvous with them at Charles Company for supper (the food is better there than here).

Today we have routes one and two again with the boys doing the longer route one in the daylight; we save the shorter route two for the evening.

This evening we pulled up on a mountainside to check out the bunker, and spent some time watching the sun go down. The view was spectacular. Our viewpoint was high on a hill, which dropped away steeply, down into the valley and a large bay on the Adriatic. As you looked left there were numerous islands and bays that dotted the coastline. To the right were the coastal mountains and foothills. There was just enough cloud in the sky to reflect the brilliant colours of orange, pink, and red as the sun went down. This was truly a beautiful sight to behold and the perfect end to a wonderful spring day.

On patrol in spring, with the almond trees in bloom

As we drove to Charles Company, the locals could be seen cleaning up their yards, and working in their gardens. Just outside Benkovac we passed a group of people on the roadside that were cleaning and laying out to dry winter onions they'd just harvested. The smell of onions was in the air.

The water is running in the ditches, the almond trees are in bloom, the grass is turning green, and tiny newborn animals are running about all over the place. There is a smell of fresh clean air about and the earth is a rich, dark colour. It won't be long now and the earth will dry out and the war will start again. But, for now all we have to do is worry about the rocks that get thrown at us regularly.

This evening's patrol was rather pleasant despite the almost uncontrollable urge I had to go to sleep at the first couple of stops. These past two nights, for the first hour or so of the patrol I've had an increasing desire to crawl into a corner of the carrier and rack for a few minutes. I guess the patrols are taking their toll on me. Certainly my back and legs feel it more than usual.

I forgot to mention a funny incident that happened on last night's patrol. We'd just driven through a Croat bunker, and defence in depth position, when we decided to pull over and make a quick stop to take a leak. We'd just dismounted when all of a sudden we heard whistling and yelling about 50 metres to our left within the defensive lines. Alarmed by the fact that the UN stopped near them, the Croatians had called a stand-to. Based on the night's experience, Henry decided it was best we not hang around, so he quickly zipped up and got into his carrier. After he closed the door, I heard him tell Jim to get them the hell out of there. Jim hadn't heard Henry's order and John noted this point, and said rather loudly "Jim, get us outta here" No sooner had John uttered the words than Jim fired up the carrier, released the tiller bars, and took off down the road.

The first carrier's sudden departure had caught Robert completely off guard, as he was only half finished what he was doing. Ted anticipated our departure and fired up the carrier, Robert tried to cut himself off and put everything away. As he was climbing in through the back door, George told Ted to go, where upon the carrier jumped and took off down the road. Robert was almost thrown back out the door and was hanging on for dear life. George had to climb down and physically haul Robert into the carrier, and the two of them fought with the steel door to get it closed as we bounced around on the road. In his haste to get into the carrier Robert lost control of his bladder and wound up pissing all down one of his legs. By the time we started moving Jim was 100 metres down the road, Robert was uncomfortable, and George and I were rolling in the isles with laughter. What can I say? We find our humour where we can.

The rest of tonight's patrol went off without a hitch and we were back in the camp by nine fifteen and in the mess by nine twenty-five. That was some of the finest tasting beer I'd ever had. We could only have a couple, but they sure went down well. So well in fact, I didn't even hear John stumbling around when he came into the ISO after I'd gone to bed.

A curious thing I've noted is the fact that others and I find it easier to deal with days left rather than weeks left. 42 days sounds easier to handle than six weeks. Not long now!

Wednesday, 22 Feb., Patrolling I was wrong about the rain. Today was another incredibly lovely day. Crisp and clean, and no caffeine, as the saying goes. This morning at ten we all gathered at the carrier to do a change around. We had to take everything out of 1-3 Bravo, and transfer it to 1-4. This took about an hour and had to be done so our carrier could go in for its maintenance check.

After laying out all the kit in 1-4, Jim did a first parade on the vehicle. That's when we discovered the problem and Ted lost it. The belts that drive the alternator and fan tower were off the pulley wheels, and one of the pulleys was ready to fall off. Instant grounding.

We found out that the driver from 3 Section, had been the last to drive the vehicle and had declared it workable. Clearly he hadn't done his job.

Ted was livid, and was going to kill him, but cooler heads prevailed, and the driver was told to sort himself out. Ted really lost it again, when he discovered that

The Second Half of the Tour   233

the guy had gone back to SC 50 instead of working on the carrier like he was supposed to. The rest of us worked on the carrier to get it serviceable and tried to ignore Ted as best we could.

Henry told me something interesting last night in the mess about Ted. It seems that Ted has been on C&P (counselling and probation) for a very poor P.E.R. last year. The reason? His attitude! His performance on the tour has been duly noted, and is one of the reasons we don't say, or complain much about him.

Counselling and probation is the military's last ditch effort to save a soldier's career. When you're on it you aren't eligible for promotion or courses for a period of six months. It also stays on your record for the rest of your career. I understand this is not Ted's first visit to the C&P hurt locker, which makes one wonder how he's managed to survive so long.

We all broke and went for lunch around 1130 and after lunch I mailed out three t-shirts to Cat's sister's kids. They have "my uncle is a peace keeper" on the front with the UN symbol. A nice touch and something for the kids to wear to school and brag about.

I also filled out another questionnaire for the military. What a waste of time and paper (and I put that down under "comments"). It had three questions on it and all they wanted to know was whether I was a visible minority and if so what type. What a crock! I should have put down that I was an endangered species in Canada, a WASP. That would have got their attention.

When it was over, Henry told us he was thinking seriously of applying for minority status as a Newfoundlander. There aren't but 250 thousand Newfies in Canada, and there are more Italians, Chinese, and other groups who have the status. He had us in stitches as he explained his grand plan for guaranteeing his rights to unemployment insurance, and special compensation.

Tonight's patrol got off to a bit of a shaky start. Because of the repairs needed to 1-4, Henry took the HQ carrier out at 1300 to start the patrol. Before he left, we noticed that on of the 10 bolts, one of the drive sprockets had sheared off. No big deal really. There are 9 others left to hold the sprocket on. But when our mechanic heard about it he tried to ground the vehicle. This proved a waste of time, as the patrol was already a couple of hours old when he found out about it, so there really wasn't anything he could do until the patrol came back. Then our mechanic became very upset when he learned the vehicle wouldn't be back in camp until 2100. This is another good example of why you want to stay the hell away from headquarters at all costs. The mechanic at Charles Company said to carry on and fix it when we got back. After all, "you've got nine other bolts holding the sprocket on." Still the vehicle got grounded until it was fixed.

As a result, we had to take our now empty carrier along with us to Charles and transfer enough kit from the HQ carrier into it, so that we could take it on patrol with us. The only good point was that we now had two very fast carriers to fly through the patrol with.

Tonight's patrol, aside from a wrong turn at the very beginning, was uneventful. So uneventful, that as we drove down one of the roads by a vineyard I began to dream of some of those things that I look forward to when I get back. Like using a toilet seat that doesn't bend when you sit on it. Or being able to use the bathroom undisturbed (if you're married or have kids it's a near impossibility anyway, but nice to dream about). How about eating a meal that doesn't come in a box, that'd be nice. Or maybe getting a good night's rest without having someone come crashing in in the middle of the night. But especially sheets! Being able to actually sleep between clean sheets —on a bed I can stretch out on, and have a nice warm body to snuggle up to, and play with. God that'd be nice. What about being able to make a decent meal, maybe with a little home-made wine, some good music, good company and . . . WHACK! Sorry, reality check, that was a bump in the road that knocked the wind out of me. Yes, going back to a normal life will be a nice change.

The remainder of the patrol went off without a hitch, nothing to see nothing to report. There was a short beer at the mess when it was all over, a long shower, and a quick pack for our trip to SC 50 tomorrow, then into the bag. I really need the rack. These past seven days have gone fast but it's taken its toll. My back, legs, and calves are sore, and I'm just plain tired. This break is well placed; everyone looks a little dopey.

I wanted to call Catherine tonight because it's the last chance I'll have for a week, but the damn phones were out. It'll have to wait until I get back to camp now.

Ah yes, Sierra Charlie Five Zero, the hottest spot in the Zone. The place where Reid nearly got himself killed over a bloody video camera. Also home to lots of rack, down time to read, and . . . basketball? Yup! Since 3 Platoon's arrival on the scene, a game of pickup basketball has started between the Croats and us. This should be an interesting interlude.

Thursday, 23 Feb., Pristeg Up at 0600 to clean up and have breakfast. By 0800 all eight of us (and our kit) were stuffed into the carrier on our way to SC 50. We pulled in and dropped our kit, and then Ray Labell, Henry and I went for a foot patrol of "the zone" outside the gates of our new abode.

You know things are a little more tense when the first thing they tell you is "don't step off the path." Mines surround this place on all four sides. Pristeg was the area of some of the hottest fighting, and both sides mined their positions heavily, and to tell the truth, I don't think either side either knows, or can remember, where all the mines are. The JNA had a tactical mine field established here before the war broke out, and these mines are still in place, though no one kept record of their exact position.

Our first stop on the all expenses paid tour of the area was to a Serb position about 500 metres up the road from us called The Waterworks. It's called this because that was the excuse the Serbs used when they were asked about all the digging going on on the hill. "Never mind," they said, "it's just some waterworks we're installing." It didn't fool anyone. In fact, it's a long trench system on the crest of a low rising hill with several bunkers and numerous fire positions along its several-hundred-metre length. We patrol along it to ensure that the position is unmanned and hasn't been worked on recently. We have to be careful not to piss off the locals, as they have enough firepower stashed in the village that an antipersonnel mine might magically appear along our route overnight.

The next point of interest was the local destroyed cemetery. Every town has to have one, and this place is no different. Back in November, we came here to provide security for their All Saints Day vigil. We skirted the outside of it, not going inside because our engineers haven't cleared it, and based on our experience in November, it's almost certain that there are a few errant mines left in there somewhere.

Our last stop on the Serb side was the small bunker outside a Serb section house, where Reid nearly got himself killed. Ray pointed out where the Serbs had placed themselves during the "camera" incident, and it was quite clear he wouldn't have lasted

"The Waterworks" in Pristeg

ten seconds if they opened up. They had three anti-tank weapons on the second floor of a burned out building looking straight down into his carrier, and they had a full platoon of men deployed in an arc with every support weapon you could think of pointed at him and his deployed men. In spite of this, Reid had the audacity to imply that the Serbs might have gotten him, but his carrier would have gotten away. What an ass! Nobody on our side would have survived that fight. This is the type of officer everyone dreads. There are two sayings that come very close to describing this man. They are: professionals are predictable, amateurs are dangerous, and never do anything to attract enemy fire if it annoys everyone around you. Personal bravery is respected; stupidity is not tolerated. This is the man who starts a patrol by telling you not to walk off the path, then wanders all over the place kicking stones and walking down trails that the locals have told him are booby trapped (this describes the christening of the ground that Ray got from Reid).

Any time our people have come in contact with him, they refuse to follow where he goes because they never know if it's been cleared. In Rodaljice he went against direct orders and went into non-cleared buildings, that ended in a recorded warning for endangering his troops.

Finally, relations with the locals of the Pristeg area have improved 1000% simply because we bother to stop and say hello how are you in their own language. We also don't engage in the 2 Platoon practice of cutting landlines on the waterworks, or intimidating the locals. As I said earlier, since our arrival, a basketball game is an ongoing thing with the Croats, and we even stopped one day to play bocce with the Serb garrison, much to their surprise and delight.

The people have told us that they know that a very professional and nicer platoon is now stationed here. While you can talk with them, don't mess with them. Like the saying goes, be firm, fair, friendly, and professional. There are some that could learn from that saying.

The remainder of the day was pretty quiet. The platoon commander stopped by to check things out while I was on duty in the OP. He was going to ask me if I knew the short briefing we were to give to visitors, but he saw that I was ready, so he didn't ask, much to my relief, because I hadn't even looked at it yet.

The food situation here is, like Bruska, out of hand. Not only is there way too much of it, they expect us to cook for eight guys on a Coleman two burner stove and makeshift barbecue. A challenge for even a good cook. The day ended with a night shift for me from 0000 to 0300. I'm on again at 1000 so the most rack I'll get is six hours, and right now any rack will feel good.

Friday, 24 Feb., Pristeg Six hours is definitely not enough rack, and these damn cots don't help my back at all. I got up at nine to be ready for a 10–12 shift in the bunker. Just as I came on shift, our carrier pulled in having passed the maintenance inspection. Now the work of changing everything over and doing a serialized kit check began. My timing to go on duty was perfect. The shift went quickly and John relieved me at noon.

Shortly after John came on, he spotted some people in the Zone on Bulldozer hill. It's about 2000 metres from our position and on top of it is a Serb bunker under construction. We keep a spotting scope trained on it and check periodically to see if anyone is working on the bunker. According to the cease fire agreement the Serbs are not allowed to make any improvements to it. Today we spotted some people, so John called it into Charles. Our fearless and peerless leader, Lt McConnell, dashed off from Zero to investigate. He found not a few, but 14 people working on the structure of the bunker. By the time he got there they'd built a cement block wall about waist high in the shape of a small room, about 10' x 10'. When the lieutenant arrived they stopped work, and after some discussion agreed not to continue for the rest of today and tonight—which they probably would have done anyway because it started to rain after supper, and didn't let up until the next morning. The lieutenant then came by our position and gave us a quick SITREP, and went on his merry way. John gets a pat on the back for a job well done.

After the platoon commander left, Henry had some work to do, so he asked me to take Bruce and Jim for a tour of the Croat half of the patrol route in his stead. We suited up and went for the short ten-minute stroll down the road.

Remember I told you about the basketball game? Well we had one on the way back. Two on two, myself and a Croat vs. Jim and a Croat (My team kicked butt!), while Bruce kept an eye on our kit. For twenty minutes or so we played around, then suited up again, and walked through the Croat line of defence and into our camp.

Nothing much else happened today. For supper I cooked up barbecue ribs and a salad for everyone. Then later in the evening 3-9er and 3-9 Charlie showed up briefly. They were scoping the place out for a visit to be made by the Regimental honorary Col in the next few days. More fun and games. It's now 6 A.M., my shift is over and you'll never guess where I'm headed?

Saturday, 25 Feb., Pristeg Ah, another glorious rain soaked day. The clouds actually decided to take a break about mid morning, and the sun managed to put in an appearance for the afternoon, but by six, it clouded over again and by nine it was raining intermittently.

I went to bed shortly after 0600 this morning, but Henry decided that since the platoon commander was coming for a visit we should all be up. Our regular supply run did not show up yesterday, so there was no water to shave with (they bring us a regular supply of water and diesel fuel, plus any ADREPS we might have requested the day before) so I got dressed. I then lay back down on top of my sleeping bag to grab a few more hours rack before my shift.

At 1400, shaved and in my best bib and tucker, I went on duty, and that was when the day got interesting. At 1430 the platoon commander showed up with a film crew from the BBC World Service. They were in the area filming a segment on UNPROFOR's potential pulling out of the Krajina, and what affect it would have on the Croats. To get that angle, they brought the mayor for the Croatian side of Pristeg into the compound and interviewed him on camera. We were all disappointed. I always knew that interviews were constructed, but this was a little extreme. It seemed that the reporter didn't really care what the mayor thought. He kept asking the same question every possible way he could, in an effort to get him to say what he wanted. By reinterpreting what the mayor said each time, he answered a question, he tried to twist his words to his own ends. What the British reporter was after, of course, was for the mayor to say that it was not a good thing for UNPROFOR to leave "particularly when things are just starting to get better." To his credit, the mayor held his ground. He maintained that things could only get better if UNPROFOR left, and that "the world knows that it is the Serbs who started the war and they are the ones who will decide if they want to live peacefully with us."

On shift at the gate in Pristeg

The translator was Marilla (who worked with us at Rodaljice) and when she had to translate what the mayor had said, you could see she wasn't impressed (she's Serbian). Even from 50 feet away, I could see her expression change to ice. It made me smile.

The interview was abruptly cut off when the BBC reporter finally got the mayor to say that Croatia did not want UNPROFOR to leave.

The filming then progressed into the village. We all became movie stars at that point. John took three takes opening the gate for an Iltis that kept driving in and out of the compound. They got me looking in various directions with the binos up in the bunker. And Robert and Jay were filmed ad nauseam walking back and forth in the village. Finally around 1700, with waning light they called it a wrap, and left us in peace and they motored back to Rastivic.

It was odd, during the interview it seemed that everyone wanted something. A patrol from 2 Platoon stopped by, but had to be turned away because there wasn't enough room at the inn for all the vehicles. I don't think they were impressed. A second DP run with pallets and coco matting for our sleeping area had to wait outside the gate for the interview to end, so as not to disturb them. And the Serbs decided to pick this afternoon to review the work done on the defensive emplacements on the waterworks. Ted and John had to do a patrol of the area to ensure that they weren't up to no good, but found nothing.

To tell the truth, I'm kind of surprised the whole thing came off at all. Not twenty minutes prior to the arrival of the entourage, a mine exploded on the Croat side of the village. It just so happened that two Croat policemen, an interpreter, and two UNCIVPOL police had just arrived in the village and were congregating outside their vehicles when the blast went off. I had the bino's on them at the time trying to figure out who they were. The Croats, with interpreters in tow, and the UNCIVPOL, came to our compound.

The two policemen stayed for twenty minutes or so, and were up in the OP with me the whole time. From the moment they arrived, it was clear that something was amiss. It was obvious from his attitude, that the Nigerian senior officer was less than impressed with his Bangladeshi counterpart. The two conducted an animated discussion about what to do in this type of situation and I think the Nigerian would have shot the other guy, if he'd had a gun, for being the idiot he was. It was clear he was at the end of his tether. It was most amusing to watch.

After everyone had left, we laid out the pallets and put down the coco matting that came with the days supply run so that we were finally out of the water that constantly streams under the tent when it rains.

My next shift was at midnight to 0300, so I racked after cooking up a meal for the section, of hamburgers and salad. When I got up no one had cleaned up so I spent a few minutes doing that too. I hate doing clean up under these conditions; it's a pain in the ass, and the prime reason I choose to do the cooking.

Tomorrow is medals parade for those who have not yet received them. In our case that's everyone but John and Bruce. I hope the parade won't too be long, I'm not sure my back can handle it.

Sunday, 26 Feb., Medals/Rastivic
At 0800 this morning, half of us, Henry, Ted, Jay, Robert, and myself, piled into the back of the ML and went into Rastivic for our medals parade. We arrived early so everyone quickly changed and headed for the showers. Four days without showering can make one feel somewhat uncomfortable.

Pristeg doesn't even have a rudimentary shower set up like Bruska did, and with all our water having to be brought to us in jerry cans every day, we avail ourselves of every opportunity to go into Rastivic to shower.

As soon as we'd formed up, my back started to hurt. I don't know what it is, the way I'm standing, my boots, or what, but if I don't shift my weight around and bend my knees some during the parade, they'd have to carry me off in a stretcher at the end of the parade.

My medal was presented to me by Col Skidmore. A verbal pat on the back, a handshake, and on to the next guy. I'm actually surprised at the number of people who would rather have the medal sent to them, or pick it up in the orderly room. I always considered parades for handing out awards important recognition of the troops and therefore necessary. I never understood the other viewpoint.

Mercifully, this parade was but a half-hour or so long, so I was still able to walk off without too much pain. When we were dismissed we went straight back to our lines to get ready to disperse to the various OPs. We're going to fill in at some of the other OPs while the other platoons come in to receive their medals. George called out a list of OPs and who was assigned to them, and when he came to me he said "sorry big guy, you get stuck with the platoon commander today." I felt a little letdown because I was looking forward to seeing the landscape from a new perspective so to speak, from the top of a mountain.

When I reported to the lieutenant, he told me to respond to direction from the platoon warrant, who promptly tasked me to do a garbage sweep of the company lines. What a contrast! An hour before I was getting a medal for my work over here, and now I'm picking up garbage. Oh well, life in the army, it could be raining I guess.

The tasking lasted until lunch, after which things started to get more interesting as the platoon commander grabbed me to join himself, a driver, and George as they went into the Zone to sort out some kind of dispute.

Our first information was that the Croatian side of the town of Pristeg had recorded an official protest, claiming that there were supposed to be thirty Serb soldiers on their side of the village in uniform.

The protest was right, but when we arrived we talked to the locals (one was my teammate during the B-ball game) and discovered the protest was over some work being done on bulldozer hill. So off we sped to see what was happening on the hill.

When we arrived we found that 1-3 Bravo (our carrier) had been dispatched earlier, and was sitting at the base of the hill where the road ended and the foot trail began. Henry was out, and trying to sort out the situation. I counted 16 men sitting around taking a break, as their commander went back to the village to drop off his pistol, which is not permitted in the Zone, and get permission from his commander to carry on working. Construction on defensive positions is strictly forbidden by the Cease Fire Agreement, and this was one more in the ever-increasing number of violations we get each day.

On the scene, our platoon commander negotiated a temporary halt to the construction. Actually he bullied the hell out of them. Yelling and screaming until they relented—they probably thought he was as crazy as Reid and simply gave in—and all the workers walked down the hill. He then left Henry, Bruce, and myself (carrying the radio) while he went off to find the local brigade commander to try and sort things out.

Sitting on top of the hill would have been nice if it hadn't been so damned windy. We had to sit down to keep from being blown over. While we waited, we heard AAP get dispatched to our location, and the QRF go to 15 minutes' notice to move in case things got out of hand.

We were there maybe half an hour, when we spotted the work crew returning—all seventeen of them—from what amounted to a lunch break. As they approached, Henry tried to stop them from continuing work, in keeping with our orders from the platoon commander. He was told flat out by Dracula (the nickname we gave the guy in charge because he looks like a vampire) that they had permission from his commander to continue working. I called in a SITREP to higher, and was told to wait for a reply. Meanwhile, Henry tried to convince the workers to stop what they were doing.

It was frustrating as hell. Henry was beside himself because everyone was ignoring him. He kept trying to get Dracula to stop working, and Dracula kept giving him excuses. Bruce wanted to jump in and start throwing bodies around, but was reduced to pacing back and forth along the rim of the construction hole. And I couldn't believe what I was hearing on the radio. 3-9er wanted us to "have them stop construction now," he said, "but DO NOT escalate the situation." Well what the fuck does that mean???? Every time we tried to talk to the Serbs, they'd completely ignore us, hiding behind a barrier of language, or pretending to focus on their work. We couldn't make physical contact. That constituted escalation. Besides, if a shoving match ensued, sure as shit one of those bastards was going to pull a pistol. The likelihood was just too great. They'd all gone home at lunch, and knew full well that when they came back a confrontation was likely to ensue. We had a minimum of one in seventeen chance that someone had a pistol, and the odds were high that more than one of them was carrying. Even if we were carrying automatic weapons, in a close quarter situation such as this, it just wasn't worth it to take a chance and press the point; you'd never see the bullet coming. Besides, three against seventeen is not good odds no matter how you cut it.

At one point Dracula told Henry "this is a very complicated situation, war is coming soon, we must work fast." How do you argue with a man trying to defend his home and family? Yet how do you get them to stop without tossing bodies around and maybe cracking a few heads? Clearly they are breaking the rules but unless you escalate things a little (or a lot) there was no way to get them to stop working.

It was frustrating to the point that I'm still angry about it as I write this a day later. Higher clearly has no balls and/or desire to stop the work that is going on all over the Zone for fear of retaliation. Like corralling a large bull, how far do you go before it turns and attacks you?

It was agony to sit and watch these guys work. AAP had taken up positions of support on the next hill some 750 metres from us, but the work continued. I felt like I was tied to a stake, trying to convince the natives not to build the woodpile at my feet any higher. An equally futile gesture!

—Three, this is One Three Bravo, SITREP, over

—Three, Send, over

—One Three Bravo, the work on the bunker has stopped and the workers are taking a break, over

—Three, why have they stopped work, over

—One Three Bravo, they've stopped work because they have to wait for the cement to dry before they can put the roof on, over

—Three, Roger out.

I tried hard, but I don't think I could hide my utter contempt for Three at the time.

Finally, at long last, the platoon commander and the local battalion commander showed up, but by then it was too late. The work was complete. Oh they agreed to stop work all right. They had to, because they couldn't go any further.

Clearly, the platoon commander was not impressed. In fact he nearly had a bird when he discovered how much work had been done. I could see him fighting with himself not to say something to us, but he turned to the battalion commander and let him have it instead. The battalion commander tried to justify the work by pointing out various Croatian positions on the other side of the valley that they had been recently working on. This of course was a moot point, because the positions are well outside the Zone and do not fall under the Cease Fire Agreement, thus have no bearing on the obvious violation we were trying to clear up. Nonetheless, the damage had been done, and we'd been hung out to dry by Three. It is true our platoon commander had told us clearly not to allow anyone to continue working, but then we'd been given equally clear directions not to escalate the situation. Henry, who was concerned that if we started pissing the locals off they might retaliate, chose to err on the side of safety, and thus we stood back and let them continue working.

I suppose we could have handled things differently. We could have blocked the path and not let them near the place. We could have raised our voices and ordered them off the hill, which is what the platoon commander did the first time, and it worked. But hindsight is 20/20 and not ever having had any experience at this kind of thing, it's difficult to know how to react when faced with someone who simply doesn't want to listen, and conflicting orders to boot. Without doubt, the next time will be different.

Sitting in the Iltis on the way back to Rastivic, the platoon commander told me that digging in the Zone is going to skyrocket in about three days' time. This directly from the Serb battalion commander he'd just talked to. There's no doubt these people are scared and are preparing to defend themselves. I can't say I blame them, it just makes our job that much harder.

We got back in time for supper and were told to be ready to go out again at 2000. The platoon commander was keen to visit the OPs our boys had taken over for the night, the rest of us thought it was foolish and unnecessary, but didn't say anything. In the end common sense won, and we didn't go out. The problem was no one told the driver or me, so we spent twenty minutes waiting by the Iltis, until the lieutenant showed up and apologized for forgetting about us.

I was glad we didn't go out, I wanted a beer and needed to call Catherine, but the damn phone lines were down in Canada, so I couldn't get through. I wound up going to the mess and having a few beers instead.

It was a long and rather interesting day, and when I went to bed, I had little trouble getting to sleep. It still bugs me the way things on bulldozer hill were handled, but then one could ask why should I care when higher doesn't? There are never any easy answers without the big picture, but from where I'm sitting, it seems like no one wants to put his foot down, which is a shame. I'd hate to have to tell people our mandate was unfulfilled due to lack of balls. That's enough to make a man get out of the army.

26 Feb 95
My dearest Catherine
    Forgive me my love for not having written to you sooner. While I was in camp I had come to rely on our near daily phone calls to remain in touch with you.

Your letter with "chicken scratch" on it troubled me somewhat. It was painful to think of you working so hard to produce something that was in places illegible. However I do fully agree with you that we must continue to maintain our elegance of lifestyle (and not letting the scotch go to waste) so as to retain our dignity in the face of our disease (I say "our" because it is something that I feel strongly we must bear together).

It has been said that one must occasionally step back from a situation in order to see it more clearly, I always knew we had something special but by comparing what I have to others, I now have a new appreciation for our situation. You were, of course, quite right in that observation. However, my dilemma is the price we have paid for that separation. I cannot help but feel guilty over not being with you when you needed me most. I think we both knew this tour would be hard on us, but perhaps we were caught off guard by just how hard it would be. When I get back we'll work on spending more time together.

To that end, this is what I know. I'm flying out on the 4th of April, and will be released sometime before noon on the 5th. I'll have three weeks off, and must report back on the 1st of May. I'm on base until the 12th, home on weekends, and on Saturday the 13th there's a big family type party and barbecue. I leave it to you if we should go, but as it stands now, I'm disinclined to go. I understand I'm paid till the end of the month—this to be confirmed—so I hope to work on the house and garden for the rest of May. With any luck I'll be able to find work by then and can start back the 1st of June.

I hate to say it but all of this is subject to change depending on how the situation unfolds over here. But for now this is the plan.

It's an odd thing I've observed, but since we've changed taskings, time seems to fly by. It seems only yesterday I put "60" at the top of the page in my diary to indicate the number of days remaining. I'm now down to 37. At this pace I'll be home tomorrow.

I wanted to say something about our friends. We've been incredibly fortunate in their selection. Not one has forsaken us in our time of need, and were it not for them, I'd have asked for a compassionate discharge last month. We must do something to thank them, and no doubt you have it all arranged by now. Without them I/we would not have been able to go on. How does one say thank-you to such wonderful people?

I just received a letter from my mother, she said I was a great hit with the German side of the family when I visited after leaving you. I'm still at a loss as to what exactly I did, but I like these people, and perhaps that came through.

The time is passing quickly for me my sweet, I hope it is for you too. Tomorrow I get my medal, and by rights it should go to you, you certainly have earned it.

> *I love you my sweet, and will call you soonest.*
> *My love to all.*
> *Kurt*

Monday, 27 Feb., Rastivic/Pristeg At 0900, I was lying in bed having a wonderfully pornographic dream about my wife when I heard George outside the ISO asking around for free people. I knew damn well he had a work party in mind, and I

The Second Half of the Tour

prayed he found someone to fill it before he got to my trailer. When I overheard that no one was available from the other sections, I knew I had to think fast. I needed a place to hide. Looking around the ISO, I pondered the possibilities. The weapons locker was too narrow, my barrack boxes were full of kit, and there was no room under the beds. I had one option and one option only. Just as the door opened, I pulled the sleeping bag over my head, if I can't see him he can't see me. George walked in and burst out laughing. "Mister Grant" he said in a large well-humoured voice, "I have a tasking for you." I'm beginning to get the impression he enjoys that phrase. "This," I thought as I lay there under the covers, "is going to be a long day."

George wanted me to help unload a beaver tail full of sandbags, but suggested I shave first if I was going to get into uniform. The act of dressing and shaving just took three times longer than usual.

By the time I got to the beaver tail, I discovered four civilian workers had all but finished unloading it. It was terribly muggy, and I had worked up a sweat getting ready, so I went back and took a shower.

After cleaning up I buggered off to the JR's mess to do some writing, stopping off to mail a package with the T-shirts in it to for the relatives. I spent the rest of the morning in the mess writing, then went for lunch.

After lunch everyone was back from the OPs and ready to go back out to Pristeg. Jay and I were to go with the platoon commander in two Iltis to Charles HQ (he had to attend an Ogroup) and then on to SC 50. It struck me as odd that everyone was wearing helmets and we were doing a two-vehicle move. When I asked, I discovered that this morning in the Bravo Company's AOR, some Serb stepped out from behind a vehicle and fired thirty rounds from an AK over the cab of a passing Canadian 5/4-ton truck. It got the driver's attention, and gave his sphincter a serious workout. The alert status was raised.

At Charles we sat around for forty-five minutes until the lieutenant was finished, then we piled into the vehicles and got ready to leave, it was then that the platoon commander said something very telling. "Gentlemen," he said with a distant look, "over the next two weeks you are going to witness the gradual disintegration of the Zone of Separation. In fact, it wouldn't surprise me if the Serbs asked for two weeks of unrestricted digging." Now there's something to chew on.

Here are some points to ponder along the way. In the last couple of months, the number of VCFAs has tripled. This tells you that the Serbs are getting more and more worked up over what the Croats have said and appear to be doing. The Croatian president has threatened to cancel the UN's mandate when it comes due the end of next month. Clearly, with the Germans' help he has re-equipped and retrained his whole army, and it's quite likely he'll be ready to move come the first of April, about a week before we are scheduled to leave.

The Serbs of course know this, and are preparing for the coming fight to the point of ignoring the UN. To them we are becoming an increasing inconvenience in the face of what they consider to be the obvious.

It is fairly clear that the Croatians are strong enough to overrun the Krajina, but the question remains if they are capable of holding it. The Serbian Serbs, and the Bosnian Serbs, have sworn to support the Krajina should they be attacked. My understanding is that the only thing keeping the Croats from acting has been the words "economic sanctions."

Looking at it strictly as an infanteer, this is not a land I would want to try and take, or hold. It continues to amaze me that more people don't suffer from ankle or leg injuries due to the terrain. As for as I'm concerned, these people can continue to pound each other into oblivion, just as long as they wait until we're outta here. There are only thirty-six days left in the tour, and nothing would piss me off more than to have to stay longer than necessary because someone jumped the gun and decided to start the war early.

There is, of course, every possibility that war will never come. The Croats have grown fat and happy from their coastal economy, where the Serbs are much poorer but considerably more willing to fight to defend what they have. As with all agrarian societies, the land is very important to them. I do not believe this is necessarily the case in Croatia. Perhaps the Croat mayor was correct when he said that peace lies in the hands of the Serbs. Who's to know? Like the scorpion who stung the frog halfway across the stream, war may simply be everyone's nature. It will be interesting to see what happens after I get back to Canada.

When we got to Pristeg, I was just in time to work on the gabions. They've been given to us to fortify our position by building a temporary wall around our tent, and the carrier. Fortunately, instead of having to hand fill each one with sandbags, someone had the kindness to send us a front-end loader and several truckloads of dirt and rock. All that remained for us to do was clean up around them and level the tops off, but even that took an hour to do.

SC 50. Our home at Pristeg as seen from the OP

Just before supper we spotted a guy on bulldozer hill who we thought was working. We called it in to Charles, and the merry goose chase began. Charles dispatched us to investigate, so Bruce, Henry, Jim and myself raced down the road to put an end to this flagrant violation of the cease-fire agreement. Either the native telegraph got to

The Second Half of the Tour 245

him first, or he heard all 14 tons of us coming, because by the time Bruce and Henry made it to the top of the feature, he was nowhere in sight (would you be?). When they returned to the carrier we had to wait to call in our report. 4-7 had spotted three guys in uniform on the Malaclav feature (the next bunker down the road). We just looked at each other and knew what our next tasking would be.

Sure enough, no sooner had we called in our SITREP on bulldozer hill, than we were dispatched to check out the next feature. While Charles whined on over the radio about not letting these people on the feature without their commander being present, Henry and Bruce went off up the hill to investigate.

At least this time the soldiers didn't run away. A little while after going up the hill, everyone came down the hill with smiles on their faces, another round of the game completed.

As we stood around the carrier talking to the locals, a bottle of surprisingly good wine appeared and the glass was passed. Not content with just a sip, the habit here is to drain the glass (about the size of a whisky tumbler) in one go. I think we were all just fed up with the bullshit of the situation, so to a man we had a glass each. One glass wasn't going to kill us anyway, and we put it down to détente, which is as good an excuse as any I suppose.

Supper consisted of macaroni and cheese and some ham, then around 2100 Henry and I went on duty in the bunker until midnight. Tomorrow I'm going to be giving an OP brief to the honorary Colonel of the Regiment. This should be interesting; the OP brief has been changed about three times this week by the CSM of Charles Company. It's to the point now where we have to know names of features, the distance to it, the bearing to it in mills, and its grid on the map. For example, "the feature you are looking at is called the waterworks. It is on a bearing of 5850 mills, 500 metres from our location, and is at grid 507678." There are five of these features. So instead of memorizing them like the CSM wants us to, we've written them on the wall in places only we can see when giving the brief. That way at least we don't look like total idiots when we're reciting the numbers.

Tuesday, 28 Feb., Pristeg Last night I did not sleep that well. I was just that little bit too cold, and I kept waking up shivering. It was a nippy night out. But today dawned clear and without a cloud in sight. I relieved Henry at the gate a little past 0800, then hunkered down to review the OP brief in earnest. Nothing like a little cramming before the big performance.

We had all expected at least three CSMs, an OC or two, the Battalion commander, the RSM and a few extra officers thrown in for good measure, in a cavalcade of vehicles touring the countryside. It was anyone's guess who'd show up for the OP brief.

As it happened only three vehicles showed up. One with the CO, one with the RSM and one with the honorary Col. I was mildly surprised when the old guy and a liaison officer were the only two who showed up for the brief.

As for the brief itself, it didn't quite turn out as planned. The liaison officer wound up using the briefing map to explain the layout of Charles Company AOR, and point out the various OPs relative to our position. That in essence covered half of my job. Thinking quickly, I modified the brief and tied it into what the LO had just said. Out the window went the grids, bearings, and distances. This was going to be a simple discussion that pointed out the major features and talked about the people and the job. It turned into about a half-hour talk about the area, the conflict, and the geo-political situation in a historical and present day context. The Canadian army is nothing if not well educated.

The visit didn't last much longer after that. The two Cols, the RSM and a couple of our guys went for a quick walk down the road to see the Croatian lines, and a bombed-out church, then they left to visit another position. That's what we like; short sweet visits.

The remainder of the morning was uneventful and lazy. I actually got in some sun tanning when I came off duty. About mid afternoon, John and I went for a patrol of the area. It turned into a photographic expedition. I must have taken about two dozen shots, and considering you're not supposed to have cameras in the Zone that's pretty good.

A couple of interesting things happened on this patrol. The first occurred when we got up on the waterworks and discovered five guys up there. One of them was Dracula, and the other was the local Serb battalion commander, who was wearing a uniform and carrying a sidearm.

We approached, and started the meeting with handshakes all around, no point in being an asshole right away. We quickly ascertained that only Dracula could understand English (though in truth, I suspect that the battalion commander was more fluent in English than Dracula was, even though he didn't let on) so we asked him to translate for us. I asked Dracula to tell his commander that he was not permitted to wear a sidearm while in the Zone (he of course knew this, but it had to be said anyway). He did, and the answer came back "I don't trust my enemies." So I told him "sir, if you were carrying an AK, I might understand the need for a weapon, but a pistol is a waste of time, it's inaccurate and has very limited range. Besides, by international agreement you have agreed not to be in the Zone with weapons, or in uniform either." This was translated and the guy thought for a moment, then nodded, smiled, and said, "we were just leaving anyway." Whereupon they all packed up and left. Another successful round played out, chalk one up for us.

One of the local women tending the flock and carding wool to pass the time

One of the many desecrated graves in Pristeg

A house barricaded with bio-degradable sandbags

Land mines were used to knock out the wall and bring down the roof

The other thing of interest was the cemetery—destroyed like the one in Rodaljice. John and I stood outside its short walls and looked in. This was the place I'd heard so much about. The place where our platoon came to do the security during the All Saints' Day visit back in November. The place had been declared off limits to everyone because it hadn't been fully cleared by the engineers. Also, because there was every chance that someone had snuck back in and planted a few new booby traps in the past few months, just for good measure. Still, all it took was for John and I to look at each other, and together we said, "fuck it" and over the wall we went.

Always careful to step on hard surfaces, we hopped from grave top to grave top, as we began to explore. We searched around, and found a lot of the usual things. Broken headstones, open graves, dashed bones, and pieces of anti-personnel mines. I came across a capstone on a grave that had an intricate design inlayed in the cement with coloured stones and shells. I took a picture.

John was moving a few feet ahead of me, when he came to a complete stop, accompanied by a short, sharp exclamation. I stepped onto the grave beside him and was immediately assaulted by a smell like none I'd ever encountered before. Before us was a grave that had been opened, and the casket inside broken open. Nothing unusual about that, only it appeared that the body inside had not been in the grave very long, a couple of months maybe, and was still in the process of decomposing. The bitter sweet smell of rotting flesh floated up to our noses, and almost made my eyes water. This, despite the appearance that most of the decomposition had taken place already and what we smelled was residual.

We both just stood there for a moment, then we each took a picture, and carried on, there wasn't much point in commenting.

We wandered around for a while longer, found some more open graves, took about a dozen photos, then hopped the wall, and carried on with our patrol. Our justification for walking through the graveyard was "man has a natural curiosity about life and death, and we were just satisfying our curiosity." It's not much, but that's our story.

The open grave and casket, complete with occupant, that we encountered on patrol

This evening we had an interesting discussion about what's going on in the Zone. It went back and forth for a while, but the essence of it was this: we feel that the Zone is beginning to crumble. It's only minor right now, but it will likely get worse rather than better. The UN is increasingly being ignored, or not consulted, prior to something happening. For example, Camp Alpha conducted an anti-aircraft firing exercise without informing our higher (scared the shit out of the 2 Platoon guys). The feeling is that when we do act tough, someone gets shot, or shot at, and we respond by running to our bunker and hiding. The result has been the UN trying not to "escalate" the situation, which leaves the guys on the ground frustrated and angry.

We can't act too tough for fear of local retaliation; both from here and back home if we start sending people home in body bags. This is not an easy situation, and we feel our current mandate must change to accommodate what's really happening. Either we get out, back up our threats with more troops, or we discontinue our patrols and revert to an observe and report role. Any way you cut it, what we're doing right now isn't working and is a pain in the ass for everyone.

Wednesday, 01 Mar., Pristeg The day was just breaking at 0600, and I was preparing itself for another one of those clear skied, warm weathered days, when, the generator died.

It had been throbbing on and off all last night, and finally gave up the ghost this morning. It's a good thing it quit when it did; otherwise we would have been left quite literally in the dark.

No amount of coaxing would convince it to start, so we called in a repair and recovery request, and waited. Another fortunate thing was that we called in early, because it took all day and several visits by Bluebell to finally get the thing going.

The problem, we discovered in talking to the repair guys, was the fuel filter. It seems some dirt got into the system while we were filling the gabions and clogged the lines. The result of that finding was that our fuel barrel was declared condemned, and we have to order in new fuel. Just as well, he told us that as much as 20% of the fuel by volume is water anyway. It seems whoever is supplying us with diesel, is siphoning off and selling the fuel, and replacing the missing volume with water. Over time, the fuel barrel has become more and more saturated, to the point where it is now almost useless. A new barrel was promised to us today, but it never showed up. So what else is new? We've jury rigged the system so that the fuel line comes right out of a jerry can, which we refill every three hours. It's simple but it works.

Today was the first totally relaxing day I've had since coming here. We all sat around the bunker and sun-tanned and talked.

The highlight of the day came when Henry announced that he had finally caught the rat that he shared the bunker with. He would go into the bunker sometimes with a loaded pistol and lie on his bunk and wait for the bugger to present itself then try to take a shot at it. This had been going on for days, and was the source of some considerable humour for us. Finally Henry set out a trap with peanut butter instead of cheese (previous attempts proved too easy as the rat got the cheese the first time without setting off the trap), and when Henry got off shift he was rewarded with a sprung trap and a dead captive.

Henry figured he'd cleaned out all the rats, but when he went down later today, he discovered the first rat had a friend. The trap has been reset.

The platoon commander came out briefly today to pass on a couple of points. He said the honorary Col was quite pleased with the briefing he received from us. He said it was good to talk to someone his own age. This brought down the house, and I just waved and said, "thank you, Sir" (little shit). Smiles all around.

The lieutenant announced that the Canadian Press would be making the rounds in the next few days and he left us a sheet of possible questions and approved answers. We've been told not to comment on policy, but if you read the questions, they are all about policy, which is a bit of an oxymoron. We won't be here for the interviews, but the boys don't seem to mind. They'd much rather avoid talking to the press altogether. I don't understand that attitude at all. I don't look forward to talking to them, but I wouldn't run from them either. Not that I have much respect for the press anyway, but they do represent another viewpoint.

Tomorrow's the big change-around. We go in to become QRF and start doing odd jobs for a week. Something we're all just dying to do. John and Robert went in today to pack for their UN leave, they leave tomorrow which means the warrant is back, George rejoins the section, and David returns to the fold. These past three weeks have just flown by. It feels like only a couple of days ago David went on leave. Hard to believe he's back already.

I do believe the Partiburg dinner is tonight. Darn that means we won't do QRF for 24 hours. That's too bad.

Thursday, 02 Mar., Change-Over This morning I was on the 0600–0900 shift, but seeing as we were going to leave around 0900, Jay was sent to relieve me at 0800 so that I could pack up my kit. He needn't have bothered though, our relief didn't leave Rastivic until 0900 and didn't get into our position until 9:40, so I could have completed my shift and still had lots of time to pack.

Henry was a little slow on the handover and we didn't get off until 10:15, which was fine by me, because it was nearly 11 before we got back to camp and too late to be assigned to do special tasks for the CSM.

After lunch John and Robert boarded their bus to start their UN leave. Just as well for John. He was starting to get on my nerves. He developed this "I don't give a shit" attitude these last three weeks and it manifested itself in ways that weren't like him at all. For instance, he would leave long notes on our door that could get us in shit, or he'd verbally attack people over the smallest things. I had to tell him to back off several times; he was simply losing control.

We signed our assessments this afternoon as well. The points that Henry put down for me were all above average stuff. "Excellent worker, can be relied on, willing to learn, good attitude, blah, blah, blah." What caught me off guard were the platoon commander's comments. He wrote "wealth of talents, excellent worker, tends to annoy his peers sometimes (who doesn't) but makes up for it by his dedication and knowledge of the job" or words to that effect.

Assessments are to be directed at job performance only. That shit about "annoying his peers" is both unprofessional and uncalled for. Besides, how the hell would he know if I annoyed anyone anyway? He's never around long enough to know.

David is back, and he is much relaxed. We were betting football would call him away and he'd go AWOL. We weren't serious of course, but it gave us a few laughs.

MCpl Parry (our platoon CQ) and I made a run back to Pristeg this afternoon to drop off fuel and extras to make life easier out there. We took our time and got back around 3:30, once again dodging the CSM's bullet. I ducked out to call Catherine, but the damned phones were at Bravo Company. It'll have to wait till tomorrow.

The Partiburg dinner I had hoped was today is on for tomorrow. We'll work half the day then have 24 hours off. Tomorrow night there will be a lot of tired and drunken bodies in our lines, with any luck I'll be one of them.

I have it on good authority that if we are to remain past our scheduled return dates; it will be for no longer than three weeks. The Vandoos will be brought in to do the teardown, but no one really believes we'll be staying.

You recall the thirty-round burst incident a couple of days back? Well, Ted talked to the driver in the mess tonight. What happened was, the guy was on a run of some sort and had to take piss, so he pulled over. While he was around the side of the vehicle doing his business, the two guys with him decided to get out and snap a couple of pictures, as the scenery was particularly appealing for whatever reason. Unbeknownst to them they had stopped in front of a Serb section house. The Serbs thought they were taking pictures for intelligence purposes and came running out of the house. One of them grabbed an AK and fired off the rounds in an effort to scare the guys off. Scare them it did. The poor guy relieving himself nearly shit himself at the same time. There was a mad dash by all to get in the vehicle and get the hell out of there. Higher is going to charge those involved for having cameras and taking pictures of the Serbs. These boys are with SIG, and you can bet there'll be a few personal phones that won't be working if the charges go through. Typical 1 RCR, the infighting continues.

Friday, 03 Feb., QRF Last night I was tired for some reason, so I hit the sack around nine thirty, and got the first really good sleep I've had in a week. This morning got off to an unexpected start. At 0730 we all gathered with our UAB, and barrack box by barrack box they were inspected. This would have been done so much easier at a platoon level, but no, as per SOP with 1 RCR everything has to be done the hard way. In this case we stood around for two hours while the MPs went through our kit. I would tell you it could be worse by raining but in this case I'd be wrong. It was only raining on and off as our boxes were opened. Once again the military strikes with excellent pre-event planning. There was much grumbling in the ranks.

Still very few people were caught with odd things in their kit. For example, one guy got caught trying to bring oversized glow sticks back. John had a mountain stove with a full tank of naphtha in it (I took his kit through). There was zero tolerance on pornography, so a lot of guys took their magazines out, as well as knives, which also weren't allowed (though no one knows why). I'd like to say something suitably satirical but nothing comes to mind just now. It's just another example of the bizarre set of rules we labour under on this tour.

Right after I was done, I went for a quick ride to Pristeg with the platoon commander. On the way we spotted a large backhoe we'd been keeping an eye on (the one parked outside Charles Company a while back), in a field beside 100 yards of new trench line that had been dug in the last 24 hours.

The incidents of digging have increased markedly on both sides of the Zone. Things are getting tense and in two places shots were fired back and forth between the sides. Both sides are on edge. We see new digging every day.

We're off at noon today, but we had an Ogroup at 1300. In it we were told that all reservists are now on advanced party, and as soon as we get back and hand in our kit we're being cut free. No contract extension, no Battalion party, nothing. This is not 1 RCR's doing, but LFCA's efforts at saving money. A lot of us are pissed about it. We put a lot of money into the company fund and expect at least something in return but now we can kiss the money goodbye. "It's being looked into" was the last word we had; I'm not inspired.

I've just called Catherine, and she really sounds good. Her doctor said she's in better shape than she was in July. She's a lot stronger and much of her balance has returned. Still, it's been an exceptionally hard month on her. She was unable to leave the house to work even for a single day, and if it weren't for our friends, I likely would be sitting at home now. I can tell you I'm chomping at the bit to get home. Only four and a half weeks left. It's hard to believe we've been here nearly half a year.

Before the party started, I managed to get in another call to Catherine. The Reverend Doctor Andrew Stirling was there and I talked to him for 5 or 6 minutes. It was nice to hear his voice. He was kind enough to offer to edit my diary and recommend a publisher. I'll have to be extremely careful with exactly what goes into the final product.

Tomorrow I'll try to call Catherine again. It is so good to hear her voice, and know that she is well. I very much look forward to seeing her again.

Now then, off to the party!!!!

Saturday, 04 Mar., QRF Oh my God, oh my God, oh my God. Wasn't that a party! Blow-out would probably be a better word. The bar certainly made some money last night that's for sure.

Two beers and a half bottle of wine were the free issue; steak and lobster was on the menu. Foregoing the beer, I went with wine all night, very few people were drinking it so there was lots of it around.

This was a necessary party. Dukes feel like they've been kicked around and treated like shit for so long that we needed this just to blow off some steam.

In all honesty last night I had a really good time. I didn't drink enough to do something really stupid (though I did try to call Catherine, thank God I got the answering machine. I hope my speech wasn't too slurred. Rule number 17 of bar edict: Never call anyone when you are drunk, as it tends to leave a bad impression). I seemed to have been the only one to have brought a camera to the mess, though I took a few shots, I know the vast majority of the shots were taken by others. I went in with a new roll, and came out with a fully exposed one.

Everyone in our platoon had a really good time. I cannot say the same for the other two platoons. 3 Platoon was by far the rowdiest of all, in spite of which no one in our platoon got charged.

At every party there are always wet noodles, and this party was no exception. Two MCpls from 2 Platoon excelled last night at being assholes, the likes of which I've rarely seen before. Their efforts were focused on trying to control us, and when that failed they ran like little children to the duty sergeant and started tattling on people who had gotten themselves drunk.

One, who had gone on about how bad this battalion was during the CIS training, was the worst of the two. For a guy who hates blades (back stabbers), he is by far the worst I've ever seen, not content to keep it in the company and protect his own, he was the first to talk to the duty sergeant and threaten people with being charged. Everyone I've talked to agrees that this guy is seriously fucked up. I don't think I've ever seen him smile and he walks around with an enormous chip on his shoulder. He has no idea how close he came last night to getting pounded into the dirt. At one point four guys had to restrain Ted from having a go at him.

In the end, one guy will be charged for taking a beer to the phones with him, the CSM has gone over to see the RSM about the party and this morning a bunch of us had to go clean up the mess (spilled beer and such).

What I fail to understand is this paranoiac need the battalion has for charging as many people as possible. It's not as if they didn't know this was coming. What else do they expect from a company that's been treated the way ours has, or been as dry as long as we have. Of course we're going to cut loose; of course we're going to get drunk and do silly things; the least they could do is protect us in case something dumb happens, instead of waiting to pounce when it does. Besides, nothing bad happened anyway, nothing got broken, nobody got hurt, and aside from being a lot too loud, we all had a good time.

The Second Half of the Tour 253

This battalion does not look after its own and it does not foster a sense of family, yet in spite of that, we all continue to work hard and do the job as best we can.

This morning I woke up at 0700 and tried to have breakfast, but succeeded only in drinking a lot of juice and by noon downed about eight Tylenol. Midmorning I went over and helped a bit with the cleanup but for the most part it was a quiet morning. Hell, it was a quiet day. I slept part of the afternoon, and chatted with the guys the rest.

This afternoon's Ogroup was somewhat interesting. More shots have been fired in Bravo's AOR, and one of their OPs that confiscated a .50 cal and a recoilless rifle yesterday, got another machine gun and something else today.

Things are pretty tense over there. JORBAT I believe had one of their trucks hit by a flying-holy-fuck-wakeup-call (anti armour missile) from the Serbian AAP boys. No one was hurt. KENBAT had a couple of mortar rounds dropped near them. Digging is increasing on both sides of the Zone.

I called Catherine again today. The first thing she said to me was something she couldn't tell me yesterday because Andrew was there, "Come home soon honey, I'm horny." This from a woman who can be best described as a true lady, and who wouldn't say shit if she were buried in it. After I picked myself off the floor, she explained that she is feeling much better and that would I please come home soon. If only she knew how many times I've gone to sleep at night or woken up in the morning with a tent in my sleeping bag from thinking of her. One of the true joys of marriage is the enjoyment of each other's body. Deprived of that pleasure, one becomes antsy and all the more desirous of your partner. The pleasure I gain from knowing she's healthy again, is matched only by the anticipations of many passionate nights to come.

30 days and a wakie.

Sunday, 05 Mar., QRF Today began with a shudder, literally. At 0645 an explosion (I thought it was a mortar round) went off close enough to shake the ISO. Virk rolled over and I went to shave, and so starts another day in Croatia.

The morning was spent working for the CQ. It wasn't hard work, just a lot of little jobs piled together. We stacked water boxes, loaded an ML, and resupplied the ablution ISOs with water then weaseled our way out of any more work for the morning. When CQ found out that his work party had been released he nearly lost it. Jay and I have to go back tomorrow and you can bet it won't be a short day.

In the afternoon I got in a really good workout, and a call to Catherine. About 6 minutes into the call we got cut off because the phone lines went down. This pissed me off because I never got a chance to tell her I need a new diary.

Catherine did tell me about the letter I wrote to the kids in 4N. They liked the bit about why I got into the army and not paying lip service to your beliefs so much that they put it in the yearbook.

Tonight's Ogroup glossed over the fighting—no one cares—and focused on new rules. A new rules of engagement card came out a couple of days ago and the big change is you are now not permitted to fire on someone to protect UN property. This means if a Serb sneaks up to your carrier and starts to run off with your .50 cal, you can't shoot him. Of course the odds of that ever happening are virtually zero, but it illustrates my point. Other interesting restrictions include belt knives can no longer be worn (except a Leatherman, and a C-5 knife which is a poor replica of a Swiss army knife), and all tattoos offensive to women must be removed at the wearer's expense.

On the first point, I wear what is called a rigger's knife. It is an army issue knife, and I have used it every day I have been on tour. I consider it a tool and therefore I refuse to remove it. If they want to charge me so be it. I'll gladly stand in front of the CO, RSM, or whomever and say the same thing. The second point about tattoos is pure bullshit, and would never survive a human rights hearing. Enough said. Both of these rules come from a General, who, conjecture has it, likely never spent a day of his life in the field.

After the Ogroup, George asked each of us privately if we felt we were suffering from combat incident stress. When he asked me I burst out laughing. The only stress I've suffered from lately has been trying to avoid the CSM's work parties, and avoiding higher ups so I don't get in shit over dumb things—like having a knife on my belt.

In reality though, I must admit that there have been times when this tour has been less than easy for me. Catherine has been on my mind every waking minute, and the separation from her has been hard. To say that sexual frustration is a way of life over here is only just beginning to describe it. Though I must confess that more people speak openly about masturbating than when I was in the military ten years ago. Sign of the times I guess.

Ray Labell paid me the highest compliment the other day. He's been moved into the section commander's position for 3 Section—formerly Sgt MacKinnon's section, and one of his guys was down in the dumps about a girl he met on leave. This guy had gone off to the Cayman Islands for his UN leave, met a beautiful blond, they'd screwed themselves silly for the entire three weeks, then gone their separate ways. They thought it was love, and he was planning on getting hitched. She sobered up and sent him a Dear John letter. He's been in the dumpster ever since. So much so that it affected his job performance. Ray told me that he had to counsel the guy to get him back on track. And yet, he said, when he looked at me, "you were someone who had a legitimate reason to let his job performance waiver and never have." I was quite moved by it. Truth is, if I didn't have this diary, or the more than regular phone calls home, I think the going would have been a lot tougher. Who's to say?

Certainly the young man I heard on the phone the night of the party was close to losing it. Two of us standing outside couldn't help but over hear the short, sharp, conversation that went like this: "Shut up . . . shut up . . . shut the fuck up bitch . . . shut up. I will call you when I see fit to call you and no sooner . . . shut up . . . if I don't hear what I want to hear out of you, the next time you hear from me, it'll be through my lawyer!" SLAM! The guy then got up and stormed past us.

How much of it was alcohol, how much of it was real, we'll never know, but it left the two of us dumbstruck and looking at each other. One wonders if he'll have a marriage to come back to. No doubt he needs to talk to someone. Soon!

If stress manifests itself sometimes in excessive sleeping or a change in sleeping habits, then I must be suffering some stress. Everyone tells me I've started snoring. I cannot confirm this of course, as I am never there when it happens, though I have caught myself once or twice just as I was drifting off, making some bloody strange noises. It will be interesting to see if this new trait goes away, or if it's another sign of old age, like this bloody spare tire I can't seem to get rid of.

Monday, 06 Mar., QRF Today felt like a bloody long day. Jay and I spent the whole day working for QM, and while the work was not overly hard, it was continuous, which meant come 4:30 I was bagged.

I worked today with a couple of reserve guys from 1 Platoon. One of them wound

The Second Half of the Tour 255

up with seven extras for having a beer with him by the phones during the party. The worst part is that not only does he do the seven extras, his section commander (Sgt Thompson of Knin fame) has told him he'll get every shit job that comes up for the section for the rest of the tour. To add insult to injury the two of them are the only reservists in the section and as a result get every Joe job that comes their way. I thought that kind of discrimination went out with the dark ages, but in 1 Platoon it appears to be alive and well. Fortunately, I can tell you that in the rest of the company, the standard is very different. Reservists are treated as equals, which is as it should be. Is it any wonder morale in that platoon is so bad.

The Ogroup was quite short tonight. Tomorrow we're to stay in combats and remain in the company lines in case the call comes in for us to move. My understanding is that our platoon commander had another run-in with the Serb battalion commander in Pristeg over the digging issue, and tomorrow it may come to a confrontation. No doubt tomorrow we'll end up sitting around most of the day watching TV. At least we won't be working for the CSM.

The other big thing in the Ogroup was about the battalion party on the 13th of May. It appears the Reservists have not been invited. The reason given was that it's a catered affair, and higher didn't want three hundred people saying they were coming, and only thirty show up. We've been with these people for a year now, and this is the thanks we get. RCR family my ass thanks for nothing!

George is planning to hold a party at his place on the 12th for everyone in the section. It's a bring your wives and a sleeping bag and I'll supply the booze kind of get together. No doubt the drinking will last all night, and there was even the suggestion of playing golf the next morning before the battalion thing. As I write this, it becomes clear to me that I will likely not attend either function. The simple reason is it's not my style when I'm with my wife, to get drunk and stupid and pass out in a tent. I would never subject her to that, though I may consider coming alone. There are so many good men that I've met on this tour that it's a shame not to continue the relationship. George, Henry, Jay, and Ray who, when I told him at the Partiburg dinner that I was really glad I'd met him, reached out and gave me a hug.

Though a part of me wants to come and see them all again, I think this is one of those times where it's best just to walk away, and get on with my life. I've done what I've come here to do, and now it's time to close the book, so to speak, and move on. My mind is not fully made up, and I expect this place is having an effect on my judgement, so I'll leave it till closer to the time.

Virk and I chatted again today about our wives. He too had a real rough go of it yesterday. We both find that thinking of home takes all the steam out of us. On the wall above my writing space, I have taped a picture Graham took of Catherine and I only moments after our arrival at his flat in London. Each time I look at it I smile and reach out to touch Catherine's image. We had a grand time, the best time we've ever had together, and yet as I look at it now it seems a lifetime away. I have trouble remembering what we did, save for a few snippets of images, which sadly lack emotion. The steady sound of the rain on the roof of the ISO is a constant reminder that like a prison sentence, I still have time to serve in this place. It is by far too easy to let the doldrums creep up on you, and sink into a foul mood. Each day I fight to keep a good attitude and go about my work with cheer. But I must confess I grow weary of the battle, and with each passing day it becomes that much harder to see the humour in things, and be unaffected by the ever changing situation we find ourselves in. Perhaps it's just the gloomy weather, or the fact that I'm tired and in a pissy mood, but it seems that these past couple of days have been a little rougher than most. Forgive me if I sound like I'm whining, if you pass the cheese I'll shut up.

There are still things to smile about though. Sector South HQ suspected that we were lying to them about the number of accidents the battalion has had to date. It seems the PPCLI had 18 in one month, and we've only had four thus far in the tour.

This close to the end of the tour people are inventing new and unusual ways of counting down the time remaining. 28 days and a wakie, four more Saturday Barbecues, three more rotations, or the most unusual, one more period. I don't think that last one would work for the guys.

Tuesday, 07 Mar., QRF Last night as I was making my diary entry, I heard what I thought was a single .50 cal round go off. There was a carrier approaching the gate at the time and 4 or 5 of us stuck our heads out of the window to see what the commotion was. Like something out of a cartoon, all these heads popped out of the windows at once, and asked the same questions. "Did you hear that?" "I heard that," "Was that a 50?" "I thought it was a 50, do you think it was a fifty?," "well if it was, someone's in kaka now."

We found out in tonight's Ogroup that last night as the Engineers came off patrol, the Sergeant at the gun had an accidental discharge and fired a round (armour piercing tracer) right over the camp. Scared the shit out of the poor guy at the gate. It's a good thing it was a Sergeant on the gun, otherwise more than one guy would have burned for it.

Today was one of those blah, rainy, slow days. I couldn't even get motivated to do a workout. We were supposed to be on call in case we were needed, but the only thing they needed us for was a garbage sweep of our lines. Most of the day was spent reading, watching TV, or writing. I finally got a letter off to one of Catherine's students who wrote to me, but I had difficulty keeping it upbeat, and not satirical.

Henry came around and gave us all our warrior badges. Once again I was awarded the gold. It's going to be a challenge as I get older to continue to keep getting gold. I'm not sure I can stay in good enough shape each year to keep running under 18 minutes. Only time will tell on that one.

The Ogroup this evening had some interesting and funny points in it. And one sobering thought. For days now it's come down in orders that withdrawal plans are being formulated. We didn't think much of it because it falls into the category of contingency planning, and on the grand scale of things it was only one of the many options available to us. Tonight a little more emphasis was put on it; as the date for the renewal of the UN mandate grows nearer it's looking more and more like we'll either fly out of here as planned, or fight our way out. There are other options which fall in between the two, but that's for higher to consider. Right now we're thinking about the latter option, hoping for the former, and barely touching the ground as we mentally dance back and forth between the two. No one wants to fight his or her way out, but it certainly gets the blood going thinking about it.

The best option is not to think about it. The less you think the easier and faster time passes. Thinking is like a sea anchor to a sailboat. All you want to do is skim over the surface without giving any thought as to how deep the water is and what dangers it might contain.

A Serbian officer was put in jail the other day. Why is that important? It's important because he was the man in charge of a Serb artillery piece that was captured in the Zone last week. We didn't think much of it, but it's come out that this officer had left the piece unattended, and it was found that way by a Bravo Company officer who happened to be in the Zone at the time. Realizing what he had, the young officer hooked up the gun and drove home with it. The Serb battalion commander was pissed when he found out. Not that the gun was in the Zone, he ordered it there, but for the fact that it was lost without anyone being there to put up a fight. Hence, the Serb officer in charge was put in jail and the battalion commander offered to drive Bravo Company's OC to the jail to prove it. That's one Serb I don't envy.

All this week and next we're going to be overrun by media. Tomorrow the CBC is in camp, and then one after another the major news agencies will show up. Most of the guys don't want to have anything to do with them. As for myself, I don't much care one way or the other.

Finally, at long last, the rumour has been killed. All Reservists are invited to the Battalion party on the 13th. In spite of what was passed in orders before, the CO has gone out on a limb and said that we can come. I say gone out on a limb, because we're told when the CO asked Brigade back in Petawawa if he could have us back for the stress debrief and party, he was told "no." So he went to area and asked again. He received the same answer. Still not satisfied he went to NDHQ and was given the wackiest answer of all. They were worried that if the Reservists were put back in the military environment they might suffer some kind of delayed stress reaction and flip out, therefore, no he could not have his Reservists back (think about that for a second).

The CO decided that this wasn't good enough so he invited the Reservists to the party, but they'd have to make their own way there, and find a place to stay. To make things easier for us, WO Fuller, George and Ray have offered up their homes for the Reservists in the platoon for the weekend ("there will be no drinking and driving!"). I have an overwhelming urge to go to this party just to spite the people in higher command.

It's decisions like these that kill morale in the Army. I joined this organization because I love what it does. I love the adventure, the roughing it, and the physical aspects of it all. Hell, I'm in this godforsaken place because of my love for the Army. But the longer I'm in, the harder it gets to do the job. The Army today is not the Army of the past, not fifteen years ago, not even five years ago. I think back, with envy now, on some of the stories my dad used to tell about the sense of family that used to be in the military. There was a time when you could go to the Mess and have a few drinks, find your superior, give him a piece of your mind, and clear the air between you. Christ, if you did that now you'd be up on charges the next morning before you could brush your teeth.

Today's Army is more concerned with PER's and blaming others than with protecting its own, and creating a sense of belonging. Why else would they charge three people for an accidental discharge, rather than making the one responsible pay?

There was an article some time ago in the Infantry Journal called "Where have all the tigers gone?" In it, the author, a retired officer, lamented the fact that in order to get ahead in today's Army you had to speak French, and have a degree. What ever happened, he asked, to the officer who came up through the ranks and stuck up for his men because he understood where they were coming from? A guy like that goes nowhere in today's Army. The same can be said for NCOs. Time and again I've come across good men, Sgts, WOs, MCpls, all of whom have been stuck in rank longer than they should have because they stood up for their boys when higher was looking to burn someone.

What all this does is create a sense of disillusionment within the ranks. I wish I could adequately describe my pure and utter disgust at the situation, but I feel my writing ability falls well short of the mark. Suffice it to say that decisions like the one from NDHQ make it exceedingly hard for anyone to take any pride in what they do. It's not that I necessarily want to come to the party. It's that I'd like to be offered the choice, for someone to say, "hey buddy, thanks for all your help, it was good to have you with us, come on out and have a brew and we'll look after you."

Wednesday, 08 Mar., QRF What an incredibly beautiful day it was today. The air was crystal clear, and hardly a cloud in the sky. I saw mountains today to the north and west that I've never seen before because the air wasn't clear enough.

The whole day I stayed in PT kit. I did some writing in the morning, then after lunch I lay about for a while then strapped on my combat boots and went for two laps for the camp. It's going to take some time to get my back conditioned to running again. The whole first lap I was so tight that I had to stop and stretch it out. The second lap wasn't so bad, but after completing it I figured that was enough for today.

Around 1500 I went over and called Catherine. It would be very easy for me to go over nearly every day and sit for ten minutes talking to her. Some days I'm so bored I could easily talk to her three or four times a day. I've had to guard against letting on how down I've been, but I have the feeling she knows anyway. Now that I think of it, I have to say that my admiration for Catherine continues to grow. No matter how bad things are, she's always been upbeat. At times though the separation has gotten the better of her. I'm reminded of Knin when she came apart on the phone. It was one of the hardest things I've ever done, listening to her cry and not being able to help. I had the same feeling when she told me she was on drugs again in January. I remember walking away from the phone both times with a knot the size of a softball in my stomach, and both times it took quite a while for that helpless feeling to go away. When that happens it's hard as hell to focus on the job at hand.

On the bright side, there are less than four weeks left in the tour, and when we finish our cycle of patrols (which should go quickly) we'll be down to under three weeks.

In talking to one of the guys in CQ at lunch today, I found out that part of the reason we have to hand carry and account for all our Gortex kit, is because of what the VanDoos did. It appears of the 5000 or so pieces that were issued, only 2700 or so pieces were recovered at the end of their tour, the remainder was "lost." They also tried to send back one tonne, the equivalent of a full sea container, of coffee. I can't imagine what they'd do with it all. The PPCLI blew the whistle on them, and being the Regiment we are, we have to do everything better than everyone else, so no Gortex kit will be accepted as lost. Apparently the VanDoos are under investigation for their transgressions.

I heard today on CNN that the EEC has offered a substantial economic package to Croatia if they will be good little boys and don't play with their guns. If this is the case and Croatia accepts, then perhaps war will not come, and Croatia can renew the UN mandate without any loss of face. That in turn means that our rotation home should go off without a hitch. We are all hoping Tutman agrees.

On another note, the rear party is going to be in a bit of kaka. Jay came to my ISO the other night hopping mad. He'd just talked to his dad (also in the military) who told

The Second Half of the Tour 259

him that when he called Petawawa housing to check on Jay's PMQ he discovered his son's name wasn't on the list. Jay had been offered a PMQ in November, but there was no way he could return to Canada to move his wife from Winnipeg to Pet and get things set up in the middle of a tour. So, he turned it down. When he did that, Petawawa housing dropped him from the list (instead of putting him on the bottom of it). For the past three months he's been inquiring about getting a PMQ, and has repeatedly been told by the rear party that it was being taken care of. It now appears this was not the case. The past few days Jay has been firing memos and PMQ applications into our company office to try to get things sorted out.

I gotta say I feel for the kid. Here's a guy who's been married for a year and a half, and because of the Army, has only spent about three months of it with his new bride. All he wants is to have his wife by his side in Petawawa, and have a place to call home. Yet due to an administrative oversight, he's been sidetracked. Wouldn't you be a little red under the collar too?

Thursday, 09 Mar., Patrolling I woke up this morning to the sound of a heavy rain beating on the roof of my trailer. Virk and I looked outside to find we were right on the edge of a weather front that couldn't make up its mind whether it wanted to overrun us or not. By noon we were in the midst of a steady downpour, but by supper it had cleared enough that there was just some high cloud left.

The morning was pretty quiet, as was part of the afternoon. At 1300, Henry, George Tim, and Jay went out to do the first half of the patrol. At 1500 Jim, David and myself went over to our carrier and started to get ready.

This particular carrier gets passed from section to section and as a result it gets the shit kicked out of it, and is usually left in a mess for us. Because of all the rain we've been having lately, I wanted to put a little extra oil on the gun before tonight's run. You should have seen this thing. The boys hadn't wiped her down after last night's run and she was a mess. They'd used 15W40 to oil her down instead of regular machine gun oil or WD40. This isn't as easy as it sounds, because 15W40 (or regular engine oil) sticks like shit to a Hudson's Bay blanket, and doesn't come off in the rain like the other, lighter oils. The down side is that dirt sticks to it like contact cement, and in this case she was covered. I spent half an hour cleaning the gunk off the inner workings and exterior before putting it back together and giving it a good going over with WD40. WD40 is a very light oil but has penetrating oil characteristics, which allow it to cut through crap for easy cleanup. If it's raining we keep a can if it handy and liberally and regularly douse the gun with it to try and fend off rust. It actually works pretty well.

At 1600 we started to move to the carrier to get the show on the road. We'd picked up Ingersol from 1 Section to make up our fourth man for the patrol, and when we all arrived at the carrier the fun began.

The previous section had taken all the newer headsets out of the track and stashed all the older ones. Jim had brought his helmet so he had comms but no one else did. This was a problem as the carrier wasn't supposed to move without at least two people having comms, one of them being the driver—it's a safety thing.

For 20 minutes we, that is Ingersol and David tried to find headsets. Finally Jim lost it. This was his first command role as a Cpl, and I wasn't going to get involved unless asked, so I pulled my feet up in the hatch and watched. David was dispatched to try and find the previous section to try and borrow their headgear, but they'd all gone to supper so that idea got canned. For ten minutes Jim and Ingersol rummaged around inside the track trying to find the headsets that were supposed to be left in the carrier. Finally, stuffed in a bag in the bottom of one of the boxes he found a set.

At long last we were on the road, a little late, but we were moving. It was quite entertaining to watch Jim lose it, I'd never seen it happen before, and it was fun to watch him throw things around and cuss as he tore the track apart. I suppose I should have helped, but I was having too much fun watching the show, and besides, there wasn't enough room in the carrier to have all four of us looking for the bloody things.

Tonight we were taking George around on the patrol route for the first time. He's been away from the section for nine weeks, and isn't familiar with the routes yet, so naturally we had to stop at every bunker and check them out. Fortunately it had decided not to rain tonight and stayed reasonably warm so it wasn't that big a deal. The patrol ran a little long as a result of all the stops, but that was OK, we still made it to the mess before closing for a beer.

When we came off patrol, and as we were putting things away, Warrant Fuller came up to chat with George. We overheard him say that the Americans have cut off talks with the Croats and that it's looking more and more like we'll have to do a tactical withdrawal. I have two things to say about that. First, all talks of this nature are always on again, off again. I see no reason to flinch at this point because there's still nearly four weeks left for the Croats to renew our mandate. Undoubtedly they'll try and hold out as long as possible and make it look as if they were forced into signing to avoid a war.

The second point is, it sounds like Fuller is flinching again. Virk and I had a long talk about this, and he's holding true to form. I've said it before and I'll say it here again, I'm very disappointed with Fuller. The feeling within the platoon is that he's big, fat, lazy, and doesn't come out of his ISO. Only some of that is true of course, but it tells you people are starting to, or already have, dismissed him as a warrant. He's also known as a flinch, which I believe to be true. Warrant Fuller doesn't work as hard as he might for his troops; as a result we do without much of the time, Bruska after the tear-down is a good example.

This, I feel, is sad because he so easily inspires and motivates his troops to work for him. There isn't anything we wouldn't do for him, we just wish he would do more for us.

Tonight in the mess we had live entertainment. It was the Newman and Drew show, and it had the whole mess in stitches. Nothing was sacred with those two. Both these guys are career Cpl types and from the east coast. When they went at it everyone listened in, they even turned down the music so we all could hear them better. Drew's quite a joker and Ted had been into the sauce and turns bright red when he gets going, it was like watching a standup comedy routine. It was a great way to end the day and we all left with smiles on our faces.

The days are starting to pick up speed now. I hope we stay on afternoon patrols, it breaks the day up nicely and there's plenty of time to do what you want or need to do.

Friday, 10 Mar., Patrolling Lately I've been making a point of getting up just before 0700 so that I can have breakfast. There's no call for it, I could easily sleep till noon, but getting up early allows me to enjoy a quiet morning and do my diary entries. Besides, if I'm tired I can always go back to bed for a while.

I finished up yesterday's diary entry around 1000, and decided to clean the gun on

1-3-B, which was the carrier we were supposed to take out on today's run. After I cleaned it up, Henry came over and told me that we were taking 1-3 because Ted was back off leave and Jim, being the driver, has requested that Ted not take his carrier (1-3-B) because every time he does something breaks on it. I can't say as I blame him really, Ted is a good driver but he tends to be a little tough on the carriers he drives. After cleaning 1-3-B's gun I now had to go back and clean 1-3's gun. Max flex as they say.

After lunch we started to gather at the carriers to get things ready to go. This afternoon's patrol would be Route One, with Route Two being done after supper. Ted, David, George, and myself were just about to leave the company lines when Warrant Fuller came blasting over the radio.

"Three, this is One-Three Sunray Minor. We're taking enemy fire just outside Benkovac."

We just looked at each other and chuckled. Here we go, we thought.

As we left the gate of the camp, Fuller came driving up in the ML. He got out and gave us a quick rundown on the situation then said "George, I want you to get that son-of-a-bitch for me." We drove off, then burst out laughing. If you wanted an example of Fuller's flinching, here it is. The old adrenalin was just humping through the big guy's body, and it was hilarious to watch.

Fuller had stopped to check out what he thought was a body in a field, and the shots were fired at him while he was away from the vehicle. The rounds had landed on the shoulder of the road in front of the vehicle. This meant whoever was shooting had no intention of hitting him. After all, how hard can it be to hit a truck the size of a small house? Clearly someone had fired in his direction, but the chances of him being in REAL danger were fairly low, certainly low enough that he needn't have reacted the way he did.

On our way through Benkovac we picked up the platoon commander, who thought it prudent to wait for us to escort him to Charles Company rather than risk the passage alone.

In spite of our best efforts to scour the countryside to find whoever did the shooting (and perhaps hoping he'd take a shot or two at us so we could shoot back) we never saw a damn thing. Mind you, you don't see much at 30 mph, no matter how hard you look.

We pulled into Charles to get the patrol briefing, and before we'd left the order came over the radio that all soft skinned vehicles had to move in pairs, and helmets were to be worn at all times. They also said to avoid the Benkovac area if at all possible, which is tantamount to closing the barn door after the horse has bolted.

The mountain peaks hung in the air as if suspended by some heavenly thread, their lower slopes shrouded in the mist that was the product of the morning's hot sun. The sky was clear and blue as we moved off from Charles Company to begin our patrol on Route One through the Zone. It was in short, a grand large day, and it was the perfect weather for a drive in the country. There was softness in the air brought on by the spring runoff, and as we rumbled over hill and dale our carrier got covered with more and more mud as we splashed our way along the route. At one point Ted hit a large puddle a bit too fast and a wall of water covered the front of the carrier and thoroughly soaked him. We came to a complete stop and all Ted could say rather sheepishly was "I think I underestimated the depth of that puddle." That put smiles on everyone's face as we wiped ourselves off and carried on.

On patrol in the hills

The route took close to four hours to complete and when we pulled into Charles Company for supper the wear and tear of the afternoon's activities was beginning to show. We had linked up with Henry and the second vehicle, and as we were shutting down we started to get snippets of airplay between TOW (7-4) the Engineers, and call sign two (Bravo Company). Not knowing what it was about, we shut down and had supper.

After supper we were standing by the vehicles waiting to get our Ogroup from Henry, and the second half of the patrol brief from George. It was then that we found out that something big had gone down over in Bravo's AOR. George gave us a quick rundown. One of our vehicles had hit a mine on one of the patrol routes, and the Engineers had gone out to support. When they got there the Serbs opened fire on all four vehicles, and we fired back. A full-fledged firefight ensued, and then it broke off. All we know is that our boys took no casualties, and they went by the book. The general feeling was yeah; finally someone got to shoot back! Good for them! Hopefully tomorrow we'll get the details in the Ogroup, but it was good to vicariously release a little frustration, and cheer "our team" on. I can't wait to get the details.

This evening's Ogroup was less inspiring. The Croats have agreed to renew the UN mandate IF we move to the Bosnia-Krajina border. What they want is for us to get out of their way so they can retake Krajina, and at the same time act as a buffer between them and the Serbian and Bosnian Serbs. If they really think we're going to do that they're in for a biglet down. If we do it though, I think I'll quit and go home now.

Route Two is a short route, but tonight it was even shorter. We'd just pulled into Pristeg (SC 50) when we got the call to come home. All night patrols have been cancelled for the next 24 hours in light of the current situation, and ours had just been called off. Nothing like running to hide each time you hear a twig snap in the woods.

We dutifully mounted up and returned to Charles to refuel and put in the patrol report, then headed for home. The bright side of this is that we got to go to the mess early, which is exactly what we did. I had hoped to call Catherine tonight, but the phones are out at Bravo Company so I couldn't. I gave some thought to doing a workout, but that's about all it wound up being, a thought. The idea of having something to drink was much more appealing.

Saturday, 11 Mar., Patrolling Can you believe it? They cancelled patrols during the daylight hours too. You gotta wonder what the hell higher is thinking when they do things like this. It certainly doesn't inspire confidence amongst the troops. The only good point is that it's another great day, and we might actually get some sun tanning in.

Warrant Fuller came around at 0900 and told us there was a heavy weapons inspection at 1500. We figured, fine, we'll go over to the tracks around 1300 and start cleaning up. Five minutes later the inspection was bumped up to 1330, so we figured we'd go over around 1000 then have lunch. Not! The timing got moved to 1300 so we said fuck-it and went over right then, and for the rest of the morning we worked on the weapons. I muckled onto the 50, and Jay and Henry worked on the Karl-G and the 60mm mortar.

Just before lunch George came to us with the good news, daylight patrols are back on, two-vehicle movement and we're to leave at 1300. At least now we don't have to do the weapons inspection. We cleaned up quickly, and went to lunch.

Both David and Bruce went on their 96-hour leave this morning, so when we gathered for the Ogroup at 1230 we picked up two guys from one of the other sections to round out our numbers. The only thing in the Ogroup was the shooting incident in Bravo's AOR yesterday. Here's what happened.

Call sign 7-4 (AAP boys) were on patrol in Bravo's AOR, when one of their vehicles hit a mine. The lead vehicle apparently ran over the edge of it, tipping the mine so that the second vehicle ran over it. Fortunately only the detonator went off, and aside from a loud bang, and a puff of smoke, no damage was done. Suspecting someone had snuck in and mined the whole road, 7-4 sent in a MINEREP and called for Engineering support to clear a route out.

The area they were in was a stretch of open road between two wooded areas. The Engineers arrived and began to prod their way up to the two trapped vehicles. Just as they reached them, the group came under effective enemy fire from a Serb section house about 800 to 1000 metres away (this means the rounds were landing close enough to get your undivided attention). Later it was said that they suspected that the Serbs had positions closer to them than the section house, because of the concentration of fire. Our guys immediately called into higher for permission to return fire with their co-axial mounted C-6s.

It should be pointed out here that asking permission to return fire is normally not what would happen. The first rule of engagement states that every soldier has the right to self-defence. But in all cases we are obligated to return fire with "like fire." Which means, if someone were to shoot at me with a pistol, I couldn't return fire with a .50 even if I was leaning on it. I'd have to hunt around for my personal weapon, then shoot the bastard. In this case, the Serbs had opened up with small arms fire and the only weapons the AAP boys could respond with were the co-axial 7.62 machine guns. Not exactly "like fire, "but these are the rules we are saddled with.

The Croats, who were roughly in line with the receiving end of the Serb fire, thought they were coming under fire, so they opened up on the Serb section house, by firing over the heads of our boys. This caught our guys off guard and effectively put them in the middle of a firefight.

At this point AAP and the Engineers had a choice to make—stay where they were with fire coming from both sides, or brave 100 yards of potentially mined road to the cover of trees. They chose to move, and made the dash in record time.

It should be pointed out that radio traffic was hot and heavy between the guys on the ground and Bravo Company's CP. Naturally crowds gathered around the CP and every other available radio at all the OPs around the Zone, everyone cheering our guys on. AAP had requested permission to return fire, and everyone held their breaths as they waited for the answer from higher. When the words "permission granted" came over the air the crowds burst out with wild cheering and cries of "yea, get some," and "go get'em." 7-4 began to manoeuvre for position and let go with a burst that apparently landed only a few metres short of the target.

While all of this was on going, QRF were dispatched for support, and in Italy 8 aircraft were scrambled and sent down the "race track" along the Croatian coast to be called in as "fast air" support at a moment's notice.

The firefight didn't last all that long. Once the rounds AAP fired landed close to the Serb position, they scurried back to their hole and stopped firing. "Check fire" was called, and everyone waited. But the show was over. QRF were recalled, the planes sent home, and 2-9er went in search of the Serb battalion commander to sort out the mess. When he found him, the only thing the guy would say is "it was your men's fault and I don't want to talk about it." Case closed. The fool knew damn well they'd made a huge error but weren't willing to own up to it. Typical.

It was because of this incident that things got shut down. Our patrol this afternoon was with two carriers, and I think everyone paid a bit more attention then usual. Even so, it was a quiet time as we covered Routes Two and Three for the first time during the daylight.

Tonight is barbecue night at the JR's mess, so there was an extra incentive to fly through the routes and get back by 5:30. In an effort to meet the self imposed timing, we blew past our usual stops, and OPs in what amounted to a high-speed (if you can call 40 miles an hour high speed) run through the Zone. Any digging on that hill?" (The hill was 200 metres off the road.) "Nope, I don't see any." "Right then, carry on."

We pulled into Charles around 1700 to refuel and grab a quick bite, in case we missed out back at Rastivic. By 1520 hrs we were on the road again, 1550 hrs we were through the front gate at Rastivic, and by 1805 hrs we all were in the mess.

Saturdays are always a good time because everyone comes in from the outlying companies to drink and mix. Tonight was no different. When I got there the place was packed, and stayed that way until 2330 hrs when we all got booted out. The crowd was particularly jovial this evening, and I had a bit over my limit, but had a great time.

One of the best stories of the evening (aside from the AAP one) was about a Sergeant out at SC54. He and all his troops (eight in all) were drunk on duty—and got caught. No word yet as to his punishment, but that will come.

After leaving the mess I wandered over to the TV tent and watched some TV until our phones were installed, then waited in line (while freezing my ass off) until 0100 hrs to call Catherine. I must have sounded like shit. My voice was hoarse from singing in the mess, and the alcohol didn't help matters. I must make a point not to go to the phones after a few drinks. It leaves entirely the wrong impression, like I'm having a good time or something.

Sunday, 12 Mar., Patrolling What a lazy, hazy, relaxed day this was. I spent much of the morning getting caught up on my writing. People were sitting out in front of their trailers enjoying music and trying to get a tan.

We had to be at the carriers for three, so just before two I decided to strap on my combat boots and go for three laps of the camp. The first two laps were fine, but the third one seemed to take it out of me. Though I finished with no problem, the rest of the day I felt like shit, and kept wanting to lie down, which eventually I did after the carriers were prepped.

Supper was undercooked roast beef, Yorkshire pudding, and mashed potatoes. It sounds good, but it sat like a lump in my stomach for the rest of the night and was damned uncomfortable.

We left the camp at 1745 hrs, and as we pulled through the gate and stopped to load our weapons, adjust our kit and make sure everything was ready to go, Anna Maria Tremonti, from the CBC was there with her cameraman filming our every move. Though outwardly no one paid her any attention, I will confess that I noticed we overplayed the load procedures a whole lot. There was a lot more strike and drive, and our movements were more crisp than usual. When I turned to let George know I was ready to go, I gave him a real positive thumbs up gesture which he returned aggressively with a smile, as we laughed at what we were doing. I wonder if any of this will make the air back home? As we moved off down the road we each tried to get into the fact that we were going to be standing up for the next eight hours. So starts another long patrol.

Charles Company wanted us to do Routes Two and Three tonight. These are short

SC 54 in the middle of the Zone

routes that take no more than two hours each if you drive really slowly. Seeing that we had to be out in the Zone for a minimum of eight hours, we were in no hurry as we checked out the various stands and bunkers.

Our first stop was Malaglave stand. George, Jay, and Henry went for the twenty-minute walk up the hill and back to see if any digging was going on. There is an agreement with the local commander that none of his troops are permitted on the hill in uniform or with weapons, but each time we've stopped we've caught someone with one or the other. Tonight there were just three guys in civies, which was permitted. We had driven past a large party on the side of the road a couple of hundred metres from our stop at the Malaglave stand, and when our patrol came back along the road, two of the men dressed in fatigues approached us and started a conversation with George.

One of the men had had his machine gun taken away from him because he got caught with it in the Zone. He wanted to know if he could get it back to defend his family. He was told, "sorry, that's out of our hands." He went on to tell us that the Ustashi (Croats) were sneaking up on their positions and taking pictures. "They are terrorists, why do you not stay on the Malaglave 24 hrs?" Again the answer was "sorry that's out of our hands." He understood but suggested that he goes to Canada and we stay here. The offer was politely declined.

Our next stop was hill 48, otherwise know as flag hill, for its enormous Serbian flag made of painted stones on the hillside. The thing has to measure at least 50 metres by 30 metres, and can be seen for miles. George and I did this one. I needed to get out of the carrier because I was starting to fall asleep. The view from the top of the hill is quite impressive. For five miles in any direction nothing can move without you seeing it. The hilltop is laid out in a maze of bunkers and fire positions, and as an infanteer I'd hate to be charged with taking it. You'd never get near it without a full artillery barrage in support. Even at night it'd be hard, there's no cover anywhere. When you see a position like this, it drives home the nature of the game you're involved in, and it can make the hair stand up on the back of your neck.

Bulldozer hill, and hill 47 followed in quick succession, then it was over to SC 50 to kill a couple of hours before starting Route Three.

We pulled into the camp around 2300 hrs and immediately put the kettle on and made ourselves some soup and coffee. While we were sitting around eating, a call came through from Charles asking us to leave our current position and move to the area of the Arrowhead on Patrol Route One. We were to patrol the south half of the route and investigate a SHOTREP in the area though what we were looking for at night was beyond us. We mounted up and headed south. Actually north, it's one of those "you can't get there from here" things.

Midnight found us at the Arrowhead checking out the Croatian OP at the intersection of the three roads that form the point of the arrow. A short while later we were down the road to OP Colt, the Croatian OP at one end of a branch of the arrowhead. George and Jay got out to chat with the people there and wound up getting an earful. "You drink with the Serbs and let them continue digging," the guy said, "this is not right." Nothing like getting it from both sides! Standard reply #27 I think works best in this situation, "sorry that's out of my hands."

They kept going on about it, so we didn't get the information about the shooting we'd come for. The next stop would have to be SC44 who'd reported the shots.

SC44 is an OP smack in the middle of the Zone, and is surrounded by open fields. It's run by Mortar platoon and in the middle of the compound is a great big mortar pit that is surrounded by sandbags. The observation post is a little over two storeys high and gives you a real good view of the surrounding terrain. To get to it we had to drive along the side of several farm fields, cross a creek in two places, and drive alongside a minefield. The ten-minute drive to the OP from OP Colt was, at least we thought, uneventful. The road's in pretty bad shape, so most of your concentration is on keeping yourself from getting knocked around. As we came up to the OP they called in another SHOTREP. Two shots this time and "they appear to be directed at the patrol coming towards us."

Wait a minute. That's us!!

Usually it's very easy to tell you've been shot at. Either there is a loud clang as the bullet hits the carrier somewhere; there's blood everywhere, in which case you know you've got a problem; or in the most likely case, you hear a loud crack-thump, indicating the bullet passed very close by. In our case none of these things happened, which lead us to doubt severely that the shots were directed at us. Of the eight guys in the two carriers, not one of us heard anything above the sound of the engines.

After a brief consultation at the OP, we decided to do our best duck in the shooting gallery impression and drive back over the route (suitably hunkered down of course) to see if the "sniper" would try again.

Ten minutes later we were back at the arrowhead with no holes in the carriers or us. I guess whoever it was got bored and went home—that, or he passed out in a ditch somewhere from too much drink. We on the other hand still had an hour to kill, so we went to check out the Popavich and Lubichen stands.

If the Croatians ever wanted to take the Krajina back, all they'd have to do is wait until two in the morning, and they could walk over the place without ever firing a shot. We drove up to Popovich stand, 26 tons of carrier, several hundred horsepower of unmuffled engine blaring, parked by the front door, and had to wake up the guys in the hut to let them know it was the UN stopping by. At Lubichen they didn't even get out of the bag to open the door. Some front line troops! Thank God they're not defending MY country.

We pulled back into Charles Company around 0200 and did the refuelling thing while George gave in his patrol report. Everybody was bagged. Sitting around drinking lukewarm coffee no one said a whole lot. Sitting for the first time in hours was truly a wonderful experience. It felt so good to take the weight off my feet and ease the pain in my back. Everything seemed to ache.

The big news of the day has been the announcement that Croatia has agreed to renew the UN mandate IF the force is reduced from 12000 to 5000 men, and the troops are thinned out along the Zone and put along the Bosnian border. We're not strong enough to do the job now, so thinning us out will only make things easier for the Croats if they do decide to attack. Moving us to the Bosnian border will effectively give them a 5000 man early warning or recce force. I can't believe the UN went for it.

I predict as soon as the new troop deployment is in place the Croats will take the Krajina and use the UN as a buffer to keep the rest of the Serbs off their back. The only good thing is that it looks like we're going home as per schedule.

I got to bed at 0300. My sleeping bag never felt so good.

Monday, 13 Mar., Patrolling Last night was a rough night. Despite being very tired from the patrol, I only managed to sleep for five hours, and spent the last two hours tossing and turning before I finally decided to get up. For the rest of the morning

I struggled with my diary entries, then finally packed it in and went and had lunch.

After lunch it was over to the carriers for our regular cycle of maintenance in preparation for the evening's patrol. It takes me about 40 minutes to strip the .50 and give it a light coat of oil. After I was finished with the guns, I pitched in and helped change two road wheels on 1-3. Changing these things is definitely a team effort; even so it took us a good forty minutes to get the job done.

Around 2:30, I went over to call Catherine and see how things were. It's hard to believe, but there are only three weeks left. Three weeks! I can't believe I've been doing this shit for nearly a year. It feels like a lifetime, like nothing exists outside this job. It'll be a bit of a shock to go home and have to do things for myself again.

Supper was its usual uninspired fare and around 5:30 we started to suit up for the patrol. I chose not to wear my longjohns which proved to be a mistake, because it was bloody cold out there. Thank God for my rain pants, they made the difference.

Since Warrant Fuller's shooting incident, we've taken to carrying two hand grenades on our person. I keep mine in a pouch with the candies I snack on during the patrol (I'm sure there's some social commentary in that action). I'm not quite sure when we're supposed to use them, but we carry them nonetheless. We also have the Karl Gustav out of the bag, which completely baffles me because it takes two men to operate, when you could fire 2 M-72's at different targets in the same amount of time it takes to get one Karl G round off. Oh well, soldier on.

We rumbled out of the camp on schedule and were told at Charles the evening tasking would be Routes One and Two, so off we went.

Our first stop was Popavich stand. The usual pleasantries were passed around as they were actually awake this time, but as we were coming down the hill in the carriers two guys stopped us. They didn't ask us to stop; they just stepped out into the middle of the road and basically told us to stop. Then one guy produces a bottle of white wine from his little tractor and gives it to us, implying that we can't go anywhere unless we have a drink first; so we did (the stuff tasted like shit) and smiled and complimented him on how good it tasted. Diplomacy has its price.

The rain I thought we were going to get never materialised, but the wind did, and when we went into the valley to check out the Arrowhead OPs it got real cold. Every time we go down into the valley, I notice about a five-degree difference in temperature, and it's always colder. It got so that on particularly cold nights, like tonight, I rue the fact that we have to go there at all.

We pulled into OP Colt and George and Jay dismounted to check things out. They walked up the road a bit, over the bridge and into the bunker, located under the bridge. It seemed like they were gone forever for those of us left outside, as there was no hiding from the wind. When finally they came out, they were all smiles. The buggers had been drinking wine in there; the kind you get in a bottle…with a label…and a bloody cork. I hate it when I miss out on the good stuff. The patrol carried on.

Sometimes when I'm patrolling I'll tune out different senses as my mind wanders. As we went past the place where we were supposed to have been shot at, I tuned in my hearing to listen for the crack-thump indicating we'd been shot at. When it didn't materialise, I turned up the music I was listening to in my mind's ear. It's kind of like your body is a great big house and you're in an upstairs room looking out the windows of your eyes. Your body just goes about its business hanging on for dear life, but your mind wanders around looking into different topics to pass the time, coming back only when necessary.

OP Colt on the Croatian side of the Zone

SC 43 on the Serb side of the Zone. This is where the young private committed suicide

Your eyes are always looking, and your ears are listening closely, but your mind can dwell on other things. Like figuring out my financial situation, or making love to my wife (a popular topic). But then something will catch your eye and bring you back, like the flares we saw. We'd just passed through SC43 when, through the trees, we spotted orange flares in the sky. We stopped to observe for a moment, then spotted a second set. At first we didn't know what they were, but then Jim put forward a possible option; they were chaff flares. Chaff flares are dropped behind an aircraft at regular intervals to confuse ground to air missiles. But it seems bloody odd to be out tonight. We didn't know of any operations with aircraft that were on going, so George called it in, and we carried on.

As we rumbled down the road I had an interesting reaction to a situation that caught me off guard. It's the time of year when all this years' wildlife is big enough to start wandering from the nest. Tonight alone, I spotted seven small rabbits, three of which were silly enough to be on the road and tried to outrun us, before smartening up and getting out of the way.

One of the little buggers decided to make a marathon of it and for 500 metres or so stayed directly in front of the carrier. At first I thought it was funny. But then something strange happened; I had this overwhelming urge to stop the carrier and let the little guy catch his breath and carry on back to where he came from. The further down the road we went the worse I felt. I suppose the fact that the other three guys in the carrier were laughing and hooting at the little guy didn't make it any easier. My uneasiness got to the point where I was about to tell Jim to slow down, when the little rabbit, who clearly was running for his life and starting to tire from it, turned off the road and into the bushes, whereupon we carried on down the road. Damned odd feeling that!

Not ten minutes later we came across an entirely different situation.

We were coming up to a Croatian defensive position on their side of the Zone. As we approached, the headlights of the carrier picked up something in the middle of the road up ahead. As we got closer, it became clear that someone had dragged an old stove out to block our way. Two things immediately come to mind; it's an inconvenience, or it's booby trapped with a mine. We stopped short.

I crawled out of the hatch, and worked my way out to the front of the vehicle, standing on the barbed wire we had coiled on the front. We approached slowly. With flashlight in hand, I began scanning the stove looking for any obvious trip wire or signs of fresh digging. We slowly advanced until we were about three feet from it. I could see no evidence of either.

Stepping down from the carrier I approached and began to do a thorough search of the area and the insides of the stove. I could see nothing untoward. So, climbing back into the carrier, I hunkered down in the back of the carrier with George and Jay as Jim advanced on the stove to move it. Nothing .

It appeared to be a prank, but there was only one way to be sure. Advancing very slowly, Jim drove over the stove so that it would pass underneath the centre of the carrier. When nothing happened, the carrier behind us did the same.

A couple of moments to catch our breath, and return to our positions, and down the road we went. The remainder of the patrol was uneventful, but cold. We pulled into Charles Company and went through the usual routine of refuelling, and drinking coffee to warm up. George was taking a little longer to do his patrol report because of the various incidents so to pass time, Jim and I decided to make up orders to get us to bed.

Gentlemen, orders.
Situation:
Enemy—the wind, the cold, the distance to the bag, and any nasty Serb who wants to delay us by taking a shot at us.
Friendlies—the bag.
Mission—you will advance from Charles Company to the bag as fast as possible.
Execution—this mission will be executed in three phases:
    Phase 1—move from Charles to Duke's Company lines
    Phase 2—put away all kit
    Phase 3—get into the bag
Service and Support—your carrier
Command and Control—no change
Gentlemen, synchronize your watches!
A tired military mind works in strange ways. I was in the bag by 03:00.

Tuesday, 14 Mar., Patrolling I slept like a log. In fact, I don't even think I moved until 11:00, the cold is really taking it out of me.

Today's maintenance cycle was very short, and right after it was done I slipped off to call Catherine for the third day in a row. I won't be able to call her for the next week, because we'll be at SC 50, so I figured I'd take advantage of the situation. She didn't sound too good. She'd just woken up and her voice was gravely from her cold. She'd sent me a card that had "warning pornographic material" written on the outside. Yeah right, I thought, how pornographic can it be? She never says anything along those lines ever. So I casually opened it and read. WOWA!!! For the next hour I had a tent in my pants. "Excuse me sir, I'd like to go home, NOW!" When I got her on the phone I called her a wanton woman, and if she'd hold on just a little longer I'd fulfil all her wantons. It made her smile. I can hardly wait.

While at the phones I ran into Ray Labell. We chatted for a while, and he told me of his experience with the press. For the most part he said his experiences have been bad. They're pushy, opinionated, manipulative, and generally out of line. But, he said, his experience with Mrs. Tremonti was polar opposite. She was courteous, well informed, helpful, and professional. In short, all the things you'd hope to find in a reporter. Quite clearly he was impressed with her. And that respect was returned. Though he did not ask her directly, Ray was left with the impression that she had a great deal of respect for the professionalism of our troops. She even said the best course she ever took was our combat first aid course. It's nice to know we're well respected somewhere in the press.

After our calls, Ray and I wandered back to my room and carried on the conversation. It was here that he floated one of the most interesting observations I've ever heard about the army. He contends that we are the last five years of what he calls the "programmed thinkers." These are people who got in 20 years ago and have risen through the ranks to the levels of senior NCO. Coming into the army with little education, they have learned everything the army way, and now are incapable of keeping up with the younger guys who have far and away better education and new and innovative approaches to situations.

Our group respond to situations in a programmed way, which took them their entire careers to learn. "By Jesus that's the way I learned it, and that's the way you will too" appears to be the battle cry for this group. If there isn't a standard operating procedure for it, they don't know how to respond.

Of course not all senior NCOs are like this, and certainly there is a new crop of young NCOs who fit into the old mold. But, by and large, it's these old dogs that are causing the problems in today's army. Frankly I think Ray's hit the nail on the head. Ray also had a chat with Warrant Fuller about his shooting incident. It would appear the story is getting better for the telling.

What actually happened was Warrant Fuller, MCpl Parry, and Mark Newson (one of the troops in Ray's sections and the source of much of the true story), were driving along in the ML when they spotted what they thought was a body lying in the field. The warrant, who was driving, stopped the vehicle and got out to see what was going on. Two shots were fired at them while the warrant was in the field, and a third as the warrant made his way back to the ML. The good warrant high tailed it out of there and started blathering on the radio.

Mark who was in the back of the ML and was watching everything through the open flap at the front, contends that the rounds landed within 20 metres (60 feet). To hear the warrant tell it, it was a "burst of fire" and he "could feel the splash of the bullets," whatever the hell that means.

Mark is just a private, and has no reason to exaggerate his story, MCpl Parry was in the cab of the ML, so he had nothing to add. Therefore, the evil eye of suspicion falls upon our good warrant officer.

All day today there's been a nasty cold wind blowing. It's sunny out but I've had to put my long johns on to keep from getting too cold. For our patrol we bundled up big time. I felt like a Michelin man for all the kit I had on. It was tough just bending over.

Tonight's run was Routes Three and One. Our plan was to fly through Route Three, then take an hour or two break at SC 50, and then carry on with Route One. After an hour in the wind though, that plan got amended and we pulled into SC56 on top of the hill and took an hour to warm up.

With coffee in our bellies and sweets in our pockets, we loaded up and headed out to complete the route, and pause again at SC 50. The moon was full and the wind biting, when we finally got to Pristeg, and it was good to stand by the fire and warm up.

Ted was into one of his moods again, and George finally told him to take some Prozac and calm down, much to our relief. It didn't help matters at all though.

Route One is a long one. It takes four hours to complete, and if we were cold after only one hour, you can imagine how bad we all were after four.

At one point I started running on the spot to try and take the numbness out of my feet and generate a little heat and circulation. As I was bouncing along in the hatch, I got a tap on the shoulder. I turned to see Henry and David running on the spot behind me. Henry came on the intercom and asked, "Where you going? Wait for us." I guess you had to be there.

To end the patrol on an up note, just as we were coming into Rastivic, we blew another inner road wheel. More fun for tomorrow.

A couple of interesting points in tonight's Ogroup. Recce spotted a battalion of fresh troops in Benkovac. New uniforms, fresh young faces, and clean leather belts were the dead give-aways.

The UN mandate has yet to be ratified. Both sides have to agree to the proposal before it goes through, and frankly none of us see the Serbs agreeing. Time will tell.

Remember the Sergeant who got drunk on the OP with his troops? He got caught because one of the troops was messing around on the radio and the CSM came out to investigate. He's now a Cpl.

The Sergeant who had the .50 cal discharge at the gate a few nights back, has been fined $1000. Let's see, if a 5.56 round is worth $1500 fine, and a .50 cal is worth $1000 fine, does that mean that a TOW missile is worth about $100 fine?

And today's funny: Our wondrous CSM broke his foot while jogging around the camp today. It appears he stepped on a rock and gave himself a stress fracture (it's a wonder he didn't do more damage, considering his size). Dangerous thing, running with too much weight. And only three weeks to go, too! What a shame!

Tuesday, 15 Mar., Patrolling Again I slept the sleep of the dead. I didn't get up until nearly 11:00, and slowly wandered over for something to eat.

In spite of my rack time, I was still very tired, and cleaning the guns today took a little longer than usual. The cold, biting wind we've been having for the last couple of days has died down considerably this morning, and it was almost pleasant to work outside. Thankfully I didn't have to work on the road wheel we blew last night as there were enough guys to take care of it, so I focused on the guns.

To tell the truth, I've felt the absolute pits since I got up. When I finally finished the guns, I went back to my ISO and slept for a couple of hours to try and beat this thing before having supper.

While I was getting ready to go out, the platoon commander came by and told me that I was on the BBC report that had been filmed at Pristeg during our last rotation there. The report will be included in the tape we get of the tour. So too will the report that Anna Maria Tremonti filed I understand. Next stop, Hollywood.

When we pulled out tonight, the wind had dropped nearly to zero, and the first couple of hours on the road were nearly pleasant.

Our first stop on Route Two took us to the V. Umac feature. From there you can see the Arrowhead valley and the islands in the Aegean. As soon as we stopped we could hear a bulldozer working somewhere to the east of us along our patrol route. George called it in and we got the go-ahead to check it out.

It didn't take us long to find it, and in conversing with the operator, he told us that he was working on the water main in front of his house. Ted was convinced he was lying and said as much to those of us in the carrier who could hear him. One look in the hole and you could see the pipe he was talking about, which shot Ted's theory all to hell. We called it in.

3-9er got on the radio and made two points. First, and quite rightly, that most of the defensive positions start out as work on "water works," and "well done all involved." Hey, we got a "well done" over the radio, we're heroes now.

The rest of Route Two was quiet. The Malaglave, hill 47 (flag hill), bulldozer hill, and hill 49, all were unoccupied and untouched. An hour after spotting the dozer, we were in SC 50 enjoying a hot cup of soup.

We'd only been in Pristeg twenty minutes, when 3-9er came back on the air and asked us to check out some digging sounds that Recce had heard when they passed through our area. The position given was right on the beginning of Route One, which we were going to start in a little while anyway, so we took our time finishing up.

The new digging was not at all hard to find. We'd just crossed the MSR and pulled up for a listening halt. As soon as we shut off the motors, we could hear this thing— working quite clearly within the boundaries of the Zone, off to our right somewhere.

When we told 3, they came back with the usual response. "Tell them to stop digging, but don't escalate the situation." In other words, go and have a look but don't touch.

Every now and then Ted will hit the nail on the head. Tonight it was with his definition of patrolling. "Patrolling: running around in a Zone we've lost control of, for eight hours burning fuel and not being able to do a damn thing." Couldn't have said it better myself.

One of the Serb bunkers on Flag Hill overlooking the Zone and countryside

On the road in to the digger, we passed two bunkers, about 8 feet high and 10 or 12 feet around (they looked sort of like an igloo made of rock with a flat top). As we passed, in the moonlight I spotted tripod on the top of one of them. At the time I was the only one who saw it so when we got to the digger, I told George and we made a note to check it out on the way back.

We found the digger with no problem. It was at the end of the road we were on, working away larger than life, clearing a new line of trenches in the scrub brush. What transpired next was something out of a comedy routine. George and Jay dismounted to talk to the operator, stopping about 20 feet from him. "How's the digging going boys?" George opened. The Serb operator could either not hear him, or was choosing not to, either way he just looked at George with a blank stare then kept working.

"I'll bet you don't want to stop do you?" the unmuffled sound of the digger's engine drowning out everything George was saying, and the operator continued to studiously ignore him. "Oh well, have a good night." George smiled, waved, and walked back to our carrier.

In spite of the local commanders' agreement not to do any digging, it was clear this guy was under orders to do his work and wasn't going to stop until he got the job done.

George called in and gave a SITREP, adding at the end "digging is progressing nicely." The subtlety of the humour might have been missed by the Rad Op but it left us in stitches.

As we were turning around, Henry wondered aloud if the area in front of the new trench line had been mined. This is SOP in front of a defensive position, which is where we were, but then the hoe was out here so it should be safe. Right?! We took our time turning around.

On the way out we stopped at the bunkers and lo and behold, not only was the tripod there, it was for a .50 cal Browning like the one I was leaning on. Before seizing it we confirmed the position was actually in the Zone, by looking at our map, and when we found out it was, we jumped on it and stashed it in the back of the carrier.

Henry spotted two guys coming down the trail from the main road, so we had to work fast. George climbed the bunker and heaved the tripod down to David, who quickly folded it up, and tucking it under his arm like a football, made the dash from the foot of the bunker to our carrier. Just as we closed the back door of the carrier, the two Serbs came around the corner, and like kids playing a prank we fired up the carriers and headed off into the night, giggling like idiots.

We could have snagged three cans of .50 cal ammo that were in the bunker, but in the dark it was too hard to spot any potential booby traps, so we chose to leave the ammo in place. Though it's an unlikely possibility, it still needs to be considered. Score one for the guys in blue.

I didn't see much of the next four hours. We were the second carrier and because there's been no rain for seven days, the dust was terrible. The three of us in the rear carrier just stood there the whole time with our eyes closed as the miles clicked by. Ted was the only one with his eyes opened because he was driving, and quite frankly I don't know how he did it without goggles.

It's been said before that there are too many patrols in the Zone. When we started Route One tonight, AAP had just finished it, and as we approached OP Colt, we pulled in beside two carriers from Recce who were doing Route One from the other end.

It is the way of the infanteer to make things easy for himself, so as we sat on the road we traded the information we'd gathered from the part of the route we'd completed, with the info Recce had gathered on the other part. Then we both broke the overland speed record driving the routes without stopping, to get back to Charles.

As I said earlier, I didn't see much of the route, but I sure felt it. My feet went numb about two hours into it, and by the time we got to Charles I had trouble getting off the carrier.

With all of tonight's activity, George was grilled for an hour in his patrol brief, and it wasn't until 02:30 that we got back to camp.

We're going out to Pristeg tomorrow and I didn't want to hand over the gun in bad shape. The other sections are in the habit of handing it over without cleaning the weapons, but I'll be damned if I'm going to do the same, so after we got in, I spent twenty minutes wiping down the .50. This was something of a futile effort because like Pig Pen from Charlie Brown, every time we moved in the back of the carrier there was cloud of dust that covered the area we'd just cleaned. The final cleanup will have to wait until tomorrow. I hit the sack at 03:20.

Thursday, 16 Mar., Day Off I was supposed to go to Pristeg today, but Henry came into my ISO at 9:00 and told me that I had the day off and that I'd be going out there tomorrow.

We were supposed to leave on the change at around 11:00, but got that got moved to 10:00 and Henry asked if I could spend some time on the gun before they left.

It took me forty minutes to get all the dust and crap off it, and put everything back together. When I was done I let Henry know, then went and took a shower.

These past two days I've been a little down in the dumpster about things, and it occurred to me last night, as I bounced down the road with my eyes closed, that I'm very tired. I'm tired of this place, and I'm tired of the bullshit. For the first time since returning to the military, I seriously contemplated getting back out. For a couple of hours anyway, the thought of getting out held great appeal, even though I know that's not the right answer.

I don't think it's the job. I've proven, to myself anyway, that I'm capable of doing it. Lord knows it doesn't take brains to be uncomfortable, and suffer the slings and arrows of outrageous fortune. It's all the little things, like the food, the living conditions, the bullshit, and the personalities, that end up piling up and eventually start to get to you. A quick look around the platoon, and you'd see that I'm not the only one who feels this way. It seems that being where we are, living and doing what we do, is like living in a pressure cooker. The longer we're here, the worse it is, and the greater the feeling of animosity.

Now some fella who gets paid entirely too much for his opinion will likely tell you this is a stress reaction to my environment. No doubt one of the stress guys would have a field day with this one!

I went to the mess tonight, and being in an antisocial mood, I sat alone and watched. It's amazing what you see when you look. Someone had the decency to play Pink Floyd's Dark Side of the Moon album, and for three marks, I had three beer and closed my eyes and let my mind wander with the music.

Tomorrow I shall again pick up my sword and my shield, and do battle against the forces of evil—but only for 17 more days. For now, to sleep.

Friday, 17 Mar., Pristeg I'm in a better mood this morning. Most of the cynicism has returned to the depths from whence it came. It's a bright sunny day today, and perhaps because of it, I can better deal with this place. I've noticed that I'm not the only one affected by the weather. The mood in general tends to get down when it rains, or threatens to. I've also noticed a difference in attitude between the Reservists and the Regs. Perhaps difference is too strong a word; subtle variance would be closer to the mark. As a Reservist I feel I'm holding on to a life outside of the military, and thus I'm not fully committing myself to this place or this job, the same way the lifers do. Slight though it may be, I've noticed a rebellious streak in others and myself that does not accept what's going on at times. This can be both good and bad. At times it can help you through a task, and other times it can hinder you. It's no big deal really, just an observation.

This morning when I was getting ready to come out to Pristeg, I thought I saw Henry walking towards the company offices. It struck me as odd because I had to go out to the OP before anyone could come in.

A short time later I spotted Henry again and he came over to me with some things to give to George. We chatted for a bit and then he dropped a bombshell. His mother

The Second Half of the Tour 277

has just been diagnosed with terminal cancer, and she hasn't got much time left, so the Army's flying him out today or tomorrow to be with her.

To say that it caught me off guard is an understatement. What do you say to a guy who's mother is going to die in the next little while? It was clear by his face that he was shaken, but was trying to understand the magnitude of what had, and was about to happen. I really felt badly for him. We chatted for a while longer, then he went to pack.

Out at Hawaii 5-0, little had changed. Another section of the modular was added to give a bit more space to the living quarters, and bring the rations indoors, but otherwise everything was the same. Ted has been appointed our 2IC for now, to fill in for Henry. People are quietly resigned to this decision.

Around 1300 hrs, David spotted four guys working on bulldozer hill, and called in a SITREP to higher. The platoon commander came by at 1400 hrs with an interpreter just as I was coming on duty, and picked up one of our guys to help him sort out the issue on the hill. Once again the Serbs are continuing to work in spite of us. You'll be pleased to note that the latest reports have the roof now on the bunker.

The only interesting thing in the Ogroup this evening was that we were right to snatch the .50-cal mount the other night. An officer drove out to the sight and confirmed, using the GPS, that the bunker was indeed in the Zone, therefore we were not giving it back no matter how loud the Serbs screamed. I understand we're not giving it back until the digging stops. I can just see it now, two guys in a firefight, "OK Boris, it's your turn to hold the barrel."

And from the annals of burdensome tasking, 1 Section had the pleasure of the CSM and OC's company on their patrol tonight. Fortunately they didn't stop in to see us, but I did notice that Routes One and Three took about an hour longer than usual, so they probably didn't have time to stop anyway. Just being a bit more thorough than usual I guess.

Saturday, 18 Mar., Pristeg At 8:00 this morning we were awakened by Ted and told of a lovely plan 3-9er had cooked up for us. It seems they want us to do a twenty-minute standing patrol at 09:00 and 11:00 on bulldozer hill to deter the Serbs from building any further. Frankly I'm at a loss as to what this is to achieve. SC47, SC51, and ourselves all have a clear view of the hill, and we know when people are on it. Sending us out there when there's no one on the feature is a substantial waste of time and resources. No one in the section is impressed with this idea, least of all George who tried to get the tasking canned—to no avail. Ted of course had his say as well.

Undeterred by silly orders, the boys mounted up and drove out to the hill to wave the UN flag. Ted, Bruce and I stayed behind to man the fort. An hour later they were back in our position, none the worse for wear and very unimpressed with the whole situation.

The morning DP run brought news of a change. Because Henry has gone home, and Ted is not 6A (section commanders course) qualified, MCpl Parry will replace Ted as section 2IC. It is the CO's policy that there be a Sergeant and a 6A qualified person in the section at all times. This of course flies in the face of the fact that George was away from the section for nine weeks and Ted was the 2IC and Henry the section commander the whole time. With roughly three weeks left in the tour and no one left to go on leave, one is left to wonder why they're even bothering to make the change. The platoon warrant will be out tomorrow and I'm sure George will argue the case. As much as we don't care for Ted at times, we all see it as a travesty to change things now.

The 11:00 patrol to bulldozer hill was cancelled but was replaced by a 12:00 run to the Malaglave feature to investigate 12 guys who were working there. Upon arrival, the first thing George did was ask the two men carrying weapons (AKs) to leave, which they did with no argument as a sign of good faith.

George was going to leave things as they were because he couldn't legitimately ask these guys to leave. They were all in civic dress and not breaking any rules. Then the platoon commander arrived wearing his UN cape, and two hours later the situation was diffused, with no change to George's original assessment I might add. God saves us from keen officers!

While they waited on the feature for the platoon commander to negotiate with the local commander, George and Jay talked with the Serb soldiers. The Serbs asked about the C7 and C9 they were carrying, and then to contrast they started pulling out their pistols for a show-and-tell. Now, you have to see the humour in this; we just booted two guys off the hill for carrying weapons, yet when asked nearly every one of the men remaining were carrying handguns. All George could do was laugh and thank God the platoon commander had left the feature temporarily to talk to the local commander. Still, you can see now that Henry, Tim, and I were right to back down when we were surrounded by these guys on bulldozer hill. The fact that all these guys had weapons hidden on their person only illustrates how dangerous the situation really was.

It's obvious that the Serbs are taking us for granted and are becoming bolder as the deadline for the mandate draws closer. The other night SC54 and SC56, two of our best OPs for observing the Zone, were approached by Serb soldiers who asked permission to use the OPs to observe the Croats. Right, would you like coffee while you use our scopes? Their requests were politely denied.

George did make one telling comment upon his return from the Malaglave, he said, "I wish we'd train our officers before they come here instead of teaching them on the job. I'm tired of taking orders from dweebs with only two years in." No truer words were ever spoken.

Shift tonight was from 2100 to 2400 hrs with George. We spent the entire shift playing Gin Rummy. Things are quiet out here. If we could just get higher to leave us alone they'd be great!

Sunday, 19 Mar., Pristeg Life out here is quite relaxing. No one came by today to give us a hard time, though the lieutenant did come by in the morning with the Ogroup for us.

I came on shift at 8:00 and was supposed to be relieved at 10:00, but because everyone was sleeping, I chose not to wake them and stayed on until noon.

The morning DP run saw the departure of Ted, and the arrival of MCpl Philip Parry. He'll stay with the section until the tour's over now, and do Henry's job. As much problem as we've had with Ted, I'm really not sure how I feel about his leaving. True he was a right proper pain in the ass at times, but some how this whole thing doesn't seem right. Time will tell I suppose.

As usual the remainder of the day was laid back. The weather wasn't half-bad, but not warm enough for tanning. There's a cool wind blowing and by the looks of the sky, it's likely it's going to rain tonight or tomorrow, which is going to make things inconvenient for us because we have to clean all the weapons in preparation for 3-9er's inspection some time this week.

The reason that the lieutenant gave us for the inspection was "I'm an Lt and he's a major." Sound military reasoning. What's going on here, is a fight to see who has the right to inspect the equipment prior to departure. The lieutenant feels that because we belong to Dukes Company, and we're his platoon, he should not have his troops submitted to an inspection by another company commander. 3-9er believes that because we are occupying one of his positions, he has the right to inspect the troops and their equipment. Highest rank wins. Both Dukes and Charles Company of course will subject us to an inspection and, as usual, there will be two standards to which we must adhere. Funny how the troops always lose when officers fight.

The Ogroup tonight held a couple of interesting points. One of the Kenyan OPs got caught between a Serb and Croat mortar duel. No more details on that.

Two mortar rounds dropped into the village near where SC44 is located. No casualties reported.

Later on in the evening when George and I were on shift, SC44 took three five-round bursts of harassing fire from two drunk Croats outside their section house some 700 metres away. The rounds passed by harmlessly, but it got our boys' attention.

The funny story of the day seems to fall to the Serbs. It appears they LOST some old lady's body that they were supposed to deliver for burial. No details other than that, but you got to admit it's funny. It seems army administration is a universal nightmare.

I'm on the 2100 to 2400 hrs shift with George again. The shift list has pretty much stabilized and we all have the same shifts from one day to the next. George and I have taken to playing Rummy the entire shift. It's a boring game, but it makes the three hours go quickly.

Monday, 20 Mar. Pristeg As predicted, it's pissing with rain today. Sometimes a torrential downpour, other times just drizzle or nothing at all. We were told that March is supposed to be a hot month, but I haven't seen it. So far it's the coldest and wettest month we've had since our arrival. I am thankful it's not snowing though.

The regular daily routine hasn't changed much; up to do the 8–10 shift; shave and clean up some, and have a bit to eat; lunch; watch some movies and nap; supper; watch another movie; then 2100–2400 shift; and to bed.

Today we were graced by a visit from the CSM (now nicknamed "Hop-a-long"), the OC, Warrant Fuller, with the morning DP run, and the lieutenant with the Ogroup—which didn't get passed on because there wasn't anything interesting in it.

The warrant brought out our leave passes to sign, and passed on admin points, like everyone on advanced party must go to the pay office to pick up a check so admin can close the records. The leave passes are for the end of the tour. As soon as we get back home, we've been granted three weeks' leave, and this is the standard Army way of knowing where you are or at least, where you're supposed to be. . . .

The visit by the other three was brief and came just as we were sitting down to have lunch. Neither the OC nor the CSM chose to stay, but the lieutenant did, and joined us for a bowl full of pasta and sauce.

With two full meals a day we usually end up with quite a pile of dishes by the end of supper. There are no rules here for doing the dishes and as a result the pile gets quite high. George came off duty at noon and wanted something to eat, but all the pots were dirty, so taking matters into his own hands he spent an hour slaving over the pile until they were all done—cursing and swearing the whole time.

Tonight's supper was another matter. We had an unexpected treat of steaks sent out to us today, so we made a marinade of Jambalaya spices, Heinz 57 sauce, Tobasco sauce, and Chili sauce. I did the honours on the barbecue, and they cooked up beautifully and tasted truly delicious. But as good as the meal was, the results were just as inevitable. Thank God it was windy tonight and the OP is drafty, otherwise none of us would have survived very long in there. The air was truly blue at times.

The lingering smells of the Jambalaya, HP, and steak combination, I'm sure, worked their way into the woodwork of the OP, and served as a constant reminder for each successive shift change, of the evening's meal. Even the blue rockets took on the smell, but in a more concentrated form. You took your life in your hands each time you had go to into one of them. Whoever was downwind from us this night must have been tossing their cookies when they caught a whiff of the odour that wafted so unpleasantly from our little UN encampment. Fighting for the free world has its price.

Tuesday, 21 Mar., Pristeg, 14 Days What a grand and glorious day it is today. Crisp, clear air, unlimited visibility, and hardly a cloud in the sky. Coming on shift at 0800 there was a lingering reminder in the air of last night's meal, despite the open windows. Though I'm not certain if it's the OP or my clothes I smell. I haven't changed my uniform in five days so it's tough to tell. There are no shower provisions here as there were in Bruska. We come out here and don't shower for the entire eight days we are on duty. Usually we'll make a run into Rastivic once during the rotation to use the showers, but that can easily get waylaid if something more important comes up.

Today was considerably more active than the past few days have been, and it started early. SC43 spotted two Croats with weapons coming towards their village in the Zone, shortly after I came on shift at 0800. A foot patrol was dispatched to intercept them, and as they approached the area where the Croats were last seen, two five round bursts were fired over their heads (though the patrol reported they could not be certain from where the shots came). A flurry of radioactivity followed, ending with the patrol being recalled until 3-9er Bravo could get to the scene.

When he arrived, he and the foot patrol went out and had a look around, but no one was found. Quelle surprise! It's kind of like chasing ghosts. Sometimes you see them, sometimes you don't.

Shortly after 1000, SC51 spotted two people on hill 48 (flag hill). We were dispatched to investigate, and Parry, Jay and myself stayed behind. Again, after about an hour no one was found and the boys returned to camp.

Things calmed down some after that for the best part of the day. SHOTREPS were coming in from various OPs, and around our OP alone we've counted at least six land mines going off because of the weather; as the ground warms up in the spring, the shifting earth sets off the mines.

In the afternoon Jay and I went for a foot patrol of both sides of the village. It took us about an hour, and was a pleasant walk and talk.

Later on this evening hill 48 acted up again. 6-2 was on patrol in the area with 3-9er Bravo on board. They had dismounted below the hill and a foot patrol was on its way up the trail when three five-round bursts were fired at it from the village. Quickly returning to their carriers, the patrol mounted up and headed into the village. Instead of staying in their carriers, they dismounted a foot patrol to walk 100 m in front of the carriers as they worked their way through the village, to see if they could find the culprit.

They met up with a local commander, and after a brief discussion it was revealed that the shots were fired from another village down the road and some names were given to be brought up at the next joint meeting with command (read: "It wasn't us, it was them!"—as he hides the smoking gun behind his back). Chasing ghosts again. It can be terribly frustrating. The odds are always stacked in their favour.

Now here's a point. George got in shit the other day for passing "tactical" information over the radio to 3, even though the information in question was part of a standard report format. Tonight 3 was so keen to get the goods on what went on with 6-2 and 3-9er Bravo, that he OK'd "tactical" info to be passed to him, even though 3-9er Bravo initially objected by pointing out that the info could wait till he got back. No dichotomy there is there? When an officer gets keen, anything goes. Nothing like making the rules up as you go.

The Ogroup tonight had a couple of interesting points about Rastivic and one that makes you shake your head. Two girls went up on charges before the camp CSM for partying too loud in their ISO. More to follow.

The water supply for Rastivic has been shut off in Benkovac. Did I not mention that? We get our water from the Serbs. Water rationing is now in effect. I'll have gone seven days without a shower by the time I get back, a couple of days more won't matter.

Get this. The Croats walked into a portion of the Zone in KENBAT's AOR and simply said "this is ours now" and took some positions away from the Kenyans. Why do they bother sending the Kenyans over here? They're worse trained than the Serbs or Croats, and the Serbs are hillbillies compared to us. This is your UN at work.

Wednesday, 22 Mar., Pristeg Last night I felt like I hardly slept at all. It was just cold enough to be uncomfortable, and I kept tossing and turning the night through.

At quarter to eight, I got up and got dressed to go on shift, only to discover just as I was going to the door that the shift list had been changed, and I was on at ten instead of eight. No one had bothered to tell me. I could still be in the bloody sack getting some rack for Christ's sake!

I didn't even bother to undress, I simply lay down on top of my bag and tried to grab some shuteye.

Shift was quiet until the lieutenant stopped by. He didn't come into the camp but stopped on the road so I had to go down to him.

Working the OP I sometimes leave my flack vest undone to make it more comfortable to sit. When I went down to the Iltis, I started to do it up and was immediately challenged by the lieutenant and questioned if I was just putting my vest on.

"Putting it on sir?"

"Yes, you heard me, were you putting your vest on?" As he watched me continue to do it up.

" Why no sir, I wasn't putting my vest on," as I smiled at him. I wasn't lying; merely bending the truth a little.

He then asked for some information, which I went and got for him. When I returned with it he thanked me then quietly reproved me for not having my vest done up. I told him I'd get right on it, and he left.

Mr. McConnell is an under-trained, over-confident, strutting peacock, who's keen as punch. Which, now that I think of it, describes most of the junior officers I've ever come in contact with. Still, I like the guy, his heart's in the right place and he's done right by me, so I have no problems going along with whatever he wants.

In talking to him and watching him for the last ten months, I see in him many of the things I was and am. I like the guy, but I think his keenness gets the better of him most of the time and he comes across the wrong way sometimes.

Today's funny story comes to us care of David. I call this little story "David and the Fire," but before I tell you what happened, you have to know that fire and David don't mix. He's always burning himself when he lights a fire, or when he's around the stove. It's so common an occurrence that it's become a running joke; keep this in mind.

We decided we were going to barbecue the remainder of the steaks from the other night, so David volunteered to start the barbecue. He efficiently cut and piled the wood, then arranged it neatly in the barbecue. He stuffed paper in all the right places. For fire-starter he decided on using gas instead of naphtha; this necessitated getting a jerry can from the POL point, which he carried carefully back to the Barbecue area. After pouring a generous amount of gas on the wood, he cautiously moved the gas can a good ten feet away from the barbecue, setting it down beside the gabions near the entrance to the tent. Unbeknownst to him, in moving the gas can to a safe area, he had dribbled a trail of gas from the barbecue to the gas can.

Standing well back he carefully lit the match and tossed it onto the gas-soaked wood, which lit up with an almighty WOOF. Looking through the flames David watched aghast, as a modest trail of flame travelled from the fire, along the gas-dribble, the whole "safe" distance to the gas can.

The exterior of the can caught fire of course, and immediately recognizing the danger, David, in a valiant effort to separate the burning can from the tent, leapt over the flames of the barbecue, dashed to the burning can. In a movement resembling an Olympic discus-toss, he spun and heaved the can with all his might to the open centre of the compound. An impressive quick response on David's part; except that he had not re-capped the can after prepping the fire, so when the jerry can landed, gasoline sprayed out everywhere, creating an instant fire ball. Flames reached twenty feet high.

The sudden flash drew the rest of us outside in a mad rush to see what had happened. SC51, who are on a hill some 3km away, spotted the flames and enquired over the radio if we needed any assistance. Jay, who was on shift at the time, called back and, displaying an uncommon cool under the circumstances, casually thanked them for their enquiry, but no thanks, we're just preparing dinner and everything's under control. The flames quickly burned themselves out as David, silhouetted by the dying light, stood hands in pockets, thoroughly embarrassed.

The final irony came when we gathered at the barbecue. The fire had completely burned itself out when the gas burned off. The wood itself had not ignited. We ended up using the stove to cook our steaks.

Yesterday was Jim's birthday, he's now 24, and he started the day by doing all the dishes—an interesting, if somewhat bizarre, way to start celebrating your birthday.

The two girls, who were up before the CSM for partying, I understand, made the mistake of partying in the ISO directly across from the camp CSM. It baffles the mind that people in their 30s can still act like teenagers and do things as stupid as having a party across from the CSM, when everyone in camp knows that it's against standing orders to have alcohol in your ISO. That's tantamount to waving a red cape in front of a bull. No sense of responsibility at all.

1-3A stopped by tonight on their patrol, the poor guys were out only an hour and they were freezing. Admittedly these past two nights have been extremely cold.

It was passed on that the Croats plan to take over the Zone as of 01 April. That means with 3 or 4 days left in the tour things might get interesting. I hope it's not true but in this place anything is possible.

Thursday, 23 Mar., Change Around In spite of the cold again last night, I actually didn't sleep all that badly. I was up an hour before shift to clean up and pack all my kit away, with a little extra time on my hands I took the opportunity to grab a bite to eat as well, since supper would be my next meal.

I went on shift from 10–12, and during that time the guys did a general clean up of the area for the incoming section so they wouldn't have too much more to do for the OC's inspection on Friday.

From all accounts, the OC Charles is going into great detail when inspecting his troops. He's apparently checking everything, going as far as to check spare parts for ALL serialised kit, and ensuring everything is cleaned and oiled. With us though, he's going to be a little more lenient as we're only attached to his command. He therefore, will only inspect the camp and "operational" kit like the NODLR and C-6 we keep in the OP. The track he won't go near.

While I was on shift the warrant came in with the DP run for the day. I hate it when I don't get to listen in on Ogroups, it makes me feel detached somehow. As it turned out, the only thing of importance was that we were to stop at the range on the way home to test fire all weapons. There was something about a prisoner exchange coming up in the Zone in a couple of days, but it doesn't affect us so I didn't miss anything. Before we left, I had a quick chat with the warrant about the Croatians' intentions on April 1st. He confirmed that the general consensus is that they're planning to make their move April first, but there is no way to confirm anything. Like so many things in the army we'll just have to wait and see what happens.

At 13:30 1 Section showed up to relieve us so we packed up and headed for the ranges. A forty-minute carrier ride later we pulled into the range off the road to Rodaljice and took out all our weapons. Today we were going to confirm sighting on everything! The .50, C-6, C-9, C-7s, C-3, 60mm mortar and Karl Gustav meant that tomorrow would be spent cleaning said same weapons.

With 3 rounds I quickly confirmed that Robert's C-9 was on target (he took my C-7 on leave with him) then went over to get the .50 ready to shoot.

A bit of a competition broke out between the 3 Karl Gustav teams, with headquarters surprising everyone by scoring two for two on the tank we were all shooting at some 650 metres away. The other two teams took a lot of ribbing for that embarrassing performance. Beat by headquarters. Man, it just doesn't get any worse than that.

Last to shoot were the .50s. We were supposed to only shoot 50 rounds—half a box—but I can't recall anyone telling me that. Besides, I had "technical difficulties" and was forced to shoot the entire box to ensure that the weapon was working properly. Who knows when I'll ever have the opportunity to fire a .50 cal from a carrier, and we must maximize our training opportunities whenever we can, mustn't we? *Wink*.

An hour or so after we arrived on the range, we were finished and headed for home, the one thing on everyone's mind: shower. We arrived back at camp at 1600 and by 1605 all the weapons had been sprayed down and the track closed up, and we were heading for our trailers to get out of our clothes.

As I was sorting my kit, George came around and told us not to shower before supper. Our alert status had been bumped to "green and a half," and we were to be ready to move. So instead of taking a shower we all went over to have supper. I felt bad for the guys who had to sit beside us.

At 1800 I was in my room sorting through my kit again getting ready to take a shower when George again came to the door. 1-3, the second vehicle on patrol tonight, was down and he needed a work party to get it working. He paused for a moment then asked if I'd taken a shower yet. When I said no, he told me to carry on, he'd get someone else. At the Ogroup, which was held at the disabled carrier, I found that everyone in the section but me was working on it. Damn decent of George to give me a break I thought, but I could tell from the looks of some of the younger guys, it pissed a few of them off.

The Ogroup tonight was interesting, and Robert and John were back from leave so they joined us. The two girls who were partying, were given two extras each (I should say something snide about the number of extras handed out, but nothing comes to mind immediately).

In KENBAT, six Serb soldiers hijacked a Kenyan Land Rover. One wonders if the Kenyans offered to sell them some diesel at the same time.

In CZECHBAT, three people were killed in a car accident on the coastal road. That's the road we took to get to Budapest. It's a wonder more accidents don't happen on that road, with the way people drive around here.

An odd thing happened as I was writing tonight. I started to think about Cat's body. The curve of her hips, the softness of her skin, the feel of her lips. The feelings and images were so intense that I was quite overwhelmed, and aside from immediately creating an uncomfortable sitting position, it sent a shiver up my spine. Thank God we live in the country, I'd hate to have neighbours when I get home.

I consoled myself by going to the mess, where I met Robert, whose first comment to me was "Kurt, you look ten years older." Thanks buddy. I went to bed early (we old folks need our beauty sleep don't ya know).

Friday, 24 Mar., QRF Today was a day to work and work we did. It started at 0800 at the HQ carrier, where everything that could come out of it did. We stripped it down completely, and washed out the insides, then cleaned and oiled everything before putting it all back in. We even took the box of .50 cal link ammo that was regularly used while on patrol and delinked it all, and cleaned each round before reassembling the belt and putting it back.

To completely clean the whole carrier took ten guys three and a half hours of steady work. At 11:30 we broke for lunch and at 1300 we started the whole process again with our own carrier, 1-3-B.

By 16:15 we were finished, and glad of it. 1-3 had been in pretty rough shape. The carrier technically belongs to HQ, but it gets passed from section to section to be used on patrols as the second vehicle. The result is that it has three times the amount of miles put on it but nobody has time to do any maintenance to keep it going. I know for a fact that Ted never did anything more than a morning parade on it, and sometimes he never even did that. Each week it seems we're changing major components on it just to keep it going.

Just before lunch, the warrant came over to chat with us and see how things were going. He told us of the procedure the RSM and CO have to go through during the POW exchange, which is scheduled for tomorrow at the Zemenic crossing.

The first to be handed over will be the dead. These are people who were killed in fighting in the Bihac. A body bag will be brought from a truck into a tent and put on a table. The CO, RSM, and MO will open the bag, account for all body parts, including fingers and toes, take a photo as a record, then hand the body over. Accounting for the fingers and toes is important, because some of the soldiers have been hacking them off as souvenirs, or as proof of a kill, not unlike the British practice of scalping an Indian during the seventeen and eighteen hundreds as proof of a kill.

The walking prisoners, some of whom are said to be in such bad shape that they are expected to die as they are handed over, will be the last to be transferred.

A grizzly task at any time, I expect some of the dead will be particularly ripe as it's more than 80 miles to the Bihac from here, and it's quite likely they've been in the bag for a while. The weather's been hot these past two days, and I can just imagine what it will be like in that tent. No thank you.

I am told the prisoners are currently being held less than a kilometre from here in the Benkovac barracks—in light of the hatred between these people—not to Geneva Convention standards I'll wager. We also found out that the inspection at SC 50 did not fare well for 1 Section. Apparently the .50, which we were told would not be inspected, was found to be "wanting."

The remainder of the camp, of course, did not meet muster so Warrant Fuller was called up in front of the Charles Company CSM. The carrier's condition was only part of it. In the POL bunker someone had written on one of the beams "all civvies must die." I know for a fact that no one in 3 Platoon put it there, because it was there when we first arrived. When higher found out about it they lost it, which is why Fuller got called out. Not a good day for the boys out there.

After work I called Catherine. Damn it felt good to hear her voice. I've been dreaming about her more and more lately, in obvious anticipation of my return home. To hell with the stress debrief; just don't stand between my wife and I. You're liable to get hurt.

One call wasn't enough, so I checked outside to confirm no one was there waiting for the phone, then called her back. Right in the middle of the call a MCpl opened the door and stood there staring at me... Then he had the indecency to start coming on to me for taking too long on the phone. I told him to "close the fucking door, and we'll sort this out when I'm done."

Admittedly it was not our company's phone day, and I did make two calls back to back, but on the other hand, I haven't been in camp for the past eight days, like these guys, and I do have permission to use the phone anytime I feel fit to. The resulting confrontation was short and sharp. All it took was for me to tell him I'd just spent eight @#$%^&* days in the Zone, my wife was ill, and this was the first opportunity I'd had to call her. The guy shut up in an awful hurry and had no comeback. What was he going to do? Make me join the Army? Not likely! REMFs (Rear Echelon Mother Fuckers) really get on my nerves some times. They forget they're here to support the rifle companies who do the real work.

Tomorrow will be a rather interesting day. There's a company commander's hour laid on and then a giant all ranks barbecue to mark the end of the tour. Unfortunately we're QRF so we can't drink. Bummer! It means we'll have to waste valuable drinking time to decant our beer into pop cans.

In tonight's Ogroup, a Czech OTR 64 was stopped and surrounded by 14 Serbs on Route 147. They were detained for a while then let go. No doubt their sphincter muscles got a good workout.

Tomorrow our section will be tasked to do a standing patrol at one of the Serb section houses on Route One. I won't be going out until Monday. At least we won't be stuck in camp to do shit jobs.

The big news in tonight's Ogroup involves the end of the mandate on the 31st. Because we don't know how anyone is going to react—or what the new mandate will entail—all OPs will go to 100% manning, and maximum daylight patrols will occur. No night patrols will happen; this last point is good, because we're scheduled to start our patrol cycle on the 31st, and I'd hate to be shot at and not be able to see where it came from.

The end of this month is going to be a tense time for everyone. We'll see what it brings.

Just after I went to bed Virk showed up from his patrol—5 hours early. 1-3 broke down again. I'll have to get the details from him tomorrow.

Saturday, 25 Mar., QRF I'd been given today off, but this morning I got up at 6:45 with Virk to go with him to the weigh-in for the big power lifting competition scheduled to be held tomorrow. Virk has been training for two months now to get in shape, and the odds are very good that he'll actually win. At 190 lbs, he is lifting a combined weight in the bench press dead lift and squat of almost 1300 lbs, and by all reports nobody can even come close. But these reports could be skewed. Part of the fun of the training has been misleading others into thinking Virk's been hurt. Everyone in the platoon is in on it, from the lieutenant on down. Each time we stop in at Charles Company, the main hotbed for the opposition, we drop a rumour that Virk's hurt himself, or that his workouts have gone badly as of late. It's a lot of fun really, but they give as good as they get. Trying to get information on the other competitors is next to impossible, but then that's what the games all about. Only the actual competition will sort this all out, and it should be a good time.

At breakfast Virk told me what happened to last night's patrol. It appears that when they pulled into Charles Company for the patrol brief, oil and diesel started to come out of the engine well. An investigation found that diesel was getting into the engine through one of the crossover tubes and they had to ground the vehicle and call back to Rastivic with a Repair and Recovery request (even though Charles Company mechanics are 50 yards away).

A carrier showed up with a tow bar and hooked up to 1-3 to tow it back to our lines where it could be repaired. Just as they were pulling into Benkovac, the tow vehicle erupted in a cloud of white smoke and broke down, much to everyone's delight, and another two vehicles had to be called in to tow the broken carriers home. With all the abuse they take, I'll be surprised if these things last out the year. The patrol as you might imagine was cancelled and the guys actually got to have a night off.

As I got back to our lines I ran into Ray who was just heading out his door all kitted up. His section has been assigned to provide security for the Czechs who were going to clear Route 147. The Serbs, after stopping the OTR 64 yesterday on the route, had threatened to mine the route. Not taking any chances, the Engineers were dispatched to clear the route. Ray was to tell me later in the day that the Czech Engineers showed up with a T-72 with a mine roller on the front, a section of troops, our Engineers, the medics, the liaison officer, and Ray's section. For the most part they just sat around and waited as the T-72 rumbled down the route and back.

Earlier this morning, George, Jim, David and Bruce went out to do a standing

The Second Half of the Tour 287

patrol on a Serb section house at Kapela in the Zone. The house is located about 1000m from the Croatian lines (the same place where the stove blocked the road and Robert pissed on his leg). It's the only high piece of ground around and the Serbs have been sitting on it for a year and a half, which leads one to ask why the hell this late in the tour, we're putting a 24-hour picket (split between Recce and us) on it. There's been more than a little grumbling throughout the platoon over this one, but this is the Army, and we just do as we're told.

Marshalling the vehicles for quick dispatch. Here we are on five minutes' notice to move

The morning was pretty quiet so I took the opportunity to get in a workout and a haircut. It's the first workout I've had in about two and a half weeks, and I felt stiff and weak, but I'm going to try to get in every day for the rest of the tour.

As I was walking back from the gym, I saw a line of five carriers with all the QRF suited up ready to go. That's odd, I thought to myself, I wonder what's up? As I got closer I realised that the first carrier had all my guys in it. Parry spotted me and told me to get dressed quickly. I ran to my ISO and in five minutes flat was out of PT strip and into my uniform and vest.

As we sat around the carrier, two things came out. First that this morning the Serbs had told the UN to fuck off and that they were going to take whatever measures necessary to protect themselves. And that a mortar round had dropped about 250 metres from George's carrier, which was why we were suited up.

George had called in and said that everything was under control, but SC43 had flinched badly and got somewhat excited when they called in a similar report (they were about 400 metres from George's position). 1-9er decided to get in on the show and put the QRF on five minutes' notice to move.

Because our section is under 3-9er's command, we were called out as well.

Warrant Fuller placed a call to 3-9er to ask for direction, upon which he was told that he didn't think we were needed anymore, and we were told to stand down.

1-9er, our company commander, kept his guys in the HQ carrier ready to move while we went and had lunch.

This is a good example of every man and his dog wanting to get in on the action. The Ops O and the Ops warrant, as well as the OC, and CSM have no need to be involved in this kind of operation, yet they were all suited up and ready to roll, probably afraid they might miss something. A point that wasn't missed by the watchful eyes of the troops!

The afternoon was pretty quiet. We unloaded 1-3 of all kit so it could go in for repairs, and filled some jerry cans for the morning DP to Pristeg.

At 1500 we had a company commander's hour. These things for the most part are a waste of time. Nothing ever said at them ever makes a difference, and everyone knows it, which is probably why no one ever says much, preferring instead to sit stone faced. Today's topic was "morale in the army," and how we all responded to the Brigade commander's paper on the matter.

The brigade commander contends there is no morale problem. But I don't know of any organisation that holds its people to a pay freeze for four years, rotates them in and out of theatre every 18 months and is regularly subjected to trial by misinformed press. Because of the training schedule it does not offer advanced courses, thereby effectively stopping promotions, and to top it all off, does not permit smokers (company parties) unless it is requested and approved by the Brigade commander himself (as if he has nothing better to do).

And they wonder why the humour is so often sarcastic, sardonic, and black.

In spite of this, CANBAT 1, ROTO 5, has set the standard for how a tour should be run (much to everyone's surprise). There have been no deaths—accidental or otherwise—hardly any repatriation due to problems back home (CANBAT 2 has had over 40 so far), and we are still the only battalion in theatre that patrols 24 hours a day. This is without doubt testament to the professionalism, hard work, and pride of the individual soldier to get the job done.

There can be no doubt that the average soldier is under tremendous stress from forces beyond his control (i.e.: the yearly Personal Evaluation Review system), which is why he suffers from a lack of faith in his superiors. Listening to the OC rattle on, it occurred to me that his stock answer to any question he was asked, "It's a command decision." Is it any wonder everyone stonewalled him, they all just turned off after his first couple of answers? I sometimes wonder how stupid they really think we are. Everyone walked out of the tent agreeing it was another waste of time.

On a lighter note tonight was the night of the big barbecue. There were steaks, two roast pigs, shish-ka-bobs, chicken, ribs and lobster. As well, there was a large salad spread and three six-foot tables full of desserts. As is the Canadian way, there was entirely too much food. Is it any wonder the Brits call us "FOODBAT?"

I met up with Ray, and Padre Rembaldie and we sat and chatted over dinner, the subject was again the stress and morale problem, and probably was one of the best discussions I'd been involved with in quite a while.

Afterwards I went and called Catherine. We had a good chat, but just as I was telling her what I was planning to do to her body when I got home, we got cut off early, and I wound up talking to myself for about a minute before I realised no one else was there. Most embarrassing!

On the way back to the shacks I popped into the mess and had a pop, and chatted with some of the guys. Parry found me and told me I was on patrol tomorrow because Bruce had to compete in the weightlifting competition. I was looking forward to watching Virk compete, but I'll gladly stand in for Bruce.

Before going to bed I visited with Ray. We haven't had the chance to just sit and talk in a long time so that's what we did for two hours. I like him, he's a real nice guy and I'm glad I met him. But 4:00 AM comes early and I had to cut it short. It looks like rain tomorrow.

Sunday, 26 Mar., Standing Patrol This morning got off to a racing start, then slowed to a dead crawl. It started when George came by at 04:30 and said, "get up, we're VERY late." This didn't make sense until John pointed out it wasn't 4:30 but 5:30. We'd completely forgotten about the clocks going ahead one hour and as a result were an hour behind schedule. It was a mad dash as George, Jim, David, and myself headed for the carrier carrying everything we needed for the day.

It didn't take us long to get organised and by 5:50 we were rolling out the gate. Fortunately, the Recce guys we were to replace had forgotten about the time change as well, so when we showed up at 6:30 they thought it was 5:30 and we were early.

What can I say about 12 hour shifts that you haven't already heard in Knin, aside from the fact that we all thought we'd put them behind us.

I volunteered for the first hours watch while the rest of the guys went to ground. I started writing in my diary and when the first hour passed I decided to keep going until I'd finished the entry. Besides, it was overcast and cold, and it looked like it was going to rain so I wanted to take advantage of the lack of rain while it held off.

The day in general was pretty damn quiet, to be honest. We slept some, read, played cards, and cooked up food by turns to pass the time. At one point in the day, George was lying on his side with his back to me, on the bench opposite, trying to grab some rack. I was in a nice comfortable reclining position reading a book. Out of the corner of my eye, I caught George adjusting his position as he broke wind, only something was different, the sound that emanated from his nether regions, had more of a . . . wet sound.

There was a pause, as I put down the book, and George tried to figure out what happened. Then the smell hit. Not only had he managed to break wind, he shit himself at the same time. As soon as the rest of us realised what happened we started to howl with laughter. Everyone started to cut into him with comments about needing diapers, or Depends, and George, much to his credit played right along.

Being away from washroom facilities, meant cleanup was out of the question for the time being, so George did the next best thing, he dropped his drawers and cleaned up as best he could (while we opened every door and hatch on the carrier to clear the air) and stuffed some paper towel down his shorts to tide him over until we returned to camp.

Yesterday, Warrant Fuller couldn't find the location of the patrol to bring the boys box lunches the kitchen had laid on. This despite the fact that Jay had pointed out on the map the exact location of the carrier.

Today the platoon commander showed up two hours late with our lunch. Again because of apparent trouble in finding the place. He also brought the Ogroup.

The main points today were that for four days (March 30, 31, April 1, and 2) we're going to state Yellow without the helmets (sort of a greenish yellow if you will) because of the situation with the mandate. We should find out Tuesday or Wednesday what that entails.

The other point is after our arrival in Petawawa we're staying on the Mattawa plane for the night. It's probably the only available housing, but like a slap in the face, we Reservists all felt like we were getting the boot from 1 RCR. The Mattawa is a Reserve and Cadet training area, and to be relegated to stay there is like being told you're not one of us any more. A little extreme, but that's how we feel. Thanks for coming out, boys!!!

Another problem we faced is retrieving kit we took home. Prior to departure for Yugo, many of us were told to take all of the kit we were issued but would not need back home with us before we deployed, as there was no storage space for it on the base while we were on tour. This decision now created a problem because we have to clear the base stores the day we get back with no chance to get some of the kit we have to hand in.

One option put forward (I understand from talking to the padre) is to make us pay for all missing kit then give us a voucher for reimbursement when we bring the piece of kit in to our stores. If this happens, then many of us have decided that we will refuse to pay. They have to give us a reasonable amount of time to retrieve the kit. Besides why can't I hand it in through my Unit? Someone clearly wasn't thinking when he put this proposal together. Nothing like making things as hard as possible for us, is there?

The remainder of the day was quiet. We were all floored to find out that Virk had bombed out of the competition completely. He scored zero in the bench press when he failed to lift his training weight of 350 lbs. He was hoping to lift 425 plus. Bruce did the same thing at 250 lbs and both of them were drowning their sorrows in the mess when I got back. What a letdown that must have been for them.

Monday, 27 Mar., QRF What a depressing day! I got up at 08:15 thinking it was 07:15 and was greeted by another cold, windy, overcast, blah kind of day. Breakfast was from 06:30 to 08:00, but when I arrived at 08:30 the cooks were kind enough to cook up some eggs for me.

After breakfast I went to the TV tent and vegetated in front of the tube. I wasn't there ten minutes when the Care Bears descended upon me with a section from 1 Platoon for a stress debrief. I should have gotten up and left, but silly me I didn't, and for the next hour and a half I listened to these guys go on about what to expect when I got home.

If you ask me, this stress debrief thing is like killing an ant with a steamroller. This tour has been anything but stressful. My bloody infantry section commander's course was harder than this. But the word "stress "has become the new buzzword for the military. And whether we want it or not, we're all going to be debriefed, which I suppose is not such a bad thing. It just gets everyone riled when you are being told that doing your job is supposed to be stressful, when you feel it isn't.

The only stress on this tour is that which has been generated from higher, with all their weird and restrictive rules. Somewhere along the line people tend to forget that the infanteer is trained to execute his job with maximum skill and aggression. To close with and destroy the enemy under all conditions takes not only time to train, but a particular frame of mind. Today's infanteer must be skilled in no less than eight different light and heavy weapons, know radio procedure, tactics, and orders formats. He has, in short, been trained better, and knows more than the average platoon of men from

WWII. A section of men today carries more firepower than a company of men from the War of 1812. We are not only expected to survive under all conditions between -50 and +40 C, but to thrive and do our jobs better than anyone else.

And yet this does not bother us. We actually enjoy it; more accurately, we thrive on it. We thrive because of the bonds that are forged between men under adverse conditions, because of the friendships that are developed and nurtured; because of the feeling of invincibility, which grows from accomplishing an impossible task or doing a job better than anyone else. It becomes us vs. them after a while, and what the fuck do you know anyway, you weren't there.

This is where the sense of family comes from, this is why we go on and do as well as we do.

Stress comes from a sense of abandonment; abandonment by our politicians, who will not protect us, by the press, who constantly get the facts wrong and criticize us; from our leaders, who flinch and worry about their careers, and from the very system itself which is so flawed.

Stress comes from being told, "under no circumstances will you permit them to dig," and in the same breath being told, "but you will not escalate the situation."

Stress comes from confiscating a platoon's worth of weaponry from a house on one side of the road which is in the Zone, then two hours later watch an officer give it all back to the soldiers on the other side of the road outside the Zone.

And finally stress comes from being told we're trained troops and we should know our jobs, but not being trusted enough to clear, or even clean our own weapons unsupervised.

And yet, no matter how odd the orders or how bad the press, the sense of camaraderie always brings us through. The feeling of shared adversity that binds us together and fuels our sense of humour.

We few, we precious few, we band of brothers (apologies to the bard), continue to do more with less, in the strangest of places and under the worst conditions. We take pride in ourselves, we take pride in our work, and goddamn it, unlike some in our country, we take pride in being Canadian!

There are other things of course which make the job here harder. The pain of separation from loved ones being the biggest.

It has been said that a UN tour is like a magnifying glass on a relationship. It amplifies problems, or intensifies a love affair. The strain of separation will destroy a bad marriage and glorify a good one. Certainly in Catherine and my case, the latter is true. I believe that we have both grown as individuals and as a couple. Our love for each other is stronger now than it has ever been.

We in the Army love camping; otherwise we wouldn't be able to do this job. But to ask us to live out of boxes for six months is a lot to ask of anyone. Is it any wonder we get tired of it; box lunches, box juice, box water, box trailers, box shitters, and we even drive around in boxes. Things would be a lot worse if we didn't like each other. The section I was sitting with from 1 Platoon all sat separately. No two people sat on the same couch, instead they all spread out all over the tent, unlike our section who, later that day, all sat together. A most telling observation!

I don't believe the job is the cause of the stress. I believe it's the isolation. The fact that we're halfway round the world from the very things that we love most—our wives, our children, our friends, our country—makes doing our job just a little harder the longer we're away. It's been said that the military has a brutalizing effect on men.

I believe this to be true. The fact that just below the surface there lives within all of us a dark and sinister side is something that we must accept as fact and not conjecture. We like to put on airs and believe that we in the Western world are civilised, but one need only open the flap on the tent to see what happens to a country when you scratch away that delicate layer of civilisation and reveal the base nature of people. The military allows us to tap into that dark side in a controlled way in order to protect the very things we hold dear. Any time you isolate men, or women, you will find that a culture will emerge that throws away the rules of civilisation, and builds new ones based on what's been encountered. Execution of mission, and saving one's life and the lives of those around you, takes priority. There is no time for listening to the other guy's opinion or position. Survival becomes the only priority. The real stress on this tour will come when we all return home to our loved ones without some kind of detox to reacquaint ourselves with civilisation's rules of acceptable behaviour.

Right now I feel tired and about 100 years old. This may well be the accumulated stress of the tour showing itself, or it may simply be that I have been getting depressed whenever it gets cloudy out. Either way people have noticed it. Robert again commented how tired I looked when we were in the mess tonight. Without doubt the strain of worrying about Catherine alone in our big old house has taken its toll. Coming home to her and the animals will be the best possible tonic for this place that I can possibly imagine.

I know when I get back that I'll devote a fair amount of time to putting this diary on computer. If nothing else it will serve as a type of completion for the tour. A way, if you will, of summing up everything that's happened in the past year. It's some thing I know I'll have to do if I'm going to put the tour behind me. Heaven forbid that I end up like so many WWII vets, or Vietnam vets, who simply can't seem to put their war experience behind them, and talk of nothing else.

Stress. For me the best stress reliever will be to get back home and get on with my life.

Tuesday, 28 Mar., QRF It's unanimous, the weather in this place is fucked! I got up this morning at 04:00 to get ready for the standing patrol and when I opened the door I got hit smack in the face with: SNOW! I couldn't believe it; I quickly closed the door and got undressed, then put on my Gortex socks, long johns, and extra polar fleece. There was no way this puppy was going to suffer if I could help it.

By the time I got dressed there was no time left to shave so I went right over to the carrier to give John a hand mounting the gun and getting things set up to go.

Mother nature was kind enough to raise the temperature for us as we went out the gate at 05:00 (just enough to change the snow to rain) but even so the wind seemed to cut right through every layer of clothing we had on. In the end, I took refuge inside the carrier and only peeked out to see where we were.

When we got to the Kapalla section house for our standing patrol, we closed all the hatches, fired up the Coleman stove for a quick cup of coffee, then stretched out and racked, vigilant souls that we are. In fact, for a while there I'm pretty sure every one of us was asleep.

For the best part of the 12 hours I stayed horizontal, though I was awake most of the time. It was difficult to sleep anyway, because the track was literally being blown around by the wind.

When Warrant Fuller showed up with our lunch—a hot meal for a change—he told us that the wind had knocked the walls out of both the KO's trailer and the VIP trailer. All available tracks and trucks had been moved to the windward side of our trailers to act as a barrier to keep our trailers from being blown away.

What a slow shift, the whole day seemed to take forever to pass. As I lay there listening to the wind whistle through the air vents and the occasional radio transmission, I happened upon the question of whether or not I was happy. The God's honest truth to that question is, I don't know.

How does one define happiness? Certainly I am happy with my marriage, I'm not sure how I'd even begin to improve on that.

Am I happy in my work? Two-minute pause. I guess you could say there are parts of it I love and parts of it I hate. But on the whole I'd have to say I've enjoyed myself over here.

Am I happy with my house? I am. Though I would tell you that I look upon it as a never-ending project, and then there's the ever-present spectre of the mortgage hanging over my head.

I think what I'm trying to say is that I realise fully that I have it better than many people. I've even been told I'm envied for what I have or have done. The problem is that I seem to spend so much time trying to change or improve a situation that I actually fail to enjoy it fully because I'm always holding back. It seems to be a character flaw with me, probably inherited from my German side. I can, however, tell you that freezing my knackers off in a carrier in the middle of a war zone is not exactly my idea of fun. It's cool, but not fun.

By 3:00 this afternoon, every cloud in the sky was gone and the sun was out. Even so, the wind still howled past the carrier and like hibernating groundhogs, we all stayed inside the carrier until the very last minute, when we heard our relief motoring up.

The trip back didn't seem to take all that long, and as we climbed the hill to the gate at Rastivic the view was truly wondrous. The air was crisp and clear and acted like a magnifying glass, so that as I looked across the valley below the camp, the grass seemed greener and the mountains larger and closer.

Tonight was a night for all Reservists to sign their assessments. Mine, I'm pleased to say, was very good indeed. The assessment has three parts. Two narratives—one by the platoon commander and one by the section commander—and a rating based on three categories. Both the narratives and the ratings put me well above average. The lieutenant was even kind enough to say that even though he teased me throughout the tour, he always knew I was "one of the solid troops" and that he could always rely on me.

After a good hot shower and a verbal pat on the back, I decided to say bugger it to the fact that we were QRF, and I went to the Mess and had a couple of beer. After all I figure I deserved it. Fortunately I ran into Parry and he was doing the same thing, so if I needed to, I could blame my drinking on my 2 IC who was leading me astray. After two and a half hours in the Mess, I packed it in and by 11:30 I was in the bag.

A couple of parting thoughts; I could, I suppose, blame my tendency for brooding on my upbringing, or my German background, but to tell the truth I think there's more shit in that excuse than the average cow pasture. I hold a dim view of those who don't accept responsibility for who they are and their actions, and I'm not about to explain away my shortcomings by blaming someone else for them.

The quest for who we are and why we're here is a life long journey. I have found that it begins with the realisation that we are a product of our parents (both mentally and physically), and that our initial reactions to situations are usually not our own but something we learned from our parents. Some people don't seem to realize this, and go through life blaming others for their actions, rather than accepting responsibility for who they are, and finding out how, or what they feel about the things that affect them. Once you start the journey, it's hard to stop. The quest for self inevitably ends up in a quest for God, and how we fit into the grand scheme of things. For some, the journey ends there, for others—like myself—it continues on; but in the end it is the journey that is important, not the arrival. We find our clues and our inspiration where we can. And with a little luck you can solve the riddle before you die. Here endeth the sermon!

Wednesday, 29 Mar., QRF This morning I was slow getting up, but I managed to get to breakfast just before they shut the grill off. As usual though, the morning meal was the standard fare of overcooked eggs (to avoid salmonella poisoning), warmed over potatoes, and bitter coffee. The bread was good though.

After I came back and cleaned up, I was tasked with Jim to help the EMEs work on 1-3. We arrived at the maintenance bays around 10:30 to find that our job for the morning was to muck out the engine compartment after they pulled the motor. What a job! We searched around for coveralls, and I found a pair that was so small, that when I got them on over my uniform, I could barely bend over.

The bottom of the compartment was a small lake of diesel and oil, while the sides of the compartment were caked with oil impregnated mud. With the help of some putty knives and rags, Jim and I worked for an hour straight to scoop all the goop out from in and around the various nooks and crannies. It wasn't hard work, just messy. Thank God for coveralls.

One of us had to come back after lunch to help out, so because Jim is a driver I volunteered him to do it. He didn't object, and I really didn't want to come back, so it worked out for both of us.

After lunch Philip Parry found myself, Tim, and David and sent us over to the gym to help rebuild the tents after yesterday's windstorm. We three, plus three people from 1 Platoon, worked for an hour and a half rebuilding three sections of modular tenting and moving the weight equipment around, thus concluding my workout for the day.

We finished up at 2:30 and I went over to call Catherine. She was still in bed when she answered, and as soon as I heard her voice I had a warm fuzzy feeling come over me. God I love the sound of her voice in the morning. It's all soft and little-girl-like, and I get this image of her lying in bed with her silk top on and her legs spread out towards the end of the bed . . . sorry, got carried away there for a second. I have to stop torturing myself like this, but then, why? There's only four days left in country, and two in Petawawa before I see her. Ah yes, I love to go to sleep at night, I have such good dreams about her. Especially now, there's less than a week left before I see her.

Tonight's Ogroup, the first in several days, made the point again of stressing that we can not take metal mags back to Canada with us. They are considered prohibited under our gun legislation and if we're caught we could get two years in jail (though that's highly unlikely). You have to wonder about laws that have this kind of impact on your Army. Don't you find it a little odd that the bloody Army can't even have metal mags for their weapons because some do-gooder decided that the magazine should be considered Prohibited—only because it's made of metal. Instead, we have to use plastic mags that have an annoying habit of cracking, breaking, and generally choosing not to work at the most inconvenient times. It has many people in the Army shaking their heads. After all, we each carry around enough firepower to take out a small village on any given day; we just can't do it with metal mags on our guns.

Warrant Fuller was shot at again, though how or why they keep missing is quite beyond us. The man's the size of a small truck, and he rides around in a truck the size of a small house. We'll have to talk to the Serbs about their marksmanship training. No word on what actually happened.

KENBAT is tense again. The Kenyans are probably holding back their diesel, and it's pissing off the locals. Did you know that they do absolutely no patrolling and still manage to go through more diesel than CANBAT 1 who patrol 24 hours a day? Amazing!!! Their CO has to be involved in the black market. There's just no other way to sell that much fuel without him knowing.

Can you believe this? Newson and Peters are in shit again. Last night they asked the wrong person if they could buy beer after hours, and our CSM found out. Both were marched up this morning and given 14 extras each. Newson, who is a Reservist, won't have to do all of his because he's on the first lift out, but Peters will. I should point out here, that the CO always has a few cases stashed away in his ISO, and he's been making it available to whoever requests it after hours, provided he knows who it is, and it's kept quiet. Peters and Newson were in the mess when it shut down and went looking for beer to keep the party going. Only problem was, they knocked on the wrong door in their alcoholic haze, and woke up the wrong warrant by accident.

This is Peters's fourth charge in six months, at this rate they'll be giving him the boot before his contract is up in two years, and that would definitely not be good.

After the Ogroup, I was in my room filling out a debriefing questionnaire we'd been asked to complete, when some wingnut of a Serb, about 100 metres from our end of the camp, decided to let off two mags worth of AK rounds. To hear it, you would think the guy was only a few yards away, and other than being mildly annoyed at the disturbance, I didn't even get up. In fact, I told the guy to bugger off (using far more colourful military language of course), and went back to filling out the questionnaire.

Did I mention that the VCFAs are up over thirty per day now—not including tonight's incident, of course. They have been for the last two days. Both sides are getting antsy about the end of the mandate, something we still know nothing about. I'm glad I won't be around to deal with these people when they finally decide what's going to happen. I've had enough, thank you very much, time to move on.

Back to this questionnaire. Talk about a diverse line of questioning! The topic areas included biographical, political, military, topographical, demographic, foreign contingent, economic/infrastructure, and humanitarian. Some of the questions were: Could you comment on the state of the economy in your AOR? No, there is none. Could you comment on POL levels in your AOR? No, but I understand KENBAT is doing a roaring business. Could you comment on faction morale? No, other than to say they're worried about the other guy, and drunk most of the time. Could you describe the effects of weather on the terrain in your AOR? It's mostly rock, so when it rains it gets muddy, then it dries up and gets dusty.

You get the idea. Most of us simply went through and circled the "no knowledge" dot on all the questions and handed it back. While I appreciate the necessity of the questionnaire, I have to say that the questions were geared to the senior NCOs and officers more than the privates and corporals, hence all the "no" answers.

People are starting to shut down now. With only a few days or weeks left in the tour, people are doing as little as possible and fornicating the canine as much as possible. For the past week the Mess has been packed, and people are seriously looking forward to going home, which is why I had another forbidden beer tonight.

Five days and a wakie . . .

Thursday, 30 Mar., Patrolling What a way to wake up. I was lulled out of a deep sleep by the sounds of 70-mile-an-hour winds howling through the cracks and holes of the ISO, and by the irregular shaking of the whole trailer. As I lay there enjoying the warmth of the bag, Ray came crashing in and snapped on the light. "Get up, Virk!" he bellowed, "something's going on in Charles AOR and we have to do the change-around at Five-Oh early!"

So instead of being gently rocked back to sleep by the movement of the trailer, I was subjected to the crashing around of a guy in a hurry to get his shit together. The safest thing to do in situations like this is to get out of the way. There's only so much room in these damn trailers, and when someone is in a hurry, there's nothing you can do to help except stay out of the way. So, out of courtesy I stayed in the sack (that's the best excuse I've ever come up with for staying in the bag. I'll have to use it more often).

I never did find out what was going on over at Charles, but I did get to the mess for a late breakfast of coffee and cereal. We've all been scheduled for medicals prior to departure and release from 1 RCR. Mine was scheduled for 10:00, so I took my time cleaning up and tried to enjoy that which the cooks call coffee—though paint stripper would probably come closer to describing it.

At 10:00 I was at the UMS taking my shirt off getting ready to be stuck with a needle. The medic was just about to start when he told me it was the third in the hepatitis B series he was going to be giving me. Good thing he did, too. I've already had the full series of shots when I was with the fire department back home. On to the next stand.

Testing my hearing was a bit of an interesting go. It was held in an examining room but the background noise—wind, radio, people—was so great that nearly everyone complained that they couldn't hear the lower sounds. One guy registered a 25% hearing loss because of it. He may have lost some hearing, but 25% is a little drastic.

I'm pleased to report that my BP is a solid 120/80, but my heart rate is up slightly at 84, no doubt because of the 3 cups of coffee I had earlier.

The final stop was an interview with the Doc, which went well. I took the opportunity to talk about my back pain and learned that I may have a legitimate problem. Although it's rare, this is one of the few times he recommends that I see either a massage therapist or a chiropractor to have my lower back worked on. It seems I have some minor swelling caused by a hyperextension of the back, which is why I slump so much when I'm sitting. It relieves the pain. It's good to know I haven't been complaining about nothing, and that there actually is a problem.

The medical took me to lunch, and then a lazy afternoon. Jim had hoped to do track maintenance today in the form of track pads and retorqueing and tensioning the tracks. That would have meant at least four hours of backbreaking labour that no one was looking forward to. Fortunately it couldn't be done today due to the backlog at the maintenance shop, so it's been postponed—hopefully until after we've left.

We were also due to go out tonight from 7 p.m. until 4 A.M. on Route One. No one could figure out why we were given nine hours to do a route that only takes three to complete. Of course working for Charles Company one gets used to these types of taskings, no matter how illogical they may seem, and you learn not to ask questions.

Mid afternoon the patrol timings were changed back to 1800 to 0200, so we packed up early so we could eat at Charles Company before leaving for the patrol.

Ted was assigned as the second driver, and right from the outset, it was clear he was in his usual shitty mood. This was the source of knowing looks and much laughter amongst the whole section. In spite of our constant chuckling, I'm sure Ted never caught on we were laughing at him.

Our first stop of the night was at SC 50 even though it isn't on the patrol route. Someone had removed the patrol map from our carrier, so we popped into take 3 Section's, seeing as they would not need it.

Our next stop was just after we'd entered the Zone on the Goranje road. We came across an area the size of a football field where someone had cleared and buried all the scrub brush. You will recall the high hoe we came across on our last series of patrols, this clearing was directly in front of the line of bunkers and trenches they had recently completed. Like the Maginot Line between France and Germany, this trench system marks the Krajina edge of the Zone, and the cleared area is to provide an unobstructed field of view and killing zone. It's clear the work is ongoing because much of the slash is still in place, and you can see where they stopped working.

Looking at it you can see quite clearly what their plans are, and that this phase of prep for battle is not an exercise.

This discovery warranted a call to higher, and once we called in the SITREP we left the main service route (MSR) to head towards Lubichin stand on our way to SC43 on the track route. We were about 400 metres short of the Lubichin when we heard this great rumble and rattling noise, then suddenly the track lurched to the left and skidded to a halt. Oh shit, I thought, we've blown a track. Sure enough not only had we tossed a track but also both idler wheels on the left side had come off and the track itself was wedged in amongst the shocks of the undercarriage. All 8 bolts holding both idler wheels on had sheered off right at the hub, and the wheels were lying in the puddle ten yards behind us.

The time now was 18:45. This was going to be a long night!

The first thing we did was call in a SITREP to Charles Company to apprise them of our situation. To our surprise and delight, they actually offered to help, and after some discussion with their maintainers, callsign 8-8 was dispatched to effect repairs.

Their arrival wouldn't be for at least an hour as they ran around trying to find the parts they needed, so to pass time and make things easier for the maintainers when they arrived, we got out the track kit, and tried to dig the track out of the undercarriage.

I've learned, on this tour, to stand back when something breaks, and let the younger members of the section burn themselves out working on whatever the problem is. Either David, Bruce, or John will get in there and start swinging, and quite frankly, I couldn't be bothered to get in amongst them and fight for elbow room just so I can say that I've helped out. John in particular, when he gets annoyed—as he was tonight with Ted—likes to get in and start swinging with the sledge hammer and try to figure things out for himself. When he starts swinging, it's prudent to stand back and give him the room to move, it's also safer. Tonight, I noticed the older guys in the section—George, Philip, Ted, Jim, and myself—were standing back some, watching the younger guys fight it out with the track. Jim and Ted were offering sage advice and pointers at opportune moments, while George and I kept our flack vests on and stood back some in an effort to offer at least the semblance of local security.

It was getting dark and the boys were still hard at it, when Philip asked me to go up the road a couple of hundred metres, to act as a contact point for 8-8C when they showed up. I walked up the road, found a convenient bush out of the wind, and plopped myself down on a sturdy branch and proceeded to smoke my pipe, as I watched the sun go down. Might as well enjoy the break, I figured.

19:30 rolled around and Bluebell showed up with a carrier and an Iltis, and what they hoped were the right parts. The guys dropped ramp, took a look at the situation, grabbed their tools and got right to it. For them it was going to be a long night. The ramp on our carrier dropped in the middle of a mud puddle, which we thankfully had passed through and were on the high side of.

They started by taking the hub for the idler wheel off. That took twenty minutes. Because all the bolts had sheered off right at the face of the hub, they thought they would remove the inner and outer bearings from the old hub and use them in the new hub they brought with them. First they had to hammer bolt studs into the new hub. This is achieved by flipping the hub over and running the bolt through from the inside. The hole in the hub is tapered, as is the end of the bolt, so when the bolt is driven home from the inside, it stays in place largely because of friction. Also because the head of the bolt stops it from being pulled all the way through the hole. To remove the bolt you need only beat on the threaded end of the bolt to drive it back through the hole. Unfortunately this destroys the bolt, so you only get one go at it. With the new bolts in place on the new hub, it was over to our carrier for a test fit.

They discovered, to their annoyance that the bolts they drove into the new hub were too short, so back to their ramp they went to drive the short bolts out and long bolts in.

Half an hour later they were back for a second test fit. The hub slid on nicely, then things went wrong. The inner bearing slid into place properly, but the outer bearing wouldn't go. Thinking they were the same, the spare they had brought was the hub for a road wheel, and not an idler wheel. Kneeling in the mud in the cold and windy backwoods of Croatia, the maintainers were to discover that there is a $1/32$" difference in the opening for the outside bearing, hence the old bearing would not slide home. Good lesson to learn, tough place to learn it. Back to the ramp.

Now they had two problems. If they were going to use the longer bolts in the old hub—the one we broke—they would have to reclaim the bolts from the new hub. They couldn't drive the new studs out without damaging the threads, and they didn't have a punch to drive out the broken off studs from the old hub.

After some choice comments directed at the questionable lineage of the designer of the hub, they solved the problems. Because there are 8 bolts on the hub they chose to sacrifice one of the nuts to act as a cap. They'd only brought just enough to do the job; parts are very scarce. By threading the nut onto the end of the bolt, they could safely beat on the nut without damaging the threads. This took half an hour.

Now it was on to the old hub. By taking an old bolt from their tool kit, and pounding the end threads down, they devised a punch, and then proceeded to pound the broken studs out of the holes. I should point out that it is necessary to use a sizeable sledgehammer to knock these things out of place, but because of the size of the hammer, it becomes a two-man operation. Tentative looks were exchanged between the two involved each time the need arose to remove a bolt. Hushed comments about what would happen to the guy swinging the hammer if he missed his mark always accompanied these occasions, much to the delight of everyone gathered. Each operation lasted about half an hour.

With the old studs removed, the new studs went in quickly, and it was back to our carrier to bolt everything back together. By now it was pushing 2200, and we still had to put the track back on. For the next hour we laboured to get the track in place. This involved breaking track by removing two end connectors at an opportune location; slowly advancing the carrier to free the track; rethreading the track and backing the carrier up so the track ends line up; and replacing the end connectors. This operation, while simple enough in description, was made more difficult by the fact that we were beside a puddle, it was dark and there wasn't much light to work with, and the fact that the track itself weighted a ton. Literally. It was also more frustrating because Ted, who was driving, seemed utterly incapable of following the simplest of instructions, much to everyone's aggravation.

David and Bruce were both covered in muck, as they alternated turns crawling under the carrier trying to pound the inside end connector into place. It was nearly 2300 when we finally finished and were starting to move.

I, for one, was starting to shake from the cold, but I can just imagine what David and Bruce were feeling like, they were both wet from being under the carrier, and with the wind blowing I'll bet it went right through them. Thankfully the patrol was canned and we were headed for home, otherwise it would have been an extremely uncomfortable night for both of them.

On the ride back, I was thinking how tonight had been one colossal waste of time. It occurred to me then, that not only was tonight a waste, but I feel like most of the tour had been also, and that this was the reason I'd been depressed or down this past week. I'm sure some of it is due to the fact that I feel I haven't been at all challenged while over here.

I guess I expected to be put into the shit, and I'd finally put all my training to good use. Unfortunately, this tour saw anything but shit, and the constant waiting for something to happen has taken its toll. Also it's tough to feel good about something when there's no tangible evidence of your having made a difference. Only history will be able to sort that one out.

Friday, 31 Mar., Patrolling I was up early this morning so I could have breakfast prior to working on the carrier. Last night's repair was only supposed to get us back to camp—which it did well enough—not to be permanent.

At 0900, John and I went over to 1-B and broke track on it. We removed the idler wheels, and prepared the hub for removal. That took all of half an hour or so, then we waited for the EME to show up with the right part.

To pass time, we went over to the TV tent and watched the latest on CNN. By lunch the mechanic still hadn't returned with the part so we went and had something to eat.

After lunch we had the Ogroup. Apparently last night two kids were caught trying to breach the wire in camp here. They were caught and handed over to the local police.

Surprise, surprise, the mandate has been extended for an additional two to four weeks. After that the formula will change somewhat as soon as both sides agree to what they want. I'm not at all surprised that the Serbs agreed. From all estimates the UN represents 70% of the economy in the Krajina, and they'd be fools to give us the boot.

The Croatians on the other hand, want the name UNPROFOR changed to something that has Croatia in it. What a bunch of wingnuts! They should take all the bloody politicians out and shoot them, it would probably eliminate half the problems right off the bat.

We are reminded to address all personnel by their rank, "you're still in the army after all!"

Ted is back in the section again. At least, as long as we're patrolling. Everyone is oh so pleased about that, most of all Ted, who hates driving. Each time he goes out, he swears it will be the last time. And each time he shows up for the next patrol we laugh at him. Heaven forbid that he actually does his job.

Our patrol came very close to being cancelled for the second day in a row. 1-3B was still down with no idler wheels; 1-3 was still in the shop getting a new engine; 1-3C was out at SC 50, which left 1-3A which, half an hour before we were due to leave, was still out on patrol.

Charles Company, not wanting to lose another patrol, had 1 Section cut their patrol short and come back so we could take their vehicle out. They showed up at 13:50 and we did a quick switch around and literally spun the vehicle around and headed back out the gate.

Today was a good day for patrolling. The sun was out, the wind was down, and the air was crisp, though I was glad I had my long johns on. Once again we were given several hours to complete Route One, though why still remains a mystery to all of us.

I've noticed that as soon as I get into the hatch of the vehicle, and we start off down the road, I immediately begin thinking of home. It's some kind of Pavlovian response thing. I suppose when I get home I'll start thinking of patrolling.

Being the second vehicle in a patrol is the pits. If it rains you get covered in mud; if it's dry—like now—you can hardly see for the dust. The second vehicle is usually the borrowed vehicle so you never really know what you'll get, but you can usually depend on it being pretty beat up. The most important thing is to know where all the appropriate ammo is, keep your personal weapon close at hand, and don't worry about the rest.

Our first stop on today's tour of the countryside was the Kapella section house where we did our recent standing patrols. George dismounted to talk to the soldiers and was told that the Croats had just shot at them from their bunker system at Viterinci about a kilometre away. Great! Our last couple of days on patrol and these idiots are shooting at each other. It's starting to look like it's going to be one of those days.

We took down the particulars, called in a SITREP (conveniently forgetting to mention the shooting. None of us believed them anyway, because we all know an AK round would hardly be able to hit the target after 1000 metres), and carried on. Our next stop was Viterinci anyway, so rather than being told by higher to check it out, we chose to do it on our own.

Viterinci hadn't changed at all, in fact everything looked positively docile. We only saw two men on duty, and the likelihood of them admitting to shooting at the Serbs was non-existent, so we didn't even bother to ask.

SC43 was the next stop only ten minutes down the road. We pulled in, undressed and proceeded to brew up in order to kill some time. We were just settling in when Charles Company got a hold of us on the radio and told us to return to Viterinci and check out some digging the Serbs had reported. George tried to explain to higher that we'd just been there not twenty minutes ago and hadn't seen anything, but no we had to go back. As we mounted up and moved out I thought that this really was turning into one of those days.

Back at Viterinci nothing had changed. We motored through the position and came to a halt on the other side. We knew the Serbs were watching through their binoculars so we all stood up on the carriers and waved to them. That's when Philip Parry noticed that he wasn't wearing his flack vest. Oooppps!! Whadda mistak-a to make! So for the third time in forty minutes, we rumbled though the Viterinci defensive position. I'm certain the Croats on duty thought we were right out of it. Lord knows we did. Smiles all around.

Back at 4-3, an embarrassed MCpl Parry dismounted to collect his flack vest, and we then carried on with the patrol. As we approached the Arrowhead, a call came through from Charles to proceed to OP Colt and check out some Serbs one of our OPs had spotted entering the Zone. When we got there we couldn't see anyone so we back-tracked a ways and took another road, which put us more to the north. There, we came across three guys in a field by a stream. We didn't think these were the guys we were looking for but just in case we stopped and checked it out. Turns out the guys were fishing. One of them had an army jacket on so George made him turn it inside out—no uniforms permitted inside the Zone—so once again UNPROFOR exerts its vast might, and wins another battle against the forces of evil.

We called in our report and were given another grid reference in the area to check out for soldiers. We moved down the road to find the location in question. According to our map, we'd come to the edge of the Zone, and as we came to a stop along a road at the base of a hill we spotted an OP 200 metres up the side of the hill. A bun fight nearly broke out between higher and us, as to whether the OP was in the Zone or not. At George's suggestion it was finally agreed that they'd sort it out back at Charles when George gave his patrol report.

After the prolonged delay caused by trying to figure out what to do, Ted was peaking. As we sat at the base of the hill waiting for direction from higher, Ted subjected our carrier to a never-ending litany of complaints about where we were, and who we were working for. It was pushing the end of our patrol timing and we still had at least an hour's driving to do. Ted wasn't going to get his supper, and this pissed him off. The fact that it's our job to be out here checking these things out never enters into his picture of things. For him it's a matter of driving the route as fast as possible so he can get to the drinking mess. There's only so much of his shit I can put up with, and when I reached my limit I told him to lighten up. This of course did not help matters.

Nobody likes to work for Charles Company, but that doesn't mean you bludgeon the fact every chance you get. It means you keep your mouth shut and get on with things. But not Ted, who can be as thick as a rock.

The trip home was slow. Our carrier kept lagging behind every time we had to go up a hill, which continued to aggravate Ted, (and delight the rest of us). At one point, the first carrier sped ahead up and over the crest of a hill. Our carrier kept slowing down as we climbed up towards the crest. Finally, as we made it to the top of the hill, we spotted the first carrier sitting in the middle of the road, with David, John, and George, all standing on top of it smiling and slowly waving at us. Ted nearly lost it, and even without the intercom on, you could hear him swearing, which only served to crack everyone up even more.

At long last we pulled into the Charles Company compound and did the refuelling and patrol report thing. We were all watching Ghost Busters on the tube when I heard some carriers start up. I looked around and suddenly realized these were my carriers, the buggers had all slipped out without my noticing and were about to leave without me. I think I cleared the front steps of the building in a single bound, and virtually leapt aboard the carrier, as it sat idling just outside the gate. Most embarrassing!

Back at Rastivic I stayed behind to clean the .50 for the guys we borrowed it from. After brushing down the outside and removing the barrel I tried for twenty minutes to get the bolt out. The last guy to assemble the weapon had neglected to put the cocking lever forward on the bolt, and as a result it was almost impossible for me to remove the bolt without a weapons tech.

I got so frustrated, that I just grabbed the whole receiver group, threw it over my shoulder and went to Sgt Gray's ISO. When I got there I dropped it on a bed and turned to Sgt Gray and said, "this thing is fucked! I need help taking it apart." What I wanted to do was give the gunner who was bunking with him, a blast of shit for not looking after the weapon and telling me that it was in working order when he handed it over. We'd done the change around so quickly that there was no time to confirm it was working. My fault really, I should have gone through the load and unload drills and dry fired it before we left the camp. Instead together the sergeant and I worked on it for twenty minutes, then I went to collect the rest of the parts and close up the carrier.

The good sergeant didn't need me to help him fix the gun, and seeing it was one of his guys who had screwed things up in the first place, he told me to take a shower. By the time I was done the problem was fixed and out of my hands. Thank God for that, I wasn't looking forward to working on that thing till the wee hours of the morning.

On the way back from the shower I ran into Ted who said, "have you heard? The tour's over for you guys, all Reservists are confined to camp." Holy shit, the tour's over! I'd go to the mess for a beer but the camp is dry right now. Bummer!

Saturday, 01 April, Rastivic At twenty to nine, Gaetz came into my room and woke me up. "Kurt, I need you to go over to CQ for 9:00, you've got twenty minutes." I knew I should have gotten up earlier and had breakfast.

Everyone had all anticipated patrolling right up to the day before we were due to leave, at least that was the plan. That way the time would go faster and we wouldn't get tagged for shit jobs. I was definitely not into working for CQ, and I was going to use any excuse I could to get out of it. As it happened I still had to go to the UMS for a TB test, so when I got to CQ I told the guy in charge that I'd have to leave. Fortunately he had nothing big for me to do so I just slipped away and didn't bother going back. The TB test takes all of two minutes to do, but thankfully no one else seemed to know that, so when I didn't show back at CQ they didn't come looking.

The rest of the morning was lazy and relaxed. I drove 1-3 over to the maintenance bay, under the supervision of one of the drivers, where we discovered when we arrived that we'd brought over the wrong carrier. So I drove back.

The afternoon, the rest of the day for that matter, was quiet and to be honest, boring as hell. All the Reservists in the platoon gathered in one of the ISOs and we spent an hour cleaning weapons and talking. When I was done with my weapon, I went back to my ISO and tried to catch up on my diary entries, but found I could only work twenty minutes at a stretch before I had to take a break.

By 4:00 I was burned out, so I went to the phones and waited in line for forty minutes to call Catherine. When I finally got through, she was terribly excited that I'm coming home, she's got all kinds of things planned for me, the best of which is two days alone with her. I must confess I'm looking forward to coming home very much. The thought of being able to do my own thing for a while is very appealing.

Today's Ogroup highlighted two idiots. The first is a young man who tried to defraud the government by claiming that he was living common law with his girlfriend. This entitled him to the separation allowance from the Army, while she at the same time was collecting welfare but not claiming his income. Our company clerk picked up on it when he noticed the guy had put down his parents instead of his girlfriend as next of kin. The clerk could have overlooked the situation, but he wasn't willing to put his butt in the sling for someone he didn't know, so he turned the guy in. The guy is now in jail for 14 days, and has to pay a $2,000 fine. He was slated to leave in two days with us, but now he'll remain in jail for two days after the last flight leaves and the VanDoos have replaced us. There you have it, military justice in action. He's lucky though, if the civvies had got hold of him, the fine and jail time would both have been bigger.

If this next bit is true, what this guy did truly defies logic. We're told a Reservist from Bravo Company was stupid enough to write an article for a university newspaper back in Canada, in which he called down 1 RCR for the way things were run. Phrases like "I have trouble working for people with less education than me" were quoted by the RSM in the sergeants' mess, as he read the article.

It's OK to write this stuff, but do it after you leave. Clearly despite his much-touted education, this guy has no common sense if he writes this kind of defamatory article while he's still in the bloody Regiment. He didn't even have the smarts to cover his tracks by leaving the article unsigned. When the RSM gets a hold of him he's going to be in a whole different world of hurt.

George and Sgt Gray were talking with me about it and both were livid. Some of the things they would have this guy doing if they got a hold of him would truly define tedium, cleaning all the ISOs with a toothbrush until they gleamed, or washing all the carriers with a toothbrush were just two of the suggestions.

I can't say as I blame them really. True, many of the troops in the military do not have post-secondary education, but that is not to say that these people are stupid. Their education comes in the form of Battle School, Jump courses, Recce courses and Leadership training. If they have risen at all in rank they will be capable of teaching a lecture on nearly any subject the infantry deals with, from hygiene to sighting a machine gun, they can lead and control an attack, or deploy weapons systems. To my mind that requires not only smarts but a healthy dose of common sense as well. Something this guy appears to lack. That is not to say that the Army doesn't have more than its share of dolts, but then what organisation doesn't?

Although I have been hard on this guy, I have the feeling the paper may well have misquoted him. It's hard to form an opinion when you have only bits of information. Yet my distrust of the media still remains.

Sunday, 02 April, Rastivic It was a very early morning as I was up at 0400 to get ready for a 4:45 shift at one of the bunkers. One of the problems with being confined to camp is that you suddenly become available for all kinds of little jobs.

The shift was just over three hours long, yet I think it was one of the fastest shifts I've ever done. My shift partner, a guy from 3 Section and I started talking about vampires and Anne Rice's books on the subject. Before we knew it the shift was over.

When our shift ended, so too did the enhanced alert status. I've heard it is called high-speed green, green at 25000 RPM, plaid, and orange without helmets. It is really Orange without helmets because of the potential of something happening at the end of the mandate. Truth is, no one here is paying much attention. For the Reservists anyway, the tour is over, and for the most part no one really cares what either side does to each other, we'd just as soon nuke and bypass the whole country.

We had an early Ogroup this morning before the patrol went out. The bad news was that we are dry for the remainder of our stay here. No one is impressed with that bit of news.

The Croatians and Serbs have agreed to a new name for our peacekeeping force, they haven't told us what it is yet, but we've all nicknamed it UNCROCK, and I'm sure by now you can figure out why. The mandate has been extended for eight months, which isn't so good for the VanDoos. I don't have details on what's in it, but if it's like anything they've been talking about (reduced forces, moving back to the Bosnian border) it's going to mean a shitload of work for them when they get on the ground. I almost feel sorry for them. The tear down process will be long and tedious, and done in the heat of the summer.

We were told, reminded, that we are to wear helmets at all times when in the carriers. Someone at Bravo had 11 stitches on his chin when the carrier he was riding in stopped suddenly, and he was thrown off balance. Of course how something on top of your head is going to protect your chin is a little beyond us. Unless there is a way of wearing the helmet on your chin that I'm not yet aware of.

Change #442. We have now been informed that we will be leaving here in the wee hours of the fourth; fly out of Split sometime in the afternoon; arrive at Trenton that evening; spend three hours at customs; then 4 hours on a bus to Petawawa. The earliest we'll arrive on base, we're told, is 0200 on the fifth.

I have no doubt that this plan will be extended as soon as the ball gets rolling, and it will turn into another episode of "planes, trains, and automobiles."

After the Ogroup I caught up with Warrant Fuller and asked about the no drinking policy. I wasn't the only one to approach him so he called us all together and read us the riot act. "OK boys," (his favourite saying), "I'm NOT going to tell ya you can't drink. I AM going to tell you not to get stupid, because if any of you fuck up, you're going straight to jail without passing go." Sound advice and good news, we were all looking forward to having a good party.

And what a party it was. The barbecues were fired up and the food laid on. The beer was plentiful, and the mess was hopping to the music. I can't remember the last time I had that much to drink—wait, yes I can, it was that night in Knin (pick one). That was a wild night, but then so was tonight.

I stayed for about four hours, and had a great time talking to people, and playing cards. By about 10 o'clock though I sort of hit a wall and couldn't drink any more beer. Of course running out of money didn't help matters, so instead of sticking around I staggered off home through the darkness. I'm pleased to report that I made it all the way back without tripping or falling down once, and I even managed to crawl into my top bunk without assistance—which is no mean feat I might add considering my alcohol induced state. Sleep mercifully overtook me before the speed of the room's spinning got up over twenty miles an hour, though I suspect I passed out before I actually fell asleep. Fortunately, before that happened I had the foresight to drink a load of water in an effort to stave off the impending morning hangover. We'll see if it helps any.

Monday, 03 April, Rastivic   I was awakened this morning when Virk walked through the door carrying all his kit. This was not a good sign. Virk had already come in once in the past few days because his child went into hospital a couple days ago with bronchitis. He was brought in from SC 50 to use the phones and get the lowdown on how the little guy was. He was fine a couple of days ago, but the fact that Virk was standing in the doorway meant that something was amiss.

After calling home, Virk was told that he'd been bumped from main one (the first lift of reg personnel) and was now going home with us. His wife was ecstatic, as you might imagine, and I'm pleased to say that the little guy is recovering after a minor reaction to some medication. That's one thing I have to say about the military. The welfare of its dependants is sacrosanct. They will stop at nothing to get a man to a phone, or out of the country if something threatens his family. It's something to see really. Everyone will put in extra effort and stop at nothing to get the guy home. It's like an unwritten rule; you just do it, no questions asked.

From one bit of bad news to another: Warrant Fuller called us all out for another talking to. He wasn't mad at us, but once again 3 Platoon and alcohol didn't mix. This time it was Ted's turn to get in shit—why are none of us surprised? Fuller went on about looking after each other when we're drinking, and if we see someone getting stupid to muckle onto him and put him to bed, because "When Ted drinks, he gets stupid!" Couldn't have said it better myself.

Last night he got into an argument with a MCpl in the JR's mess. The end product was that Ted slapped the guy in the face, and although there's supposed to be no rank in the mess, this guy went off the deep end and got the Duty Sergeant and asked to have charges brought against him. Sadly three other people saw it happen and wrote up statements that made Ted look pretty bad. He went up before the CSM this morning and was charged with striking a superior, and given 14 extras. Ted's career is proceeding as per normal.

What a way to start an otherwise incredibly beautiful day.

The morning was not hectic, but certainly active. We went and collected our thanks for coming out gifts. There was a mug, a statue, and a laser print, all of which had to be packed into any available remaining space in our kit. Then it was over to CQ to turn in our personal ammo, and the load bearing vests we wore over our flack vests. The army doesn't have enough vests to go around for the next tour, so we have to leave ours behind for the VanDoos. With roughly twenty pounds of kit removed from the vest, we veritably floated back to the ISOs. I can remember when putting the flack vest on was an ordeal, now with it being so light, it feels like a spring jacket.

Once that was completed, our section went over to the carrier and did the section photo thing. Then it was to the TV tent where we formed up and were presented with an official "Dukes Company thanks for coming out certificate," followed by the obligatory speech by the OC and CSM. All of this took us up to lunch.

After lunch we were supposed to have a barrack box inspection at 1300, but because the MPs were being so thorough, the inspection was delayed until 1500.

One of the things they were checking for was the European porn mags that nearly everyone had. They are outlawed in Canada because they show full penetration, and if you're caught trying to bring them into the country, you could end up getting some jail time for trying to import pornography, not to mention what the Regiment would do to you.

In the Army one comes to expect delays and our inspection, delayed once, was also very thorough. Patience is a virtue in this man's Army.

As we sat around waiting to have our kit inspected, George helped to pass the time by reading the article written in the Toronto university paper. George's delivery was beautiful. As we reclined in the sun, he rose to the occasion by reading the article aloud, and carrying on a running commentary of sarcastic diatribe, much to the delight and humour of all gathered.

The DAG was next (don't ask me what this one stands for, in more than a year I haven't been able to find anyone who knows what it means). We were given our passports, leave passes, ID cards, a check for our UN pay, and our yellow vaccination books. The most important part of the DAG of course was the stop at the duty free shop (cleverly disguised as a sea container) where I picked up a litre of Drambuie for 24 marks (roughly $25 CDN). That's what I call a good deal.

Once our kit and all the paperwork had been taken care of, all the Reservists had a muster parade at the JR's mess for a thanks for coming out speech from the CO. He was kind, and gracious in his thanks, without sounding too sappy, and he invited us all back for the next tour in March of 1996. Then he saluted us, and it was off to the mess for two free beers and yet another steak and shrimp barbecue. At this rate it's going to take a while for me to get used to the idea of having something green on my plate.

Tonight for some reason I didn't much feel like partying, the beer was going down well enough, but I felt that I did my partying yesterday, and frankly I didn't feel up to going overboard again tonight. I must be getting old.

I hung around till about 2000 then wandered over to the CP, where I sat and started watching Danny De Vito in Renaissance Man in the radio room, until we were interrupted by an incident report being called in by SC 44.

44 had spotted eight men in Serb uniforms in the Zone carrying at least one RPG, and a 60mm mortar and bombs. It appeared they were practising manning a bunker. The radio operator informed the Ops O and the CSM, and because our platoon had a patrol in the area, as well as being QRF, Warrant Fuller and Lt McConnell were brought in on things.

The order came down to put the QRF on 15 minutes notice to move, and Warrant Fuller, true to character, leaped into action trying to get people rounded up.

Just before I left the radio room, an LO—a Liaison Officer—and our patrol track, which happened to be at 44 at the time, were dispatched to the area to sort out the mess.

Quite frankly I couldn't have been bothered to stick around to see how things turned out. I still had some small things to pack away in my kit, I wanted to take a shower and I needed to spend some time writing.

By 22:30 I'd completed all of what I wanted to do, so I crawled into bed. Lying there awake for a while, I listened to the sound of the Serbs firing off their machine guns in the night. Isn't it amazing what we can get used to? That's one sound I'll be glad to replace with the chirping of crickets.

I nearly forgot to mention a discussion I had in the mess with one of the guys from Bravo Company. I asked about the guy and the incident with the article in the university paper. The guys in question were part of his company so I thought if anyone knew the lowdown on the story he would.

He told me first, that there were two of them involved, and that the guys have had a bit of a rough go the past few days, but in spite of the threats against them, they both have been vindicated by the RSM. As predicted, both were promptly hauled up before the RSM to explain their actions. It would appear the editor took some artistic licence with the truth, and decided to spice things up a bit for the naive and politically idealistic student body.

Turns out that it was an interview that had been conducted which resulted in an article being written. And, it was conducted in the presence of the PAF O (public affairs officer) who edited their comments prior to answering the questions put to them over the phone.

Right from the beginning the truth was in danger when the interviewer phrased his questions in such a way that it had everyone wondering. Phrases like "the carrier that was shredded by a mine," and that one of the four injured was "still in a coma," clearly indicated that this guy had his info all mixed up. This last comment was referring to the incident when the carrier slid off the road back near the beginning of the tour.

Once the RSM realized the boys were interviewed, and didn't actually write the article he gave them his blessing. He then sat down—I'm told by another source—and wrote a letter to the editor that absolutely blasted him for writing the article incorrectly, and misquoting "his troops."

This brings up some points I'd like to make about the press both on campus, and in general.

To my way of thinking, there needs to be more accountability in the press, for what they publish. That is NOT to say they should be censored, on the contrary, I am a firm believer in freedom of speech. The old saying "I may not agree with what you say, but I shall defend to the end your right to say it" still holds true. Papers like the *Enquirer* get their dicks slapped regularly for printing misleading information, either by intent or by accident. Reputable papers like the *Globe* and the *Washington Post*, even get their wires crossed from time to time, and have to print retractions. University papers too, should be held accountable. These papers represented a direct pipeline into the minds of our future leaders, and when misleading or incorrect information is published it can lead to all kinds of problems.

I don't know what the answer is, but I do know some kind of guidelines need to be enforced. They can be as left or right as they want, and often are, but once they cross the line, punishment should be swift and hard. How one goes about enforcing something like that is beyond me, but it sure would save a lot of heartache for people like our two guys.

Tuesday, 04 April, The Never Ending Day And once again the game is afoot. The starting gun went off at 0300 but John, Virk and I were already up. Virk swears that both John and I snored up a storm last night, but I refuse to believe it. I felt like I didn't sleep any of the four hours I lay there, and judging by the smirk on Virk's face, I think he's yanking my cord.

To say that anticipation was high for the day's activities is an understatement. The three of us didn't take very long to get cleaned up, and pack up the last of our kit. Breakfast wasn't due to start until 04:30, which makes you wonder why we had to get up at 3:00. So that left us with an hour and twenty minutes to kill. Everyone in our lines who was set to leave on this lift was up and outside in the cool night air. We all talked, walked back and forth, and tossed pebbles at each other. Killing time was very hard for us, adrenaline was high and we were fresh from a night's rest, or at least the semblance of a night's rest. I don't think any of us really slept at all.

I'm disappointed to say that John's attitude is still the pits. It was bad before he went on leave, but since his return it's continued to go downhill. He contends that he's just fed up with people not listening to him. Unfortunately, the result has been that he's crabby, pushy, and bossy. He snaps back at everyone for the smallest perceived slight. A couple of times now I've come close to giving him a piece of my mind, but haven't because I know damn well that it will do absolutely no good. And also I realize for the most part he's as fed up with this place as we all are, and this is just the way he deals with the stress. The best, and only, solution is for all of us just to get the hell away from it all for a while.

Finally at 4:10 we all said the hell with it, and headed for the mess. Leaving our carry-on kit on our bunks, we took our duffel bags with us, and on the way threw them in the back of the five-ton truck allocated to our company, and continued on to the mess.

We'd arrived early and thus were right at the front of the line. I spotted George sitting at one of the tables, and could tell instantly that he was hurting big time. He was slumped over in his chair with his arms crossed in front of him on the table, and his eyes were barely open. He'd been out drinking last night and it was clear he was still drunk. The huge cup of coffee he was nursing was an indication that he was at least trying to regain some semblance of sobriety prior to departure. When he saw us laughing at him, he smiled sheepishly, then came over to chat with us.

The food wasn't going to be served until 4:30, but it was good we got there early. People from Bravo, Charles, Echo, and Foxtrot Company had to be fed out of the same mess, that meant that when all the seats in the mess were full, the line still went out the door and around the building.

Breakfast was quickly inhaled so we could make room for the other guys still in the line. We returned to our ISOs to collect the last of our kit, and go around to the guys staying behind to say our final farewells. Now that I think of it, I never even bothered to take one last look at the place I'd called home for the last three months. Instead, I just suited up and walked out the door. The flack vest hardly weighed anything at all, we'd handed in all our ammunition save one mag of thirty rounds. There was a spring in my step as I walked down the line of trailers. I was going home.

In the dark we gathered and formed up in our companies. The platoon commanders came by and shook hands with their departing troops, then we waited for our buses to be assigned. Once allocated, the rush was on to find a seat and get settled, as if sitting down faster would somehow speed the process of departure.

I swear these buses were built for people no taller than 5'6," yet despite the fact that some of us had our knees jammed up against our chest, buddy's elbow in our ribs, and there was no place except the aisle to put any of our kit, nobody complained. For someone from the back of the bus trying to get out, it was a major operation falling just short of requiring climbing gear and safety ropes. Despite the inconveniences, we were going home, everybody knew it, and we were prepared to endure any amount of hardship to get there.

Leg One, Rastivic to Sibenik —At long last we were on the move. As we pulled out of the front gates of the camp hardly anyone said anything. It was as if we were all holding our breath, scarcely able to believe that it was all over and hoping that nothing would happen on this, the final ride out. There were the usual jokers of course, but for the most part things were pretty quiet.

The bus ride to Sibenik would require about two hours, and as it was still dark out, those who had decided to party last night and were still in a state of inebriation were trying to get some sleep. For myself sleep was out of the question, so I just watched the countryside speed by. We drove past bombed out buildings, deserted villages, barren and abandoned farmland, vineyards, cemeteries and mine fields. Through all of it no one said a thing.

After a time we came to the town of Zeminic. The fighting had been fierce here, and there wasn't much left of it. Yet the Serbs were still in control of their side of it and as we approached the crossing you could see the new fortifications and bunkers that had been built since January, the last time we'd passed this way.

Without a word, or a command, we all began to move. Ball caps were replaced with kevlar helmets, and the familiar click of magazines being pushed home echoed throughout the bus.

The gate was raised and once more, and for the last time we entered the Zone. First we drove past the Serbs, who were armed to the teeth and ever vigilant. We drove on for a piece, until we came to our UN positions. The buses slowly worked their way through "S" in the road created by the roadblocks, and, as if watching over us, our boys in the OP stood guard sullenly as we passed below them.

Another hundred yards down the road and we came to a ninety-degree turn, where, on the left side there was a large modular tent. It was here that the prisoner exchange took place only a few days ago.

More driving, and we came to the Croat side of the Zone. We stopped, and the Croatian policemen went about their business of checking papers, in an orderly and quiet fashion.

Once through the checkpoint, the helmets came off, and the ball caps went back on. There was a subtle change in the feeling and appearance of the landscape, I noticed. The further away from the Zone you got, the more "normal "the environment looked. At first you can't tell one side of the Zone from the other, they've both been destroyed. But as you approach the coast and move South towards Zeminik, things begin to appear as if nothing ever happened. It was daylight now, and as we crested one hill and began a parallel run with the coast, all kinds of expensive boats came into view nestled into small harbours. We're talking forty-foot plus yachts, with brightwork everywhere, and looking for all the world as if they just came off the factory floor. On land there were brightly painted houses, greenhouses, and new BMWs in the drive. There was nothing at all to indicate that this had once been one of the hottest and most dangerous war zones in the world.

The instant the boats came into view, the whole mood of the bus changed. Where once we were all glad to be going home, the feeling of euphoria was forgotten, and replaced with pure vitriol for what they were seeing. Here we'd been busting our butts for the past six months, patrolling through minefields, and the backwoods all hours of the day and night, and these bastards were sitting here sun-tanning and driving their Beamers around as if we were some kind of servants for them. Jesus, it pissed us off. "Can you believe it?" one guy said. And to George, that kind of summed it up. If ever there was a reason to leave the people to fight it out, here it was. The sheer arrogance of it all was staggering. In an instant it became clear that we'd all been used, and it only fuelled our desire to get the hell out of there.

As we rumbled along in the coast, my mind started to drift to Catherine. Looking around you could see the smiles were coming easier to people, as some of the guilt of being in the advanced party began to wear off.

Now, if I were writing a comedy, it is at this point that something would have to happen. "Just when they thought it safe to get their hopes up . . . the bus broke down." Sometimes it's astounding how much truth is stranger than fiction.

It was on a lovely little hill that it happened, so it did. What caught everyone's attention, was the gradual deceleration of the bus. There was a collective groan as the engine started to sputter, cough, hack, and finally give up the ghost in a cloud of black smoke. Time and again the bus driver tried to get the beast started. Each time he tried, our hopes went up. Each time he failed, our hopes sank lower.

Snide comments wafted up and down the bus as people became more and more frustrated with the situation. Another bus pulled up beside us and snippets of conversation between the two drivers drifted back to us at the back of the bus. Everyone had their ears tuned to the front.

Various options were talked about for about five minutes, then finally it was decided. The remainder of the convoy would proceed to Sibenik, then a bus would be sent back for us. Great! Ten km short of the destination, we get stranded on the side of the road. Nobody could believe it. We could bloody force march the distance before the second bus came back for us. Yet, as inevitable as the rising sun, we knew the plan was set when the last bus in the line sped past us and we were left on the side of the road, all dressed up and no place to go.

One final attempt to start the engine convinced a young man at the very back of the bus to make a difference. As he worked his way forward, he was overheard to say "I am not going to spend one minute longer in this country than I have to." The frustration in his voice was evident, and I half expected him to drag the driver off the bus by the scruff of the neck.

A small gaggle of people gathered at the back of the bus as the engine compartment was opened and the young man went to work, Leatherman in hand. Not five minutes later, the bus was running and our intrepid hero was working his way to the back of the bus again, to the cheers of everyone.

As we made our way down the road the truth was revealed. Whoever we had purchased our diesel fuel from, had watered it down. The result was that the fuel filter was full of accumulated water from the tank, not the go-juice that makes buses run. All our hero did was drain the line and filter until he hit diesel, then reconnected everything. This was maintenance the driver should have been doing each morning. I'll not repeat what our hero had to say about the driver, and the questionable way he maintained his bus, but as you can imagine, it was full of wonderfully militaristic language, and completely uncomplimentary. I guess he would know—he was a maintainer from Bluebell.

Never content to let you let off easy, life threw another curve at us as we drove through Sibenik, on the hill overlooking the bloody base no less. As we rolled to a stop the general consensus was that we should just push the damn thing until it started to roll downhill, and coast into the base. The driver politely declined this. Our hero came to the rescue, yet again, and, as he returned to this seat, the "S"embossed on his chest was starting to show through his uniform.

At long last we pulled into the base that had offered us our first look at Croatia so many months ago, and would now offer us our last. Leg two of the operation was about to begin.

Leg Two, Sibenik Base to Split Airport—As we stepped off the buses, the object of the exercise now became find your duffel bag. All the MLs pulled up in a line, and we began to offload the bags and lay them out by company. The stop on the base was supposed to be short, just long enough for us to pack away our flack vests and helmets, and put our rifles into the section rifle bags. This accomplished, we turned our ammunition in to a central collection point, and then it was back on the buses for the ride to the airport.

The trip to the airport took another hour and a half, and when we arrived, we were told to collect our gear, and gather in the parking lot. The charter from Canada was late and wouldn't be there for at least another hour, so we were to cool our heels and wait for further instructions.

Looking around at the area where we gathered, it occurred to me that six months prior we had gathered in the same spot, and were desperately trying to acclimatize to the heat and environment. Now as we gaggled about, it seemed as if hardly any time had passed at all. Still, it was a lovely day, so I parked my butt on my kit, pulled out my pipe and my book, and proceeded to read, and occasionally chat with George who'd parked himself beside me.

Waiting at the Split airport for our flight home

Eventually, word was passed to bring our kit—duffel bag and carry-on bag—into the terminal. We lined up and checked our kit through the check-in counters so it could all be weighed, and loaded onto a panel truck for transport to the aeroplane when it arrived. All of this took time of course, which meant there was lots of standing around to be done after your kit was handed in. I hooked up with Padre Rembaldie, and we chatted for more than an hour as we waited for the plane to arrive.

When told of its arrival, we all gathered at the windows overlooking the runway and watched as the Tower Airways 747 landed and taxied to its place below the terminal. We all watched as the VanDoos off-loaded and went through the same bewildering adjustments that we all had done.

They filed past us in the terminal and I was reminded of our arrival here. Is it possible we looked as fresh and new as these guys did? And is it possible that we now look as old and tired as the PPCLI had? Certainly there was a bitterness that we'd acquired, which may well have been the same look we saw and wondered about. Then again, perhaps it was the personification of what we were all thinking, just you wait, you'll see.

About half an hour after the last VanDoo had left the terminal and gone to the buses, we were told to line up and prepare to go through customs and load the plane. We lined up by company and Dukes was at the front of the line. The first fourteen of us through the checkpoint were asked to go out onto the tarmac to help with the loading of the kit. As it turned out, it was everyone from 3 Platoon who wound up outside. We all grabbed our carry-on kit and went straight up into the plane and grabbed seats for ourselves. Then it was back out onto the tarmac to wait for the truck with the kit to arrive. This took another half an hour or so.

A self-propelled conveyor belt to help with the loading preceded the truck's arrival. When the truck got there, we formed a chain and began loading the kit. It must have been the fact that we were leaving, because the four French soldiers who were up in the hold of the aircraft couldn't keep up with the pace we'd set. They kept stopping the conveyor as they tried to position the kit inside the hold, and they kept shooting us dirty looks every time we restarted the conveyor.

Eventually the truck was emptied, and we all went up into the aircraft to get out of the heat. That's when it was discovered that about fifteen of the barrack boxes wouldn't fit into the hold. For some unknown reason, the chief steward came to me and asked my advice. I suggested that he just load the stuff inside the aeroplane on the seats that were empty at the back. Air Regs wouldn't allow this, for fear that the kit break loose and fly about in a crash situation—of course the fact that no one would give a damn at that point is irrelevant, but we still couldn't do it. A sergeant appeared and the matter was taken to higher.

I found out later that the kit belonged to Charles Company, and that the kit would be on the next lift out, and forwarded to the people at various home Regiments around Ontario about a week after they got back. I quietly thanked my lucky stars that mine was not in the kit involved.

The plane loaded up with people, and because there weren't that many of us on the first lift, I wound up with a group of three seats to myself. That was fine by me, because I intended to stretch out on this trip.

When the engines started, it got everyone's attention, and things got quiet in a hurry. The next leg of the trip was about to begin.

Leg Three, Sibenik to Shannon Ireland, and Shannon to Trenton—We sat there on the tarmac for quite a while as the pilots went through their checklists. The delays seemed to take forever. Finally someone at the back of the plane yelled "release the parking brake!" This sent a ripple of laughter throughout the plane and lightened things up a bit.

Finally! The plane started to move. We taxied down the ramp and to the end of the runway, where we began a large 180-degree turn. Again someone yelled, "Oh God, they're taking us back. We're not going home!" More laughter. The engines started to rev up, and the parking brakes were applied. Everyone went quiet. The engine RPMs increased, and still no one said anything. The RPMs increased again, and the plane started to shake. Quiet.

The parking brake was released and the engines roared with additional power, and we began to move down the runway. Everyone held their breath. The giant 747 rumbled, and shook, as it accelerated down the runway, and you felt you were being pressed back into the seat. Still, no one said anything. It seemed to take forever, but finally the nose began to rise. It kept going up, until I thought we would surely scrape our tail on the runway. Then it happened. There was a thunk that reverberated throughout the aircraft as the landing gear left the runway, and as if on cue, the entire aircraft broke out into one spontaneous cheer. Yes, I thought to myself, I'm outta here.

The gear came up, and locked into place accompanied by the usual mechanical noises, and we continued to be pressed into our seats as the plane climbed for altitude. We completed a large clockwise turn that brought us out over the Adriatic to run parallel along the coast of Croatia as we continued to climb. Sitting by the window, I looked down to find the countryside where I'd spent the past six months spread out below me. My first thought was that it all looked like a 1:50,000 map. All the pertinent points were easily recognizable. The Arrowhead, Rastivic, Benkovac, Camp Alpha, and if you looked Rodaljice. Karinslana was easily found by the water, as were Charles Company HQ and Bravo Company. Yes, it was all there, and as far as everyone on the aircraft was concerned, it could stay there. I don't think anyone would argue that "thank God that's over with" was the general motto for the passengers of this aircraft.

We reached cruising height fairly quickly, and everyone settled in for the flight to Shannon, Ireland. I read some, tried to sleep (but couldn't), then settled into something of a daze as I looked out the window and watched first the Alps, then the rest of Europe pass below us.

Time seemed to float by, and it was the dropping of the nose, and the throttling back of the engines that alerted us to the fact that we were beginning our decent into Ireland. Great, this is going to be a good chance to stretch my legs, I thought as I reached down to put my combat boots back on.

We came in low over the landscape as we approached the airport, and looking out the window, I couldn't believe the incredible intensity, and variations on the colour green I was seeing. When we had lifted off and flown along the Mediterranean coastline, everything on land had looked brown or sand coloured. There wasn't a dot of green to be seen. Here, there wasn't a single brown dot to be seen. Everything was green. It was like looking at a different world. And I suppose in a sense we were.

Before we got off the aircraft, we were given timings to be ready to go again, which amounted to an hour. We were free to shop the duty free shops and buy anything we wanted, just don't get lost.

Thus cut loose, I set off to wander around the airport, and eventually wound up at the bar, where a large contingent of our boys had gathered. It's got to be a rule or something, but any time you have infanteers and bars in the same building, you will rarely find one without the other. I lucked in and managed to order a Guinness, and found a table with some of the 3 Platoon boys as we waited for what was left of the hour.

There was a bit of a kafuffle at the bar, and when we looked over, we saw one of the sergeants speaking directly to the bar manager. After a moment, there was an announcement. "No beer will be served to Canadian soldiers." Bloody hell, the guys were lined up three deep around the bar trying to order. There were a lot of evil looks directed at the sergeant. We at the table thanked our lucky stars that we'd got in when we did.

Padre Rembaldie wandered up and joined us, and when he found out that we'd all been cut off, he was MOST disappointed. He'd been shopping for pipe tobacco (Three Nuns actually—something Freudian there I think), and missed the beer call. He probably has to work on his priorities. But then, after six months in country, you'd think he'd know better. Beer first, shop later. His loss.

Back on the plane and back in the air. It would be about seven hours to Trenton with nothing much to do but look out the window. Time seemed to pass very slowly.

Leg Four, Trenton to Petawawa—As we approached the runway, it was clear the pilots had their hands full. The lower it got the bumpier the ride became, and as we came over the end of the runway, the pilot had one wing lower than the other trying to stay in control while dealing with the crosswind. The catcalls began to multiply as we approached the landing, and as with the departure, the instant the wheels touched down the plane erupted into another great cheer.

It was now 12:30 A.M., and we were taxiing up to the hanger where we'd go through customs. We were all quietly mumbling along getting ready to get off when one of the stewards opened the door. Holy shit! It was ten below out there, and there was a thirty-mile-an-hour wind. Not one of us had thought to bring a jacket, or long johns. That was all packed below in the hold. OK, I thought, it's only fifty yards to the hanger. I can tough it out. That thought lasted until I got to the door and the guy ahead of me let out a groan. The bloody brigade commander and RSM were standing at the main door shaking everyone's hands, welcoming them back as they came into the hanger. The resulting line went from the hanger to the door of the aircraft. So, instead of a sensible mad dash to the hanger to get out of the cold, we wound up standing for ten minutes or more in the freezing wind as we waited for our turn to shake the hand of the brigade commander.

More than a few choice comments were made about the questionable parentage of those in command as we worked our way up to the door. By the time I got there, I didn't care much. I couldn't feel much of anything.

Inside the hanger we all stood under the overhead blowers, de-frosting. For efficiency's sake, we were herded into a caged-off area the size of a small gymnasium so wouldn't be in the way of incoming luggage. Then several of us were asked to help unload the kit and stack it in orderly rows. All the rucksacks were lined up, then the duffel bags, and finally all the barrack boxes were stacked three deep. Customs then worked their way through the piles and pulled pieces of kit at random. The name of the person who owned the kit was called out, and he had to open the kit and have it searched by the customs official. This went on for about an hour.

Standing in the waiting area with George, John, and David, I realized the adventure of the past year and a half was coming to an end, and it bothered me that I couldn't find the words to tell these guys how I felt about them. We just made small talk as we waited for customs to finish, then, by Company; we collected our kit, grabbed one of the famous military box lunches, and boarded the bus for the two-hour ride to Petawawa.

Time seemed to pass quickly, as we zipped through the lunches, and settled in for the ride. It was dark and cold outside, so most of us simply took the opportunity to grab some sleep.

We pulled into Petawawa at 03:30 unrested and cramped.

All the kit had to come off the bus. One barrack box, your rucksack, and the duffel bag were all brought into the drill hall, and stacked by company. Despite the late hour, when we stepped into the lights of the drill hall, we were greeted by people who were wide-awake, and directing traffic. Families were kept out of the drill hall proper, and were all gathered in the long hallway that defined the centre of the building.

Once we found our company's designated area and where the kit was stacked, the search was on to find your other two barrack boxes from the pile laid out in that area of the floor. With all our kit together, we next had to unpack our helmets, flack vests, and any Gortex clothing we had. Stations had been set up to receive the various pieces of kit, and our battalion sign out cards were all there waiting for us. We moved from station to station, handing in kit and having it struck off our cards. The final stop was to pick up a print the battalion had commissioned. This I carefully packed away in one of my barrack boxes.

The last thing to do was to say goodbye to some of the Regs I'd worked with. Virk was met at the drill hall by his wife, and I managed get in a handshake before he got dragged off by her (but to be honest, I'm not sure who did the most dragging, him or her). People were running back and forth, and the last I saw of George was the backside of him and his wife as they went arm in arm down the hallway. Standing there amidst all the women and children, and watching all the families being reunited, I was suddenly struck by a sense of loneliness. I'd half expected, no, I found myself actually hoping that Catherine would be there to greet me, but knew that it wasn't realistic to expect her, she had no way of knowing when I'd be back. Still, I felt left out of it all, and wished somehow she'd been able to make it. The loneliness and the exhaustion of the last two days' travel all caught up to me then as I stood there surrounded by the echoing sounds of laughter and happiness. I wearily made my way back into the drill hall to collect my gear, and loaded it onto the back of one of the waiting MLs for the shuttle run to the Mattawa plain.

All the Reservists were bunked at the Mattawa in the old barracks. We pulled up outside our assigned barrack block in the wee hours of the cold April morning and unloaded our kit, went into the barracks, and found a bunk space. It was now 04:45, and I was cold, tired, and feeling kind of down. Rather than go to sleep, I stripped off, and made my way to the showers for a nice long soaking, and a shave. They say that a shower is worth two hours' sleep, and once the sun's up you don't care anymore. I'd been on the go for well into my third day now, with nothing much in the way of sleep. I figured there was no point in trying to get any now, you'd just get settled in and you'd have to get up again for breakfast.

The two hours we had to wait before the mess opened passed quickly as a few of us sat around and chatted about the tour. When the first shuttle run to the mess arrived, those of us awake piled on and as soon as I got to the mess, I called Cat. She was overjoyed to hear me, and said she'd leave right away. That meant another three hours at least before I saw her, so I settled in for a large breakfast.

We'd all essentially been cut free after we turned in our kit. Some of the guys had collected their cars in the night, and buggered off home. The majority of the remainder had to wait for their Regiments to lay on transport for them to get home. For me, it was a matter of waiting for Catherine to pick me up, and I was free to go.

Cat and I had agreed to meet at the local cafeteria, so I went straight there after breakfast and picked a table by the window to wait for her arrival. It was a grey overcast day as I sat there in front of the large window, and my mind seemed to be stuck in neutral, not really being able to focus on any one thing. The coffee tasted stale, the air smelled of smoke, and time seemed to pass more slowly than ever. When finally I saw Catherine's familiar red Jetta pull into the parking lot, my heart leapt into my mouth. I went outside and waited for her to make her way to me. She'd brought both Rascal and Molly, and when she opened the back door, both dogs scampered out and ran to my side when I called them. As much as I love them my focus was on her. She covered the distance between us quickly, and when she landed in my arms we both had tears in our eyes. It was a very long, and much anticipated hug.

There is an unwritten rule on military bases that says you don't disturb a couple when they are in the throes of a reunion. You don't stare, or make comments; you just let them be. It is a courtesy that everyone extends because it is so personal. Everyone knows when the battalion is coming home, and for a while anyway everyone allows each other a little extra space. As we stood in the middle of the parking lot, few people paid much attention to us. For Cat and I, as we stood wrapped in each other's arms, time stood still.

Leg Five, The Ride Home—Loading the car was something of a challenge. Two dogs, two people, three barrack boxes, a duffel bag, a rucksack, and carry-on kit required some inventive packing. But in the end everything fit and there only remained one thing left to do.

As we left the base I pulled into a tiny strip mall just outside the main gate and went inside to have something done. When I came out, I sat in the front seat beside Cat, and opened the tiny box. "Here," I said, presenting the contents of the box to her, "I want you to have this, because you deserve it as much as I do," whereupon, I removed a miniature replica of my UN medal from the box, and proceeded to pin it on her. If the tears were any indication, I think for once I did the right thing. The drive home was a blur.

The last thing I remember of that day was going to bed. I'd been awake nearly sixty-five hours, and Catherine swears I let out a long low groan as I slipped between the cool, crisp, cotton sheets of our queen-sized bed. With my wife in my arms, the dogs by the bed, I drifted off to sleep the sleep of the weary. The tour was over.

EPILOGUE

> "There is a wreck in your head, part of the aftermath, and you must dismantle the wreck. But after many years you discover that you cannot dismantle the wreck, so you move it around and bury it. It took years for you to understand that the most complex and dangerous conflicts, the most harrowing operations, and the most deadly wars, occur in the head."
>
> Anthony Swofford
> JARHEAD, p 247–8
> 2003, New York

Within 48 hours of our arrival in Canada, the reservists who were part of the 1RCR Battle Group had returned to their own homes. With our three-week leave passes in hand to take us to the end of our contract, we emerged from the front gates of CFB Petawawa and re-entered a world that seemed at once both familiar and utterly alien. Leaving behind a world of single-minded dedication to the achievement of the mission, we entered one that seemed to have no mission at all.

For the most part, a reservist coming off tour was left to deal with the "mental wreckage" from the tour in his own way. For many young and single men, it was not uncommon for drinking binges and heavy partying to be the norm for months after they returned home. With no one to be responsible for, or to, it became difficult for some to find a sense of purpose to keep them on track. A study of veterans of UN tours conducted in the late 90's showed that 15% of returning regular force soldiers suffered from some kind of delayed stress syndrome from their experiences. For reservists the number runs closer to 25%. Both these figures have since been revised downward, but are far higher than officials ever anticipated, and I suspect falls well short of the real numbers due the soldiers' natural reluctance to seek help for their emotional distress or confusion. My wife will attest to the fact that it took nearly eight months for me to stop talking in my sleep, and longer still to be as demonstrative with her as I was before I left. It was, in fact, nearly three yeas before I started to talk to her about some of the things that happened over there, and that was just the funny stuff.

Support structures for returning reservists at the end of my tour were few. Unlike returning WWII soldiers, hardly anyone outside our immediate family knew we were even away. For the regs, the base offered a protective cocoon within which they could unwind. Being isolated from the rest of society, the soldiers were able to speak openly with comrades or find support within the system for matters that troubled them. Even so, the return home for many was a bumpy one. Of the roughly 300 married regular force men in the battalion, more than 40 had divorce papers waiting for them upon their return. For others, divorce was only delayed, coming after weeks or months back home. Then there are the countless unrecorded cases of men in common law relationships coming home to empty houses, and empty bank accounts. I suspect that puts the divorce/separation rates at close to 30%, and likely quite a bit higher.

That's not to say that it was all bad news. For many of us, we came home to understanding and loving relationships, and it's fair to say that more than a few children were conceived within the first week of a soldier's return home. Nevertheless, making the transition from war zone to civilian life was tough. The aggressiveness I developed during training has softened over the intervening years, and the writing of this memoir has been a huge help in sorting through my own "wreckage." Though the first months were rough for Catherine and I, it can be said that without her love, understanding, and infinite patience, it would have taken me longer to return to civilian life than it did. Still there are days I feel caught between the tough, mission-oriented world of the infantry, and the less directed civilian life I surround myself with. As a reserve soldier I live in neither.

Based on my own journey I can more deeply appreciate the reasons why older combat veterans have no desire to speak of their experience. So few things in civilian life can begin to compare to the physical hardship and the sheer sensory overload they were subjected to on the battlefield, that it becomes extremely difficult to explain their experience to the uninitiated. Where do they begin? The military has long been known for its plethora of acronyms, and it can become frustrating to constantly have to explain oneself. Simple comments they thought were self-explanatory have the effect of leaving the unversed listener completely baffled as to their meaning. Also, most soldiers don't acknowledge that there is a problem. Many feel they were just doing their job and they'd just as soon forget about it and get on with things. It is far easier to bury the wreckage of their experience and throw themselves into the work at hand, than to deal openly with any feelings they might have, thereby risking embarrassment or the perception of weakness.

My greatest struggle however, came with my unexpected discomfort at being called a veteran. To me, a veteran is someone who saw action in places like Normandy, Sicily, North Africa, Dieppe, and Kap Yong. These were men who saw combat and in my eyes are worthy of respect. Not ever having fired a shot in anger, it was difficult to reconcile being grouped in with these men. Having since learned more about the scope of the UNPROFOR mission, I'm now more comfortable with it.

Looking back I'm very proud to have done the tour, and honoured to have served with so many fine men and women. Many of the men I served with are still in the military, and over the years I've managed to catch snippets about them. George and Peters are both officers now, and both Ray and Philip are warrant officers. John left the reserves and went on to complete a PhD in chemistry, and David went on to a pro ball career while staying with his old regiment. I've lost touch with the rest.

The tour has afforded me the opportunity to see my world from another perspective and this, I feel, has had a positive affect on me. For one thing, I find I am far more grateful. Grateful that I live in a country where the words peace, human rights, ethnic diversity, and freedom, actually stand for something. I am grateful that I am healthy, and that my wife can get the medical care she needs to stay healthy. And above all, I am grateful to be Canadian.

As I draw this final entry to a close, I am reminded of a poem posted on the wall of the company radio room in Rastivic. The author is unknown, but whoever it was got

Epilogue 319

it right, because it so eloquently sums up what a lot of us felt about what we were doing over there, and how many of us as see ourselves as soldiers. It is the most appropriate ending I can think of for this book.

I was that, which others did not want to be,
I went where others feared to go,
And did what others failed to do,

I asked nothing from those who offered nothing,
And willingly accepted the burden of loneliness,
Suffering the strain of deprivation that constant vigilance demands,

I have seen the face of terror, felt the stinging cold of fear, cried,
Felt pain and sorrow, and tasted the sweetness of a moments love,

But most of all,
I have lived in times that others would say were best forgotten,

And after it all,
I am able to say that I am proud of who I am...

A Soldier
In the service of peace.

SERGEANT KURT GRANT is a serving member of the Brockville Rifles. He completed an eight-month peacekeeping tour with The Royal Canadian Regiment in Croatia. While completing a BA in Military Science at Royal Military College, Kingston, he is developing an operations database for the Department of History and Heritage, Ottawa.